First published in 1999 by MBI Publishing Company, 729 Prospect Avenue, PO Box 1, Osceola, WI 54020-0001USA

MBI Publishing Company books are also available at discounts in bulk quantity for industrial or sales-promotional use. For details write to Special Sales Manager at Motorbooks International Wholesalers & Distributors, 729 Prospect Avenue, PO Box 1, Osceola WI, 54020 USA.

Library of Congress Cataloging-in-Publication Data

Sessler, Peter C.
Ultimate American V-8 engine data book / Peter C. Sessler.
p. cm.
Includes index.
ISBN 0-7603-0489-0 (pbk. : alk. paper)
1. Automobiles–United States–Motors
2. Automobiles–Motors–Specifications. I. Title.
TL210.S4224 1998
629.25'04–dc21
98-40460

Edited by Keith Mathiowetz
Designed by Tom Heffron and Rebecca Allen

On the front cover: Deviating from the 1950s Chrysler Spitfire engines were the Dodge and Plymouth "A" engines. Like the Chrysler powerplants, these engines also used scalloped valve covers. The best known "A" engine was the 318cid version which was used on various Dodge and Plymouth vehicles until 1966. *Gary Stauffer*

On the back cover: A collection of V-8 components, including a Ford 370cid truck cylinder block, a Pontiac cast iron four-barrel intake manifold, a high-performance Chevrolet cylinder head, and a high-performance Corvette exhaust manifold.

Printed in the United Sates of America

Contents

Acknowledgments

This book could not have been put together without the help and assistance of all the people who helped with this book in one way or another. Special thanks goes to the following, who went out of their way to help: Mike Brattland; Brad Burnett; Doug DeShong; Carmen Faso; Charlie Gluck; Jerry Heasley; Bill Haenelt and Quality Engine Rebuilders, Middletown, New York; Andre "A. J." Jacobs; Don Keefe; Joe and Joannie Koryicki; Jim Mattison; Paul McLaughlin; Chuck Mill; Alan Mills and Star Crankshaft, Port Jervis, New York; Jim and Julie Moore; Mile Odell; Bob Palma; Gary Stauffer; and Frank Tomjack.

All photos by the author, except where indicated.

Introduction

The King is dead! Long live the King! That pretty much sums up the situation with the good old American V-8 engine. For all intents and purposes, it's dead and gone. Sure, there are a few holdouts—namely the Chevy small block—but the V-8 engines that are still around are really living on borrowed time. They too will eventually be retired. Even the gas engine as an entity is bound to be replaced with electrics sooner or later. (Sooner if there is another gas crisis.) Looking back, it does seem like the V-8 era was an age of excess—the engines got bigger and thirstier as time went by—but even so, if you lived through the era, it really was an exciting time for the American automobile. In the end, though, the American V-8 made sense only if cars were big and gas prices remained low.

The *Ultimate American V-8 Engine Data Book 1949–1974* is an attempt to categorize the roughly 30-year span when the American V-8 was king. The era started when Cadillac and Oldsmobile introduced their overhead valve V-8s in 1949. Chrysler followed suit with their hemi-head engines in 1951, while Buick brought out their V-8s in 1953. Chevrolet and Pontiac released their engines in 1955. Lincoln brought out their V-8 in 1952 and, finally, Ford retired the old flathead V-8 in 1954 and replaced it with the Y-block V-8 in the same year.

Then there were the independents: Packard, Studebaker, and AMC. Packard folded by 1958, but not before they introduced their V-8 engine; Studebaker brought out their well-designed V-8 in 1951; and AMC eventually proved that its V-8 engine was as good as any after a successful racing career in the late 1960s and early 1970s. To its credit, the AMC V-8 engine outlasted AMC itself as Chrysler continued to use the engine in the Jeep line until 1991.

Although many of the engines covered in this book continued into the 1980s, I have chosen 1974 as a general cutoff point; however, with some engines I continued until their eventual demise if it was only a few years past 1974. I chose 1974 because by that time the emissions era was well into its own and the V-8 engines produced after that were shadows of their former selves. The industry kept them in production more as a stopgap measure until new four- and six-cylinder engines were developed to power the next generation of downsized cars.

Each chapter of this book covers a single engine family. Within each chapter you will find a brief history of the engine, and a chronological listing of the engine and its power ratings. After researching 23 engine families, it is my opinion that the horsepower ratings the manufacturers assigned to their engines were bogus most of the time. They always seemed to be increments of 5 or 10 horsepower and calculated to either make good advertising copy, satisfy a particular race sanctioning body, or to look good to the insurance industry. There were some exceptions: it seems that Pontiac reported actual horsepower figures until at least the mid-1960s when the power ratings for most of its engines started to have nice, round numbers.

The industry also seems to have fixated around certain horsepower figures for their most powerful engines. That number, more often than not was 425. You've got the Chrysler 426 Hemi, the 426 Max Wedge, the Ford 427 Low and Medium Riser, and the Chevrolet 409 and 427 big blocks, which all rated at 425 horsepower. At the other end of the scale, the Chevrolet 302 Z28, the Ford Boss 302, and the Chrysler 340 6V engine were all rated at an identical 290 horsepower. Some engines were also rated unrealistically low. The best known example of this was Ford's 1968–1970 428 Cobra Jet rated at 335 horsepower.

You'll also find an engine identification guide within each chapter. Wherever possible, I've listed engine ID codes, engine serial numbers, and casting numbers for cylinder blocks, heads, and intake and exhaust manifolds. If casting numbers weren't available, I've listed part numbers, and sometimes I listed both. The photographs used in this book generally show a typical part and are not meant to show every possible variation of a particular part.

A word about casting numbers and, actually, any other number that is associated with a particular part. Generally speaking, you will find that the guidelines in each chapter hold true. However, in the final analysis, the manufacturers did whatever they wanted to do. There are no rules set in stone, just guidelines because there are exceptions (and sometimes very many) when it comes to identification. For example, a casting number might be in a particular position most of the time but at other times the number might be located at another area of the part or even not at all. The manufacturers followed the rule of expediency.

And you really can't rely on just one ID number. For example, if you think that a casting number is that last word when it comes to identifying a part and its application, you'd be wrong. There are many times when several different cylinder heads, for example, will all have the same casting number, yet will have obvious visual differences between them. You might have to measure valve size, check the date code, and so forth in order to identify a particular head. And so it is with all the parts listed in this book.

Every effort has been made to make sure that the information in this book is correct; nevertheless, I cannot assume any responsibility for any loss arising from the use of this book. However, I would like to hear from any enthusiast with corrections, clarifications, or any interesting additions.

Peter C. Sessler
Milford, PA 18337
November 1998

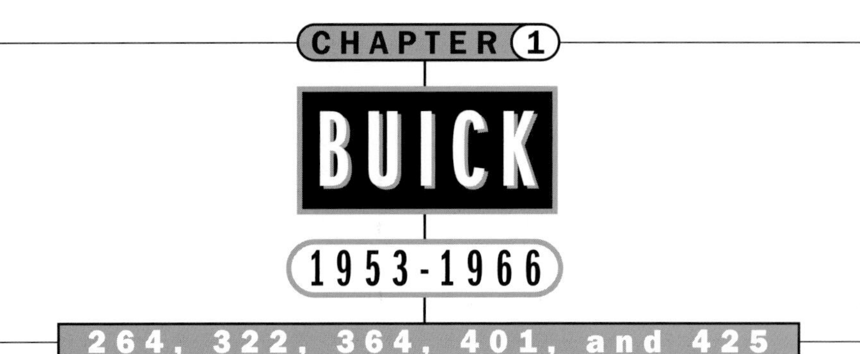

Buick introduced the Fireball V-8 engine in 1953. The overhead-valve (ohv) V-8 was similar in many respects to other recently introduced V-8 engines by GM, Chrysler, and Ford. The engine was a 90-degree V-8 with a centrally located hydraulic-lifter camshaft that actuated the inline valves via rockers mounted on a rockershaft. The crankshaft was supported by five main bearings, and compared to the engine it replaced, the Buick V-8 certainly was smaller, lighter, and more powerful.

There were differences, however. Buick, too, used a wedge-type chamber, but it had features of the hemi-type combustion chamber. The combustion chamber was conical in shape with the spark plug located at the center of the chamber. The pistons were domed, thereby compressing the mixture in the pentroof or semi-hemi (as it was called) combustion chamber. Another departure from the norm was the Buick's not using slipper-type pistons. (Slipper pistons have cutaways on both sides to provide crankshaft clearance when the piston is at the bottom of its stroke.) Instead, the crankshaft's counterweights were molded to clear the pistons.

Probably the most controversial aspect of the engine was its valve angle. The two valves for each cylinder were perpendicular, each at a 45-degree angle in relation to the cylinder's axis. Because the combustion chamber was small, the valves, too, were small. Intakes measured 1.75 in. while the exhausts were minuscule, measuring 1.25 in. Eventually, the engine became known as the "nailhead" V-8 because of the small valves.

Buick pointed out the small valves' advantages: They made possible a smaller combustion chamber, provided better valve cooling, reduced manufacturing costs, and provided excellent part throttle flow characteristics. While this may have been true and the engine was a good torquey design, its weak point was that it still couldn't breathe at high rpm. As the engine displacement increased over the years, valve size didn't (and couldn't) keep up in relation to displacement. The nailhead description stuck.

The first Buick V-8 to go into production was the 322 cid version. The 322 was around until 1957, when it was replaced by a larger 364 cid V-8. In the meantime, a small 264 cid variation was available during 1954–1955. The 364 lasted through the 1961 model year. A larger 401 cid version was introduced in 1959 and the largest, the 425 cid V-8, was finally released in 1963. Both were available through the 1966 model year.

264 cid

This was the smallest of the original Buick V-8 engines, and it was used on the 1954–1955 Buick Special. It had a bore and stroke of 3.625x3.20 in. The engine had the two-bolt main-bearing block, hydraulic camshaft, forged-steel rods and crankshaft, and a two-barrel carburetor. The 1955 version had the greatest output, at 188 hp.

322 cid

The first Fireball V-8 in 1953 had a bore and stroke of 4.00x3.20 in. for a 322 cid. It was available with a two-barrel carburetor for 164 hp and with a four-barrel for 188 hp. The engine came with a forged-steel crankshaft, forged-steel connecting rods, hydraulic camshaft, and either a two- or four-barrel carburetor.

The 322 cid engine was putting out 255 hp by the time it was phased out in 1956.

364 cid

The 322 cid V-8 was replaced in 1957 by a bored and stroked version of the engine, 4.125x3.40 in., for 364 cid. Because of the original engine's compact dimensions, the block's deck height had to be increased by 0.25 in. and the engine also used longer connecting rods. The cylinder heads were carried over, but the valve sizes were increased to 1.875 in. intake and 1.50 in. exhaust. The engine was in production through the 1961 model year.

401 cid

In 1959, the nailhead was once again bored and stroked, 4.1875x3.64 in. for 401 cid. Again, this required a taller deck engine block, different crankshaft, longer rods, and a wider intake manifold, so there isn't much that can be interchanged with earlier versions of the engine. However, the cylinder heads used the same size valves as before. With a four-barrel intake manifold and dual exhausts, the 401 cid was rated at 325 hp, and it was available through the 1966 model year.

The 401 V-8 was the standard engine in Buick's 1965 Skylark Gran Sport. However, Buick advertised the engine as a "400." The redesigned 400 cid big-block wasn't produced until 1967, and it should not be confused with the nailhead V-8.

With the exception of the dual four-barrel intake setup, this is a fairly stock 364 cid Buick nailhead V-8.

425 cid

The largest permutation of the Buick nailhead V-8 occurred in 1963 with the release of the 425 cid engine. The 425 cid engine had a bore of 4.3125 in. and a stroke of 3.64 in. The single four-barrel version was rated at 340 hp. The highest output version, with two dealer-installed four-barrel carburetors and manifold was rated at 360 hp in 1965–1966. As with earlier Buick engines, the 425 cid V-8 used a forged-steel crankshaft, forged-steel connecting rods, hydraulic camshaft, and the same cylinder heads as the 401 cid engine.

Engine Blocks

All Buick engine blocks had a two-bolt main-bearing cap bottom end. Besides the various bore sizes, there were different deck heights differentiating the 322 cid blocks from the 364 cid blocks and the 401- and 425 cid blocks. All had the same crankshaft main journal size of 2.499 in. and rod bearing journal of 2.250 in.

Cylinder Heads

The Buick cylinder heads had the unique pentroof combustion chamber. The 264- and 322 cid heads had the smallest valves, 1.75 in. intake and 1.25 in. exhaust. All other engines used 1.875 in. intake and 1.50 in. exhaust valves. Piston top shape was used to control compression ratio. All engines used conventional shaft-mounted rocker arms.

Intake Manifolds

All Buick intake manifolds, whether they were two- or four-barrel, or dual four-barrel, were cast in iron. They are all similar in design, but because of block deck height differences, they are not interchangeable.

Exhaust Manifolds

All manifolds were made of cast iron. Differences in outlet size and shape between manifolds was due to application variations.

Engine Identification

Buick's system for numbering parts and castings was similar to that used by other GM divisions. The casting number is found on the part itself, but its location has varied over the years. On engine blocks, it can be found on either side. On manifolds, it's on one side or the other. On cylinder heads, the casting number is found under the valve cover area.

Buick was a bit more thorough than most manufacturers when it came to coding engines. The number used from 1953 to 1956 was a consecutive number followed by a single-digit number that indicates what series or Buick line the engine belonged to. It did not connect a particular engine with a specific car. That all changed in 1957, when Buick started to inscribe the vehicle's vehicle identification number (VIN) on the block itself. This was located on the left front side of the block and from 1959 on, on the right side of the block.

From 1959 on, Buick also included a specific two- or three-digit code (listed here) that identified the engine and a number that indicated the production sequence of the engine. Buick also included a date code that indicated the date on which the engine was assembled. A typical engine date code might be 11 22, for November 22. The engine identification (ID) number was located on the right front side of the block.

Although Buick's engine codes weren't as specific as those used by Chevrolet, for instance, Buick's addition of the VIN connected the engine to the particular vehicle it was installed in.

Engine Identification Codes

Code	Engine
1953	
V-2415-5 and up	322 cid 164/172 hp
V-2001-5 and up	322 cid 188 hp
1954	
V273956-4 and up	264 cid 143/150 hp
V273956-5 and up	322 cid 177/182 hp
V273956-6 and up	322 cid 195/200 hp
V273956-7 and up	322 cid 200 hp, Roadmaster
V273956	322 cid 200 hp, Skylark
1955	
V-720080-4 and up	264 cid 188 hp
V-720080-5 and up	264 cid 188 hp, Super
V-720080-5 and up	322 cid 236 hp, Super
V-720080-6 and up	322 cid 188 hp, Century
V-720080-6 and up	322 cid 236 hp, Century
V-720080-7 and up	322 cid 236 hp, Roadmaster
1956	
V-14600023-4 and up	322 cid 220 hp
V-14600023-5 and up	322 cid 255 hp, Super
V-14600023-6 and up	322 cid 255 hp, Century
V-14600023-7 and up	322 cid 255 hp, Roadmaster

1957

Engine ID code is the same as the car's VIN
1st digit, series: 4 Special, 5 Super, 6 Century, 7 Roadmaster
2nd digit, model year, D 1957
3rd digit, plant code
Last six, numerical sequence

1958

Engine ID code is the same as the car's VIN
1st digit, series: 4 Special, 5 Super, 6 Century, 7 Roadmaster, 8 Limited
2nd digit, model year, E 1958
3rd digit, plant code
Last six, numerical sequence

Code	Engine
1959	
3F	364 cid
4F	401 cid
1960	
3G	364 cid
L3G	364 cid 235 hp
4G	401 cid
1961	
3H	364 cid
L3H	364 cid 235 hp
4H	401 cid
1962	
L2I	401 cid 265 hp
2I	401 cid 280 hp
L4I	401 cid 315 hp
4I	401 cid 325 hp
1963	
JS	401 cid 265 hp
JU	401 cid 315 hp
JT	401 cid 325 hp
JW	401 cid 340 hp
1964	
KT	401 cid 325 hp
KW	425 cid 340 hp
KX	425 cid 360 hp
1965	
LT	401 cid 325 hp, "400" Gran Sport
LW	425 cid 340 hp
LX	425 cid 360 hp
1966	
MR	401 cid 325 hp, "400" Gran Sport

Engine Identification Codes

Code	Engine
MT	401 cid 325 hp
MW	425 cid 340 hp
MZ	425 cid 360 hp

Engine Specifications

	Displacement	Carburetor	Horsepower	Torque	Compression Ratio	Notes
1953						
	322	2V	164@4,000	286@2,200	8.0	
	322	4V	188@4,000	300@2,400	8.5	
1954						
	264	2V	143@4,200	228@2,400	7.2	
	264	2V	150@4,200	240@2,400	8.1	
	322	2V	177@4,100	295@2,000	8.0	
	322	2V	182@4,100	300@2,000	8.5	
	322	4V	195@4,100	302@2,400	8.0	
	322	4V	200@4,100	309@2,400	8.5	
1955						
	264	2V	188@4,800	256@2,400	8.4	
	322	4V	188@4,800	296@2,400	8.4	
	322	4V	236@4,600	330@3,000	9.0	
1956						
	322	2V	220@4,400	319@2,400	8.9	
	322	4V	255@4,400	341@3,200	9.5	
1957						
	364	2V	250@4,400	380@2,400	9.5	
	364	4V	300@4,600	400@3,200	10.0	
1958						
	364	2V	250@4,400	380@2,400	9.5	
	364	4V	300@4,600	400@3,200	10.0	
1959						
	364	2V	210@4,000	340@2,400	8.5	m/t
	364	2V	250@4,400	384@2,400	10.5	
	401	4V	325@4,400	445@2,800	10.5	
1960						
	364	2V	210@4,000	340@2,400	8.5	m/t
	364	2V	235@4,400	362@2,400	9.0	
	364	2V	250@4,400	384@2,400	10.25	
	364	4V	300@4,400	405@2,800	10.25	
	401	4V	325@4,400	445@2,800	10.25	
1961						
	364	2V	235@4,400	362@2,400	9.0	
	364	2V	250@4,400	384@2,400	10.25	
	401	4V	325@4,400	445@2,800	10.25	
1962						
	401	2V	265@4,200	395@2,800	9.0	
	401	2V	280@4,400	415@2,800	10.25	
	401	4V	315@4,400	435@2,800	8.75	
	401	4V	325@4,400	445@2,800	10.25	
1963						
	401	2V	265@4,200	395@2,800	9.0	
	401	2V	280@4,400	415@2,800	10.25	
	401	4V	315@4,400	435@2,800	8.75	
	401	4V	325@4,400	445@2,800	10.25	
	425	4V	340@4,400	465@2,800	10.25	
1964						
	401	4V	325@4,400	445@2,800	10.25	
	425	4V	340@4,400	465@2,800	10.25	
	425	2x4V	360@4,400	465@2,800	10.25	
1965						
	401	4V	325@4,400	445@2,800	10.25	"400" in Gran Sport
	425	4V	340@4,400	465@2,800	10.25	
	425	2x4V	360@4,400	465@2,800	10.25	

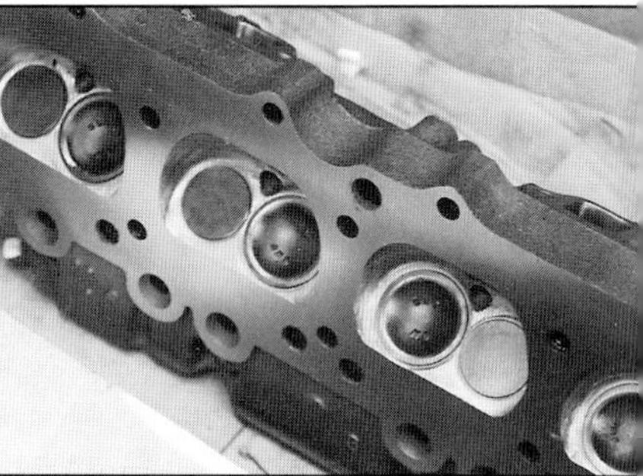

The 1953–66 Buick V-8s were unusual in many respects; the pentroof combustion chamber and the small valves were unique. *Carmen Faso*

	Displacement	Carburetor	Horsepower	Torque	Compression Ratio	Notes
1966						
	401	4V	325@4,400	445@2,800	10.25	"400" in Gran Sport
	425	4V	340@4,400	465@2,800	10.25	
	425	2x4V	360@4,400	465@2,800	10.25	

Engine Internal Dimensions

Displacement	Bore and Stroke	Rod Bearings	Main Bearings	Intake/Exhaust Valves
264	3.625x3.200	2.125–2.126	2.5625–2.5635	1.75/1.25
300	3.750x3.400	2.000	2.992	1.625/1.313
322	4.000x3.200	2.249–2.250	2.498–2.499	1.75/1.25
364	4.125x3.400	2.249–2.250	2.498–2.499	1.875/1.50
401	4.1875x3.640	2.249–2.250	2.498–2.499	1.875/1.50
425	4.3125x3.640	2.249–2.250	2.498–2.499	1.875/1.50

Block, Head, and Manifold Part and Casting Numbers

Year	Engine	Part or Casting Number
Engine Blocks		
1954	264	1391629 w/ Dynaflow, 1391871 w/o
1953	322	1390972
1954	322	1391753, Series 50/60/70
1955	322	1392101 w/ Dynaflow to eng. no. 1145218, Series 40
1955	322	1392290 w/ Dynaflow after eng. no. 1145218, Series 40
1955	322	1392102 w/o to eng. no. 1142556, Series 40
1955	322	1392291 w/o after eng. no. 1142556, Series 40
1955	322	1392101 w/ Dynaflow to eng. no. 1058464 and no. 1058494 and to no. 1058504, and w/o to eng. no. 1063628, Series 50/60/70
1955	322	1392292 w/ Dynaflow to eng. no. 1058494 and after no. 1058504, Series 50/60/70 and w/o Dynaflow after eng. no. 1063628, Series 50/60
1956	322	1392734, 1392586 w/Dynaflow, 1392734 w/o
1957–1958	364	casting 1173201, 1174372
1959–1960	364	casting 1173201
1960	401	casting 1172889
1961–1966	401	casting 1185404, 1185485
1963–1966	425	1349046, 1354704, 1364704, 1364705
Cylinder Heads		
1953	322	1344214
1954	322	1391745
1955	322	1391947
1956	322	1392351
1957–1960	364	1392747, casting 11722889, 1185485,1190415, 1196914
1959–1963	401	casting 1172889, 1185485, 1190415, 1196914
Intake Manifolds		
1953	322 2V	1165308
1953	322 4V	1162286
1954–1955	322 2V	1165308
1954–1955	322 4V	1163206
1955	322 2V	1165308, 1169189 m/t, 1170624
1955	322 4V	1165384
1956	322 2V	1170624
1956	322 4V	1170625, 50/60/70 Series
1957–1961	364 2V	1175327
1957–1961	364 4V	1175328
1959–1962	401 4V	1187708
1962	401 2V	1349425
1962	401 4V	1187708
1963	401 2V	1355410
1963	401 4V	1353531
1964	401 4V	1375548
1965	401 4V	1375548
1966	401 4V	1375548, 1375118
1963	425 4V	1375548
1964	425 2x4V	1357106
1965	425 2x4V	1370316
1966	425 2x4V	1370316
Exhaust Manifolds		
1953	322	1345564 right, 1345564 left
1954–1955	264/322	1165212 right, 1345564 left
1956	322	1168110 right, 1169265 left
1956	322	1175576 right, 1175575 left
1956	322	1168110 right, 1169001 left, duals
1956	322	1175576 right, 1175581 left, duals and Series 70
1957–1958	364	1187336 right, 1185463 left, Roadmaster and Limited
1957–1958	364	1185463 right, 118546 left
1957–1958	364	1185463 right, 1185463 left, duals
1959–1960	364/401	1185602 right, 1185603 left
1959–1960	364/401	1185602 right, 1186291 left, duals
1961	364/401	1196974 right, 1196457 left
1962	401	1351702 right, 1348477 left
1963	401/425	1396568 right, 1348477 left
1964	401/425	1377480 right, 1348477 left
1965–1966	401/425	1377480 right, 1367159 left
1965–1966	401	1377476 right, 1372319 left, Gran Sport

CHAPTER 2

BUICK BIG BLOCK

1967-1976

400, 430, and 455

Buick finally retired the nailhead V-8 engines and introduced an updated big-block V-8 in 1967. Although the block had a similar design with the same bore spacing of 4.75 in., few parts interchanged with the earlier blocks. The block had much larger two-bolt crank bearing journals, measuring 3.250 in. vs. 2.500 in. on the older blocks, and the cylinder heads were also different. They were basically the same cylinder heads that were used on the 300–340 cid small-block engines introduced in 1961. A quick way to visually identify the new series of engines was the front distributor location; the older engines had the distributor in the rear.

There were two displacements of this engine between 1967 and 1969. The smallest was the 400 cid V-8 with a 4.04 in. bore and 3.90 in. stroke. Increasing the bore to 4.1875 in. resulted in the 430 cid engine. The 400 cid engine was used on the Buick GS 400 and rated at 340 hp. The 430 cid engine was used on the full-size cars and was rated at 360 hp.

In 1970, the 400- and 430 cid engines were replaced by a 455 cid big-block. This largest Buick engine yet had a bore and stroke of 4.3125x3.90 in. The highest horsepower-producing 455 cid engine was the 1970 Stage I, which put out an advertised 360 hp. The Riviera 455 cid was advertised at 370 hp, but the Stage I put out more power. The Stage I used a different camshaft and also had cylinder heads with larger valves. From this high point, the engine produced less and less power due to reduced compression ratios and emission controls until it was retired after the 1976 model year.

400 cid

The 400 cid Buick was in production for three model years, from 1967 to 1969. The engine came with a cast nodular iron crankshaft, forged-steel connecting rods, cast-aluminum pistons, hydraulic-lifter camshaft, and a four-barrel carburetor with a dual exhaust system. In such trim, the engine was rated at 340 hp.

There was a dealer-installed Stage I package on the 1968 400 cid engine; it consisted of a different camshaft, higher compression pistons, and other modifications for a 345 hp output. The Stage I group became a bona-fide option on the 1969 400 cid engines, and it included a higher performance hydraulic camshaft, different valve springs, heavy-duty fuel pump, some oil pump modifications, and chrome valve covers.

A Stage II package, which included a hotter camshaft, higher compression pistons, an Edelbrock aluminum intake manifold, Mickey Thompson exhaust headers, and other items, was available on a dealer-installed basis. The Stage II package was basically a collection of high-performance parts that could be purchased individually or in groups on an over-the-counter basis.

430 cid

The 430 cid V-8 was a bored 400 cid engine, and like the 400, it was available from 1967 to 1969. It was similar to the 400 cid engine, except for displacement. It was rated at 360 hp.

455 cid

The largest Buick V-8 was the 455 cid engine, which had a 4.3125x3.90 in. bore and stroke. In 1970, there were three versions of the engine: 350 hp, 360 hp Stage I, and the 370 hp Riviera 455. As was the other Buick V-8 that preceded it, the 455 cid engine was equipped with a cast nodular iron crankshaft, forged-steel connecting rods, cast-aluminum pistons, hydraulic camshaft, four-barrel intake induction, and dual exhausts.

By 1974, the 455 cid Buick engine could have been had with a single exhaust system and a two-barrel carburetor. The last Stage I was rated 245 hp, and it, too, was a 1974 engine.

Engine Blocks

All Buick big-block engines had two-bolt main-bearing caps. The main-bearing cap journals were larger than those of the previous big V-8s, measuring 3.250 in. The 455 cid blocks also had 0.25 in.-thicker main-bearing caps.

There is a difference between 1967 and 1972 and 1973–later blocks. The 1973 and later cylinder heads have different water passages, and accordingly, the block's deck surface is also different. Later blocks are the so-called double-scallop blocks, due to the shape of the intake side of the deck. Accordingly, cylinder heads aren't immediately interchangeable among the blocks, unless a relatively simple modification is made to plug the extra water passages.

Cylinder Heads

All of the late big-block engines use cylinder heads similar to those used on the small-block Buick engines. The previous pentroof combustion chambers of the older big-blocks were replaced by a more conventional wedge-shaped combustion chamber. Valve sizes were larger, too, 2.00 in. intake and 1.625 in. exhaust.

The 1970 Stage I cylinder heads had larger ports (the same as those used on the 1967 430 cid engine) and larger valves, 2.12 in. intake and 1.75 in. exhaust.

The 1970 and later engines used a different system to lubricate the rocker arms. Instead of the oil passage running the length of the cylinder head, the rockers were lubricated by oil from the hydraulic lifters, which was routed via tubular pushrods. All 1970–1972 engines had 1.59:1 ratio rockers, which were lighter aluminum die castings; these were replaced on 1973 and later engines with stronger 1.54:1 ratio stamped steel rockers.

The Buick 455 was a great street engine, with lots of low-end torque. This is a 1971 Stage 1. *Jerry Heasley*

Although the big-block heads are similar to the 300/340/350 cid small-block heads, the big engines have a five-bolt valve cover, while the smaller engines use a six-bolt cover, and the heads do not interchange.

There were a few special Stage II D-Port heads cast by Buick in 1970. Because of production problems, only 75 to 100 sets were made. There were also a few Tunnel Port heads made for drag racing.

Intake Manifolds

All Buick engines used cast-iron two- and four-barrel intake manifolds. The Edelbrock aluminum intake manifold was an over-the-counter option.

Exhaust Manifolds

All Buick engines used cast-iron exhaust manifolds in various configurations. Stage I exhaust manifolds had freer-flowing passages and larger outlets.

Engine Identification

Buick's system for numbering parts and castings was similar to that used by other GM divisions. The casting number is found on the part itself, but its location has varied over the years. On engine blocks it can be found on either side, while on manifolds it's on one side or the other, and on cylinder heads the casting number is found under the valve cover area.

Buick was a bit more thorough than most manufacturers when it came to coding engines.

Buick stamped the vehicle's VIN on the right front side of the block until 1970 and on the left side from 1970 on.

Buick also included a specific two- or three-digit code (listed here) that identified the engine as well and a number that indicated the production sequence of the engine. In 1969, Buick also included an engine plant code (F for Flint) and a date code that indicated the date the engine was assembled. A typical engine date code might be 11 22, for November 22. The engine ID number was located on the right front side of the block and on the left side from 1970.

Engine Identification Codes

Code	Engine
1967	
NR	400 cid 340 hp
ND, MD	430 cid 360 hp
1968	
PR	400 cid 340 hp
PD	430 cid 360 hp
1969	
RR, RS	400 cid 340 hp
RD, RO	430 cid 360 hp
1970	
SR	455 cid 350 hp
SS	455 cid 360 hp
SF	455 cid 370 hp
1971	
TR	455 cid 310 hp
TA	455 cid 335 hp
TS	455 cid 345 hp
1972	
WF	455 cid 225/250 hp

Engine Identification Codes

Code	Engine
WA	455 cid 260 hp
WS	455 cid 270 hp
1973	
XF	455 cid 225/250 hp
XS	455 cid 260 hp
XA	455 cid 270 hp
1974	
ZI	455 cid 175 hp
ZH	455 cid 190 hp
ZF	455 cid 210 hp
ZK	455 cid 230 hp
ZS	455 cid 245 hp
ZA	455 cid 255 hp
1975	
AF	455 cid 205 hp

Engine Specifications

	Displacement	Carburetor	Horsepower	Torque	Compression Ratio	Notes
1967						
	400	4V	340@5,000	440@3,200	10.25	GS 400
	430	4V	360@5,000	475@3,200	10.25	Buick
1968						
	400	4V	340@5,000	440@3,200	10.25	GS 400, Sportwagon
	430	4V	360@5,000	475@3,200	10.25	Buick
1969						
	400	4V	340@5,000	440@3,200	10.25	GS 400, Sportwagon
	430	4V	360@5,000	475@3,200	10.25	Buick
1970						
	455	4V	350@4,600	510@2,800	10.0	GS 455, Buick
	455	4V	360@4,600	510@2,800	10.0	GS 455
	455	4V	370@4,600	510@2,800	10.0	Buick, LeSabre, Riviera GS
1971						
	455	4V	315@4,600	450@2,800	8.5	GS 455, Buick
	455	4V	330@4,600	455@2,800	8.5	GS 455
	455	4V	345@5,000	460@3,000	8.5	Buick, LeSabre, Riviera GS
1972						
	455	4V	250@4,600	375@2,800	8.5	Buick
	455	4V	260@4,600	380@2,800	8.5	Riviera GS
	455	4V	270@4,400	390@3,000	8.5	Gran Sport
1973						
	455	4V	225@4,000	360@2,600	8.5	Century, Regal, LeSabre, Centurion
	455	4V	250@4,600	375@2,800	8.5	Century, Regal, LeSabre
	455	4V	260@4,600	380@2,800	8.5	Buick, Riviera
	455	4V	270@4,400	390@3,000	8.5	GS
1974						
	455	2V	175@3,400	360@2,600	8.5	Century, Regal, LeSabre, Centurion
	455	2V	190@3,600	370@2,000	8.5	Century, Regal, LeSabre, Centurion, GS
	455	4V	210@3,600	335@2,200	8.5	Century, Regal, LeSabre, Centurion, GS, Riviera
	455	4V	230@3,800	355@2,200	8.5	Century, Regal, LeSabre, GS, Riviera
	455	4V	245@4,000	360@2,400	8.5	Buick, Riviera
	455	4V	255@4,400	370@2,800	8.5	GS
1975						
	455	4V	205@3,800	345@2,000	7.9	LeSabre, Electra, Riviera

Engine Internal Dimensions

Displacement	Bore and Stroke	Rod Bearings	Main Bearings	Intake/Exhaust Valves
400	4.040x3.900	2.249–2.250	3.250	2.00/1.625
430	4.1875x3.900	2.249–2.250	3.250	2.00/1.625
455	4.3125x3.90	2.249–2.250	3.250	2.00/1.625, Stage I 2.12/1.75

Block, Head, and Manifold Part and Casting Numbers

Year	Engine	Part or Casting Number
Engine Blocks		
1970	455	casting 1231738
1971	455	casting 1231738, 1238861
1972	455	casting 1238861, 1241735
1973–1974	455	casting 1241735
1975	455	casting 1241735
Cylinder Heads		
1967	400	1382720
1968	400/430	1385649
1969	400/430	1245713
1970	455	1240150, casting 1231786, 360 hp
1970–1971	455	1240144
1971	455	1240146, casting 1237661
1972	455	1238530, Riviera GS, Stage I
1972	455	1242448, casting 1242445, 1238148
1973–1974	455	1242001, casting 1241860
1975	455	1250489, casting 1246332
Intake Manifolds		
1967	400 4V	1374068
1967	430 4V	1374068
1968	400 4V	1383438
1968	430 4V	1383438
1969	400 4V	1386003 (casting and part no.)
1969	430 4V	1386003 (casting and part no.)
1970	455 4V	1231718 (casting and part no.)
1971	455 4V	1236403 (casting and part no.)
1972	455 4V	1245375, casting 1239925, 1243020
1972–1973	455 4V	1245059
1973	455 4V	1245375, casting 1239925, 1243020
1974	455 2V	1244302
1974	455 4V	1245059
1975	455 4V	1247330
Exhaust Manifolds		
1967	400/430	1238094 right, 1245433 left
1968	400/430	1383648 right, 1384089 left
1969	400/430	1238094 right, 1245443 left
1970	455	1238094 right, 1233451 left
1971–1974	455	1238094 right, 1233451 left
1975	455	1238094 right, 1246715 left

CHAPTER 3

BUICK SMALL BLOCK

1961-1977

215, 300, 340, and 350

Buick brought out its first small-block V-8 in 1961. The engine was used on the 1961–1963 Buick Special Skylark, 1961–1962 Pontiac Tempest, and 1961–1963 Oldsmobile F-85. The engine, which displaced only 215 cid, was quite unusual for Buick at the time. It was an all-aluminum engine, which weighed in at about 320lb.

In 1964, Buick came out with a new small-block engine to replace the 215 cid aluminum engine. The 215 cid V-8 was redundant because of its small displacement (the Buick 225 cid V-6 filled that slot just as easily and it was a lot less expensive to manufacture). The aluminum engine also proved to be generally unreliable, and there were many production problems associated with it. There was also just too much of a gap between the 401 cid big-block and the 215 cid small-block.

So Buick took its existing iron-block V-6 engine and added two more cylinders at the back, and the result was a 300 cid small-block V-8 engine. The 300 cid V-8 had the same bore spacing (4.24 in.) and the same bore and stroke (3.75x3.40 in.) as the V-6. The new engine was a much better choice for the redesigned 1964 Buick Special, which because of its larger size, was now classified as an intermediate. The four-barrel version of the engine, with its 11.0:1 compression ratio, put out a healthy 250 hp.

In 1965, the engine was stroked to 3.85 in., creating an "undersquare" design, but displacing 340 cid. Both the 300- and 340 cid engines were replaced by a 350 cid small-block in 1967, which remained in production through 1977. The 350 cid engine was similar to the previous small-blocks.

215 cid

The 215 cid small-block V-8 was in production from 1961 to 1963. It had a bore and stroke of 3.50x2.80 in. and used a cast-iron crankshaft and forged-steel connecting rods. The engine was cast in aluminum, including the two- or four-barrel intake manifold, and the cylinders were fitted with cast-iron liners. The cylinder heads followed Buick practice of using shaft-mounted rocker arms.

300 cid

The 300 cid V-8, introduced in 1964, was an enlarged version of Buick's V-6. The engine used a cast-iron crankshaft, cast connecting rods, and cast-aluminum pistons. The intake and exhaust manifolds were also cast in iron, and like all Buick engines, a hydraulic-lifter camshaft was used. The cylinder heads were a new wedge design but still used shaft-mounted rocker arms. In the Buick tradition, the valves were on the small side, 1.625 in./1.313 in. intake/exhaust; however, they were enlarged on the 1966–1967 engines to 1.8175 in./1.38 in. The 1964 two-barrel engine was rated at 210 hp, while the four-barrel put out 250 hp. The two-barrel engine continued on through the 1967 model year at the same 210 hp output, while the four-barrel was discontinued after the 1965 model year.

340 cid

Buick saw the need for a bigger displacement small-block and introduced the 340 cid engine in 1966. It was available in both two- and four-barrel versions. The engine was essentially a stroked 300 cid, as it had the same 3.75 in. bore but a longer 3.85 in. stroke. The longer stroke necessitated the use of a taller engine block, so the intake manifolds of the 300- and 340 cid engines do not interchange, although both engines used the same cylinder heads.

350 cid

Both the 300- and 340 cid engines were replaced by a larger 350 cid engine in 1968. The 10 cid increase was achieved by increasing the bore to 3.800 in. The 350 cid engine used the same block and cylinder heads as the replaced 300–340 cid engines. The most powerful version of the 350 cid V-8 was the 1970 315 hp edition. The engine took a dive in power output from 1971 on, like all Detroit engines, and it was finally retired after the 1977 model year.

Cylinder Blocks

The small-block Buick engines, with the exception of the 215 cid aluminum engine, all used a cast-iron block with two-bolt main-bearing caps. The 340- and 350 cid variants have a taller deck height than the 300 cid engine. All engines used a cast nodular iron crankshaft, cast malleable iron connecting rods, and cast-aluminum pistons.

Cylinder Heads

After taking a lot of heat for the nailhead pentroof cylinder heads on the big-block engines, Buick used a conventional wedge-chamber cylinder head design on the 1961 V-6 and therefore on the subsequent small-block V-8 engines. Valve sizes varied—1964–1965 engines used 1.625 in./1.313 in. intake/exhaust valves; they were increased to 1.8175 in./1.38 in. on the 1966–1967 engines; 1968 and later 350 cid engines have gigantic 1.88 in./1.50 in. valves.

The 1970 and later engines used a different system to lubricate the rocker arms. Instead of the oil passage running the length of the cylinder head, the rockers were lubricated by oil from the hydraulic lifters, which was routed via tubular pushrods. The 1970–1972 engines had 1.59:1 ratio rockers, which were lighter aluminum die castings; these were replaced on 1973 and later engines with stronger 1.54:1 ratio stamped steel rockers.

Intake Manifolds

All (except those for the 215 cid V-8) small-block intake manifolds were made of solid, premium-grade cast iron.

A Buick 350 cid cylinder block. The block resembles the original Buick V-8 blocks in that it is a Y-block design, with its deep side skirts. However, there is no interchangeability between the two designs. The 400 and 455 blocks are similar.

Exhaust Manifolds

All Buick engines used cast-iron exhaust manifolds of different sizes and outlets.

Engine Identification

Buick's system for numbering parts and castings was similar to that used by other GM divisions. The casting number is found on the part itself, but its location has varied over the years. On engine blocks it can be found on either side, on manifolds it's on one side or the other, and on cylinder heads the casting number is found under the valve cover area.

Buick was a bit more thorough than most manufacturers when it came to coding engines. Buick inscribed the vehicle's VIN on the block itself. This was located on the right front side of the block. In 1970, the VIN was moved to the left side of the block.

Buick also included a specific two- or three-digit code (listed in the tables) that identified the engine and a number that indicated the production sequence of the engine. In 1969, Buick also included an engine plant code (F for Flint) and a date code that indicated the date the engine was assembled. A typical engine date code might be 11 22, for November 22. The engine ID number was located on the right front side of the block and on the left side from 1970.

Although Buick's engine codes weren't as specific as those used by Chevrolet, for instance, Buick's addition of the VIN connected the engine to the particular vehicle it was installed in.

Engine Identification Codes

Code	Engine
1961	
H	215 cid
1962	
LI	215 cid 145 hp
I	215 cid 155 hp

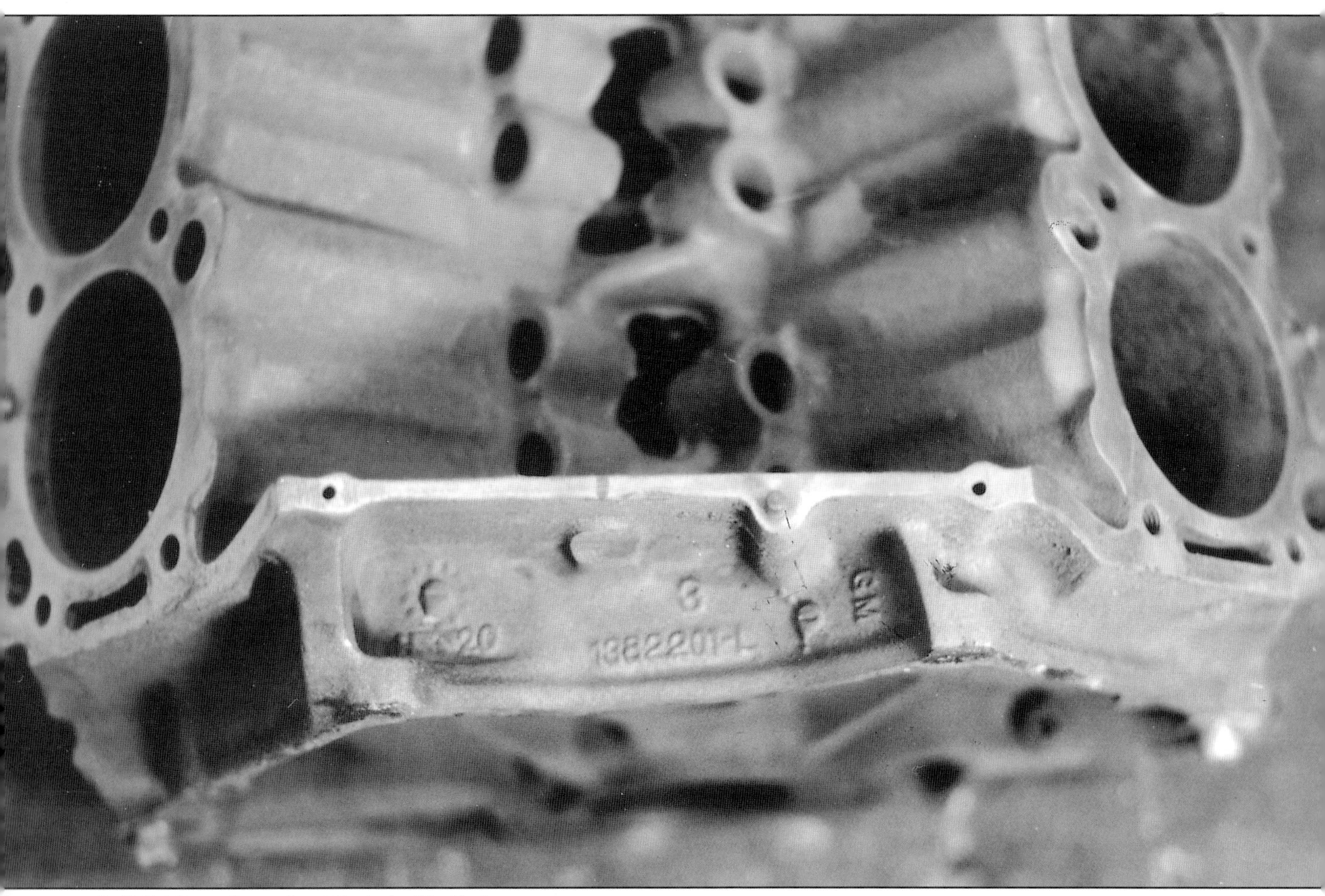

You'll find the casting number at the back of the block.

Engine Identification Codes

Code	Engine
HI	215 cid 190 hp
1963	
JP	215 cid 145 hp
JM	215 cid 155 hp
JN	215 cid 200 hp
1964	
KL	300 cid 210 hp
KP	300 cid 250 hp
1965	
LL	300 cid 210 hp
LP	300 cid 250 hp
1966	
ML	300 cid 210 hp
MA	340 cid 220 hp
MB	340 cid 260 hp
1967	
NL	300 cid 210 hp
NA	300 cid 260 hp
1968	
PO	350 cid 230 hp
PP	350 cid 280 hp
1969	
RO	350 cid 230 hp
RP	350 cid 280 hp
Code	**Engine**
1970	
SO	350 cid 260 hp
SP	350 cid 315 hp
1971	
TO	350 cid 230 hp
TD	350 cid 260 hp, TH a/t
TB	350 cid 260 hp
TC	350 cid 230 hp, TH a/t, LeSabre
SP	350 cid 315 hp
1972	
WC	350 cid 150/155 hp
WB	350 cid 180/175/190 hp
1973	
XC	350 cid 150 hp
XB	350 cid 175 hp/190 hp
1974	
ZC	350 cid 150 hp
ZP	350 cid 150 hp
ZB	350 cid 175 hp
ZM	350 cid 175 hp
1975	
AB	350 cid 145 hp
AM	350 cid 165 hp

Engine Specifications

	Displacement	Carburetor	Horsepower	Torque	Compression Ratio	Notes
1961						
	215	2V	155@4,400	220@2,400	8.8	Special, Skylark
	215	4V	185@4,800	250@2,600	10.25	Special, Skylark
1962						
	215	2V	155@4,400	220@2,200	8.8	Special, Skylark
	215	4V	190@4,800	235@3,200	11.00	Special, Skylark
1963						
	215	2V	155@4,600	220@2,400	8.8	Special, Skylark
	215	4V	200@4,800	240@3,200	11.00	Special, Skylark
1964						
	300	2V	210@4,600	310@2,400	9.0	Special, Skylark, LeSabre
	300	4V	250@4,800	335@3,000	11.0	Special, Skylark, LeSabre
1965						
	300	2V	210@4,600	310@2,400	9.0	Special, Skylark
	300	4V	250@4,800	335@3,000	11.0	Special, Skylark, Sportwagon, LeSabre
1966						
	300	2V	210@4,600	310@2,400	9.0	Special, Skylark
	340	2V	220@4,000	340@2,400	9.0	Sportwagon, LeSabre
	340	4V	260@4,000	365@2,800	10.25	Special, Skylark, Sportwagon, LeSabre
	340	4V	260@4,000	365@2,800	10.25	Special, Skylark, Sportwagon, LeSabre, GS 340
1967						
	300	2V	210@4,600	310@2,400	9.0	Special, Skylark
	340	2V	220@4,000	340@2,400	9.0	Sportwagon, LeSabre
	340	4V	260@4,000	365@2,800	10.25	Special, Skylark, Sportwagon, LeSabre, GS 340
1968						
	350	2V	230@4,400	350@2,400	9.0	Sportwagon, Skylark, LeSabre
	350	4V	280@4,800	350@2,400	10.25	Special, Skylark, Sportwagon, LeSabre, GS 350
1969						
	350	2V	230@4,400	350@2,400	9.0	Sportwagon, Skylark, LeSabre
	350	4V	280@4,800	350@2,400	10.25	Special, Skylark, Sportwagon, LeSabre, GS 350, California GS
1970						
	350	2V	260@4,600	360@2,600	9.0	Skylark, LeSabre, Sportwagon
	350	4V	285@4,600	375@3,000	9.0	Skylark, LeSabre, Sportwagon
	350	4V	315@4,800	410@3,200	10.25	GS 350
1971						
	350	2V	230@4,400	350@2,400	8.5	Skylark, LeSabre, Sportwagon
	350	4V	220@4,600	360@2,400	8.5	Skylark, LeSabre, Sportwagon GS
1972						
	350	2V	150@3,800	265@2,400	8.5	Skylark, LeSabre
	350	2V	155@3,800	270@2,400	8.5	Skylark, LeSabre
	350	4V	175@3,800	270@2,400	8.5	Skylark, LeSabre
	350	4V	180@3,800	275@2,400	8.5	Skylark, LeSabre
	350	4V	190@4,000	285@2,800	8.5	Skylark, LeSabre
1973						
	350	2V	150@3,800	265@2,400	8.5	Century, Regal, LeSabre, GS
	350	4V	175@3,800	270@2,400	8.5	Century, Regal, LeSabre, GS
	350	4V	190@4,000	285@2,800	8.5	Century, Regal, LeSabre, GS
1974						
	350	2V	150@3,800	270@2,000	8.5	Apollo, Century, Regal, LeSabre, GS
	350	4V	175@3,800	260@2,000	8.5	Apollo, Century, Regal, LeSabre, GS
1975						
	350	2V	145@3,200	270@2,000	8.0	Skyhawk, Apollo, Century
	350	4V	175@3,800	260@2,000	8.0	Skyhawk, Apollo, Century, LeSabre

Engine Internal Dimensions

Displacement	Bore and Stroke	Rod Bearings	Main Bearings	Intake/Exhaust Valves
215	3.500x2.800	2.000	2.2992	1.625/1.313
300	3.750x3.400	2.000	2.992	1.625/1.313, 1.8175/1.38 (1966–1967)
340	3.750x3.850	2.000	2.995	1.8175/1.38
350	3.800x3.850	2.000	2.995	1.88/1.50

Block, Head, and Manifold Part and Casting Numbers

Year	Engine	Part or Casting Number
Engine Blocks		
1961–1963	215	casting 93724
1964–1966	300	1357943
1967	340	1374557
Cylinder Heads		
1961–1963	215	1193743
1964	300	1394280
1965	300	1374720
1966	340	1396788
1967	340	1396788, casting 1366379, 1383984 w/ A.I.R.*
1968	350	1382720
1971	350	casting 1382546
1972	350	1242457 w/A.I.R., 1238532 w/o A.I.R.
1973	350	1242457
1974	350	124498
1975	350	1247716

Tall, rectangular intake ports typify the Buick cylinder head.

Block, Head, and Manifold Part and Casting Numbers

Intake Manifolds	Engine	Part or Casting Number
1961	215 2V	1195360
1962	215 2V	1354966
1962	215 2V	1396950
1963	215 4V	1195360
1964	300 2V	1358504
1964	300 4V	1359122
1965	300 2V	1377507
1965	300 4V	1367299
1966	300 2V	1378707
1966	300 4V	1379948
1967	340 2V	1378707
1967	340 4V	1379948
1968	350 2V	1382616
1968	350 4V	1382615 (casting and part no.)
1969	350 2V	1386845 (casting and part no.)
1969	350 4V	1387069 (casting and part no.)
1970	350 2V	1231381 (casting and part no.)
1970	350 4V	1231924 (casting and part no.)
1971	350 2V	1236402 (casting and part no.)
1971	350 4V	1236839 (casting and part no.)
1972	350 2V	1244945, casting 1238643, 1242014 w/ A.I.R.
1972	350 2V	1238643, casting 1238578, 1238578 w/o A.I.R.
1972	350 4V	1244947, casting 1238647, 1242015 w/ A.I.R.
1972	350 4V	1238647, casting 1238586 w/o A.I.R.
1973	350 2V	1244945, casting 1238643, 1242014
1973	350 4V	1244947, casting 1238647, 1242015
1974	350 2V	1245057
1974	350 4V	1245058
1975	350 2V	1249166
1975	350 4V	1246677, California
1975	350 4V	1249168
Exhaust Manifolds		
1964	300	1364178 right, 1359689 left
1965	300	1369310 right, 1359689 left
1966–1967	340	1375910 right, 1375917 left
1968–1970	350	1246658 right, 1383427 left
1970	350	1381750 right, 1231359 left
1971–1974	350	1246658 right, 1243457 left
1975	350	1246656 right, 1246713 left

* A.I.R. is for Air Injection Reactor

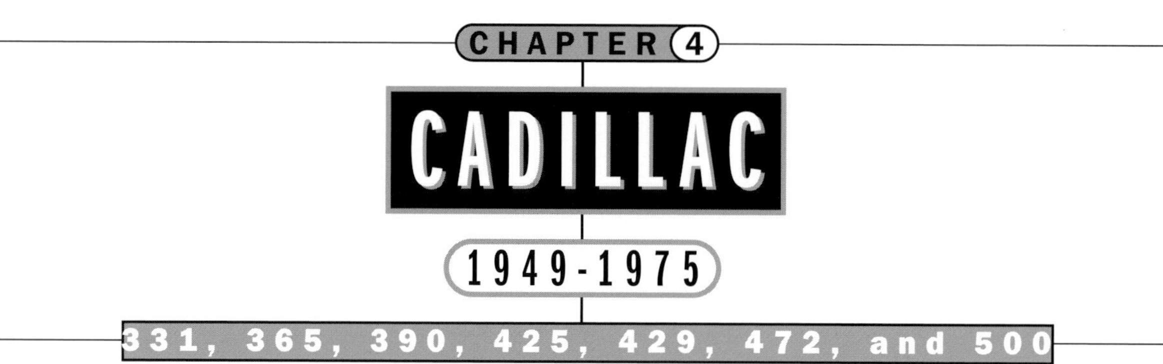

It was Cadillac (along with Oldsmobile) that brought out the first modern ohv American V-8 in 1949. The ohv V-8 set the pattern for the rest of the industry and would dominate American engine design until the early 1980s.

At the time, the Cadillac engine was considered to be an engineering marvel. Here was an engine that was smaller and lighter than the previous Cadillac V-8 and yet it produced more power. The engine design has been credited to three men—Harry F. Barr (the staff engineer who was in charge of Cadillac engine design and later helped design the Chevrolet small-block V-8), Edward N. Cole (chief engineer at Cadillac, who also went to Chevrolet along with Barr and later became president of GM), and John F. "Jack" Gordon (Cadillac's general manager, who also became GM's president).

The 331 cid Cadillac V-8, with a bore and stroke of 3.8125x3.625 in., put out 160 hp with a 7.5:1 compression ratio. The engine was 4 in. shorter and 4 in. narrower than the Cadillac flathead V-8, and it also weighed 188lb less. The reason for the engine's more compact dimensions was the new type of "slipper" piston design used on the engine, which was credited to Byron Ellis, a piston designer at Cadillac. The new slipper piston design, which had its sides cut away, enabled the piston to fit in between the crankshaft's counterweights at the bottom of its stroke. The use of this type of piston enabled the use of shorter connecting rods and therefore a shorter engine block.

The Cadillac V-8 engine had some interesting features that made it quite different from anything else offered in Detroit at the time. First, the engine's valves were located in the cylinder head, over the combustion chamber. The overhead valves were actuated by a camshaft located in the center of the engine, through a system of hydraulic lifters, pushrods, and shaft-mounted rocker arms. The engine also had an "oversquare" bore and stroke dimension, meaning that, unlike the flathead engines, the bore was larger than the stroke. Previously, it was thought that an engine, in order to produce enough low-end torque, would need to have a longer stroke and a smaller bore. (When an engine has the same size bore and stroke, the engine is said to be "square.") The oversquare design meant less piston travel (and therefore less wear) when compared to the long-stroke flathead. Another benefit of the new engine design was the possibility of using higher compression ratios, better engine breathing through larger and more direct porting and valves, and a more efficient combustion chamber design.

It took years for other manufacturers to come up with their own ohv V-8 engines. Chrysler came out with its Fire Power Hemi engines in 1951; the Lincoln V-8 was first used in 1952; and Chevrolet finally came out with the famous small-block V-8 in 1955 (it didn't break any new ground, but was rather a refinement of a previous design concept).

The 331 cid Cadillac V-8 was replaced by a bored-out version of the engine in 1956 that displaced 365 cid; in 1959 the engine was stroked to produce 390 cid.

The engine went through a complete redesign in 1963, yet it still had the same bore and stroke, for 390 cid. It was bored again in 1964 to 429 cid, and this displacement was in production through 1967.

Once again, the engine went through a makeover in 1968. Displacement increased to 472 cid and to a whopping 500 cid by 1970. These displacements proved to be too large to continue during the 1970s, so the Cadillac V-8 was reduced to a still large 425 cid in 1977. Even that proved to be too large, so the engine was again reduced in size in 1980 to 368 cid.

The Cadillac V-8's emphasis over the years was to produce enough power to move the increasingly heavier Cadillac cars in a reasonable manner and do so in a quiet, unobtrusive, and reliable manner. In that respect, the engine has proved to be a success.

331 cid

The 331 was introduced in 1949, and it had a bore and stroke of 3.8125x3.625 in. It was rated at 160 hp with a two-barrel carburetor. The engine used shaft-mounted rocker arms, a hydraulic camshaft, forged-steel connecting rods, and cast-iron intake and exhaust manifolds.

The 331 cid displacement would be in service until 1955, with increasingly higher output. This was due to higher compression ratios and the use of a four-barrel carburetor beginning in 1952.

365 cid

The Cadillac V-8 was bored to 4.00 in. in 1956, while retaining the 3.625 in. stroke. The engine kept the same basic configuration as the 331 cid engine it replaced, and by 1958, in its last year of production, the 365 cid engine was pumping out 310 hp with the four-barrel carburetor.

Cadillac also used a multiple-carburetor system in 1958. The engine used a Tri-Power induction system that featured three two-barrel carburetors for a 335 hp output.

390 cid

With the same 4.00 in. bore and a longer 3.875 in. stroke, the Cadillac V-8 displaced 390 cid beginning with the 1959 model year. The engine would remain in service until 1962. With the four-barrel carburetor, power was up to 325 hp.

The optional Tri-Power induction system continued on the 1959–1960 engines, this time putting out 345 hp.

In 1963, the "old" 390 cid engine was replaced by a "new" 390 cid Cadillac V-8. Although both engines had the same bore and stroke and even the same power output, 325 hp, the only parts that interchanged were the cylinder heads and connecting rods.

The engine featured a new engine block that was shorter by 1.188 in. and that also had a lower deck height, by 0.445 in. This resulted in a more compact engine. The engine block was lighter, by 30lb, and also featured numerous internal modifications to strengthen its structure as well as larger main bearings. Because the block was lower, shorter pistons were used. A major difference was the new front aluminum housing. Not only did it cover the timing chain but also provided mounting for the distributor, oil pump, water pump, and fuel pump. Even the oil filter was attached to the housing. The engine's intake manifold was also new. It sat lower in the valley between the cylinder heads—good for hood clearance but not good for high performance, which wasn't a primary concern at Cadillac, anyway. The new engine was 50lb lighter than the 390 cid it replaced.

425 cid

With more and more emphasis on fuel economy during the 1970s, even the Cadillac buyer became concerned with it. A 500 cid was no longer a strong selling point and no matter what you did with the engine, it would always be the definitive "gas guzzler." The Cadillac V-8 was destroked and debored to 4.082x4.06 in., for 425 cid. With an 8.5:1 compression ratio and all the usual emission gear, the engine was rated at 180 hp, SAE net. Interestingly, the original 1949 Cadillac 331 cid engine was rated at 141 hp net. The engine was in production through the 1978 model year.

429 cid

Almost immediately, the new 1963 390 cid engine was bored and stroked to 4.125x4.00 in. in 1964 for 429 cid. This was only 1 cid less than the Lincoln V-8. Power went up to 340 hp to help compensate for the Cadillac's greater weight.

The 429 cid engine would remain in service until 1967.

472 cid

The 472 cid engine was introduced in 1968 for several reasons. First, Cadillacs were still growing in terms of weight and size. The existing 429 cid Cadillac V-8 was at the limit in terms of practical displacement and the only way to get more cubic inches was through a new block that had wider bore spacing, which made bore increases possible. Lincoln also had brought out its 462 cid engine (and later in the model year, a new canted-valve 460 cid V-8), and it was important for Cadillac to have a larger displacement engine than Lincoln. It was a matter of pride. Before the gas crisis hit, Ford was going to increase the 460's displacement to 501 cid, but never did. The cubic-inch race eventually reversed itself into a contest of who could bring out the smallest V-8.

With a bore spacing of 5.00 in., there was plenty of room for a bore of 4.30 in. With a stroke of 4.06 in., the result was 472 cid. Power was at 375 hp with 525ft-lb torque.

Although all the major components of the engine (block, heads, and crank) were new, Cadillac kept the same configuration as the older V-8. All the engine accessories were driven from the front cover, and the oil filter was attached to the front of the engine.

500 cid

In 1970, the 472 was stroked to 4.304 in., for 500 cid. It was rated at 400 hp with 550ft-lb torque. It was, and still is, the largest passenger car engine made since 1949. The engine was in service through the 1976 model year when, with a four-barrel carburetor, it was rated at 190 hp, and with electronic fuel injection (EFI), at 215 hp.

Engine Blocks

The Cadillac engine block was highly innovative when it first came out in 1949. It used five main bearings to support the crankshaft, and it was compact and much lighter than the flathead blocks. All Cadillac engines used two-bolt main-bearing caps. Pre-1963 blocks have different crankshaft main-bearing and rod bearing journal sizes than the 1963 and later blocks (see the table). Cadillac V-8 engines have used cast-iron crankshafts and forged-steel connecting rods. The 1968 and later engines used cast connecting rods.

Cylinder Heads

Cadillac pioneered the wedge combustion chamber design. Cadillac cylinder heads had ports similar in configuration to those of the Oldsmobile V-8 engine—paired intake ports while only the center exhaust ports were paired. All Cadillac cylinder heads used shaft-mounted rockers. The 1949–1967 heads used a conventional rocker shaft, while the 1968 and later engines had a different system: Paired rockers were mounted on a rocker arm support.

The 1949–1967 cylinder heads used removable valve guides; later engines had integral valve guides. Valve sizes are listed in the tables.

Intake Manifolds

There wasn't much variety in intake manifolds for the Cadillac V-8. The 1949–1951 engines had a two-barrel intake manifold; all subsequent engines had a four-barrel intake manifold. The exceptions were the 1955–1957 2x4V engines, 1958–1960 Tri-Power engines, and the 1976 and later EFI engines. All Cadillac intake manifolds were cast iron.

Exhaust Manifolds

Cadillac exhaust manifolds were conventional cast-iron units. Front-wheel-drive Eldorado engines were equipped with manifolds that specifically fit those engines and do not interchange with engines for rear-drive cars.

Engine Identification

Each Cadillac engine block, cylinder head, and exhaust and intake manifold is cast with a casting number and a date code. The date code indicates the date the part was cast.

Cadillac also stamped the vehicle's VIN on the engine block, the location of which is listed in the table. Cadillac also used an Engine Unit Number (EUN), which was stamped into the left rear section of the engine block. The EUN recorded at what numerical sequence an engine was assembled, and in earlier years the number included letter(s) and numbers that indicated whether the engine or vehicle was equipped with such features as air conditioning, power steering, and/or other equipment (see the table). Gradually that practice fell into disuse, and the EUN simply recorded the engine assembly sequence in a given year. In such cases, the number started with the model year.

From 1972 to 1975, Cadillac included a letter code in the VIN indicating engine. An R code denotes a 472 cid engine; an S code denotes a 500 cid engine.

EUN Codes

Series	Code
1950	
61	8-M-1 and up, m/t
60S, 61, 62, 75	9-M-1 and up, a/t
75, 86	2-M-1 and up, m/t
86	7-M-1 and up, a/t
1951	
60S, 61, 62, 75	9-N-1 and up, a/t
86	2-N-1 and up, m/t
86	7-N-1 and up, a/t
1952	
60S, 62, 75	9-R-1 and up, a/t
60S, 62, 75	4-R-1 and up, a/t, p/s
75, 86	2-R-1 and up, m/t
86	7-R-1 and up, a/t
86	5-R-1 and up, a/t, p/s
1953	
60S, 62, 75	9-S-1 and up, a/t
60S, 62, 75	4-S-1 and up, a/t, p/s
60S, 62, 75	4-SK-1 and up, a/t, p/s, a/c
60S, 62, 75	9-SK-1 and up, a/t, a/c
75, 86	2-S-1 and up, m/t
75, 86	2-SK-1 and up, m/t, a/c
86	7-S-1 and up, a/t
86	5-S-1 and up, a/t, p/s

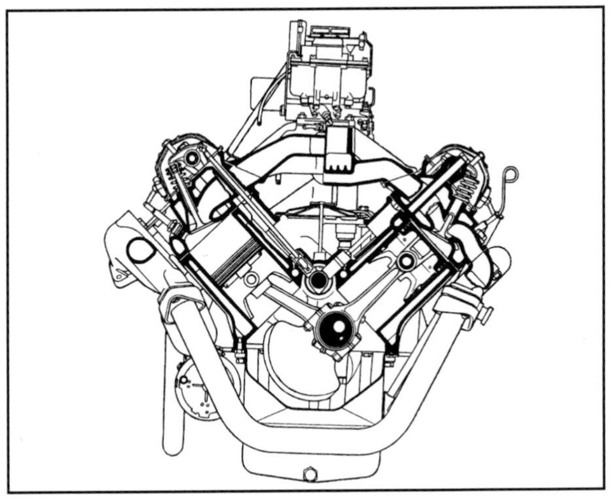

The Cadillac overhead valve V-8 was quite revolutionary when it was introduced in 1949 and set the pattern for future American V-8 engines. It was smaller, yet more powerful, than previous Cadillac engines. *Cadillac Motor Division*

EUN Codes

Series	Code
86	7-SK-1 and up, a/t, a/c
86	5-SK-1 and up, a/t, p/s, a/c
1954	
60S, 62, 75	4-T-1 and up
60S, 62, 75	4-TK-1 and up, a/c
60S, 62, 75	9-T-1 and up, m/t
60S, 62, 75	9-TK-1 and up, a/t
86	5-T-1 and up, p/s
86	5-TK-1 and up, p/s, a/c
86	7-T-1 and up
86	7-TK-1 and up, a/c
1955	
60S, 62, 75 270 hp	4V1 and up
60S, 62, 75 270 hp	4VK1 and up, a/c
60S, 62 270 hp	7V1 and up
60S, 62 270 hp	7VK1 and up, a/c
86 250 hp	5V1 and up
86 250 hp	5VK1 and up, a/c
1956	
60S, 62, 75 305 hp	4X1 and up
60S, 62, 75 285 hp	4XK1 and up, a/c
60S, 62 305 hp	7X1 and up
60S, 62 305 hp	7XK1 and up, a/c
86 285 hp	5X1 and up
86 285 hp	5XK1 and up, a/c
1957–1966	
all series	X, w/o a/c
all series	K, w/a/c

VIN Location

Year	Location
1949–1958	Upper right front corner of the engine block
1959–1967	Left side of the engine block
1968–1975	Upper part of the engine block, behind the intake manifold

Engine Specifications

	Displacement	Carburetor	Horsepower	Torque	Compression Ratio	Notes
1949–1951						
	331	2V	160@3,800	312@1,800	7.50	
1952						
	331	4V	190@4,000	322@2,400	7.50	
1953						
	331	4V	210@4,150	330@2,700	8.25	
1954						
	331	4V	230@4,400	330@2,700	8.25	
1955						
	331	4V	250@4,600	345@2,800	9.1	
	331	2x4V	270@4,800	330@3,200	9.1	Eldorado
1956						
	365	4V	285@4,600	400@2,800	9.75	
	365	2x4V	305@4,700	400@3,200	9.75	Eldorado
1957						
	365	4V	300@4,800	400@2,800	10.0	
	365	2x4V	325@4,800	400@3,200	10.0	Eldorado
1958						
	365	4V	310@4,800	405@3,100	10.25	
	365	3x2V	335@4,800	405@3,400	10.25	Eldorado
1959						
	390	4V	325@4,800	430@3,100	10.50	
	390	3x2V	345@4,800	435@3,400	10.50	Eldorado
1960						
	390	4V	325@4,800	430@3,100	10.50	
	390	3x2V	345@4,800	435@3,400	10.50	Eldorado
1961–1963						
	390	4V	325@4,800	430@3,100	10.50	

Displacement	Carburetor	Horsepower	Torque	Compression Ratio	Notes
1964–1967					
429	4V	340@4,600	480@3,000	10.50	
1968–1969					
472	4V	375@4,400	525@3,000	10.50	
1970					
472	4V	375@4,400	525@3,000	10.00	
500	4V	400@4,400	550@3,000	10.00	
1971					
472	4V	345@4,400	500@2,800	8.50	
500	4V	365@4,400	535@3,000	8.50	
1972–1973					
472	4V	220@4,000	365@2,400	8.50	
500	4V	235@3,800	385@2,400	8.50	
1974					
472	4V	205@3,600	365@2,000	8.25	
500	4V	210@3,800	385@2,400	8.25	
1975					
500	4V	190@3,600	360@2,000	8.50	

Engine Internal Dimensions

Displacement	Bore and Stroke	Rod Bearings	Main Bearings	Intake/Exhaust Valves
331	3.8125x3.625	2.2488–2.2493	2.499–2.4995	1.75/1.437 (1952–1955 1.75/1.562)
365	4.000x3.625	2.2488–2.2493	2.624–2.625	1.75/1.562
1959–1962 390	4.000x3.875	2.2488–2.2493	2.624–2.625	1.875/1.50
1963 390	4.000x3.875	2.2488–2.2493	3.000	1.875/1.50
429	4.130x4.000	2.2488–2.2493	3.000	1.875/1.50
472	4.300x4.060	2.500	3.250	2.00/1.625
500	4.300x4.304	2.500	3.250	2.00/1.625

Block, Head, and Manifold Part and Casting Numbers

Year	Engine	Part or Casting Number
Engine Blocks		
1957	365	1464819
1958	365	1467267
1959–1962	390	1469230, 1473257
1963	390	1469230, 1473267
Cylinder Heads		
1949–1951	331	3630158 right, 3630157 left
1952	331	3630263 right, 3630262 left
1953	331	3630323 right, 3630324 left
1954	331	3630458 right, 3630455 left
1955	331	3630582 right, 3630583 left
1956	365	3630634 right, 3630635 left
1957	365	3630755 right, 3630754 left (casting 1465406/1465431)
1958–1963	390	3632151 right, 3632150 left (casting 1473449/1468025)
1964–1965	429	3632907 right, 3632909 left
1966–1967	429	3632909 right, 3632908 left, w/ A.I.R.
1966–1967	429	3632907 right, 3632909 left, w/o A.I.R.
1968–1969	472	3633123
1970	472/500	3633450
1971–1973	472/500	3633544
1974	472/500	3633917
1975	500	3633979, 3633964, 3633917
Intake Manifolds		
1949	331	casting 1455104
1950–1951	331	casting 1456741
1952–1955	331	casting 1463414
1955	331 2x4V	3510439
1956	365 2x4V	3510626
1956	365	casting 1464176
1957	365	casting 1465061
1957	365 2x4V	3510701

Year	Engine	Part or Casting Number
Intake Manifolds		
1958	365	3511487
1958	365 3x2V	casting 1469889
1959–1960	390	3512079
1959–1960	390 3x2V	3512080, casting 1472225
1961–1962	390	3512079
1963	390	3512079
1964–1966	429	3632870
1967	429	3632881
1968	472	casting 1486425
1969	472	casting 1486425
1970–1972	472/500	3515328
1973–1974	472/500	3515539
1975	500	3516375 (EFI), 3516179
Exhaust Manifolds		
1949–1951	331	1453961 right, 1453754 left
1952–1955	331	1461368 right, 1461495 left
1956	365	1462987 right, 1464110 left
1957	365	1464237 right, 1464110 left
1958	365	1469298 right, 1475463 left
1959–1962	390	1475390 right, 1475463 left
1963–1964	390	1477980 right, 1475463 left
1965	429	1481668 right, 1475463 left, Fleetwood 75
1965–1967	429	1483915 right, 1482752 left
1967	429	1485556 right, 1485555 left, Eldorado
1968–1969	472	1486442 right, 1486383 left
1968	472	1485750 right, 1485749 left, Eldorado
1970–1974	472/500	1495095 right, 1486383 left
1975	500	1486442 right, 1486383 left

CHAPTER 5

CHEVROLET SMALL BLOCK

1955-1977

262, 265, 267, 283, 302, 305, 307, 327, 350, and 400

If one V-8 engine stands apart from the rest, it has to be the Chevrolet small-block. It wasn't the first ohv V-8 to come out of Detroit, but it certainly had the most innovative features. Cadillac and Oldsmobile came out with their ohv V-8s in 1949, the first of Chrysler's mighty hemi-head engines came out in 1951, the Lincoln V-8 first saw service in 1952, Buick introduced its modern V-8 in 1953, and finally, in 1955, Chevrolet and Pontiac brought out their engines. Chevrolet and Pontiac built low-line cars and, naturally, couldn't release their engines before Cadillac and the other upscale divisions had their engines out first.

What makes it even more interesting is that the last time Chevrolet had a V-8 was back in 1917, and between 1929 and 1955, the only engine Chevrolet used was an inline six cylinder! In 1952, Edward N. Cole became chief engineer at Chevrolet; before that, he worked at Cadillac. Harry F. Barr came with him as assistant chief engineer. Cole led the engineering team that designed the engine, which had to be lightweight and economical to manufacture.

And that it was. In fact, you could say the Chevrolet small-block was a work of art! In its final production form in 1955, the 575lb engine displaced 265 cid. It was very light by 1955 standards, especially for a V-8, and it actually weighed 41lb less than the Chevrolet six-cylinder engine. By refining the production process, Chevrolet was able to keep the weight of the cast-iron block as low as possible. Unlike other engines, particularly the Fords, Chevrolet felt that it wasn't necessary to extend the block's side skirts beyond 0.125 in. below the crankshaft's centerline. The crankshaft was made of forged steel, as were the connecting rods, while the pistons were cast aluminum.

It has been said that the cylinder heads make the engine, and the Chevrolet small-block was no exception. The compact small-block cylinder heads featured as-cast wedge combustion chambers, an inline valve arrangement, and exceptionally well-designed intake and exhaust ports. One of the best characteristics of the Chevrolet small-block cylinder head was that it breathed so well.

The most interesting new feature of the cylinder heads, however, was the valvetrain. Chevrolet eliminated the usual rockershaft-mounted rocker arms, replacing them with individually stud-mounted stamped-steel rocker arms that pivoted on a fulcrum ball and were kept in place by a locknut. What made it all possible was getting oil to the rocker arms. This was done via hollow pushrods that directed oil from the lifters to the rockers. Simple, neat, and lightweight. Interestingly, it was Pontiac that originated the concept in 1948, yet it seems that Chevrolet got the credit.

Again, unlike most engines of the day, the intake manifold was designed not only to direct the air-fuel mixture to the cylinders, but also to seal the lifter valley area. This saved money—fewer parts used and also less machining of the intake manifold.

The main developmental problems encountered were excessive oil consumption and valvetrain problems. The oil consumption problem was cured by designing new piston rings and putting a sheet-metal umbrella between the valve spring and spring cap to deflect oil off the ends of the rocker arms. Problems with valve float and rocker studs pulling were cured by using a damper inside the valve springs and by increasing the rocker stud's boss length and diameter. They could have used screw-in rocker studs, but that would have increased cost.

Originally, the small-block engine was designed to have its exhaust manifolds connect together at the front of the engine with a crossover pipe, much in the same way Ford's Y-block engines did. However, increased under-hood temperatures and excessive exhaust system restriction resulted in redesigned exhaust manifolds that exited below the engine into a Y-pipe.

In its original form, the 1955 Turbo-Fire small-block had a 265 cid and was available in three horsepower ratings: The two-barrel version was rated at 162 hp at 4,400 rpm with 257ft-lb torque at 2,200 rpm. The four-barrel version was rated at 180 hp at 4,600 rpm with 260ft-lb torque at 2,800 rpm. The Corvette got a more powerful 195 hp at 5,000 rpm with 260ft-lb torque at 3,000 rpm. This was due to a solid-lifter camshaft. The compression ratio was 8.0:1 on all engines.

To say the engine was a success was an understatement. In a minimum of time, the small-block Chevy had established itself as the standard by which all other V-8 designs would be judged. In addition, it was the engine to have on the street, NASCAR circuit, or drag strip.

In 1956 the engine was improved. Camshaft lift was increased from 0.330 in. to 0.365 in. An increase in compression ratio, to 9.25:1, raised power to 205 hp on the four-barrel engine. The two-barrel engine developed 162 hp with the manual transmission, but went up to 170 hp when it was mated to the Powerglide (PG) automatic. Stronger pistons were used, and the cylinder head bolts were threaded into the block deck instead of bosses at each cylinder. This minimized bore distortion. More obvious was the use of a full-flow oil filter.

Later in the model year, RPO (Regular Production Option) 411 was released. This was the dual four-barrel carburetor setup that raised power to 225 hp. For 1956 only, the small-block engine was painted red, instead of the familiar orange.

Nineteen fifty-seven was an important year for the small-block. First, the bore was increased by 0.125 in., and the result was 283 cid. Second, it was the first year of the optional Rochester Ramjet fuel injection (FI) system. The highest output 283 cid engine put out 283 hp with the FI system. The dual four-barrel intake setup was again available, in either 245 or 270 hp versions. Other changes to the engine included a higher 0.398 in. lift camshaft, improved oiling to the lifters, and substantially improved exhaust manifolds. These became known as the "Ram's Horn" exhaust manifolds.

The 265 cid small-block was still available in 1957, but that would be its last year.

The small-block Chevrolet is the most significant V-8 engine to come out of Detroit this century. This is the original 1955 265 cid. Note front engine mount, exhaust manifold that exits near the front of the engine, and lack of oil filter provision. *Chevrolet Motor Division*

For 1958, a two-barrel version of the small-block 283 cid was added to replace the previous 265 cid. Dual-quads and Ramjet FI were optional. The top FI engine got a few more horses—290 hp on the RPO 579D.

Changes to the engine itself included thicker cylinder walls and the now-familiar three-point engine-mounting system. The engine was mounted with an engine mount on each side of the block and one at the rear of the transmission.

The 283 cid engine continued to be available through the 1967 model year. In 1962, it was joined by an additional version of the small-block. With a 4.00 in. bore and a stroke of 3.25 in., the result was 327 cid. The increase in the use of air conditioning, power steering, and more electrical accessories made the addition of the 327 cid engine necessary.

With the addition of the 327 cid V-8 in 1962, the 283 cid became the smallest output V-8 that Chevrolet offered in its passenger cars. Gone were the dual quads and the FI for the 283. Although the dual four-barrel intake setup was not offered with the 327, the Rochester FI system was. Power was up to 360 hp on the RPO 582 engine, and it was offered only on the Corvette. During 1964–1965, the L84 327 cid FI V-8 was rated at 375 hp. Nineteen sixty-five was the last year for the FI system; the new big-block 396 and 427 cid V-8s could provide more power at less cost.

Nineteen sixty-seven saw the introduction of two more small-block variants. The first was the 350 cid version, which would eventually replace the 327 cid engine. In simple terms, the 327's stroke was increased to 3.48 in., but there was quite a bit of development to it because, after all, the original small-block wasn't designed to be opened up to 350 cid. In order to strengthen the bottom end, the crankshaft journals were increased to 2.45 in. and the rod-bearing journals to 2.10 in. In 1968, all Chevrolet small-blocks were built with these specs as well. The performance versions of the 350 cid and the truck engines came with four-bolt main caps and forged-steel connecting rods. The other 350s got cast nodular iron crankshafts. The 350 cid V-8, of course, is still in production today.

The other engine was the high-revving 302. To arrive at 302 cid, Chevrolet simply dropped the 283's crankshaft into the 327's block. The engine was specifically made for the Z/28 Camaro, which was built to homologate the car and engine in the SCCA's Trans Am Series. It was an all-out performance engine. More on this engine later.

The reliable 283 cid engine was finally replaced in 1968 by the 307. This was a low-performance engine that was available only with a two-barrel carburetor. In essence, it was the 283 cid engine with the 327's crankshaft, as its bore and stroke dimensions were 3.875x3.25 in.

The biggest small-block, the 400 cid, was released in 1970. With a bore and stroke of 4.125x3.75 in., this displacement stretched the small-block to its limit, and quite a bit of concern arose for the engine's durability. The main-bearing journals were increased to 2.65 in., four-bolt main-bearing caps were used, and the engine was only available with an automatic transmission. The most unusual feature of the engine was its siamesed cylinder bores. The only way to get a bore that size into the small-block was to eliminate the space between the bores, which meant the coolant didn't circulate completely around the bores. These engines can be identified by the three freeze plugs used on each side of the block. The 400 cid V-8 was used in passenger cars until 1976 and in trucks until 1980.

Given the realities of the emissions requirements in the 1970s, Chevrolet released another variant of the small-block engine in 1975. This engine was actually smaller than the original 265, as with its 3.67 in. bore and 3.10 in. stroke, it displaced 262 cid. The downsized 262 cid V-8 lacked efficiency and power, and it was dropped after only one year of production.

Surprising as it may sound, the 262 cid engine was too oversquare because it had a bore-to-stroke ratio of 1.25. This ratio is great for torque and horsepower output, as long as there isn't too much concern for emissions output. What this meant was that in order to meet emission standards, the 262's timing had to be retarded excessively. The result was loss of power output and loss of fuel economy—not exactly great selling points in an engine.

The next engine in the small-block evolution was the 305 cid version released in 1976, which is still in production today. With a 3.75 in. bore and a stroke of 3.48 in., the engine had a more favorable bore-to-stroke ratio, which resulted in better efficiency and fuel economy.

The last small-block permutation was the 267 cid version released in 1979. It had a 3.50 in. bore and a 3.48 in. stroke. This was great for fuel economy and emissions, and the engine lasted until 1982. By this time, V-6 engines based on the small-block and other GM engines precluded the need for a small V-8, leaving the 305 and 350 cid variants as the only two small-blocks in production.

262 cid

This was the smallest version of the small-block Chevrolet V-8. It was available for only one year, 1975. The 262 cid had a bore of 3.671 in. and a 3.10 in. stroke. The cylinder heads had intake/exhaust valves measuring 1.72 in./1.30 in. The engine used a two-barrel intake manifold and a Rochester carburetor. Cast-iron crankshaft, cast 8.5:1 compression ratio pistons, and forged-steel connecting rods rounded out this entirely conventional small-block V-8. It was rated at 110 hp at 3,600 rpm with 200ft-lb torque at 2,000 rpm.

265 cid

The first Chevy small-block V-8 was rather conservative compared to what was to come. It was available in three horsepower variations: 162 hp, 180 hp, and 195 hp—the biggest reserved specifically for the Corvette. That engine came with a solid lifter camshaft while the others were fitted with a hydraulic unit.

The high point for the engine was reached in 1956 when it was available with a two-four barrel intake setup for 225 hp—again in the Corvette. There were numerous improvements, which we've already touched upon. In its last year of production, 1957, only one two-barrel version was available, rated at 162 hp.

The 1955 265 cid engines had a two-bolt-main engine block. The crankshaft was made from forged steel, as were the connecting rods. Pistons were cast aluminum. The cylinder heads featured valves that measured 1.725 in. intake and 1.50 in. exhaust.

In 1956, camshaft lift was increased from 0.330 in. to 0.365 in. on the 265 cid small-block. An increase in compression ratio, to 9.25:1, raised power to 205 hp on the engine. The two-barrel engine developed the same 162 hp with the manual transmission, but went up to 170 hp when it was mated to the PG automatic transmission. Stronger pistons were used and the cylinder head bolts were threaded into the block deck instead of into bosses at each cylinder. This minimized bore distortion. More obvious was the use of a full-flow oil filter.

Later in the model year, RPO 411 was released. This was the dual four-barrel version with 225 hp. The intake manifold was cast in aluminum.

In 1957, its last year of production, there was only one version of the 265 cid engine available, the 162 hp two-barrel engine.

Chevrolet also used the new small-block in its light trucks. These were all two-barrel carbureted versions rated as follows: 1955 145 hp, 1956 155 hp, and 1957 162 hp.

267 cid

The 267 was strictly an emissions-era small-block. The 267 cid V-8 was available only during 1979–82. It had a 3.50 in. bore and 3.48 in. stroke and was available only with a two-barrel carburetor.

283 cid

In 1957, the small-block was bored to 3.875 in. to create the 283 cid.

The only two-barrel 283 cid V-8 was rated at 185 hp, while a 220 hp four-barrel version was available on passenger cars and as the base engine on the Corvette. The 245 hp and 270 hp dual four-barrel engines were available on both the passenger cars and the Corvette.

New for 1957 was the optional Ramjet FI system. It was available in two ratings, 250 hp and 283 hp, on both the passenger car line and the Corvette. Engine improvements included modifications for improved oiling to the hydraulic lifters and the new, more efficient Rams Horn exhaust manifolds.

For 1958, the 185 hp two-barrel engine continued on as the base V-8 on the passenger car line. The Super Turbo-Fire four-barrel version was uprated to 230 hp, which also became the base Corvette engine. The dual four-barrel engines were carried over with the same horsepower ratings, 245 and 270 hp. The same went for the two Ramjet FI engines, but the 283 hp engine was tweaked to put out 290 hp.

The carbureted engines continued to be offered in the same configuration through the 1961 model year; the FI engines were uprated to 275 and 315 hp.

In 1962, the 327 cid replaced the 283 as the major Chevrolet small-block V-8. As such, the 283 cid V-8 was relegated to base- or entry-level V-8 duties on the passenger car lines. In 1962, it was rated at 170 hp, and from 1963 through the 1967 model year, the two-barrel version was rated at 195 hp.

A four-barrel 283 cidV-8 was available during 1965–1966; it was rated at 220 hp. The 283 cid V-8 was finally retired after the 1967 model year.

In terms of truck applications, Chevrolet used a 160 hp two-barrel version of the 283 cid small-block V-8 in its light trucks from 1958 to 1962; from 1963 to 1967, the truck 283 cid V-8 was rated at 175 hp, with the two-barrel carburetor.

302 cid

This particular displacement of the small-block was available only on the 1967–1969 Z/28 Camaro. The engine was used by Chevrolet teams to compete in the SCCA's Trans Am Series and the Camaro was used to homologate the engine. The option code for the high output engine was Z28.

The 302 cid V-8 had the most oversquare bore-and-stroke ratio (1.33) of any small-block built to date. With its 4.00 in. bore and 3.00 in. stroke, the 302 was designed to produce power at a higher rpm. This displacement was arrived at by putting the 283's crankshaft in the 327's block.

The 302 cid V-8 came with forged-steel crank, rods, and forged-aluminum pistons that netted an 11.0:1 compression ratio. For 1967, the engine used a block that had the regular two-bolt main-bearing caps and rod/main journals that measured 2.00 in./2.30 in.; 1968–1969 blocks got four-bolt mains as well as larger rod and main-bearing journals that measured 2.10 in./2.45 in. The Z/28 engine also got an oil pan windage tray.

The 302 cid small-block also used cylinder heads that got 2.02 in. intake and 1.60 in. exhaust valves; these were essentially the same heads used on the 327 cid FI Corvette engines. The camshaft was used with solid lifters.

Rounding out the engine was an aluminum dual-plane high-rise intake manifold with a 780cfm Holley four-barrel carburetor. The engine was rated at 290 hp at 5,800 rpm with 290ft-lb torque at 4,200 rpm.

305 cid

This engine was introduced in 1976. It was arrived at by, in effect, using the original 265 cid engine's 3.75 in. bore with the 350 cid engine's 3.48 in. stroke. Starting out with a two-barrel carburetor intake system, the 305 cid engine eventually was equipped with a 1980s-style Rochester four-barrel carburetor, a high-performance throttle body injection system, the Corvette Cross-Fire FI system, and the Tuned-Port Injection system. The engine has proved its longevity, as it remains in production today.

307 cid

In 1968, the 307 cid small-block replaced the 283 cid engine as the base Chevrolet V-8. Strictly a low-performance engine, the 307 cid V-8 was rated at 200 hp from 1968 to 1971; in 1972 it was rated at 130 hp, and in its last year (1974), it was rated at a paltry 115 hp. The engine was available only with a two-barrel Rochester carburetor, hydraulic camshaft, and a single-exhaust system. The engine block was the standard two-bolt-main job; the cylinder heads had the small 1.725 in. intake and 1.505 in. exhaust valves.

There was also a truck version of the 307 cid V-8 for use in light-duty pickup trucks. As with the passenger-car engines, it was available from 1968 to 1974.

327 cid

The 283 cid small-block was bored and stroked in 1962, to 4.00x3.25 in., for 327 cid. The engine had the same two-bolt main bearings and the same main and rod journal sizes, 2.30 in. and 2.00 in. The standard cylinder heads, in terms of valve sizes, were carried over, having 1.72 in. intake and 1.50 in. exhaust valves. The optional 300, 340, and 360 hp engines got new cylinder heads with larger intake valves, measuring 1.94 in.

The most powerful 327 cid V-8 for 1962 was the 360 hp Ramjet Fuel Injected engine. The same lineup was carried over for 1963.

For 1964, the 327 cid was Chevrolet's performance small-block. Besides the 250 hp V-8, there was the 300 hp engine, with a four-barrel carburetor and hydraulic-lifter camshaft; the 340 hp version featured a solid-lifter camshaft.

In 1964 and 1965, the top two 327 cid engines were uprated to 365 (single four-barrel) and 375 hp (FI); part of the power increase was due to the use of cylinder heads that had larger valves, 2.02 in. intake and 1.60 in. exhaust. Incidentally, the 327 cid 375 hp rating was the highest factory rating of any small-block Chevrolet engine until the 1990-95 ZR-1.

By 1966, the 327 cid V-8 was beginning to be eclipsed by the bigger and more powerful big-block V-8 engines; 327s were available in 275, 300, and 350 hp versions, all with hydraulic camshafts and four-barrel carburetors. These were carried over into 1967, and another 327 cid small-block was available on the Camaro. This one was rated at 210 hp. For 1968 and 1969, a two-barrel 327 cid engine was added. Also in 1968, a 250 hp four-barrel 327 was offered. By 1969, the 350 cid small-block had replaced the 327 in most applications, just as the 327 had supplanted the 283 cid small-block back in 1962.

Regarding truck applications, Chevrolet used a 220 hp version of the 327 cid engine on 1966–1968 light trucks. It was equipped with a four-barrel carburetor. The El Camino, which was considered a truck, paralleled the engine availability of the Chevelle.

350 cid

Cars were still getting bigger and heavier in the late 1960s, so yet another small-block V-8 came into being in 1967, the 350. The easiest way to get more cubic inches out of the same old design was to increase the small-block's stroke. With a 3.48 in. stroke and the 4.00 in. bore, the engine now displaced 350 cid. Up to the 350, getting more cubic inches was simply a matter of increasing the small-block's bore or switching crankshafts from other small-block engines. With the 350, Chevrolet engineers felt that the engine had to be strengthened in several critical areas if it was to give long, reliable service. The main and rod bearing journals were increased to 2.45 in. and 2.10 in.; the numbers 2, 3, and 4 main-bearing caps received a four-bolt treatment on the high-performance and truck applications. Unlike previous performance engines, the passenger-car 350s came with cast nodular crankshafts. The exceptions were the 1967 350 cid engines, which were still equipped with a forged-steel crankshaft and two-bolt mains. The four-bolt mains did not come into usage until the 1968 model year.

The engine made its debut on the 1967 Camaro SS350. The engine, with a four-barrel carburetor, hydraulic camshaft, and dual exhausts, was rated at 295 hp.

Interestingly, the 350 cid small-block was Chevrolet's mainstay during the 1970s and 1980s. The engine powered literally millions of cars and trucks, yet the vast majority of these were so-called smog motors. These engines were generally low-output engines weighed down with relatively unsophisticated emission controls. Still, the engine has a tremendous reputation because it has been used successfully in so many different types of racing as well as in owner-modified street applications.

The only 350 cid V-8 that stands out is the 1970–1972 LT-1 (in the Corvette) and Z/28 (in the Camaro). This engine was essentially an update of the Z/28 302 cid small-block, which went out of production in 1970. Like the 302, the LT-1 came with a 11.0:1 compression ratio, solid-lifter camshaft, the big-valve (2.02 in./1.60 in. intake/exhaust) cylinder heads, pushrod guide plates and screw-in rocker studs, and an aluminum intake manifold with a 780cfm Holley four-barrel carburetor. The block was a four-bolt main unit with a forged-steel crankshaft, forged-steel rods, and forged-aluminum pistons. The 350 LT-1 was rated at 370 hp at 6,000 rpm with 380ft-lb torque at 4,000 rpm. The Camaro version was rated at 360 hp with exactly the same torque figure and at the same rpm.

The 1971 LT-1s suffered a two-point drop in compression ratio; output was 330 hp. In 1972, its last year of production, the LT-1 was rated in the net SAE method, 255 hp at 5,600 rpm.

After the demise of the LT-1, power ratings for the 350 continued to decline through the 1970s and only started to improve in the 1980s when sophisticated electronic controls and EFI became more common.

Chevrolet has used the 350 cid V-8 in trucks since 1969. Of course, it is still in production today. Generally, the 350 cid truck engines have the four-bolt main engine block and forged-steel crankshaft and rods.

400 cid

This was the largest small-block made. It stretched the small-block to its limits. With a bore of 4.125 in., the cylinder walls were siamesed, meaning they were connected to each other so there was no coolant circulating between the bores. This was deemed safe for street use, and six small steam holes were placed around the cylinder to let steam and air escape, in order to avoid overheating problems. There were also other compromises made to achieve the 400 cid. The rods were weaker than 350 cid rods because there wasn't enough space inside the block, given the engine's 3.75 in. stroke. Initially, the engine was offered with four-bolt main-bearing caps, but later they were switched to the regular two-bolt-main caps.

Still, the engine was never considered any good for high-performance applications, and it was never offered with a manual transmission. However, the 400's crank has been successfully used in the aftermarket. When modified and installed in the 350 cid block, the resulting combination yields 383 cid. The 400 was dropped from passenger car use in 1976; it was dropped from truck use in 1980.

Engine Blocks

Although it would seem that there have been a great number of engine blocks for the small-block Chevrolet V-8, there have only been three distinct engine blocks. The first was used on engines built from 1955 to 1967. This block had main and rod journals measuring 2.30 in. and 2.00 in., respectively, and all these blocks came with two-bolt main-bearing caps. From 1968 to date, Chevrolet engines have used a different block, with main and rod journals measuring 2.45 in. and 2.10 in., respectively. These could be either with two- or four-bolt main-bearing caps. The third variation is the siamesed-cylinder block used on 400 cid engines from 1970 to 1980. It had larger main journals, 2.65 in., and it was available either with two- or four-bolt main caps.

There have been minor variations made on the engine block over the years by Chevrolet. These changes were done either to improve the engine's performance or to make the engine fit into a particular application. Some of these have already been touched upon. For example, the only block that doesn't have provision for an oil filter is the 1955 block. Since 1956, all Chevrolet engine blocks have provision for an oil filter on the left rear of the block. Engines built up to 1967 use a canister (which contains a replaceable-cartridge filter element) that is bolted on to the block. From 1968 on, Chevrolet used the more common spin-on oil filter.

The 1957 and earlier blocks have their engine mounts on the front of the block; 1958 and later blocks have mount bosses on each side of the block.

The 1968 and earlier blocks have a vent hole at the rear of the block behind the intake manifold and next to the oil pressure sender. This hole was used with the Road Draft Tube to rid the engine of blow-by vapors. In 1963, Chevrolet switched over to a PCV system, but still used the opening at the rear of the block. Blocks from 1968 do not have the rear opening because the PCV system was moved to the engine's valve cover. The 1968 and earlier blocks also have a hole at the front of the block underneath the intake manifold for the oil-filler tube. Later blocks do not have this hole because the oil-fill location was moved to the valve cover.

There are also differences on the 283 and 327 cid blocks used on the 1964–1967 Chevy II. Because of a tight engine compartment, the engines used in the Chevy II have a front sump oil pan with the dipstick going through the oil pan itself. This means

The 1967–69 302 cid Z/28 engine was a real powerhouse, even with regular exhaust manifolds. Big-valve cylinder heads, aluminum intake manifold, solid lifter camshaft, and Holley carburetor were combined for an underrated 290 hp. Actual output was closer to 400 hp. *Chevrolet Motor Division*

that the tunnel where the dipstick would normally go is plugged. The oil filter boss is also located higher than on other blocks.

The 400 cid blocks can be spotted by the three freeze plug bosses per side they have, while other blocks use just two. The 400 cid blocks also have six small steam holes on the deck, which correspond to similar holes on the 400 cid cylinder heads.

Cylinder Heads

As with engine blocks, the cylinder heads used on the Chevrolet small-block engines are essentially the same. Differences occur in combustion chamber size, valve size, port size, and accessory mounting location.

Chevrolet cylinder heads came from the factory with pressed-in rocker studs and stamped steel rockers that used a ball fulcrum and hollow pushrods. The rockers are adjustable, whether the engine has a hydraulic- or mechanical-lifter camshaft. Certain high-performance engines, such as the LT-1, came with screw-in rocker studs and pushrod guide plates.

Although all small-block valve covers look the same, in terms of bolt pattern, 1958 and earlier valve covers have their top mounting bolts closer together than the bottom ones. From 1959 to 1986, the bolts are spaced equally, which is why aftermarket valve cover gaskets have both sets of holes.

The original 265 cid cylinder heads had valves that measured 1.72 in./1.50 in. intake/exhaust; the 283 cid engines also had the same size of valves. When the 327 cid engines were introduced, the intake valve size was increased to 1.94 in.; the 1964 and later high-performance 327 cid engines came with even larger valves measuring 2.02 in./1.60 in. The Z/28 and LT-1 engines also used cylinder heads with the larger valves. The 350 cid engines generally have used 1.94 in./1.50 in. valves. The 1975 262 cid engine had smaller valves measuring 1.72 in./1.30 in.

Besides using casting numbers or date codes, you can also, generally, identify cylinder heads by some of their external characteristics. For example, 1971 and later cylinder heads use smaller—14mm—tapered-seat spark plugs. The 1968 and earlier cylinder heads have the water temperature sending unit located on the intake manifold; later heads have the sender located on the cylinder head. The temperature sending unit was again relocated to the intake manifold in the mid-1970s.

In 1969, Chevrolet moved the alternator from the driver side of the engine to the passenger side and also began using a longer water pump. Mounting the engine's accessories required that the heads be drilled so that the accessories and their brackets could be mounted. The location of these holes can vary, and some 1968 heads will also have some of these holes.

There are also factory replacement cylinder heads that never came on any particular car but that have high-performance and racing applications. These include the so-called "angle-plug" heads.

Intake Manifolds

The vast majority of small-block engines came with cast-iron intake manifolds in either two- or four-barrel configuration. High-performance applications, such as all the dual four-barrel engines, all the FI engines, and the Z/28 and LT-1 engines, came with cast-aluminum intake manifolds. It should also be noted that many, if not all, Chevrolet small-block engines built since the late 1970s were also equipped with aluminum intake manifolds. These are not high-performance manifolds; rather, they are of stock design, cast in aluminum in order to save weight.

Unlike other manufacturers, particularly Ford, Chevrolet did not go into a big, involved program to develop unique and specialized intake manifolds; Chevrolet let the aftermarket do that.

Chevrolet two-barrel intake manifolds were drilled to accept a Rochester carburetor. Four-barrel intake manifolds had carburetor mounts to accept four types of carburetors: Rochester Four-Jet, Carter WCFB, Holley, and Carter AFB.

The Rochester Quadrajet four-barrel carburetor came into use in 1967, and it had a unique "spread-bore" mounting pattern—the front two barrels were considerably smaller than the secondary barrels. This design was supposed to combine fuel economy with performance.

There are also visual characteristics between manifolds that help to differentiate them. Pre-1969 manifolds have the prominent oil-filler tube at the front of the manifold. The 1969 and later manifolds also have revised alternator mounting provisions. The 1973 and later manifolds have a provision for the EGR valve, mounted next to the carburetor.

Exhaust Manifolds

Factory exhaust manifolds were cast in iron, and there have a number of designs used with the Chevrolet small-block V-8. These can be described as the overhead log type used on the early and on late engines, the distinctive Ram's Horn style, and the log type. Within each type there are a great many variations for accessory mounting bracket provision, exit location, size and type, and other characteristics, such as choke tube provision.

Engine Identification

Generally speaking, Chevrolet engine parts have various ID numbers and symbols. The best known are the casting number and date code. Both of these can be used to identify parts and usually the results are fairly conclusive. On cylinder heads the casting number is under the valve cover, on intake manifolds it can either be on the top or bottom, and on exhaust manifolds it can be on either side. Chevrolet engine blocks have their casting number on the rear of the block, on the bellhousing flange.

In addition to the casting number, there will be a casting date code on the part. This code indicates the date and year the part was cast. Most Chevrolet blocks have this code on the top part of the bellhousing flange, but the number can be located elsewhere, such as the side of the block.

Chevrolet often used the same casting number on a part for several model years. As a result, two parts with the same casting number but with different characteristics or features are common. Just because a part has the right casting number on it doesn't mean it is the correct part for your application.

Engine casting date codes consist of a letter and three or four digits. The letter appears first, with A representing January and L representing December. The next two digits stand for the date of the month, and the last one or two digits stand for the model year. For example, B 228 could stand for February 22, 1968 (or 1958, 1978, or 1988). If you're looking at an exhaust manifold that came out of a 1968 Camaro, you can be pretty sure that the 8 stands for 1968. Sometimes, Chevrolet used two numbers to designate the year, such as B 22 68. When two numbers are used for the year, they will be spaced slightly apart from the rest of the date code.

Each Chevrolet engine also has a number stamped on it to identify it and connect it with the car it is installed in. This number consists of the engine code and sometimes a part of the vehicle's VIN. The engine code consists of the Engine Plant Code, four digits indicating date and month the engine was assembled, and the engine's Suffix Code. Engine plant codes are as follows: F = Flint Motor, V = Flint Engine, or T = Tonawanda.

The Suffix Code indicates engine family, usage, and most of the time, transmission. Before 1970, this was a two-letter code. From 1970 on, this became a three-letter code. These codes are listed in the Engine Suffix Code table.

This number is stamped on a pad on the passenger side of the engine block, just where the cylinder head and block meet. The last eight digits of the car's VIN may also be on the pad. From 1969, these numbers are also stamped on a pad near the oil filter, or they may just be stamped on the filter pad alone. Most engines, however, will have the number stamped on the front of the block as indicated. As an example, the identification code F0422DZ would decode as follows: F, Flint; 0422, April 22; DZ, 302 cid 290 hp with manual transmission.

Keep in mind that the engine suffix codes are used over and over again. For example, the code CSJ stands for a 1972 350 cid small-block V-8 rated at 165 hp and used on the 1972 full-size Chevrolet cars. It also stands for a 175 hp 400 cid small-block used in the 1976 full-size Chevrolet cars. Some codes can even have five or more applications.

Most parts used on an engine should predate the assembly date code of the engine and should be within 30 days of engine assembly. There are exceptions, of course, such as parts cast for use at a later date or model year.

Engine Specifications

	Displacement	Carburetor	Horsepower	Torque	Compression Ratio	Notes
1955						
	265	2V	162@4,400	257@2,200	8.0	Chevrolet
	265	4V	180@4,600	260@2,800	8.0	Chevrolet
	265	4V	195@5,000	260@3,000	8.0	Corvette
1956						
	265	2V	162@4,400	257@2,400	8.0	Chevrolet
	265	2V	170@4,600	257@2,800	8.0	Chevrolet
	265	4V	205@5,000	268@3,000	9.25	Corvette
	265	4V	195@5,000	260@3,000	8.0	Chevrolet
	265	2x4V	225@5,200	270@2,800	9.25	Corvette
1957						
	265	2V	162@4,400	257@2,200	8.0	Chevrolet
	283	2V	185@4,600	275@2,400	8.5	Chevrolet
	283	4V	220@4,800	300@3,000	9.5	Chevrolet
	283	2x4V	245@5,000	300@3,800	9.5	Chevrolet, Corvette
	283	2x4V	270@6,000	285@4,200	9.5	Chevrolet, Corvette
	283	FI	250@5,000	305@3,800	9.5	Chevrolet, Corvette
	283	FI	283@6,200	290@4,400	10.5	Chevrolet, Corvette
1958						
	283	2V	185@4,600	275@2,400	8.5	Chevrolet
	283	4V	230@4,800	300@3,000	8.5	Chevrolet
	283	2x4V	245@5,000	300@3,800	9.5	Corvette
	283	2x4V	270@6,000	285@4,200	9.5	Corvette
	283	FI	250@5,000	305@3,800	9.5	Chevrolet, Corvette
	283	FI	290@6,200	290@4,400	10.5	Chevrolet, Corvette
1959						
	283	2V	185@4,600	275@2,400	8.5	Chevrolet
	283	4V	230@4,800	300@3,000	8.5	Chevrolet
	283	2x4V	245@5,000	300@3,800	9.5	Corvette
	283	2x4V	270@6,000	285@4,200	9.5	Corvette
	283	FI	250@5,000	305@3,800	9.5	Chevrolet, Corvette
	283	FI	290@6,200	290@4,400	10.5	Chevrolet, Corvette
1960						
	283	2V	170@4,200	275@2,200	8.5	Chevrolet
	283	4V	230@4,800	300@3,000	8.5	Chevrolet, Corvette
	283	2x4V	245@5,000	300@3,800	9.5	Corvette
	283	2x4V	270@6,000	285@4,200	9.5	Corvette
	283	FI	250@5,000	305@3,800	9.5	Corvette
	283	FI	290@6,200	290@4,400	10.5	Corvette
1961						
	283	2V	170@4,200	275@2,200	8.5	Chevrolet
	283	4V	230@4,800	300@3,000	8.5	Chevrolet, Corvette
	283	2x4V	245@5,000	300@3,800	9.5	Corvette
	283	2x4V	270@6,000	285@4,200	9.5	Corvette

Engine Specifications

	Displacement	Carburetor	Horsepower	Torque	Compression Ratio	Notes
	283	FI	275@5,200	305@4,400	11.0	Corvette
	283	FI	315@6,200	295@5,000	11.0	Corvette
1962						
	283	2V	170@4,200	275@2,200	8.5	Chevrolet
	327	4V	250@4,400	350@2,800	10.5	Chevrolet, Corvette
	327	4V	300@4,400	360@3,200	10.5	Chevrolet, Corvette
	327	4V	340@6,000	344@4,000	11.25	Corvette
	327	FI	360@6,000	352@5,000	11.25	Corvette
1963						
	283	2V	195@4,800	255@2,200	9.25	Chevrolet
	327	4V	250@4,400	350@2,800	10.5	Chevrolet, Corvette
	327	4V	300@4,400	360@3,200	10.5	Chevrolet, Corvette
	327	4V	340@6,000	344@4,000	11.25	Corvette
	327	FI	360@6,000	352@5,000	11.25	Corvette
1964						
	283	2V	195@4,800	255@2,200	9.25	Chevrolet, Chevy II
	327	4V	250@4,400	350@2,800	10.5	Chevrolet, Corvette
	327	4V	300@4,400	360@3,200	10.5	Chevrolet, Corvette
	327	4V	365@6,200	350@4,000	11.25	Corvette
	327	FI	375@6,200	352@4,600	11.25	Corvette
1965						
	283	2V	195@4,800	255@2,400	9.25	Chevrolet, Chevy II, Chevelle
	283	4V	220@4,800	295@3,200	9.25	Chevrolet, Chevy II, Chevelle
	327	4V	250@4,400	350@2,800	10.5	Chevrolet, Chevy II, Chevelle, Corvette
	327	4V	300@4,400	360@3,200	10.5	Chevrolet, Chevy II, Chevelle, Corvette
	327	4V	365@6,200	350@4,000	11.0	Corvette
	327	FI	375@6,200	352@4,600	11.0	Corvette
1966						
	283	2V	195@4,800	255@2,400	9.25	Chevrolet, Chevy II, Chevelle
	283	4V	220@4,800	295@3,200	9.25	Chevrolet, Chevy II, Chevelle
	327	4V	250@4,400	350@2,800	10.5	Chevrolet, Chevy II, Chevelle
	327	4V	275@4,800	355@3,200	10.25	Chevrolet, Chevy II, Chevelle
	327	4V	300@5,000	360@3,400	10.25	Corvette
	327	4V	350@5,800	360@3,600	11.0	Corvette
1967						
	283	2V	195@4,800	255@2,400	9.25	Chevrolet, Chevy II, Chevelle
	302	4V	290@5,800	290@4,200	11.0	Camaro
	327	4V	210@4,600	320@2,400	8.75	Chevrolet, Chevy II, Camaro
	327	4V	250@4,400	350@2,800	10.5	Chevrolet, Chevy II
	327	4V	275@4,800	355@3,200	10.25	Chevrolet, Chevy II, Chevelle
	327	4V	300@5,000	360@3,400	10.25	Corvette
	327	4V	325@5,600	335@3,600	11.0	Chevelle
	327	4V	350@5,800	360@3,600	11.0	Corvette
	350	4V	295@4,800	380@3,200	10.25	Camaro
1968						
	302	4V	290@5,800	290@4,200	11.0	Camaro
	307	2V	200@4,600	300@2,400	9.00	Chevrolet, Chevy II, Chevelle, Camaro
	327	4V	210@4,600	320@2,400	8.75	Chevy II, Camaro
	327	4V	250@4,400	350@2,800	10.5	Chevrolet, Chevelle
	327	4V	275@4,800	355@3,200	10.25	Chevrolet, Chevy II, Chevelle, Camaro
	327	4V	300@5,000	360@3,400	10.25	Corvette
	327	4V	325@5,600	335@3,600	11.0	Chevelle, Chevy II
	327	4V	350@5,800	360@3,600	11.0	Corvette
	350	4V	295@4,800	380@3,200	10.25	Camaro
1969						
	302	4V	290@5,800	290@4,200	11.0	Camaro
	307	2V	200@4,600	300@2,400	9.00	Nova, Chevelle, Camaro
	327	4V	210@4,600	320@2,400	8.75	Camaro

	Displacement	Carburetor	Horsepower	Torque	Compression Ratio	Notes
	327	4V	235@4,800	325@2,800	9.0	Chevrolet, Chevy II, Chevelle
	350	4V	250@4,800	345@2,800	9.0	Chevrolet, Nova, Chevelle, Camaro
	350	4V	255@4,800	365@3,200	9.0	Chevrolet, Nova, Chevelle, Camaro
	350	4V	300@4,800	380@3,200	10.25	Corvette, Chevrolet, Nova, Camaro
	350	4V	350@5,600	380@3,600	11.0	Corvette
1970						
	307	2V	200@4,600	300@2,400	9.00	Nova, Chevelle, Camaro
	350	4V	250@4,800	345@2,800	9.0	Chevrolet, Nova, Chevelle, Camaro, Monte Carlo
	350	4V	300@4,800	380@3,200	10.25	Corvette, Chevrolet, Nova, Camaro, Monte Carlo, Chevelle
	350	4V	350@5,600	380@3,600	11.0	Corvette
	350	4V	360@6,000	380@4,000	11.0	Camaro
	350	4V	370@5,800	380@4,000	11.0	Corvette
	400	4V	265@4,400	400@2,400	9.0	Chevrolet, Monte Carlo
1971						
	307	2V	200@4,600	300@2,400	8.50	Nova, Chevelle, Camaro
	350	4V	245@4,800	350@2,800	8.5	Chevrolet, Nova, Chevelle, Camaro, Monte Carlo
	350	4V	270@4,800	360@3,200	8.50	Corvette, Chevrolet, Nova, Camaro, Monte Carlo, Chevelle
	350	4V	330@5,600	360@4,000	9.0	Corvette, Camaro
	400	4V	255@4,400	390@2,400	8.0	Chevrolet, Monte Carlo
1972						
	307	2V	130@4,000	230@2,400	8.50	Nova, Chevelle, Camaro
	350	2V	165@4,000	280@2,400	8.50	Chevrolet, Nova, Chevelle, Camaro, Monte Carlo
	350	4V	175@4,000	280@2,400	8.50	Monte Carlo, Chevelle
	350	4V	200@4,400	300@2,800	8.50	Corvette, Nova, Chevelle
	350	4V	255@4,600	280@4,000	9.0	Corvette, Camaro
	400	2V	170@3,400	325@2,000	8.5	Chevrolet, Monte Carlo
1973						
	307	2V	115@4,000	205@2,000	8.50	Nova, Camaro
	350	2V	145@4,000	255@2,400	8.50	Chevrolet, Nova, Chevelle, Camaro, Monte Carlo
	350	4V	175@4,000	270@2,400	8.50	Chevrolet, Monte Carlo, Chevelle, Camaro, Nova
	350	4V	190@4,400	270@2,800	8.50	Corvette
	350	4V	245@5,200	280@4,000	9.0	Camaro
	350	4V	250@5,200	285@4,000	9.0	Corvette
	400	2V	150@3,200	295@2,000	8.5	Chevrolet, Monte Carlo
1974						
	350	2V	145@4,000	255@2,400	8.50	Chevrolet, Nova, Chevelle, Camaro, Monte
	350	4V	160@3,800	250@2,400	8.50	Chevrolet, Nova, Camaro, Chevelle, Monte Carlo
	350	4V	185@4,000	270@2,600	8.50	Chevrolet, Chevelle, Camaro, Nova
	350	4V	195@4,400	275@2,800	8.50	Corvette
	350	4V	245@5,200	280@4,000	9.0	Camaro
	350	4V	250@5,200	285@4,000	9.0	Corvette
	400	2V	150@3,200	295@2,400	8.5	Chevrolet, Monte Carlo, Chevelle
	400	4V	180@3,800	290@2,000	8.5	Chevrolet, Monte Carlo, Chevelle
1975						
	262	2V	110@3,600	200@2,000	8.50	Nova, Monza
	350	2V	145@4,000	250@2,400	8.50	Nova, Chevelle, Monte Carlo, Camaro, Monza
	350	4V	155@3,800	250@2,400	8.50	Nova, Camaro, Chevelle, Monte Carlo
	350	4V	165@3,800	255@2,400	8.50	Chevrolet, Corvette

Engine Specifications

Displacement	Carburetor	Horsepower	Torque	Compression Ratio	Notes
350	4V	205@4,800	255@3,600	9.00	Corvette
400	2V	175@3,600	305@2,400	8.5	Chevrolet, Monte Carlo, Chevelle

Engine Internal Dimensions

Displacement	Bore and Stroke	Rod Bearings	Main Bearings	Intake/Exhaust Valves
262	3.67x3.10	2.0990–2.1000	1	1.72/1.30
265	3.75x3.00	1.9990–2.0000	2.2978–2.2298	1.72/1.50
283	3.87x3.00	1.9990–2.0000	2.2978–2.2298	1.72/1.50
302 (1967)	4.00x3.00	1.9990–2.0000	2.2978–2.2988	2.02/1.60
302 (1968–1969)	4.00x3.00	1.9990–2.0000	2.4479–2.4488	2.02/1.60
307	3.87x3.25	1.9990–2.0000	2.4479–2.4488	1.72/1.50
327 (1962–1967)	4.00x3.25	1.9990–2.0000	2.2978–2.2988	1.94/1.50 (exc. 325/350/365/375 hp, 2.02/1.60)
327 (1968–1969)	4.00x3.25	1.9990–2.0000	2.4479–2.4488	1.94/1.50
350	4.00x3.48	1.9990–2.0000	2.4479–2.4488	1.94/1.50 (exc. 360/370 hp, 2.02/1.60)
400	4.00x4.00	1.9990–2.0000	2.6484–2.6493	1.94/1.60

1: No.1 2.4484–2.4493, No.2,3,4 2.4481–2.4490, No.5 2.4479–2.4488

Block, Head, and Manifold Casting Numbers

Year	Engine	Casting Number
Engine Blocks		
1975	262	360851
1955	265	3703524
1956–1957	265	3720991
1957	283	3731548, no side motor mounts
1958–1961	283	3737739
1958–1962	283	3756519
1958–1963	283	3849852
1962–1967	283	3789935, 3864812
1964–1965	283	3790721, Chevy II
1958–1962	283	3794226, 3837739, truck
1958–1963	283	3849852, truck
1958–1967	283	3849852
1963–1964	283	386482
1966–1967	283	3862194, Chevy II
1965–1967	283	3834810, 3896948
1967	283	3896944
1967	302	3892657
1968	302	3914678, 2.45 in. mains
1969	302	3956618
1968	307	3931174, 3941174, truck
1968–1973	307	3914635, 3914636, 3932371, 3932373, 3956632, 3970020, 3970024, 391436
1962–1963	327	3959512
1962–1967	327	3782870, 3789817
1965–1967	327	3791362, 3791363, Chevy II, Nova
1968–1969	327	3794460, 3892659, 3914678, 3932386, 3933180, 3914660, 3955618, 3992386, 2.45 in. mains
1964–1967	327	3858174, 3858180
1964–1967	327	3892657, 3903352
1967	350	3858174, 3932442
1968	350	3914678, 2.45 in. mains
1969–1974	350	3970010, 3970014
1969–1975	350	3970010, truck
1970–1973	400	3951511
1970–1973	400	330817
1973–1980	400	3951509
Cylinder Heads		
1975	262	354434, 376450
1955	265	3703523
1955–1956	265	3837065, truck
1956	265	3725306
1956	265	3731762, 225 hp
1956–1957	265	3837064
1957	283	3731539
1957	283	3731554, 185 hp
1957	283	3740997, 220/245/250/270 hp
1958–1959	283	3748770, 3748772
1958–1959	283	3755539, 3755549, truck
1958–1967	283	3774684, truck
1959	283	3755550, 3767465 (late)
1960–1962	283	3876775, truck
1960–1965	283	3774682
1960–1967	283	3767792, 3774692
1960–1967	283	3884520, truck
1961	283	3782461, 275/315 hp
1962–1967	283	3836842
1963–1967	283	3795896, 3814480, 3814482
1963–1967	283	3767460, 3774682, 3795896, 3814480, 3814482, truck
1964–1967	283	3884520
1964–1967	283	3876775, truck
1967	302	3890462
1967	302	3890462
1967–1968	302	3917291
1969	302	3927186
1968	307	3917290, 3911032
1968	307	3917290, 3917293, truck
1969–1973	307	3986339, 3998991, 3998993, truck
1969–1973	307	3927185, 3932454
1968–1973	307	3931633
1969–1974	307	3998993
1973	307	330545

This 1970 small-block doesn't really look much different from any other, but it displaced 400 cubic inches. This really stretched the small-block to its limits in terms of durability. It didn't have any potential for high performance.

Year	Engine	Casting Number
1962–1966	327	3782461
1962–1963	327	3774682
1962–1964	327	3884520
1962–1965	327	3795896
1962–1967	327	3755585, 3767462, 3836842
1962–1967	327	3767460, 3774682, 3774684, 3782461, 3795896, 3814480, 3814482, 3876775, 3884520, 3891462, truck
1963–1967	327	3798996
1964–1967	327	3891462
1966–1967	327	3817681
1966–1968	327	3890462
1968	327	3911032
1968	327	3917290, 3917293, truck
1967–1968	327	3917291 Hi Perf.
1968	327	3917292, 300/350 hp
1969	327	3770126, 3927185
1967	350	3814482
1968–1969	350	3917291 Hi Perf.
1969–1976	350	3927185, 3927186, truck
1969–1970	350	3927186 Hi Perf.
1969–1970	350	3927187, 350 hp
1969–1974	350	3932441, 3998993
1969–1974	350	3932441, 3970126, 3998993, truck
1969–1970	350	3970126, 300 hp
1970	350	3973414 370 hp, 360 hp
1971	350	3973487, 270/330 hp
1971–1976	350	3973487
1971–1976	350	3973487, truck
1972	350	3998993, 200 hp
1972	350	3998916, 255 hp
1973–1975	350	333882, 3998991
1971–1975	350	462624 Hi Perf.
1975	350	462624, 468642, truck
1971–1975	350	468642, truck
1973	350	3991492, 330545
1970–1975	400	3951509, 3951511
1970–1973	400	399380
1971–1973	400	399380
1973–1975	400	333882, 3973493
1975	400	462624, truck

Intake Manifolds

Year	Engine	Casting Number
1955	265 2V	3704790
1955	265 4V	3711348
1956	265 2V	3735444
1956	265 4V	3735448, 3837109, Corvette
1956	265 4V	3737109, Chevrolet
1956	265 2x4V	3728725, aluminum 1st design
1956	265 2x4V	3731394, aluminum 2nd design
1957	265 2V	3732880, 3746826
1957	283 2V	3732880, 3746826
1957	283 4V	3731398, 3837109
1957–1961	283 FI	3741193
1957	283 2x4V	3731394
1957–1961	283 4V	3746829
1958–1963	283 2V	3746826
1958–1961	283 4V	3746829, Corvette
1958–1961	283 2x4V	3739653, aluminum
1964–1965	283 2V	3840905
1966–1967	283 2V	3877652 w/o a/c
1967–1968	302 4V	3917610, aluminum
1969–1970	302 4V	3932472, aluminum
1968–1969	302 2x4V	3941126, aluminum, base
1968–1969	302 2x4V	3941130, aluminum, top
1968	307 2V	3919801, w/o a/c
1969–1971	307 2V	3973465, w/o a/c
1969–1970	307 2V	3916313, 3927183, 3958622
1969–1971	307 2V	3973465
1971	307 2V	3991005
1972	307 2V	6262928, 6262936
1973	307 2V	6271060, 6271061
1962–1963	327 4V	3783244, Carter WCFB or Rochester 4-Jet
1962	327 4V	3795397, 340 hp, aluminum
1963	327 4V	3794129, 340 hp, aluminum
1962–1964	327 4V	3799349, Carter AFB
1962–1965	327 4V	3866922, Carter WCFB or Rochester 4-Jet
1963–1965	327 FI	3826810
1964–1965	327 4V	3844457, Carter WCFB or Rochester 4-Jet
1964–1965	327 4V	3844459, Carter AFB
1964	327 4V	3844461, 365 hp, aluminum

Some of the best heads made were those for the 1967–69 Z/28 Camaro and the 1970-72 LT-1 engines. These cylinder heads came with screw-in rocker studs, larger valves, and pushrod guide plates.

Block, Head, and Manifold Casting Numbers

Year	Engine	Casting Number
Intake Manifolds		
1966	327 4V	3872783, Holley
1966–1968	327 4V	3872783, Holley
1966–1967	327 4V	3890490, aluminum
1966–1968	327 4V	3905393, Quadrajet
1967–1968	327 2V	3910601, w/o a/c
1968	327 4V	3919803, Quadrajet
1969	327 2V	3927183
1967	350 4V	3905393, Quadrajet
1968	350 4V	3927184 w/o a/c
1970–1972	350 4V	3959594, LT1, aluminum
1969–1970	350 4V	3965577
1970	350 4V	3972110, aluminum
1970	350 4V	3972116, aluminum (service replacement)
1969–1970	350 2V	3916313
1971	350 4V	3972361, aluminum
1971	350 4V	3973469
1971–1972	350 4V	6262932,175/200/270 hp
1972	350 4V	6263751 (200 hp), 6262930 (165 hp)
1972	350 4V	3972114, aluminum
1973	350 4V	3997770, 3997771
1973–1975	350 2V	340266
1975	350 4V	346249
1970	400 2V	3916313
1971	400 2V	3973467
1972–1973	400 2V	6263752
1974	400 2V	397772, 397773
1974	400 4V	3997770, 3997771
1975	400 2V	343756

Block, Head, and Manifold Casting Numbers

Exhaust Manifolds

Year	Engine	Left/Right	Casting Number
1955–1956	265 2V, 4V		3704792 right, 3704791 left, Chevrolet
1955–1956	265 2V, 4V		3836968 right, 3836969 left, Chevrolet
1955–1956	265 all		3836968 right, 3836969 left, 2nd design, Corvette
1955	265 4V		3704792 right, 3704791 left, Corvette
1956	265 2x4V		3725563 right, 3725563 left, 2 outlet studs
1956	265 2x4V		3731558 right, 3731557 left, 3 outlet studs
1957	265 2V		3733976 right, 3733975 left, Chevrolet
1957	283 all		3733976 right, 3733975 left
1958–1966	3747038	R	283 220 hp
1964	3747038	R	327 250/300 hp
1962–1965	3747038	R	327 250/300 hp
1965–1968	3747042	R	283 195/220 hp
1966–1967	3747042	R	327 300/350 hp
1965	3747942	L/R	327 250/350 hp
1958–1961	3749965	L	283 all
1962–1964	3749965	L	327 250/300 hp
1958–1961	3750556	R	283 250/290 hp
1962–1966	3750556	R	327 250/275/300/325 hp
1964–1967	3780728	L	327 Chevy II
1964–1967	3790729	L	283 195/220 hp, Chevy II
1965	3790730	R	283 220 hp, Chevy II
1965	3790730	R	327 250/300 hp Chevy II

Exhaust Manifolds

Year	Engine	Left/Right	Casting Number
1965	3791162	R	283/327, Chevy II w/a/c
1966–1967	3791182	R	283/327, 210/220/250/275 hp, w/ a/c
1962–1963	3797901	L	327 300 hp/340/360 hp
1962–1965	3797902	R	327 300/340/360/365/375 hp, 2.5 in. outlet
1963–1965	3797942	L/R	327 350/360/365/375 hp, 2.5 in. outlet
1965	3834947	L	283/327 195/220/250/300 hp, Chevelle
1964	3840715	L	283/327, Chevelle
1964–1968	3840912	R	283/307/327, Chevelle w/o A.I.R.
1967–1969	3840912	R	327/350, Camaro w/o A.I.R.
1968	3840912	R	307/327/350, Nova w/o A.I.R.
1964–1971	3846559	L	327/350 250/270/300 hp, Corvette, 2.0 in. outlet
1964–1965	3846563	L	327 350/365 hp
1966	3846659	L	350
1964–1967	3849288	R	283/327, Chevy II w/o A.I.R.
1964–1967	3849290	R	283/327, Chevy II w/ a/c
1964–1968	3855163	L	283/327 195/200/220/250/275 hp
1966–1967	3872723	L	283/327, Chevy II w/ A.I.R.
1966	3872729	L	283/327, Chevelle w/A.I.R.
1967–1968	3872730	R	283/302/307/327/350, Chevelle/Camaro w/ A.I.R.
1966–1967	3872738	R	283/327, Chevy II w/ A.I.R.
1966–1968	3872741	L	283/327, Chevrolet
1966–1971	3872765	L	327/350, Corvette w/ A.I.R., 2.0 in. outlet
1966–1968	3872778	R	283/307/327, w/ A.I.R.
1966	3887186	R	283 220 hp
1964–1967	3890424	R	283/327, Chevy II w/o A.I.R.
1967–1968	3892679	L	283/302/307/327/350, w/o A.I.R.
1966–1968	3892683	L	283/302/307/327/350, w/ A.I.R.
1966–1968	3893604	R	283/327, Chevrolet w/ A.I.R.
1967	3893608	R	302, w/o A.I.R.
1967–1968	3893608	R	283/302/307/327, w/o A.I.R.
1967–1968	3896956	R	283/307/327, light truck
1969–1972	3905364	R	283/307/400, truck
1969–1970	3932376	R	307/327/350/400
1970–1971	3932461	L/R	350, Corvette
1969–1970	3932465	R	327/350, Chevrolet w/o A.I.R.
1969–1970	3932469	L	350/400, Chevrolet
1969–1970	3932473	L	307/350, Chevrolet
1969	3932481	R	350, Corvette, m/t
1967	3940972	R	350 295 hp
1969	3942527	L	302, w/ A.I.R.
1969–1971	3942527	L	307/350, w/ A.I.R.
1969–1970	3942529	L	307/350, w/o A.I.R.
1969	3946826	R	302/307/350, w /A.I.R.
1972–1974	3959562	R	307/350, Chevelle/Camaro w/ A.I.R.
1971–1972	3973432	R	307/350, w/o A.I.R.
1972–1974	3986330	R	307/350, Camaro w /A.I.R.
1970–1972	3989036	R	350/400, Chevrolet
1970–1972	3989036	R	350 200/270 hp, Corvette
1971–1974	3989041	L	307/350, Chevelle/Camaro/Nova
1971–1972	3989043	L	307/350, Chevrolet/Chevelle/Camaro/Nova w/o A.I.R.
1969–1972	3989055	L	307/340/400
1971–1975	3997742	R	307/350
1972–1975	3998902	R	307/350
1974–1975	336706	R	350
1974–1975	336707	L	350
1974–1975	336708	R	350
1974–1975	336709	L	350
1974–1975	336710	L	350/400
1974–1975	346222	R	350/400
1975	346247	L	262/350/400
1975	346248	R	262/350/400
1975	354432	R	262
1975	354433	L	262
1974–1975	372243	R	350/400

Engine Suffix Codes

Suffix Code	Engine	Equipment
1955 Corvette		
GR	265 cid 4V 195 hp	m/t
FG	265 cid 4V 195 hp	PG a/t
1955 Chevrolet		
G	265 cid 2V 162 hp	m/t
GC	265 cid 2V 162 hp	m/t, o/d
GF	265 cid 2V 162 hp	m/t, a/c
GJ	265 cid 2V 162 hp	m/t, h/d clutch
GQ	265 cid 2V 162 hp	m/t, o/d, a/c
GK	265 cid 2V 162 hp	m/t, a/c, h/d clutch
F	265 cid 2V 162 hp	PG a/t
FC	265 cid 2V 162 hp	PG a/t, a/c
GE	265 cid 4V 180 hp	m/t, o/d
GL	265 cid 4V 180 hp	m/t
GM	265 cid 4V 180 hp	m/t, a/c
GN	265 cid 4V 180 hp	m/t, o/d
FB	265 cid 4V 180 hp	PG a/t
FD	265 cid 4V 180 hp	PG a/t, a/c
1956 Corvette		
FK, GV	265 cid 4V 210 hp	m/t
GR	265 cid 2x4V 225 hp	m/t
FG	265 cid 2x4V 225 hp	PG a/t
GU	265 cid dual 240 hp	m/t
1956 Chevrolet		
G	265 cid 2V 162 hp	m/t
GC	265 cid 2V 162 hp	m/t, o/d
GF	265 cid 2V 162 hp	m/t, a/c
GJ	265 cid 2V 162 hp	m/t, h/d clutch
GK	265 cid 2V 162 hp	m/t, a/c, h/d clutch
GQ	265 cid 2V 162 hp	m/t o/d, a/c
FC	265 cid 2V 170 hp	PG a/t, a/c
F	265 cid 2V 170 hp	PG a/t
GE	265 cid 4V 205 hp	m/t, o/d
GL	265 cid 4V 205 hp	m/t
GM	265 cid 4V 205 hp	m/t, a/c
GN	265 cid 4V 205 hp	m/t, o/d, a/c
FB	265 cid 4V 205 hp	PG a/t
FD	265 cid 4V 205 hp	PG a/t, a/c
1956 3100 and 3200 Series Trucks		
A	265 cid 2V 155 hp	m/t
B	265 cid 2V 155 hp	PG a/t
M	265 cid 2V 155 hp	m/t
1956 3600 Series Trucks		
AA	265 cid 2V 155 hp	m/t
BA	265 cid 2V 155 hp	PG a/t
MA	265 cid 2V 155 hp	m/t
1956 3800 Series Trucks		
AB	265 cid 2V 155 hp	m/t
BB	265 cid 2V 155 hp	PG a/t
MB	265 cid 2V 155 hp	m/t
1957 Corvette		
EF	283 cid 4V 220 hp	m/t
FH	283 cid 4V 220 hp	PG a/t
EH	265 cid 2x4V 245 hp	m/t
FG	283 cid 2x4V 245 hp	PG a/t
EM	283 cid FI 250 hp	m/t
FK	283 cid FI 250 hp	PG a/t
EN	283 cid FI 283 hp	m/t
EL	283 cid FI 283 hp	PG a/t
1957 Chevrolet		
C	265 cid 2V 162 hp	m/t
CD	265 cid 2V 162 hp	m/t, o/d
CE	265 cid 2V 162 hp	m/t, h/d clutch
Suffix	**Engine**	**Equipment**
F	283 cid 2V 185 hp	PG a/t
FA	283 cid 2V 185 hp	PG a/t, a/c
G	283 cid 2V 185 hp	TG a/t
E	283 cid 4V 220 hp	m/t
EC	283 cid 4V 220 hp	m/t, o/d
FC	283 cid 4V 220 hp	PG a/t
FE	283 cid 4V 220 hp	PG a/t, a/c
GC	283 cid 4V 220 hp	TG a/t
EA	265 cid 2x4V 245 hp	m/t
FD	283 cid 2x4V 245 hp	PG a/t
GD	283 cid 2x4V 245 hp	TG a/t
GF	283 cid FI 250 hp	TG a/t
EJ	283 cid FI 250 hp	m/t
FJ	283 cid FI 250 hp	PG a/t
EB	283 cid 2x4V 270 hp	m/t
EK	283 cid FI 283 hp	m/t
1957 3100, 3200, 3600, and 3800 Series Trucks		
L	265 cid 2V 162 hp	m/t
LA	265 cid 2V 162 hp	m/t
LB	265 cid 2V 162 hp	h/d m/t
1958 Corvette		
CQ	283 cid 4V 230 hp	m/t
DG	283 cid 4V 230 hp	PG a/t
CT	283 cid 2x4V 245 hp	m/t
DJ	283 cid 2x4V 245 hp	PG a/t
CR	283 cid FI 250 hp	m/t
DH	283 cid FI 250 hp	PG a/t
CU	283 cid 2x4V 270 hp	m/t
CS	283 cid FI 290 hp	m/t
1958 Chevrolet		
C	283 cid 2V 185 hp	m/t
CB	283 cid 2V 185 hp	m/t
C	283 cid 2V 185 hp	m/t, o/d
D	283 cid 2V 185 hp	PG a/t
DE	283 cid 2V 185 hp	PG a/t, air suspension
E	283 cid 2V 185 hp	TG a/t
ED	283 cid 2V 185 hp	TG a/t, air suspension
CF	283 cid 4V 230 hp	m/t
CG	283 cid 4V 230 hp	m/t, o/d
DB	283 cid 4V 230 hp	PG a/t
DF	283 cid 4V 230 hp	PG a/t, air suspension
EB	283 cid 4V 230 hp	TG a/t
EF	283 cid 4V 230 hp	TG a/t, air suspension
CH	283 cid FI 250 hp	3-spd m/t
CY	283 cid FI 250 hp	4-spd m/t
EC	283 cid FI 250 hp	TG a/t
CJ	283 cid FI 290 hp	3-spd m/t
CZ	283 cid FI 290 hp	4-spd m/t
1958 3100, 3200, 3600, and 3800 Series Trucks		
M	283 cid 2V 160 hp	m/t
MA	283 cid 2V 160 hp	h/d m/t
MB	283 cid 2V 160 hp	m/t
1959 Corvette		
CQ	283 cid 4V 230 hp	m/t
DG	283 cid 4V 230 hp	PG a/t
CT	283 cid 2x4V 245 hp	m/t
DJ	283 cid 2x4V 245 hp	PG a/t
CR	283 cid FI 250 hp	m/t
DH	283 cid FI 250 hp	PG a/t
CU	283 cid 2x4V 270 hp	m/t
CS	283 cid FI 290 hp	m/t
1959 Chevrolet		
C	283 cid 2V 185 hp	m/t
CD	283 cid 2V 185 hp	m/t, o/d

The high point in single four-barrel intake manifold design came in 1967 on the 302 Z/28 engine. This highly regarded aluminum manifold, #3917610, was also used on the 1968 engines and it had a Holley carburetor mounting pad.

Suffix	Engine	Equipment
D	283 cid 2V 185 hp	PG a/t
DK	283 cid 2V 185 hp	PG a/t, a/c
DE	283 cid 2V 185 hp	PG a/t, a/c, air suspension
E	283 cid 2V 185 hp	TG a/t
EG	283 cid 2V 185 hp	TG a/t, a/c
EH	283 cid 2V 185 hp	TG a/t, air suspension, a/c
ED	283 cid 2V 185 hp	TG a/t, air suspension
DL	283 cid 2V 185 hp	PG a/t, a/c, air suspension
CF	283 cid 4V 230 hp	m/t
CG	283 cid 4V 230 hp	m/t, o/d
DB	283 cid 4V 230 hp	PG a/t
DN	283 cid 4V 230 hp	PG a/t, a/c, air suspension
DM	283 cid 4V 230 hp	PG a/t
DF	283 cid 4V 230 hp	PG a/t, air suspension
EB	283 cid 4V 230 hp	TG a/t
EF	283 cid 4V 230 hp	TG a/t, air suspension
EJ	283 cid 4V 230 hp	TG a/t
EK	283 cid 4V 230 hp	TG a/t, a/c, air suspension
CH	283 cid FI 250 hp	m/t
DP	283 cid FI 250 hp	PG a/t
EC	283 cid FI 250 hp	TG a/t
CH	283 cid FI 250 hp	m/t
CJ	283 cid FI 290 hp	m/t
1959 3100, 3200, 3600, and 3800 Series Trucks		
M	283 cid 2V 160 hp	m/t
MA	283 cid 2V 160 hp	h/d m/t
1960 Corvette		
CQ	283 cid 4V 230 hp	m/t
DG	283 cid 4V 230 hp	PG a/t
CT	283 cid 2x4V 245 hp	m/t
DJ	283 cid 2x4V 245 hp	PG a/t
CR	283 cid FI 250 hp	m/t
CU	283 cid 2x4V 270 hp	m/t
CS	283 cid FI 290 hp	m/t
1960 Chevrolet		
C	283 cid 2V 170 hp	m/t
CD	283 cid 2V 170 hp	m/t, o/d
CL	283 cid 2V 170 hp	m/t, a/c
E	283 cid 2V 170 hp	TG a/t
EG	283 cid 2V 170 hp	TG a/t, a/c
D	283 cid 2V 170 hp	PG a/t
DK	283 cid 2V 170 hp	PG a/t, a/c

Suffix	Engine	Equipment
CM	283 cid 4V 230 hp	m/t, a/c
CF	283 cid 4V 230 hp	m/t
CG	283 cid 4V 230 hp	m/t, o/d
DB	283 cid 4V 230 hp	PG a/t
DM	283 cid 4V 230 hp	PG a/t
EB	283 cid 4V 230 hp	TG a/t
EJ	283 cid 4V 230 hp	TG a/t, a/c
1960 C10 and C20 Trucks		
M	283 cid 2V 160 hp	m/t
MA	283 cid 2V 160 hp	PG a/t
1960 C30 Trucks		
M	283 cid 2V 160 hp	PG a/t
1960 K10 and K20 Trucks		
M	283 cid 2V 160 hp	m/t
1961 Corvette		
CQ	283 cid 4V 230 hp	m/t
DG	283 cid 4V 230 hp	PG a/t
CT	283 cid 2x4V 245 hp	m/t
DJ	283 cid 2x4V 245 hp	PG a/t
CU	283 cid 2x4V 270 hp	m/t
CR	283 cid FI 275 hp	m/t
CS	283 cid FI 315 hp	m/t
1961 Chevrolet		
C	283 cid 2V 170 hp	3-spd m/t
CL	283 cid 2V 170 hp	3-spd m/t, a/c
CD	283 cid 2V 170 hp	3-spd m/t, o/d
D	283 cid 2V 170 hp	PG a/t
DK	283 cid 2V 170 hp	PG a/t, a/c
E	283 cid 2V 170 hp	TG a/t
EG	283 cid 2V 170 hp	TG a/t, a/c
CF	283 cid 4V 230 hp	3-spd m/t
CG	283 cid 4V 230 hp	3-spd m/t, o/d
CM	283 cid 4V 230 hp	3-spd m/t, a/c
DB	283 cid 4V 230 hp	PG a/t
DM	283 cid 4V 230 hp	PG a/t
EB	283 cid 4V 230 hp	TG a/t
EJ	283 cid 4V 230 hp	TG a/t, a/c
1961 C10 and C20 Trucks		
M	283 cid 2V 160 hp	m/t
MA	283 cid 2V 160 hp	PG
1961 K10 and K20 Trucks		
M	283 cid 2V 160 hp	m/t
1962 Corvette		
RC	327 cid 4V 250 hp	4-spd m/t
SC	327 cid 4V 250 hp	PG a/t
RD	327 cid 4V 300 hp	4-spd m/t
SD	327 cid 4V 300 hp	PG a/t
RE	327 cid 4V 340 hp	4-spd m/t
RF	327 cid FI 360 hp	4-spd m/t
1962 Chevrolet		
C	283 cid 2V 170 hp	3-spd m/t
CL	283 cid 2V 170 hp	3-spd m/t, a/c
CD	283 cid 2V 170 hp	3-spd m/t, o/d
D	283 cid 2V 170 hp	PG a/t
DK	283 cid 2V 170 hp	PG a/t, a/c
R	327 cid 4V 250 hp	3- or 4-spd m/t
RA	327 cid 4V 250 hp	3- or 4-spd m/t, a/c
S	327 cid 4V 250 hp	PG a/t
SA	327 cid 4V 250 hp	PG a/t, a/c
RA	327 cid 4V 300 hp	m/t
RB	327 cid 4V 300 hp	m/t
SB	327 cid 4V 300 hp	PG a/t
1962 C10 and C20 Trucks		
M	283 cid 2V 160 hp	m/t

The small-block's cylinder block has seen some minor changes over the years. The block on the right is a late-model block designed to use hydraulic roller lifters. The lifter bores have been machined flat.

Engine Suffix Codes

Suffix	Engine	Equipment
MA	283 cid 2V 160 hp	PG a/t
1962 C30 Trucks		
M	283 cid 2V 160 hp	m/t
1962 K10 and K20 Trucks		
M	283 cid 2V 160 hp	m/t
1963 Corvette		
RC	327 cid 4V 250 hp	4-spd
SC	327 cid 4V 250 hp	PG a/t
RD	327 cid 4V 300 hp	4-spd m/t
SD	327 cid 4V 300 hp	PG a/t
RE	327 cid 4V 340 hp	4-spd m/t
RF	327 cid FI 360 hp	4-spd m/t
1963 Chevrolet		
C	283 cid 2V 195 hp	3-spd m/t
CL	283 cid 2V 195 hp	3-spd m/t, a/c
CB	283 cid 2V 195 hp	3-spd m/t, police
CD	283 cid 2V 195 hp	3-spd m/t, o/d
D	283 cid 2V 195 hp	PG a/t
DK	283 cid 2V 195 hp	PG a/t, a/c
R	327 cid 4V 250 hp	3- or 4-spd m/t
RA	327 cid 4V 250 hp	3- or 4-spd m/t, a/c
S	327 cid 4V 250 hp	PG a/t
SA	327 cid 4V 250 hp	PG a/t, a/c
RB	327 cid 4V 300 hp	m/t
RK	327 cid 4V 300 hp	m/t
SB	327 cid 4V 300 hp	PG a/t
SG	327 cid 4V 300 hp	PG a/t, a/c
1963 C10 and C20 Trucks		
M	283 cid 2V 175 hp	m/t
MA	283 cid 2V 175 hp	PG
1963 C30 Trucks		
M	283 cid 2V 175 hp	m/t
1963 K10 and K20 Trucks		
M	283 cid 2V 170 hp	m/t
1964 Corvette		
SC	327 cid 4V 250 hp	PG a/t
SK	327 cid 4V 250 hp	PG a/t, a/c
RC	327 cid 4V 250 hp	4-spd m/t
Suffix	**Engine**	**Equipment**
RP	327 cid 4V 250 hp	4-spd m/t, a/c
SD	327 cid 4V 300 hp	PG a/t
SL	327 cid 4V 300 hp	PG a/t, a/c
RD	327 cid 4V 300 hp	4-spd m/t
RQ	327 cid 4V 300 hp	4-spd m/t, a/c
RE	327 cid 4V 365 hp	4-spd m/t
RR	327 cid 4V 365 hp	4-spd m/t, a/c
RT	327 cid 4V 365 hp	4-spd m/t, TI*
RU	327 cid 4V 365 hp	4-spd m/t, a/c, TI
RF	327 cid FI 375 hp	4-spd m/t
RX	327 cid FI 375 hp	4-spd m/t, TI
1964 Chevrolet		
C	283 cid 2V 195 hp	3-spd m/t
CB	283 cid 2V 195 hp	3-spd m/t, police
D	283 cid 2V 195 hp	PG a/t
R	327 cid 4V 250 hp	3- or 4-spd m/t
S	327 cid 4V 250 hp	PG a/t
RB	327 cid 4V 300 hp	3- or 4-spd m/t
SB	327 cid 4V 300 hp	PG a/t
XE	327 cid 4V 300 hp	Service replacement block
1964 Chevy II		
CH	283 cid 2V 195 hp	3-spd m/t
CJ	283 cid 2V 195 hp	3-spd m/t
CF	283 cid 2V 195 hp	4-spd m/t
CG	283 cid 2V 195 hp	4-spd m/t
DE	283 cid 2V 195 hp	PG a/t
DF	283 cid 2V 195 hp	PG a/t
1964 Chevelle		
J	283 cid 2V 195 hp	3-spd m/t
JA	283 cid 2V 195 hp	4-spd m/t
JD	283 cid 2V 195 hp	PG a/t
JH	283 cid 4V 220 hp	3- or 4-spd m/t
JG	283 cid 4V 220 hp	PG a/t
JQ	327 cid 4V 250 hp	3- or 4-spd m/t
SR	327 cid 4V 250 hp	PG a/t
JR	327 cid 4V 300 hp	3- or 4-spd m/t
SS	327 cid 4V 300 hp	PG a/t
JS	327 cid 4V 365 hp	4-spd m/t
JT	327 cid 4V 365 hp	4-spd m/t, TI
1964 C10 and C20 Trucks		
M	283 cid 2V 175 hp	m/t
MA	283 cid 2V 175 hp	PG a/t
MX	283 cid 2V 175 hp	m/t
MY	283 cid 2V 175 hp	PG a/t
1964 C30 Trucks		
M	283 cid 2V 175 hp	m/t
MX	283 cid 2V 175 hp	m/t
1964 K10 and K20 Trucks		
M	283 cid 2V 175 hp	m/t
MX	283 cid 2V 175 hp	m/t
1965 Corvette		
HO	327 cid 4V 250 hp	PG a/t
HQ	327 cid 4V 250 hp	PG a/t, a/c
HE	327 cid 4V 250 hp	m/t
HI	327 cid 4V 250 hp	m/t, a/c
HP	327 cid 4V 300 hp	PG a/t
HR	327 cid 4V 300 hp	PG a/t, a/c
HF	327 cid 4V 300 hp	m/t
HJ	327 cid 4V 300 hp	m/t, a/c
HT	327 cid 4V 350 hp	4-spd m/t
HU	327 cid 4V 350 hp	4-spd m/t, a/c
HV	327 cid 4V 350 hp	4-spd m/t, TI
HW	327 cid 4V 365 hp	4-spd m/t, a/c, TI
HH	327 cid 4V 365 hp	4-spd m/t, a/c

Suffix	Engine	Equipment
HK	327 cid 4V 365 hp	4-spd m/t, a/c
HL	327 cid 4V 365 hp	4-spd m/t, TI
HM	327 cid 4V 365 hp	4-spd m/t, a/c, TI
HG	327 cid FI 375 hp	4-spd m/t
HN	327 cid FI 375 hp	4-spd m/t, TI
1965 Chevrolet		
GA	283 cid 2V 195 hp	m/t
GB	283 cid 2V 195 hp	m/t
GE	283 cid 2V 195 hp	m/t
GD	283 cid 2V 195 hp	m/t
GC	283 cid 2V 195 hp	3-spd m/t, police
GF	283 cid 2V 195 hp	PG a/t
GH	283 cid 2V 195 hp	PG a/t
GG	283 cid 2V 195 hp	PG a/t
GI	283 cid 2V 195 hp	PG a/t
GK	283 cid 4V 220 hp	m/t
GL	283 cid 4V 220 hp	PG a/t
HA	327 cid 4V 250 hp	4-spd m/t
HC	327 cid 4V 250 hp	PG a/t
HB	327 cid 4V 300 hp	m/t
h/d	327 cid 4V 300 hp	PG a/t
1965 Chevy II		
PD	283 cid 2V 195 hp	3-spd m/t
PF	283 cid 2V 195 hp	3-spd m/t, a/c
PL	283 cid 2V 195 hp	4-spd m/t
PM	283 cid 2V 195 hp	4-spd m/t, a/c
PN	283 cid 2V 195 hp	PG a/t
PP	283 cid 2V 195 hp	PG a/t, w/a/c
PE	283 cid 4V 220 hp	m/t
PG	283 cid 4V 220 hp	m/t, a/c
PK	283 cid 4V 220 hp	PG a/t
PB	283 cid 4V 220 hp	PG a/t, a/c
ZA	327 cid 4V 250 hp	m/t
ZE	327 cid 4V 250 hp	m/t, a/c
ZK	327 cid 4V 250 hp	PG a/t
ZM	327 cid 4V 250 hp	PG a/t, a/c
ZB	327 cid 4V 300 hp	m/t
ZF	327 cid 4V 300 hp	m/t, a/c
ZN	327 cid 4V 300 hp	PG a/t
ZL	327 cid 4V 300 hp	PG a/t, a/c
1965 Chevelle		
DA	283 cid 2V 195 hp	3-spd m/t
DB	283 cid 2V 195 hp	4-spd m/t
DD	283 cid 2V 195 hp	4-spd m/t
DC	283 cid 2V 195 hp	m/t
DE	283 cid 2V 195 hp	PG a/t
DF	283 cid 2V 195 hp	PG a/t
DG	283 cid 4V 220 hp	m/t
DH	283 cid 4V 220 hp	PG a/t
EA	327 cid 4V 250 hp	m/t
EE	327 cid 4V 250 hp	PG a/t
EB	327 cid 4V 300 hp	m/t
EF	327 cid 4V 300 hp	PG a/t
EC	327 cid 4V 300 hp	4-spd m/t
ED	327 cid 4V 350 hp	4-spd m/t, TI
1965 C10 Trucks		
WA	283 cid 2V 175 hp	m/t
WE	283 cid 2V 175 hp	PG a/t
1965 C20 Trucks		
WA	283 cid 2V 175 hp	m/t
WE	283 cid 2V 175 hp	PG a/t
1965 C30 Trucks		
WA	283 cid 2V 175 hp	m/t
1965 K10/K20 Trucks		
WA	283 cid 2V 175 hp	m/t

Suffix	Engine	Equipment
1966 Corvette		
HO	327 cid 4V 300 hp	PG a/t
HR	327 cid 4V 300 hp	PG a/t, A.I.R.
HE	327 cid 4V 300 hp	m/t
HH	327 cid 4V 300 hp	m/t, A.I.R.
HT	327 cid 4V 300 hp	4-spd m/t
HP	327 cid 4V 300 hp	4-spd m/t, a/c, p/s
HD	327 cid 4V 300 hp	4-spd m/t, A.I.R.
KH	327 cid 4V 300 hp	4-spd m/t, A.I.R., a/c, p/s
1966 Chevrolet		
GA	283 cid 2V 195 hp	3-spd m/t
GB, GD, GE	283 cid 2V 195 hp	m/t
GC	283 cid 2V 195 hp	m/t, police
GK	283 cid 2V 195 hp	m/t, A.I.R.
GS	283 cid 2V 195 hp	4-spd m/t, A.I.R.
GF, GG	283 cid 2V 195 hp	PG a/t
GH, GI	283 cid 2V 195 hp	PG a/t
GT	283 cid 2V 195 hp	PG a/t, A.I.R.
GW	283 cid 4V 220 hp	3- or 4-spd m/t
GX	283 cid 4V 220 hp	3- or 4-spd m/t, A.I.R.
GV	83 cid 4V 220 hp	3- or 4-spd m/t, h/d clutch
GL	283 cid 4V 220 hp	PG a/t
GZ	283 cid 4V 220 hp	PG a/t, A.I.R.
HE	327 cid 4V 275 hp	4-spd m/t, h/d clutch
HB	327 cid 4V 275 hp	4-spd m/t, A.I.R
HAH	327 cid 4V 275 hp	4-spd m/t, Holley
HAR	327 cid 4V 275 hp	4-spd m/t
HCH	327 cid 4V 275 hp	PG a/t, Holley
HCR	327 cid 4V 275 hp	PG a/t
HF	327 cid 4V 275 hp	PG a/t, A.I.R
1966 Chevy II		
PD	283 cid 2V 195 hp	3-spd m/t
PF	283 cid 2V 195 hp	3-spd m/t, a/c
PE	283 cid 2V 195 hp	3-spd m/t, A.I.R.
PG	283 cid 2V 195 hp	3-spd m/t, A.I.R., a/c
PL	283 cid 2V 195 hp	4-spd m/t
PM	283 cid 2V 195 hp	4-spd m/t, a/c
PS	283 cid 2V 195 hp	4-spd m/t, A.I.R., a/c
PN	283 cid 2V 195 hp	PG a/t
PP	283 cid 2V 195 hp	PG a/t, a/c
PU	283 cid 2V 195 hp	PG a/t, A.I.R.
PO	283 cid 2V 195 hp	PG a/t, A.I.R., a/c
QA	283 cid 4V 220 hp	m/t
QB	283 cid 4V 220 hp	m/t, a/c
QC, QF	283 cid 4V 220 hp	m/t, a/c, A.I.R.
PK	283 cid 4V 220 hp	PG a/t
PP	283 cid 4V 220 hp	PG a/t, a/c
QD	283 cid 4V 220 hp	PG a/t, A.I.R.
QE	283 cid 4V 220 hp	PG a/t, A.I.R., a/c
ZA	327 cid 4V 275 hp	m/t
ZE	327 cid 4V 275 hp	m/t, a/c
ZB	327 cid 4V 275 hp	m/t, A.I.R.
ZK	327 cid 4V 275 hp	PG a/t
ZD	327 cid 4V 275 hp	PG a/t, A.I.R.
ZM	327 cid 4V 275 hp	PG a/t, a/c
ZI	327 cid 4V 350 hp	4-spd m/t
ZJ	327 cid 4V 350 hp	4-spd m/t, a/c
ZG, ZH	327 cid 4V 350 hp	4-spd m/t, A.I.R.
1966 Chevelle		
DA	283 cid 2V 195 hp	m/t
DN	283 cid 2V 195 hp	m/t, h/d clutch
DI	283 cid 2V 195 hp	m/t
DB, DK	283 cid 2V 195 hp	4-spd m/t

Engine Suffix Codes

Suffix	Engine	Equipment
DE, DF	283 cid 2V 195 hp	PG a/t
DJ	283 cid 2V 195 hp	PG a/t, A.I.R.
DG	283 cid 4V 220 hp	m/t
DL	283 cid 4V 220 hp	m/t, A.I.R.
DH	283 cid 4V 220 hp	PG a/t
DM	283 cid 4V 220 hp	PG a/t, A.I.R.
EA	327 cid 4V 275 hp	m/t
EB	327 cid 4V 275 hp	m/t, A.I.R.
EC	327 cid 4V 275 hp	PG a/t, A.I.R.
EE	327 cid 4V 275 hp	PG a/t
1966 C10 Trucks		
WA	283 cid 2V 175 hp	m/t
WE	283 cid 2V 175 hp	PG a/t
WF	283 cid 2V 175 hp	m/t, A.I.R.
WH	283 cid 2V 175 hp	PG a/t, A.I.R.
YS	327 cid 4V 220 hp	m/t
YR	327 cid 4V 220 hp	PG a/t
YC	327 cid 4V 220 hp	m/t, A.I.R.
YD	327 cid 4V 220 hp	PG a/t, A.I.R.
1966 C20 Trucks		
WA	283 cid 2V 175 hp	m/t
WE	283 cid 2V 175 hp	PG a/t
YS	327 cid 4V 220 hp	m/t
YR	327 cid 4V 220 hp	PG a/t
YH	327 cid 4V 220 hp	TH a/t
1966 C30 Trucks		
WA	283 cid 2V 175 hp	m/t
YS	327 cid 4V 220 hp	m/t
YH	327 cid 4V 220 hp	TH a/t
1966 K10 Trucks		
WA	283 cid 2V 175 hp	m/t
WF	283 cid 2V 175 hp	m/t
1966 K20 Trucks		
WA	283 cid 2V 175 hp	m/t
1967 Corvette		
HO	327 cid 4V 300 hp	PG a/t
HR	327 cid 4V 300 hp	PG a/t
HH	327 cid 4V 300 hp	4-spd m/t
HE	327 cid 4V 300 hp	m/t
HT	327 cid 4V 350 hp	4-spd m/t
HP	327 cid 4V 350 hp	4-spd m/t, a/c, p/s
h/d	327 cid 4V 350 hp	4-spd m/t, A.I.R.
KH	327 cid 4V 350 hp	4-spd m/t, a/c, A.I.R.
1967 Chevrolet		
GA	283 cid 2V 195 hp	3-spd m/t
GU	283 cid 2V 195 hp	3-spd m/t, h/d clutch
GD	283 cid 2V 195 hp	3-spd m/t
GC	283 cid 2V 195 hp	4-spd m/t, h/d chassis, police
GK	283 cid 2V 195 hp	3-spd m/t, A.I.R.
GS	283 cid 2V 195 hp	4-spd m/t, A.I.R.
GF	283 cid 2V 195 hp	PG a/t
GG	283 cid 2V 195 hp	PG a/t
GT	283 cid 2V 195 hp	PG a/t, A.I.R.
GO	283 cid 2V 195 hp	PG a/t, A.I.R
HA	327 cid 4V 275 hp	3-spd m/t
HB	327 cid 4V 275 hp	3-spd m/t, A.I.R.
KE	327 cid 4V 275 hp	4-spd m/t
HC	327 cid 4V 275 hp	PG a/t
HW	327 cid 4V 275 hp	PG a/t
HF	327 cid 4V 275 hp	PG a/t, A.I.R
KL	327 cid 4V 275 hp	TH a/t
KM	327 cid 4V 275 hp	PG a/t, A.I.R.

Suffix	Engine	Equipment
1967 Chevy II		
PD	283 cid 2V 195 hp	3-spd m/t
PF	283 cid 2V 195 hp	3-spd m/t, a/c
PE	283 cid 2V 195 hp	3-spd m/t, A.I.R
PL	283 cid 2V 195 hp	4-spd m/t
PM	283 cid 2V 195 hp	4-spd m/t, a/c
PQ	283 cid 2V 195 hp	4-spd m/t, A.I.R
PN	283 cid 2V 195 hp	PG a/t
PU	283 cid 2V 195 hp	PG a/t, A.I.R
PP	283 cid 2V 195 hp	PG a/t, a/c
ZA	327 cid 4V 275 hp	3- or 4-spd m/t
ZB	327 cid 4V 275 hp	3- or 4-spd m/t, A.I.R
ZE	327 cid 4V 275 hp	3- or 4-spd m/t, a/c
ZK	327 cid 4V 275 hp	PG a/t
ZD	327 cid 4V 275 hp	PG a/t, A.I.R
ZM	327 cid 4V 275 hp	PG a/t, a/c
ZI	327 cid 4V 350 hp	4-spd m/t
ZJ	327 cid 4V 350 hp	4-spd m/t, a/c
ZG	327 cid 4V 350 hp	4-spd m/t, A.I.R.
ZH	327 cid 4V 350 hp	4-spd m/t, A.I.R., a/c
1967 Chevelle		
DC	283 cid 2V 195 hp	3-spd m/t
DN	283 cid 2V 195 hp	3-spd m/t, h/d clutch
DA	283 cid 2V 195 hp	3-spd m/t
DI	283 cid 2V 195 hp	3-spd m/t, A.I.R.
DB	283 cid 2V 195 hp	4-spd m/t
DK	283 cid 2V 195 hp	4-spd m/t, A.I.R.
DE	283 cid 2V 195 hp	PG a/t
DF	283 cid 2V 195 hp	PG a/t
DJ	283 cid 2V 195 hp	PG a/t, A.I.R.
EA	327 cid 4V 275 hp	3-spd m/t
EB	327 cid 4V 275 hp	3-spd m/t, A.I.R.
EQ	327 cid 4V 275 hp	4-spd m/t, h/d clutch
EE	327 cid 4V 275 hp	PG a/t
EC	327 cid 4V 275 hp	PG a/t, A.I.R
EP	327 cid 4V 350 hp	4-spd m/t
ER	327 cid 4V 350 hp	4-spd m/t, A.I.R.
ES	327 cid 4V 350 hp	4-spd m/t, h/d clutch
1967 Camaro		
MD	283 cid 2V 195 hp	4-spd m/t
MJ	283 cid 2V 195 hp	PG a/t
MO	302 cid 4V 290 hp	4-spd m/t
MP	302 cid 4V 290 hp	4-spd m/t
MA	327 cid 2V 210 hp	3-spd m/t
MB	327 cid 2V 210 hp	3-spd m/t, A.I.R.
ME	327 cid 2V 210 hp	PG a/t
MF	327 cid 2V 210 hp	PG a/t, A.I.R.
MK	327 cid 4V 275 hp	4-spd m/t
ML	327 cid 4V 275 hp	4-spd m/t, A.I.R.
MM	327 cid 4V 275 hp	PG a/t
MN	327 cid 4V 275 hp	PG a/t, A.I.R.
MS	350 cid 4V 295 hp	3- or 4-spd m/t
MT	350 cid 4V 295 hp	3- or 4-spd m/t, A.I.R.
MU	350 cid 4V 295 hp	PG a/t
MV	350 cid 4V 295 hp	PG a/t, A.I.R
1967 C10/C20 Trucks		
WA	283 cid 2V 175 hp	m/t
WC	283 cid 2V 175 hp	TH a/t
WE	283 cid 2V 175 hp	PG a/t
WF	283 cid 2V 175 hp	m/t, A.I.R.
WG	283 cid 2V 175 hp	m/t
WH	283 cid 2V 175 hp	PG a/t, A.I.R.
WR	283 cid 2V 175 hp	TH a/t, A.I.R.
YS	327 cid 4V 220 hp	m/t

Suffix	Engine	Equipment
YR	327 cid 4V 220 hp	PG a/t
YC	327 cid 4V 220 hp	m/t, A.I.R.
YD	327 cid 4V 220 hp	PG a/t, A.I.R.
YJ	327 cid 4V 220 hp	TH a/t, A.I.R.
YH	327 cid 4V 220 hp	PG a/t, A.I.R.
1967 C30 Trucks		
WA	283 cid 2V 175 hp	m/t
WG	283 cid 2V 175 hp	m/t
YS	327 cid 4V 220 hp	m/t
1967 K10/K20 Trucks		
WB	283 cid 2V 175 hp	m/t
WO	283 cid 2V 175 hp	m/t
WI	283 cid 2V 175 hp	m/t
YX	327 cid 4V 220 hp	m/t
YM	327 cid 4V 220 hp	m/t
1968 Corvette		
HO	327 cid 4V 300 hp	TH a/t
HE	327 cid 4V 300 hp	m/t
HT	327 cid 4V 350 hp	4-spd m/t
HP	327 cid 4V 350 hp	4-spd m/t, a/c, p/s
1968 Chevrolet		
DQ	307 cid 2V 200 hp	m/t
DO	307 cid 2V 200 hp	m/t
DP	307 cid 2V 200 hp	4-spd m/t
DH	307 cid 2V 200 hp	PG a/t
DR	307 cid 2V 200 hp	PG a/t
DK, DS	307 cid 2V 200 hp	TH a/t
HI	327 cid 4V 250 hp	m/t
HL	327 cid 4V 250 hp	m/t, h/d clutch
HG, HH, HJ	327 cid 4V 250 hp	PG a/t
HK, HN	327 cid 4V 250 hp	PG a/t
HM	327 cid 4V 250 hp	TH a/t
HA	327 cid 4V 275 hp	m/t
HB	327 cid 4V 275 hp	m/t, h/d clutch
HC	327 cid 4V 275 hp	PG a/t
HF	327 cid 4V 275 hp	TH a/t
1968 Chevy II		
DA	307 cid 2V 200 hp	m/t
DB	307 cid 2V 200 hp	4-spd m/t
DE	307 cid 2V 200 hp	PG a/t
MB	307 cid 2V 200 hp	m/t
MC	307 cid 2V 200 hp	4-spd m/t
MD	307 cid 2V 200 hp	PG a/t
MK	327 cid 4V 275 hp	m/t
EA	327 cid 4V 275 hp	m/t
MC	327 cid 4V 275 hp	4-spd m/t
EC, EE, MM	327 cid 4V 275 hp	PG a/t
ML	327 cid 4V 325 hp	m/t
EP	327 cid 4V 325 hp	m/t
MS	350 cid 4V 295 hp	3- or 4-spd m/t
MN, MU	350 cid 4V 295 hp	PG a/t
1968 Chevelle		
DA	307 cid 2V 200 hp	m/t
DB	307 cid 2V 200 hp	4-spd m/t
DN	307 cid 2V 200 hp	m/t
DE	307 cid 2V 200 hp	PG a/t
EH	327 cid 2V 250 hp	m/t
EJ	327 cid 2V 250 hp	m/t, h/d clutch
EI	327 cid 2V 250 hp	PG a/t
EE	327 cid 4V 275 hp	PG a/t
EA, EO	327 cid 4V 275 hp	m/t
EP	327 cid 4V 325 hp	m/t
ES	327 cid 4V 325 hp	m/t, h/d clutch
1968 Camaro		
MO	302 cid 4V 290 hp	4-spd m/t

Small-block Chevrolet cylinder heads have their head casting number and date code located on the surface beneath the valve cover.

Suffix	Engine	Equipment
MA	327 cid 2V 210 hp	m/t
ME	327 cid 2V 210 hp	PG a/t
EE	327 cid 4V 275 hp	PG a/t
EA	327 cid 4V 275 hp	m/t
MS	350 cid 4V 295 hp	3- or 4-spd m/t
MU	350 cid 4V 295 hp	PG a/t
1968 C10 and C20 Trucks		
WA	307 cid 2V 200 hp	m/t
WB	307 cid 2V 200 hp	m/t
WC	307 cid 2V 200 hp	3-spd m/t
WE	307 cid 2V 200 hp	PG a/t
WF, WG, WH	307 cid 2V 200 hp	m/t
WO	307 cid 2V 200 hp	3-spd m/t
WR	307 cid 2V 200 hp	PG a/t
ZO	307 cid 2V 200 hp	m/t
ZS	307 cid 2V 200 hp	m/t
YB	327 cid 4V 220 hp	PG a/t
YC	327 cid 4V 220 hp	m/t
YD	327 cid 4V 220 hp	PG a/t
YH, YK	327 cid 4V 220 hp	3-spd m/t
YR	327 cid 4V 220 hp	PG a/t
YS , YV	327 cid 4V 220 hp	m/t
1968 C20 Trucks		
WB, WF, WG	307 cid 2V 200 hp	m/t
WR	307 cid 2V 200 hp	PG a/t
ZS	307 cid 2V 200 hp	m/t
YH	327 cid 4V 220 hp	3-spd m/t
YR	327 cid 4V 220 hp	PG a/t
YS	327 cid 4V 220 hp	m/t
1968 C30 Trucks		
WB, WG	307 cid 2V 200 hp	m/t
WO, WR	307 cid 2V 200 hp	3-spd m/t
YH	327 cid 4V 220 hp	3-spd m/t
YS	327 cid 4V 220 hp	m/t
1968 K10 Trucks		
WI	307 cid 2V 200 hp	m/t
ZX	307 cid 2V 200 hp	3-spd m/t
ZP	307 cid 2V 200 hp	m/t
YX	327 cid 4V 220 hp	m/t
YT	327 cid 4V 220 hp	3-spd m/t
1968 K20 Trucks		
WH, WI	307 cid 2V 200 hp	m/t
ZY	307 cid 2V 200 hp	3-spd m/t
ZX	307 cid 2V 200 hp	3-spd m/t
ZP, ZQ	307 cid 2V 200 hp	m/t

Engine Suffix Codes

Suffix	Engine	Equipment
YL	327 cid 4V 220 hp	m/t
YT	327 cid 4V 220 hp	3-spd m/t
YU	327 cid 4V 220 hp	3-spd m/t
1969 Corvette		
HZ	350 cid 4V 300 hp	TH a/t
HY	350 cid 4V 300 hp	m/t
HW	350 cid 4V 350 hp	4-spd m/t
HX	350 cid 4V 350 hp	4-spd m/t, a/c
GD	350 cid 4V 350 hp	4-spd m/t, TI
1969 Chevrolet		
FA	327 cid 2V 235 hp	m/t
FB	327 cid 2V 235 hp	PG a/t
FH, FC	327 cid 2V 235 hp	TH a/t
FM	327 cid 2V 235 hp	m/t
FN	327 cid 2V 235 hp	PG a/t
FG	327 cid 2V 235 hp	m/t
FZ	327 cid 2V 235 hp	PG a/t
GA	327 cid 2V 235 hp	TH a/t
FY, FJ	327 cid 2V 235 hp	m/t
FK	327 cid 2V 235 hp	PG a/t
FL	327 cid 2V 235 hp	TH a/t
GB	327 cid 2V 235 hp	TH a/t
HI	350 cid 2V 250 hp	m/t
HL	350 cid 2V 250 hp	PG a/t
HJ, HM	350 cid 2V 250 hp	TH a/t
IL	350 cid 2V 250 hp	m/t, police
IM	350 cid 2V 250 hp	PG a/t
IN, IP	350 cid 2V 250 hp	TH a/t, police
HT	350 cid 4V 255 hp	m/t
HU	350 cid 4V 255 hp	PG a/t
IA	350 cid 4V 255 hp	TH a/t
HV	350 cid 4V 255 hp	TH a/t
IW	350 cid 4V 255 hp	m/t, police
IX	350 cid 4V 255 hp	PG a/t, police
IY, IZ	350 cid 4V 255 hp	TH a/t, police
HG	350 cid 4V 300 hp	m/t
HK	350 cid 4V 300 hp	PG a/t
HH, HN	350 cid 4V 300 hp	TH a/t
IR	350 cid 4V 300 hp	m/t
IS	350 cid 4V 300 hp	PG a/t, police
IT	350 cid 4V 300 hp	TH a/t, police
IQ	350 cid 4V 300 hp	m/t, h/d clutch, police
HO	350 cid 4V 300 hp	m/t, h/d clutch
IV	350 cid 4V 300 hp	TH a/t, police
IB	350 cid 4V 300 hp	TH a/t
1969 Nova		
DA	307 cid 2V 200 hp	m/t
DE	307 cid 2V 200 hp	m/t
DC	307 cid 2V 200 hp	PG a/t
DD	307 cid 2V 200 hp	m/t
HF	350 cid 2V 250 hp	PG a/t
HD	350 cid 2V 250 hp	TH a/t
HC	350 cid 2V 250 hp	m/t
HR	350 cid 4V 255 hp	PG a/t
HQ	350 cid 4V 255 hp	m/t
HS	350 cid 4V 255 hp	TH a/t
HA	350 cid 4V 300 hp	m/t
HB	350 cid 4V 300 hp	TH a/t
HE	350 cid 4V 300 hp	PG a/t
HP	350 cid 4V 300 hp	m/t
1969 Chevelle		
DA	307 cid 2V 200 hp	m/t
DE	307 cid 2V 200 hp	m/t

This view of the Chevy small-block shows the location of the pad on the right side of the block where the suffix identification code is stamped. The size of the pad has varied over the years, but it has always been in the same place.

Suffix	Engine	Equipment
DL	307 cid 2V 200 hp	m/t
DC, DM	307 cid 2V 200 hp	PG a/t
DD	307 cid 2V 200 hp	TH a/t
HC	350 cid 250 hp	m/t
HD	350 cid 250 hp	TH a/t
HF	350 cid 250 hp	PG a/t
HS	350 cid 4V 255 hp	TH a/t
HQ	350 cid 4V 255 hp	m/t
HR	350 cid 4V 255 hp	PG or m/t
HA	350 cid 4V 300 hp	m/t
HB	350 cid 4V 300 hp	TH a/t
HE	350 cid 4V 300 hp	PG a/t
HP	350 cid 4V 300 hp	m/t, h/d clutch
1969 Camaro		
DZ	302 cid 4V 290 hp	4-spd m/t
DA	307 cid 2V 200 hp	m/t
DE	307 cid 2V 200 hp	4-spd m/t
DC	307 cid 2V 200 hp	PG a/t
DD	307 cid 2V 200 hp	TH a/t
FJ	327 cid 2V 210 hp	m/t
FK	327 cid 2V 210 hp	PG a/t
FL	327 cid 2V 210 hp	TH a/t
FS	327 cid 2V 210 hp	m/t
FT	327 cid 2V 210 hp	PG a/t
HF	350 cid 2V 250 hp	PG a/t
HC	350 cid 2V 250 hp	m/t
HD	350 cid 2V 250 hp	TH a/t
HR	350 cid 4V 255 hp	PG a/t
HQ	350 cid 4V 255 hp	m/t
HS	350 cid 4V 255 hp	TH a/t
HA	350 cid 4V 300 hp	m/t
HP	350 cid 4V 300 hp	m/t, h/d clutch
HE	350 cid 4V 300 hp	TH a/t
1969 C10 and C20 Trucks		
UA	307 cid 2V 200 hp	m/t
UC	307 cid 2V 200 hp	PG a/t
UM, UN	307 cid 2V 200 hp	TH a/t
VB	350 cid 4V 255 hp	m/t
WH	350 cid 4V 255 hp	m/t, A.I.R.
WJ	350 cid 4V 255 hp	PG a/t
WK	350 cid 4V 255 hp	TH a/t
WZ	350 cid 4V 255 hp	3-spd m/t
XA	350 cid 4V 255 hp	m/t
XC	350 cid 4V 255 hp	PG a/t

Suffix	Engine	Equipment
XD	350 cid 4V 255 hp	TH a/t
XF	350 cid 4V 255 hp	PG a/t
XG	350 cid 4V 255 hp	TH a/t
XP	350 cid 4V 255 hp	m/t, A.I.R.
ZA	350 cid 4V 255 hp	m/t, A.I.R.
ZD	350 cid 4V 255 hp	PG a/t
ZF	350 cid 4V 255 hp	TH a/t

1969 C20 Trucks

Suffix	Engine	Equipment
UA	307 cid 2V 200 hp	m/t, A.I.R.
UB	307 cid 2V 200 hp	m/t
UC	307 cid 2V 200 hp	PG a/t
UD	307 cid 2V 200 hp	PG a/t, A.I.R.
UE	307 cid 2V 200 hp	TH a/t, A.I.R.
UN	307 cid 2V 200 hp	TH a/t
UU	307 cid 2V 200 hp	m/t
VB	350 cid 4V 255 hp	m/t
VR	350 cid 4V 255 hp	3-spd m/t
WA	350 cid 4V 255 hp	TH a/t, A.I.R.
WH	350 cid 4V 255 hp	m/t, A.I.R.
WJ	350 cid 4V 255 hp	PG a/t
WK	350 cid 4V 255 hp	TH a/t
WL	350 cid 4V 255 hp	PG a/t, A.I.R.
WM	350 cid 4V 255 hp	TH a/t, A.I.R.
WR	350 cid 4V 255 hp	PG a/t
WS	350 cid 4V 255 hp	TH a/t
WT	350 cid 4V 255 hp	m/t
WZ	350 cid 4V 255 hp	3-spd m/t
XA	350 cid 4V 255 hp	m/t, A.I.R.
XB	350 cid 4V 255 hp	m/t
XC	350 cid 4V 255 hp	PG a/t
XD	350 cid 4V 255 hp	TH a/t, A.I.R.
XE	350 cid 4V 255 hp	m/t
XF	350 cid 4V 255 hp	PG a/t
XG	350 cid 4V 255 hp	TH a/t
XP	350 cid 4V 255 hp	m/t
XZ	350 cid 4V 255 hp	PG a/t, A.I.R.
ZA, ZB	350 cid 4V 255 hp	m/t
ZC, ZE	350 cid 4V 255 hp	m/t
ZF	350 cid 4V 255 hp	TH a/t

1969 C30 Trucks

Suffix	Engine	Equipment
UE, UN	307 cid 2V 200 hp	TH a/t
UN	307 cid 2V 200 hp	TH a/t
VR	350 cid 4V 255 hp	3-spd m/t
XA	350 cid 4V 255 hp	m/t, A.I.R.
XB	350 cid 4V 255 hp	m/t
XD	350 cid 4V 255 hp	TH a/t, A.I.R.
WH	350 cid 4V 255 hp	m/t, A.I.R.
WJ	350 cid 4V 255 hp	PG a/t
WK, WM	350 cid 4V 255 hp	TH a/t, A.I.R.
WR	350 cid 4V 255 hp	PG a/t, A.I.R.
WS	350 cid 4V 255 hp	TH a/t, A.I.R.
WT	350 cid 4V 255 hp	m/t, A.I.R.
XE	350 cid 4V 255 hp	m/t
XF	350 cid 4V 255 hp	PG a/t
XG	350 cid 4V 255 hp	TH a/t
XP	350 cid 4V 255 hp	m/t
ZA, ZC, ZF	350 cid 4V 255 hp	m/t

1969 K10 Trucks

Suffix	Engine	Equipment
UO	307 cid 2V 200 hp	m/t
UQ	307 cid 2V 200 hp	TH a/t
UT	307 cid 2V 200 hp	m/t
XW	350 cid 4V 255 hp	m/t
XY	350 cid 4V 255 hp	TH a/t
WN	350 cid 4V 255 hp	m/t, A.I.R.

Suffix	Engine	Equipment
WP	350 cid 4V 255 hp	TH a/t
ZG	350 cid 4V 255 hp	3-spd m/t
ZJ	350 cid 4V 255 hp	TH a/t

1969 K20 Trucks

Suffix	Engine	Equipment
UO	307 cid 2V 200 hp	m/t, A.I.R.
UP, UT	307 cid 2V 200 hp	m/t
UV, UW	307 cid 2V 200 hp	m/t
VS	350 cid 4V 255 hp	3-spd
WN, WO	350 cid 4V 255 hp	m/t
WP	350 cid 4V 255 hp	TH a/t
WQ	350 cid 4V 255 hp	TH a/t, A.I.R.
XO	350 cid 4V 255 hp	TH a/t, A.I.R.
XW	350 cid 4V 255 hp	m/t, A.I.R.
XX	350 cid 4V 255 hp	m/t
XY	350 cid 4V 255 hp	TH a/t
ZG	350 cid 4V 255 hp	3-spd
ZH	350 cid 4V 255 hp	3-spd
ZJ	350 cid 4V 255 hp	TH a/t

1970 Corvette

Suffix	Engine	Equipment
CTG, CTM	350 cid 4V 300 hp	TH a/t
CTD, CTL	350 cid 4V 300 hp	4-spd m/t
CTN	350 cid 4V 350 hp	4-spd m/t
CTO	350 cid 4V 350 hp	4-spd m/t, a/c
CTQ	350 cid 4V 350 hp	4-spd m/t, a/c, TI
CTP	350 cid 4V 350 hp	4-spd m/t, TI
CTH, CTJ	350 cid 4V 350 hp	4-spd m/t
CTU	350 cid 4V 370 hp	4-spd m/t, TI
CTK, CTV	350 cid 4V 370 hp	4-spd m/t

1970 Chevrolet

Suffix	Engine	Equipment
CND	307 cid 2V 200 hp	m/t
CNU	350 cid 2V 250 hp	PG a/t
CNV	350 cid 2V 250 hp	TH a/t
CNW	350 cid 2V 250 hp	PG a/t
CNX	350 cid 2V 250 hp	TH a/t
CNO	350 cid 2V 250 hp	m/t
CNP	350 cid 2V 250 hp	m/t, police, taxi
CNY	350 cid 2V 250 hp	m/t
CNZ	350 cid 2V 250 hp	PG a/t
CNR	350 cid 4V 300 hp	TH a/t
CNS	350 cid 4V 300 hp	PG a/t
CNT	350 cid 4V 300 hp	TH a/t
CNQ	350 cid 4V 300 hp	m/t
CGR	400 cid 2V 265 hp	TH a/t

1970 Chevelle

Suffix	Engine	Equipment
CNC, CND	307 cid 2V 200 hp	m/t
CNE	307 cid 2V 200 hp	PG a/t
CNF	307 cid 2V 200 hp	TH a/t
CNG	307 cid 2V 200 hp	m/t
CNH	307 cid 2V 200 hp	PG a/t
CNI	350 cid 2V 250 hp	m/t
CNM	350 cid 2V 250 hp	PG a/t
CNN	350 cid 2V 250 hp	TH a/t
CNJ	350 cid 4V 300 hp	m/t
CNK	350 cid 4V 300 hp	PG a/t
CRE	350 cid 4V 300 hp	TH a/t
CZX	400 cid 2V 265 hp	m/t
CRH	400 cid 2V 265 hp	TH a/t

1970 Nova

Suffix	Engine	Equipment
CNC, CND	307 cid 2V 200 hp	m/t
CNE	307 cid 2V 200 hp	PG a/t
CNF	307 cid 2V 200 hp	TH a/t
CNM	350 cid 4V 250 hp	PG a/t
CNN	350 cid 4V 250 hp	TH a/t
CNI, CNJ	350 cid 4V 250 hp	m/t

Engine Suffix Codes

Suffix	Engine	Equipment
CNK	350 cid 4V 250 hp	PG a/t
CRE	350 cid 4V 250 hp	TH a/t
1970 Camaro		
CNC, CND	307 cid 2V 200 hp	m/t
CNE	307 cid 2V 200 hp	PG a/t
CNF	307 cid 2V 200 hp	TH a/t
CNG	307 cid 2V 200 hp	m/t
CNH, CNM	307 cid 2V 200 hp	PG a/t
CNN	350 cid 2V 200 hp	TH a/t
CNJ	350 cid 4V 300 hp	m/t
CNK	350 cid 4V 300 hp	PG a/t
CRE	350 cid 4V 300 hp	TH a/t
CTB	350 cid 4V 360 hp	m/t
CTC	350 cid 4V 360 hp	TH a/t
1970 Monte Carlo		
CNI	350 cid 2V 250 hp	m/t
CNM	350 cid 2V 250 hp	PG a/t
CNN	350 cid 2V 250 hp	TH a/t
CNJ	350 cid 4V 300 hp	m/t
CNK	350 cid 4V 300 hp	PG a/t
CRE	350 cid 4V 300 hp	TH a/t
CZX	400 cid 2V 265 hp	m/t
CRH	400 cid 2V 265 hp	TH a/t
1970 C10 Trucks		
TAI, TAJ	307 cid 2V 200 hp	PG a/t
TAK	307 cid 2V 200 hp	TH a/t
TAS	307 cid 2V 200 hp	m/t
TAU, TAV	350 cid 4V 255 hp	m/t
TAZ	350 cid 4V 255 hp	PG a/t
TAX	350 cid 4V 255 hp	TH a/t
TBA	350 cid 4V 255 hp	TH a/t
TMJ	350 cid 4V 255 hp	TH
TBB, TBD	350 cid 4V 255 hp	m/t
TNT	350 cid 4V 255 hp	PG a/t
1970 C20 Trucks		
TAM, TAR	307 cid 2V 200 hp	m/t
TAH	307 cid 2V 200 hp	TH a/t
TAJ	307 cid 2V 200 hp	PG a/t
TAV	350 cid 4V 255 hp	3-spd m/t
TAZ	350 cid 4V 255 hp	PG a/t
TBB	350 cid 4V 255 hp	3-spd m/t
TBD	350 cid 4V 255 hp	m/t
TMJ	350 cid 4V 255 hp	TH a/t
TNT	350 cid 4V 255 hp	PG a/t
1970 C30 Trucks		
TTAL	307 cid 2V 200 hp	TH a/t
TAM, TAR	307 cid 2V 200 hp	m/t
TAV	350 cid 4V 255 hp	3-spd m/t
TAX	350 cid 4V 255 hp	TH a/t
TBA	350 cid 4V 255 hp	TH a/t
TBB	350 cid 4V 255 hp	3-spd m/t
TMJ	350 cid 4V 255 hp	TH a/t
TBD	350 cid 4V 255 hp	m/t
1970 K10 Trucks		
TAO	307 cid 2V 200 hp	TH a/t
TAT	307 cid 2V 200 hp	3-spd m/t
TBE	307 cid 2V 200 hp	3-spd m/t
TAY	350 cid 4V 255 hp	TH a/t
TBC, TBF	350 cid 4V 255 hp	3-spd m/t
1970 K20 Trucks		
TAN	307 cid 2V 200 hp	3-spd m/t
TAP	307 cid 2V 200 hp	TH a/t
TAW	307 cid 2V 200 hp	3-spd m/t

Suffix	Engine	Equipment
TAY	307 cid 2V 200 hp	TH a/t
TBC, TBF	350 cid 4V 255 hp	3-spd m/t
1971 Corvette		
CGT	350 cid 4V 270 hp	TH a/t
CJL, CJK	350 cid 4V 270 hp	m/t
CGZ, CGY	350 cid 4V 330 hp	m/t
1971 Chevrolet		
CGA	350 cid 2V 245 hp	m/t
CGB	350 cid 2V 245 hp	PG a/t
CGC	350 cid 2V 245 hp	TH a/t
CGJ	350 cid 2V 245 hp	PG a/t, police, taxi
CJB, CJH	350 cid 4V 270 hp	m/t
CLB	402 cid 4V 300 hp	TH a/t
CLR	402 cid 4V 300 hp	m/t
CLP	402 cid 4V 300 hp	TH a/t
CPD, CPG	454 cid 4V 365 hp	TH a/t
1971 Nova		
CCA	307 cid 2V 200 hp	PG a/t
CCC	307 cid 2V 200 hp	m/t
CGA	350 cid 2V 245 hp	m/t
CGB	350 cid 2V 245 hp	PG a/t
CGK	350 cid 4V 270 hp	m/t
CGL	350 cid 4V 270 hp	TH a/t
CJD	350 cid 4V 270 hp	TH a/t
CJG	350 cid 4V 270 hp	m/t
1971 Chevelle		
CCA	307 cid 2V 200 hp	PG a/t
CCC	307 cid 2V 200 hp	m/t
CGA	350 cid 2V 245 hp	m/t
CGB	350 cid 2V 245 hp	PG a/t
CGC	350 cid 2V 245 hp	TH a/t
CGK	350 cid 4V 270 hp	m/t
CGL	350 cid 4V 270 hp	TH a/t
CJD	350 cid 4V 270 hp	TH a/t
CJJ	350 cid 4V 270 hp	m/t
1971 Camaro		
CCA	307 cid 2V 200 hp	PG a/t
CCC	307 cid 2V 200 hp	m/t
CGA	350 cid 2V 245 hp	m/t
CGB	350 cid 2V 245 hp	PG a/t
CGC	350 cid 2V 245 hp	TH a/t
CGK	350 cid 4V 270 hp	m/t
CGL	350 cid 4V 270 hp	TH a/t
CJD	350 cid 4V 270 hp	TH a/t
CGR	350 cid 4V 330 hp	TH a/t
CGP	350 cid 4V 330 hp	4-spd m/t
1971 Monte Carlo		
CGA	350 cid 2V 245 hp	m/t
CGB	350 cid 2V 245 hp	PG a/t
CGC	350 cid 2V 245 hp	TH a/t
CGK	350 cid 4V 270 hp	m/t
CGL	350 cid 4V 270 hp	TH a/t
CJD	350 cid 4V 270 hp	TH a/t
CJJ	350 cid 4V 270 hp	m/t
1971 C10 Trucks		
THA	307 cid 2V 200 hp	m/t
THC, THK, THL	307 cid 2V 200 hp	TH a/t
TBA, TBD	350 cid 4V 250 hp	m/t
TBC, TBG	350 cid 4V 250 hp	TH a/t
TBH	350 cid 4V 250 hp	m/t
TBK	350 cid 4V 250 hp	TH a/t
TBJ	350 cid 4V 250 hp	PG a/t
1971 C20 Trucks		
THK, THL	307 cid 2V 200 hp	TH a/t

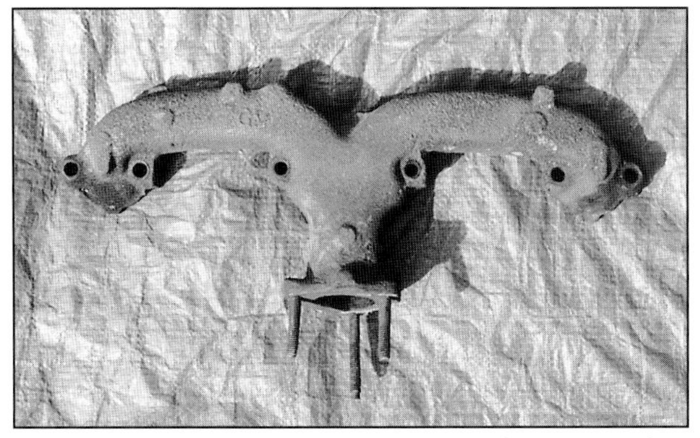

This is a typical ram's horn exhaust manifold. It can fit either side of the cylinder head as the outlet is straight down.

Suffix	Engine	Equipment
THP	307 cid 2V 200 hp	m/t
TBA, TBD	350 cid 4V 250 hp	m/t
TBC, TBG	350 cid 4V 250 hp	TH a/t
TBH	350 cid 4V 250 hp	m/t
TBK	350 cid 4V 250 hp	TH a/t
TBJ	350 cid 4V 250 hp	PG a/t
1971 C30 Trucks		
THP	307 cid 2V 200 hp	m/t
TBA, TBD	350 cid 4V 250 hp	m/t
TBC, TBG	350 cid 4V 250 hp	TH a/t
TBH	350 cid 4V 250 hp	m/t
TBK	350 cid 4V 250 hp	TH a/t
TBJ	350 cid 4V 250 hp	PG a/t
1971 K10 Trucks		
THK, THL	307 cid 2V 200 hp	TH a/t
TBA, TBD	350 cid 4V 250 hp	m/t
TBC, TBG	350 cid 4V 250 hp	TH a/t
TBH	350 cid 4V 250 hp	m/t
TBK	350 cid 4V 250 hp	TH a/t
TBJ	350 cid 4V 250 hp	PG a/t
1971 K20 Trucks		
THK	307 cid 2V 200 hp	TH a/t
THR	307 cid 2V 200 hp	m/t
THS	307 cid 2V 200 hp	TH a/t
TBA, TBD	350 cid 4V 250 hp	m/t
TBC, TBG	350 cid 4V 250 hp	TH a/t
TBH	350 cid 4V 250 hp	m/t
TBK	350 cid 4V 250 hp	TH a/t
TBJ	350 cid 4V 250 hp	PG a/t
1972 Corvette		
CDJ	350 cid 4V 200 hp	TH a/t, NB2**
CKX	350 cid 4V 200 hp	TH a/t
CDH	350 cid 4V 200 hp	m/t, NB2
CKW	350 cid 4V 200 hp	m/t
CRT	350 cid 4V 255 hp	m/t, NB2
CKY, CKZ	350 cid 4V 255 hp	m/t
1972 Chevrolet		
CSJ	350 cid 2V 165 hp	m/t
CKB	350 cid 2V 165 hp	TH a/t
CAR	350 cid 2V 165 hp	TH a/t, NB2
CSH	350 cid 2V 165 hp	TH a/t
CDB	350 cid 2V 165 hp	TH a/t, NB2
CKP	400 cid 2V 170 hp	TH a/t
CAT	400 cid 2V 170 hp	TH a/t
CDI, CDM	400 cid 2V 170 hp	TH a/t
CLR	400 cid 2V 170 hp	TH a/t, police
CTB	400 cid 2V 170 hp	TH a/t, A.I.R.

Suffix	Engine	Equipment
CTJ	400 cid 2V 170 hp	TH a/t, taxi, police, A.I.R.
1972 Nova		
CKG	307 cid 2V 130 hp	m/t
CAY	307 cid 2V 130 hp	m/t, NB2
CKH	307 cid 2V 130 hp	PG a/t
CAZ	307 cid 2V 130 hp	PG a/t, NB2
CTK	307 cid 2V 130 hp	TH a/t
CMA	307 cid 2V 130 hp	TH a/t, NB2
CKA	350 cid 2V 165 hp	m/t
CDA	350 cid 2V 165 hp	m/t, NB2
CTL	350 cid 2V 165 hp	TH a/t
CMD	350 cid 2V 165 hp	TH a/t, NB2
CKK	350 cid 4V 200 hp	m/t
CDG	350 cid 4V 200 hp	m/t, NB2
CKD	350 cid 4V 200 hp	TH 350 a/t
CDD	350 cid 4V 200 hp	TH a/t, NB2
CRL, CRK	350 cid 4V 200 hp	m/t, NB2
1972 Chevelle		
CKG	307 cid 2V 130 hp	m/t
CAY	307 cid 2V 130 hp	m/t, NB2
CKH	307 cid 2V 130 hp	PG a/t
CAZ	307 cid 2V 130 hp	PG a/t, NB2
CTK	307 cid 2V 130 hp	TH a/t
CMA	307 cid 2V 130 hp	TH a/t, NB2
CKA	350 cid 2V 165 hp	m/t
CDA	350 cid 2V 165 hp	m/t, NB2
CKB	350 cid 2V 165 hp	PG a/t
CDB	350 cid 2V 165 hp	PG a/t
CTL	350 cid 2V 165 hp	TH a/t
CMD	350 cid 2V 165 hp	TH a/t, NB2
CAR	350 cid 2V 165 hp	TH a/t, NB2, police
CSH	350 cid 2V 165 hp	TH a/t, police
CKK	350 cid 4V 175 hp	m/t
CDG	350 cid 4V 175 hp	m/t NB2
CKD	350 cid 4V 175 hp	TH a/t
CDD	350 cid 4V 175 hp	TH a/t, NB2
1972 Camaro		
CKG	307 cid 2V 130 hp	m/t
CAY	307 cid 2V 130 hp	m/t, NB2
CKH	307 cid 2V 130 hp	PG a/t
CAZ	307 cid 2V 130 hp	PG a/t, NB2
CTK	307 cid 2V 130 hp	TH a/t
CMA	307 cid 2V 130 hp	TH a/t, NB2
CKA	350 cid 2V 165 hp	m/t
CRG	350 cid 2V 165 hp	m/t, NB2
CTL	350 cid 2V 165 hp	TH a/t
CRD	350 cid 2V 165 hp	TH a/t, NB2
CMB	350 cid 2V 165 hp	TH a/t, NB2
CKK	350 cid 4V 200 hp	m/t
CDG	350 cid 4V 200 hp	m/t, NB2
CKD	350 cid 4V 200 hp	TH 350 a/t
CDD	350 cid 4V 200 hp	TH a/t, NB2
CKS	350 cid 4V 255 hp	m/t
CKT	350 cid 4V 255 hp	TH a/t
1972 Monte Carlo		
CKA	350 cid 2V 165 hp	m/t
CDA	350 cid 2V 165 hp	m/t, NB2
CTL	350 cid 2V 165 hp	TH a/t
CMD	350 cid 2V 165 hp	TH a/t, NB2
CKK	350 cid 4V 175 hp	m/t
CDG	350 cid 4V 175 hp	m/t, NB2
CKD	350 cid 4V 175 hp	TH a/t
CDD	350 cid 4V 175 hp	TH a/t, NB2

Engine Suffix Codes

Suffix	Engine	Equipment
1972 C10 Trucks		
TLB	307 cid 2V 135 hp	m/t
TDA	307 cid 2V 135 hp	m/t
TDL	307 cid 2V 135 hp	TH a/t
TRA	307 cid 2V 135 hp	m/t
TAH	307 cid 2V 135 hp	TH a/t
TSP	307 cid 2V 135 hp	TH a/t
TSS	307 cid 2V 135 hp	m/t
TBL	350 cid 4V 175 hp	m/t
TFD	350 cid 4V 175 hp	TH a/t
TDD, TDH	350 cid 4V 175 hp	m/t
TDJ	350 cid 4V 175 hp	TH a/t
TDK	350 cid 4V 175 hp	TH a/t
TAX	350 cid 4V 175 hp	m/t
VJZ	350 cid 4V 175 hp	m/t
1972 C20 Trucks		
TDA	307 cid 2V 135 hp	m/t
TDL	307 cid 2V 135 hp	TH a/t
TRA	307 cid 2V 135 hp	m/t
TAH	307 cid 2V 135 hp	TH a/t
TJP	307 cid 2V 135 hp	TH a/t
TJR	307 cid 2V 135 hp	m/t
TSP	307 cid 2V 135 hp	TH a/t
TSS	307 cid 2V 135 hp	m/t
TBL	350 cid 4V 175 hp	m/t
TFD	350 cid 4V 175 hp	TH a/t
TDD, TDH	350 cid 4V 175 hp	m/t
TDJ, TDK	350 cid 4V 175 hp	TH a/t
TRH	350 cid 4V 175 hp	m/t
TRJ	350 cid 4V 175 hp	TH a/t
TAX, TAY	350 cid 4V 175 hp	m/t
VJZ	350 cid 4V 175 hp	m/t
1972 C30 Trucks		
TDH	350 cid 4V 175 hp	m/t
TDK	350 cid 4V 175 hp	TH a/t
TRH	350 cid 4V 175 hp	m/t
TRJ	350 cid 4V 175 hp	TH a/t
TAY	350 cid 4V 175 hp	m/t
1972 K10 Trucks		
TDB	307 cid 2V 135 hp	m/t
TDP	307 cid 2V 135 hp	TH a/t
TAD	307 cid 2V 135 hp	m/t
TAJ	307 cid 2V 135 hp	TH a/t
TSR	307 cid 2V 135 hp	m/t
TFH	350 cid 4V 175 hp	m/t
TFJ	350 cid 4V 175 hp	TH a/t
TDG	350 cid 4V 175 hp	m/t
TDR	350 cid 4V 175 hp	TH a/t
TFH	350 cid 4V 175 hp	m/t
TFJ	350 cid 4V 175 hp	TH a/t
TDG	350 cid 4V 175 hp	m/t
TDR	350 cid 4V 175 hp	TH a/t
1972 K20 Trucks		
TDB	307 cid 2V 135 hp	m/t
TDP	307 cid 2V 135 hp	TH a/t
TAD	307 cid 2V 135 hp	m/t
TAJ	307 cid 2V 135 hp	TH a/t
TJS	307 cid 2V 135 hp	TH a/t
TJT	307 cid 2V 135 hp	m/t
TSJ	307 cid 2V 135 hp	TH a/t
TSR	307 cid 2V 135 hp	m/t
TFH	350 cid 4V 175 hp	m/t
TFJ	350 cid 4V 175 hp	TH a/t

Suffix	Engine	Equipment
TDG	350 cid 4V 175 hp	m/t
TDR	350 cid 4V 175 hp	TH a/t
TRK	350 cid 4V 175 hp	m/t
TRL	350 cid 4V 175 hp	TH a/t
1973 Corvette		
CLA	350 cid 4V 190 hp	TH a/t
CLC	350 cid 4V 190 hp	TH a/t, NB2
CKZ	350 cid 4V 190 hp	m/t
CLD	350 cid 4V 250 hp	TH a/t
CLH	350 cid 4V 250 hp	TH a/t, NB2
CLR	350 cid 4V 250 hp	m/t
CLB, CLS	350 cid 4V 250 hp	m/t, NB2
1973 Chevrolet		
CKL	350 cid 2V 145 hp	TH a/t
CLT	350 cid 2V 145 hp	TH a/t, NB2
CLU	350 cid 2V 145 hp	TH a/t
CLW	350 cid 2V 145 hp	TH a/t, NB2
CLX	350 cid 2V 145 hp	TH a/t
CKR	350 cid 4V 175 hp	TH a/t, NB2
CKD	350 cid 4V 175 hp	TH a/t, NB2
CKJ	350 cid 4V 175 hp	TH a/t
CSA, CSB,		
CSC	400 cid 2V 150 hp	TH a/t
CSD	400 cid 2V 150 hp	TH a/t, NB2
CSK, CSL	400 cid 2V 150 hp	TH a/t
1973 Chevelle		
CHB	307 cid 2V 115 hp	m/t
CHA	307 cid 2V 115 hp	TH a/t
CHC	307 cid 2V 115 hp	TH a/t, NB2
CHD	307 cid 2V 115 hp	m/t
CKA	350 cid 2V 145 hp	m/t
CKC	350 cid 2V 145 hp	m/t, NB2
CKL	350 cid 2V 145 hp	TH a/t
CKK	350 cid 2V 145 hp	TH a/t, NB2
CKB	350 cid 4V 175 hp	m/t
CKD	350 cid 4V 175 hp	TH a/t, NB2
CKH	350 cid 4V 175 hp	m/t, NB2
CKJ	350 cid 4V 175 hp	TH a/t
CKM	350 cid 4V 175 hp	TH a/t, police
CKR	350 cid 4V 175 hp	TH a/t, police, NB2
CMM	350 cid 4V 175 hp	TH a/t
1973 Nova		
CHB	307 cid 2V 115 hp	m/t
CHC	307 cid 2V 115 hp	TH a/t, NB2
CHD, CHH	307 cid 2V 115 hp	m/t
CKA	350 cid 2V 145 hp	m/t
CKC	350 cid 2V 145 hp	m/t, NB2
CKK	350 cid 2V 145 hp	TH a/t, NB2
CKW	350 cid 2V 145 hp	TH a/t
CKH	350 cid 4V 175 hp	m/t, NB2
CKB	350 cid 4V 175 hp	4-spd m/t
CKU	350 cid 4V 175 hp	TH a/t
CKD	350 cid 4V 175 hp	TH a/t, NB2
1973 Camaro		
CHH	307 cid 2V 115 hp	TH a/t
CHK	307 cid 2V 115 hp	TH a/t, NB2
CHB	307 cid 2V 115 hp	m/t
CHJ	307 cid 2V 115 hp	m/t, NB2
CKW	350 cid 2V 145 hp	TH a/t
CKX	350 cid 2V 145 hp	TH a/t, NB2
CKA	350 cid 2V 145 hp	m/t
CKY	350 cid 2V 145 hp	m/t, NB2
CKU	350 cid 4V 175 hp	TH a/t
CKD	350 cid 4V 175 hp	TH a/t, NB2

Suffix	Engine	Equipment
CKB, CKH	350 cid 4V 175 hp	m/t
CLK	350 cid 4V 245 hp	TH a/t
CLL	350 cid 4V 245 hp	TH a/t, NB2
CLJ	350 cid 4V 245 hp	m/t
CLM	350 cid 4V 245 hp	m/t, NB2
1973 Monte Carlo		
CKA	350 cid 2V 145 hp	m/t
CKC	350 cid 2V 145 hp	m/t, NB2
CKL	350 cid 2V 145 hp	TH a/t
CKK	350 cid 2V 145 hp	TH a/t, NB2
CKB	350 cid 4V 175 hp	m/t
CKD	350 cid 4V 175 hp	TH a/t, NB2
CKH	350 cid 4V 175 hp	m/t, NB2
CKJ	350 cid 4V 175 hp	TH a/t
CKR	350 cid 4V 175 hp	TH a/t, police, NB2
CMM	350 cid 4V 175 hp	TH a/t
1973 C10 Trucks		
TCH	307 cid 2V 115 hp	TH 350 a/t
TCJ	307 cid 2V 115 hp	m/t
TCX	307 cid 2V 115 hp	m/t
TCY	307 cid 2V 115 hp	TH 350 a/t, NB2
TJB	350 cid 4V 155 hp	m/t
TJZ	350 cid 4V 155 hp	TH 350 a/t
TDY	350 cid 4V 155 hp	m/t, NB2
TJH	350 cid 4V 155 hp	m/t
TJX	350 cid 4V 155 hp	TH 350/400 a/t
TJY	350 cid 4V 155 hp	TH 350 a/t, NB2
1973 C20 Trucks		
TCA	307 cid 2V 115 hp	TH 350 a/t, NB2
TCB	307 cid 2V 115 hp	m/t, NB2
TCC	307 cid 2V 115 hp	TH 350 a/t
TCD	307 cid 2V 115 hp	m/t
TJA	350 cid 4V 155 hp	TH 350/400 a/t
TJB, TJC	350 cid 4V 155 hp	m/t
TJZ	350 cid 4V 155 hp	TH 350 a/t
TDY	350 cid 4V 155 hp	m/t, NB2
TJH	350 cid 4V 155 hp	m/t
TJX	350 cid 4V 155 hp	TH 350 or 400 a/t
TJY	350 cid 4V 155 hp	TH 350 a/t, NB2
1973 C30 Trucks		
TCA	307 cid 2V 115 hp	TH 350 a/t, NB2
TCB	307 cid 2V 115 hp	m/t NB2
TCC	307 cid 2V 115 hp	TH 350 a/t
TCD	307 cid 2V 115 hp	m/t
TJA	350 cid 4V 155 hp	TH 350/400 a/t
TJC, TJH	350 cid 4V 155 hp	m/t
TJX	350 cid 4V 155 hp	TH 350/400 a/t
1973 K10 Trucks		
TCH	307 cid 2V 115 hp	TH 350 a/t
TCJ, TCX	307 cid 2V 115 hp	m/t
TCY	307 cid 2V 115 hp	TH 350 a/t, NB2
TJB	350 cid 4V 155 hp	m/t
TJZ	350 cid 4V 155 hp	TH 350 a/t
TDY	350 cid 4V 155 hp	m/t, NB2
TJH	350 cid 4V 155 hp	m/t
TJX	350 cid 4V 155 hp	TH 350/400 a/t
TJY	350 cid 4V 155 hp	TH 350 a/t, NB2
1973 K20 Trucks		
TCA	307 cid 2V 115 hp	TH 350 a/t, NB2
TCB	307 cid 2V 115 hp	m/t, NB2
TCC	307 cid 2V 115 hp	TH 350 a/t
TCD	307 cid 2V 115 hp	m/t
TJA	350 cid 4V 155 hp	TH 350/400 a/t
TJB, TJC	350 cid 4V 155 hp	m/t

Suffix	Engine	Equipment
TJZ	350 cid 4V 155 hp	TH 350 a/t
TDY	350 cid 4V 155 hp	m/t, NB2
TJH	350 cid 4V 155 hp	m/t
TJX	350 cid 4V 155 hp	TH 350/400 a/t
TJY	350 cid 4V 155 hp	TH 350 a/t, NB2
1974 Corvette		
CLA	350 cid 4V 195 hp	TH a/t
CLC	350 cid 4V 195 hp	TH a/t, NB2
CKZ	350 cid 4V 195 hp	m/t
CLD	350 cid 4V 250 hp	TH a/t
CLR	350 cid 4V 250 hp	m/t
CLB	350 cid 4V 250 hp	m/t, NB2
1974 Chevrolet		
CMA, CMD	350 cid 2V 145 hp	TH a/t
CMD	350 cid 2V 145 hp	TH a/t
CKD	350 cid 4V 160 hp	TH a/t, NB2
CMH	350 cid 4V 160 hp	TH a/t, NB2
CTA	400 cid 4V 150 hp	TH a/t
CSU	400 cid 4V 150 hp	TH a/t
CTC	400 cid 4V 180 hp	TH a/t, NB2
CTJ, CTD	400 cid 4V 180 hp	TH a/t
1974 Chevelle		
CMC	350 cid 2V 145 hp	m/t
CMA, CMR	350 cid 2V 145 hp	TH a/t
CKD	350 cid 4V 160 hp	TH a/t, NB2
CKH	350 cid 4V 160 hp	m/t, NB2
CTA	400 cid 4V 150 hp	TH a/t
CTC	400 cid 4V 180 hp	TH a/t, NB2
CSU, CSX	400 cid 4V 180 hp	TH a/t
1974 Nova		
CMC	350 cid 2V 145 hp	m/t
CMA	350 cid 2V 145 hp	TH a/t
CKH	350 cid 2V 145 hp	m/t, NB2
CKB	350 cid 4V 185 hp	m/t
CKU–CMA	350 cid 4V 185 hp	TH a/t
1974 Camaro		
CMC	350 cid 2V 145 hp	m/t
CMA	350 cid 2V 145 hp	TH a/t
CKD	350 cid 4V 160 hp	TH a/t, NB2
CKH	350 cid 4V 160 hp	m/t, NB2
CKB	350 cid 4V 185 hp	m/t
CKU	350 cid 4V 185 hp	TH a/t
CLK	350 cid 4V 245 hp	TH a/t
CLJ	350 cid 4V 245 hp	m/t
CMT	350 cid 4V 245 hp	TH a/t, NB2
CMS	350 cid 4V 245 hp	m/t, NB2
1974 Monte Carlo		
CMC	350 cid 2V 145 hp	m/t
CMA, CMR	350 cid 2V 145 hp	TH a/t
CKD	350 cid 4V 160 hp	TH a/t, NB2
CKH	350 cid 4V 160 hp	m/t, NB2
CTA	400 cid 4V 150 hp	TH a/t
CTC	400 cid 4V 180 hp	TH a/t, NB2
CSU, CSX	400 cid 4V 180 hp	TH a/t
1974 C10 Trucks		
TJA, TJB	350 cid 4V 160 hp	m/t
TJD	350 cid 4V 160 hp	m/t, NB2
TJY	350 cid 4V 160 hp	TH 350 a/t, NB2
TKU	350 cid 4V 160 hp	TH 350 a/t
TMH	350 cid 4V 160 hp	TH 350/400 a/t, LP gas
TMJ	350 cid 4V 160 hp	m/t, LP gas
TKT, TKU	350 cid 4V 160 hp	TH 350 a/t
TMM	350 cid 2V 145 hp	TH 350 a/t
TMR	350 cid 2V 145 hp	m/t

Engine Suffix Codes

Suffix	Engine	Equipment
1974 C20 Trucks		
TJC	350 cid 4V 160 hp	m/t
TKU	350 cid 4V 160 hp	TH 350 a/t
TKY	350 cid 4V 160 hp	TH 350/400 a/t
TMH	350 cid 4V 160 hp	TH 350/400 a/t, LP gas
TMJ	350 cid 4V 160 hp	m/t, LP gas
1974 C30 Trucks		
TKY	350 cid 4V 160 hp	TH 350/400 a/t
TMH	350 cid 4V 160 hp	TH 350/400 a/t, LP gas
TMJ	350 cid 4V 160 hp	m/t, LP gas
1974 K10 Trucks		
TJA, TJB	350 cid 4V 160 hp	m/t
TJD	350 cid 4V 160 hp	m/t, NB2
TJY	350 cid 4V 160 hp	TH 350 a/t, NB2
TKT, TKU	350 cid 4V 160 hp	TH 350 a/t
TMM	350 cid 2V 145 hp	TH 350 a/t
TMR	350 cid 2V 145 hp	m/t
1974 K20 Trucks		
TJA, TJC	350 cid 4V 160 hp	m/t
TKY	350 cid 4V 160 hp	TH 350 a/t
1975 Corvette		
CHB	350 cid 4V 165 hp	TH a/t
CHZ	350 cid 4V 165 hp	TH a/t, NB2
CRK, CRT	350 cid 4V 165 hp	TH a/t
CUB	350 cid 4V 165 hp	TH a/t
CHA	350 cid 4V 165 hp	m/t
CUA	350 cid 4V 165 hp	m/t
CRJ	350 cid 4V 165 hp	m/t
CKC	350 cid 4V 205 hp	TH a/t
CHR	350 cid 4V 205 hp	TH a/t, NB2
CRM	350 cid 4V 205 hp	TH
CRL	350 cid 4V 205 hp	m/t
CUD, CUT	350 cid 4V 205 hp	m/t
CHC	350 cid 4V 210 hp	m/t
1975 Chevrolet		
CMJ	350 cid 2V 145 hp	TH a/t, NB2
CRX	350 cid 4V 155 hp	TH a/t
CSH, CSR	400 cid 4V 155 hp	TH a/t
CST, CSS	400 cid 4V 155 hp	TH a/t
CTL, CTM	400 cid 4V 155 hp	TH a/t
CTR, CTS	400 cid 4V 155 hp	TH a/t
1975 Chevelle and Monte Carlo		
CJZ	350 cid 2V 145 hp	TH a/t, NB2
CMJ	350 cid 2V 145 hp	TH a/t, NB2
CJU	350 cid 2V 145 hp	m/t
CMU	350 cid 2V 145 hp	m/t, NB2
CMH, CMM	350 cid 4V 155 hp	TH a/t
CMN	350 cid 4V 155 hp	TH a/t
CRX	350 cid 4V 155 hp	TH a/t
CSC	400 cid 4V 155 hp	TH a/t
CTX	400 cid 4V 155 hp	TH a/t
CTB	400 cid 4V 155 hp	TH a/t
CTU	400 cid 4V 155 hp	TH a/t, NB2
CSB, CSD, CSM	400 cid 4V 155 hp	TH a/t, NB2
1975 Nova		
CZK	262 cid 2V 110 hp	TH a/t
CZM	262 cid 2V 110 hp	TH a/t, NB2
CZF, CZH, CZJ	262 cid 2V 110 hp	m/t
CZL	262 cid 2V 110 hp	m/t, NB2
CRX	350 cid 2V 145 hp	TH a/t
CMU, CMY	350 cid 2V 145 hp	m/t
CML	350 cid 4V 155 hp	TH a/t
CHW	350 cid 4V 155 hp	TH a/t, NB2
CMB	350 cid 4V 155 hp	TH a/t, a/c
1975 Camaro		
CRX	350 cid 2V 145 hp	TH a/t
CMU, CMY	350 cid 2V 145 hp	m/t
CML	350 cid 4V 155 hp	TH a/t
CHW	350 cid 4V 155 hp	TH a/t, NB2
CMB	350 cid 4V 155 hp	TH a/t, a/c
1975 Monza		
CGA, CGJ, CGK	262 cid 2V 110 hp	TH a/t
CZA, CZB, CZC	262 cid 2V 110 hp	m/t
CZD, CZE, CZG	262 cid 2V 110 hp	m/t
CZT, CZU	262 cid 2V 110 hp	m/t
1975 C10 Trucks		
TKF	350 cid 2V 145 hp	TH 350 a/t
TJG	350 cid 2V 145 hp	TH 350 a/t
TJN	350 cid 2V 145 hp	m/t
TXD	350 cid 2V 145 hp	m/t
TKN	350 cid 4V 160 hp	m/t
TME	350 cid 4V 160 hp	TH 350 a/t, NB2
TYD, TYW	350 cid 4V 160 hp	m/t, NB2
TYX	350 cid 4V 160 hp	m/t
TYY	350 cid 4V 160 hp	TH 350 a/t, NB2
TYZ	350 cid 4V 160 hp	TH 350 a/t
TZA	350 cid 4V 160 hp	TH 350 a/t
TZC	350 cid 4V 160 hp	m/t
TZD	350 cid 4V 160 hp	TH 350 a/t
TZJ	350 cid 4V 160 hp	m/t, NB2
TZK	350 cid 4V 160 hp	TH 350 a/t, NB2
1975 C20 Trucks		
TXA	350 cid 4V 160 hp	TH 350/400 a/t, NB2
TXB	350 cid 4V 160 hp	TH 350/400 a/t
TXC	350 cid 4V 160 hp	m/t, NB2
TXD	350 cid 4V 160 hp	m/t
TYW	350 cid 4V 160 hp	m/t, NB2
TYX	350 cid 4V 160 hp	m/t
TYY	350 cid 4V 160 hp	TH 350 a/t, NB2
TYZ	350 cid 4V 160 hp	TH 350 a/t
1975 C30 Trucks		
TXA	350 cid 4V 160 hp	TH 350/400 a/t, NB2
TXB	350 cid 4V 160 hp	TH 350/400 a/t
TXC	350 cid 4V 160 hp	m/t, NB2
TXD	350 cid 4V 160 hp	m/t
1975 K10		
TYW	350 cid 4V 160 hp	m/t, NB2
TYX	350 cid 4V 160 hp	m/t
TYY	350 cid 4V 160 hp	TH 350 a/t, NB2
TYZ	350 cid 4V 160 hp	TH 350 a/t
TLR	400 cid 4V 175 hp	NB2
TLF	400 cid 4V 175 hp	exc. NB2
1975 K20		
TXA	350 cid 4V 160 hp	TH 350/400 a/t, NB2
TXB	350 cid 4V 160 hp	TH 350/400 a/t
TXC	350 cid 4V 160 hp	m/t, NB2
TXD	350 cid 4V 160 hp	m/t
TYW	350 cid 4V 160 hp	m/t, NB2
TYX	350 cid 4V 160 hp	m/t
TYY	350 cid 4V 160 hp	TH 350 a/t, NB2
TYZ	350 cid 4V 160 hp	TH 350 a/t
TLL	400 cid 4V 175 hp	NB2
TLM	400 cid 4V 175 hp	exc. NB2
TLR	400 cid 4V 175 hp	NB2
TLS	400 cid 4V 175 hp	exc. NB2

* TI is transistor ignition

** NB2 is California emission system

CHAPTER 6

CHEVROLET W-SERIES

1958-1965

348, 409, and 427

Almost at the heels of the successful small-block V-8s, Chevrolet came out with a big-block engine that would develop more low-end torque for large passenger cars and trucks. Rather than just make a bigger version of the small-block, Chevrolet decided to experiment, and the result was the W-series big-block with its unusual cylinder head design. In 1958, Chevrolet released the first version of its new Turbo-Thrust engine, which measured 348 cid.

The Turbo-Thrust had a bore and stroke of 4.125x3.25 in., definitely an oversquare design. The block itself wasn't that much bigger than the small-block's—it was only 1.5 in. longer and 2.5 in. wider—but the engine weighed about 120lb more. Internally, the engine had a forged-steel crankshaft, forged-steel connecting rods, and cast-aluminum pistons. Like the small-block, the cylinder heads used stamped steel rocker arms, but unlike previous Chevrolet designs, the cylinder heads were flat—there was no combustion chamber. The engine block deck surface was milled at a 74-degree angle instead of the usual 90-degree angle. The result was that the combustion chamber was in the cylinder and shaped by the piston. One advantage of this type of design is that one cylinder head fits all. Combustion chamber design can be adjusted by changing piston top shape. Coincidentally, Ford released a similar engine family in 1958, the MEL series with this type of cylinder head design.

The base 348 cid engine was rated at 250 hp; the engine was equipped with a single four-barrel carburetor and a hydraulic-lifter camshaft. Optional was the Super Turbo-Thrust—basically the same engine but with a triple-two-barrel-carburetor system that Chevy called Tri-Power and rated at 280 hp. Also optional was the Special Turbo-Thrust, rated at 305 hp with a single four-barrel carburetor. The top engine in 1958 was the Special Super Turbo-Thrust. This engine got a mechanical-lifter camshaft and the Tri-Power intake setup, for 315 hp.

All of these were carried over into 1959 and were joined by a 320 hp Special Turbo-Thrust (single four-barrel) and a 335 hp Special Super Turbo-Thrust (Tri-Power).

Uprated 340 hp (single four-barrel) and 350 hp (Tri-Power) versions were added for manual transmission cars in 1960; in the 348's last year of production in passenger cars, 1961, the 315- and 320 hp versions were deleted from the option list.

The 409 cid engine replaced the 348 cid V-8 as Chevrolet's top engine option in 1961. With a single four-barrel carburetor, it was rated at 360 hp. Nineteen sixty-two saw two versions of the 409 cid V-8—a 380 hp single four-barrel and a 409 hp dual four-barrel setup. The Tri-Power, which was previously used only on the 348 cid V-8, was never offered on the big 409 cid V-8.

The high point in the W-series engine family was reached in 1963 when 340-, 400-, 425-, and 430 hp versions of the engine were available. This included the limited production 1963 Z11 427 cid version, which was Chevrolet's last attempt to get all the horsepower there was from the W-series. (See subsequent engine cid section.) All except the Z11 were carried over into 1964. In its last year, 1965, the 409 cid engine was available during the early part of the model year before the engine was finally replaced by the newer design Mark IV big blocks.

Neither the 348- nor 409 cid engine used in Chevrolet light trucks, but the engine did see service in medium and heavy trucks.

The 348- and 409 cid engines had a lot going for them. They had a wide bore and a relatively short stroke—both conducive to making power and, because of the large displacement, lots of torque as well. Although the engine was successful in various racing classes in its time, it did not have the same potential the small-block had. It was, in effect, almost optimized the way it came from Chevrolet, and it did not respond to traditional methods of power tuning. The problem was the combustion chamber, which was formed by the piston. Although Chevrolet wasn't officially involved in stock-car racing, it was obvious that the 409s couldn't keep up with the Chrysler Hemi or Ford's 427 cid Wedge.

348 cid

The 348 cid V-8 was available in passenger cars for only four years, 1958–1961, but in trucks through 1965. None were ever offered with a two-barrel carburetor. The low-horsepower four-barrel engines used a cast-iron intake manifold with a hydraulic camshaft and a 9.5:1 compression ratio. High-performance four-barrel engines were equipped with an aluminum intake manifold, solid-lifter camshaft, and 11.0–11.25:1 compression ratio.

The Tri-Power was available in every year the 348 cid V-8 was available. Horsepower varied from 280 hp with a 9.5:1 compression ratio and hydraulic-lifter camshaft to a high of 350 hp with a solid-lifter camshaft and 11.0-11.25:1 compression ratio. The 1960–1961 340- and 350 hp engines also came with cylinder heads that had larger valves, 2.00x1.72 in., intake/exhaust.

409 cid

The 409 cid big-block was a bored and stroked version of the 348 cid engine. It had a bore and stroke of 4.312x3.65 in. The 409 cid engines were all high-performance engines. The only engines that had less than 11.0:1 compression ratio and a hydraulic camshaft were the 1963–1965 340 hp versions. All other 409s had solid-lifter camshafts and compression ratios in the range of 11.0–11.25:1. As can be seen from the chart, power ratings ranged from 340 to 425 hp.

As with the 348 cid engines, the 409 cid V-8s got forged-steel crankshafts, forged-steel rods, and forged-aluminum pistons. The exception was the 1961 engines, which used cast-aluminum pistons.

427 cid

This was the ultimate W-series engine. Code-named Z11, this option package was a combination of the engine along with a specially

Chevrolet's 1958–65 W-series big-blocks were designed for large passenger car and truck use. They were made in only two displacements, 348 and 409 cid. This is a 348 cid engine.

prepared 1963 Impala two-door Sports Coupe. The Impala's weight was reduced through the use of an aluminum front end, saving 112lb, and the deletion of other front-end bracketry and bracing, which further reduced the Impala's weight by 121lb.

Displacement was increased to 427 by stroking the 409 cid V-8 to 3.65 in. The engine got a special aluminum isolated-runner intake manifold with two Carter AFB carburetors. The compression ratio was 13.5:1, and the engine was rated at 430 hp at 6,000 rpm with 435ft-lb torque at 3,600 rpm. Only 57 were made.

Engine Blocks

All 348, 409, and Z11 427 blocks are cast in iron, and all have two-bolt main-bearing caps. The main cap and rod journals measure 2.4985 in. and 2.200 in., respectively. All 348 cid blocks have a bore of 4.125 in.; the 409 cid and 427 blocks have a bore of 4.312 in.

There are some detail differences between the 348- and 409 cid blocks. The 348 has its dipstick on the driver side of the engine; it is located on the right side on the 409.

The date code on the 1958–1962 blocks is located on the driver side of the bellhousing flange; 1963–1965 blocks have the date code on the passenger side.

Cylinder Heads

Except for valve sizes, the 348, 409, and 427 cylinder heads are basically the same. The 1958 348 cid engine came with valves measuring 1.94 in. intake and 1.65 in. exhaust. The high-performance 348 cid heads used on 1960–1961 340- and 350 hp engines had intake/exhaust valves measuring 2.07 in./1.72 in.

The 409 and 427 cylinder heads had larger valves measuring 2.19 in./1.72 in. intake/exhaust. The exception were the 1961 360 hp and 1963–1965 low-performance versions of the engine, which came with 2.07 in. intake valves. All cylinder heads used 1.75:1 stamped steel adjustable rocker arms with pressed-in rocker studs. The 1962 and later cylinder heads had longer studs that were pushed in further into the head to prevent them from pulling out. All 409 and 427 cylinder heads also had larger pushrod holes in order to accommodate the larger 3/8 in. pushrods used by the engine.

Intake Manifolds

The base 348 cid V-8 had a cast-iron intake manifold. The optional Tri-Power intake was also cast in iron. The high-performance 348 cid engines got an aluminum four-barrel intake manifold.

The 409s were all equipped with aluminum intake manifolds, save for the 340 hp engines, the manifolds for which were cast in iron. Nineteen sixty-one intake manifolds had a four-hole mounting pad; later manifolds had undivided primary and secondary barrels only on the right side; 380 hp and later four-barrel manifolds had an open plenum chamber.

The dual four-barrel intake manifold used on the 409 hp and 425 hp engines was also cast in aluminum; both front and rear carburetors had undivided primary and secondary barrels on the right side. The left side of the mounting pads had two holes.

As previously mentioned, Z11 427s had a unique aluminum manifold with isolated runners and mounts for dual four-barrels.

Exhaust Manifolds

Exhaust manifolds for all the W-series big-blocks were cast in iron. All low-performance versions basically had the same design, with the two outside exhaust outlets meeting the center two outlets below the cylinder head. The Z11 and high-performance engines had similar manifolds but with longer runners.

All 348 cid engines used exhaust manifolds that had 2.00 in. outlets; manifolds for 409 cid and 427 cid engines had 2.50 in. outlets.

Engine Identification

Each part will have a casting number on it somewhere—on cylinder heads, it is under the valve cover; on intake manifolds, it can either be on the top or bottom; and on exhaust manifolds, it can be on either side. Chevrolet engine blocks have their casting number on the rear of the block, on the bellhousing flange.

In addition to the casting number, there will be a casting date code on the part. This code indicates the date and year the part was cast. Most Chevrolet engine blocks have this code on the top part of the bellhousing flange, but the number can be located elsewhere as well, such as on the side of the block.

Chevrolet often used the same casting number on a part that was used for several model years, so there can be two manifolds with the same casting number but with different characteristics or features on them. Just because a part has the right casting number on it doesn't mean it is the correct part for your application.

Engine casting date codes consist of a letter and three or four digits. The letter indicates the month, with A meaning January and L meaning December. The next two digits stand for the date of the

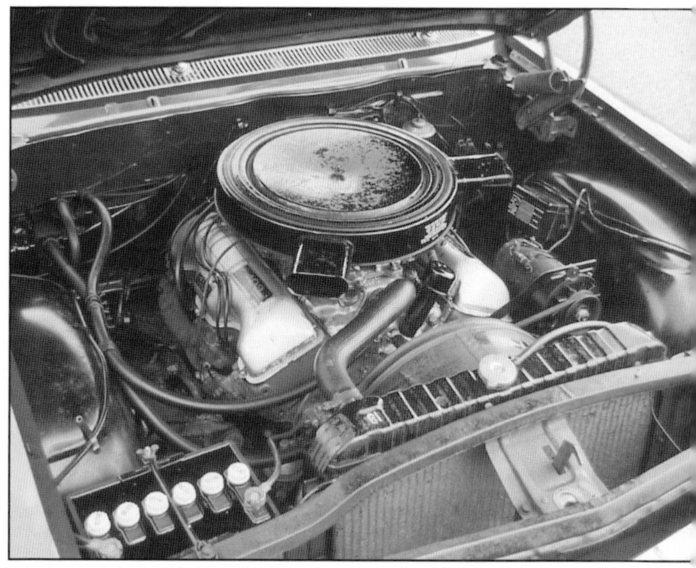

This is an original 409 cid engine in an unrestored 19,000-mile 1962 Impala convertible. Scalloped valve covers are the obvious giveaway that this is a 409 cid engine.

The intake manifolds for these big-block engines, at a quick glance, resemble those of the small-block. They are longer, but the four slots between the runners are a quick giveaway. This is a single four-barrel intake for 1962–63 engines, #3813678.

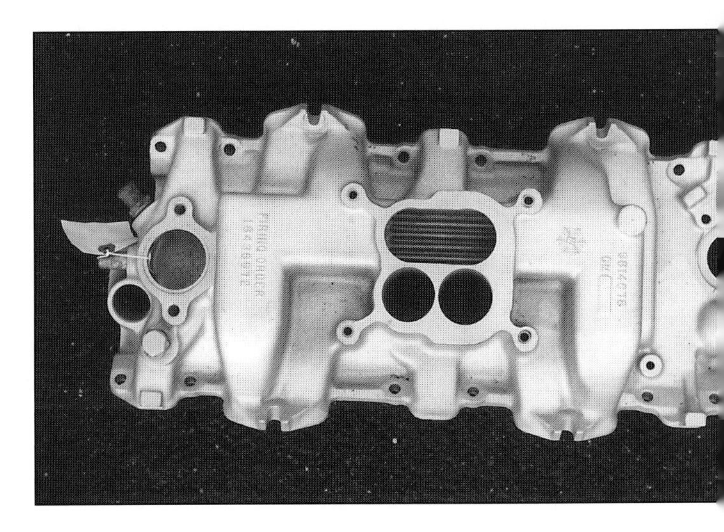

month, and the final one or two digits stand for the last number or numbers of the model year. For example, B 228 could stand for February 22, 1958 (or 1968, 1978, or 1988). If you're looking at an exhaust manifold that came out of a 1958 Chevrolet, you can be pretty sure that the 8 in our example stands for 1958. Sometimes, Chevrolet used two numbers to designate the year, such as B 22 58. When two numbers are used for the year, they will be spaced slightly apart from the rest of the date code.

Each Chevrolet engine also has a number stamped on it to identify it and connect it with the car it is installed in. This number consists of the engine code and sometimes a part of the vehicle's VIN. The engine code consists of the Engine Plant Code, four digits indicating date and month the engine was assembled, and the engine's Suffix Code. Engine plant codes are as follows: F = Flint Motor, V = Flint Engine, or T = Tonawanda. The four digits indicating date codes are broken down as follows: the first two numbers indicate the month and the other two the date. The Suffix Code indicates engine family, usage, and most of the time, transmission. On W-series engines, this was a one- or two-letter code. These codes are listed in the Engine Suffix Code table.

This number on W-series engines is stamped on a pad on the passenger side of the engine block, just where the cylinder head and block meet. Also on the pad may be found the last six digits of the car's VIN. This serves to tie in the installed engine with the chassis.

As an example, the identification code T0422QB would decode as follows: T = Tonawanda; 0422, April 22; QB, 409 cid 409 hp with manual transmission.

The only problem with this particular example was that the QB suffix was used on 1962, 1963, and 1964 409 cid 409 hp engines. You'd also have to look at the casting date codes to verify what model the engine belongs to.

Most parts used on an engine should predate the assembly date code of the engine and should be within 30 days of engine assembly. There are exceptions, of course, such as parts cast for use at a later date or model year.

Engine Specifications

	Displacement	Carburetor	Horsepower	Torque	Compression Ratio	Notes
1958						
	348	4V	250@4,400	356@3,600	9.5	Chevrolet
	348	3x2V	280@4,800	353@3,600	9.5	Chevrolet
	348	4V	305@5,600	350@3,600	11.0	Chevrolet
	348	4V	315@5,600	356@3,600	11.0	Chevrolet, Police Special
	348	3x2V	315@5,600	353@3,600	11.0	Chevrolet
1959						
	348	4V	250@4,400	356@3,600	9.5	Chevrolet
	348	3x2V	280@4,800	353@3,600	9.5	Chevrolet
	348	4V	305@5,600	350@3,600	11.0	Chevrolet
	348	3x2V	315@5,600	353@3,600	11.0	Chevrolet
	348	4V	320@5,600	358@3,600	11.25	Chevrolet
	348	3x2V	335@5,800	358@3,600	11.25	Chevrolet
1960						
	348	4V	250@4,400	356@3,600	9.5	Chevrolet
	348	3x2V	280@4,800	353@3,600	9.5	Chevrolet
	348	4V	305@5,600	350@3,600	11.0	Chevrolet
	348	3x2V	315@5,600	353@3,600	11.0	Chevrolet
	348	4V	320@5,600	358@3,600	11.25	Chevrolet
	348	3x2V	335@5,800	358@3,600	11.25	Chevrolet
	348	4V	340@5,800	362@3,600	11.25	Chevrolet
	348	3x2V	350@6,000	364@3,600	11.25	Chevrolet
1961						
	348	4V	250@4,400	356@3,600	9.5	Chevrolet
	348	3x2V	280@4,800	353@3,600	9.5	Chevrolet
	348	4V	305@5,600	350@3,600	11.0	Chevrolet
	348	3x2V	315@5,600	353@3,600	11.0	Chevrolet
	348	3x2V	335@5,800	358@3,600	11.25	Chevrolet
	348	4V	340@5,800	362@3,600	11.25	Chevrolet
	348	3x2V	350@6,000	364@3,600	11.25	Chevrolet
	409	4V	360@5,800	409@3,600	11.25	Chevrolet

Engine Specifications

	Displacement	Carburetor	Horsepower	Torque	Compression Ratio	Notes
1962						
	409	4V	380@5,800	420@3,200	11.00	Chevrolet
	409	2x4V	409@6,000	420@4,000	11.00	Chevrolet
1963						
	409	4V	340@5,000	420@3,200	10.00	Chevrolet
	409	4V	400@5,800	425@3,600	11.00	Chevrolet
	409	2x4V	425@6,000	425@4,200	11.00	Chevrolet
	427	2x4V	430@5,800	435@3,600	11.0	Chevrolet, Impala
1964						
	409	4V	340@5,000	420@3,200	10.00	Chevrolet
	409	4V	400@5,800	425@3,600	11.00	Chevrolet
	409	2x4V	425@6,000	425@4,200	11.00	Chevrolet
1965						
	409	4V	340@5,000	420@3,200	10.00	Chevrolet
	409	4V	400@5,800	425@3,600	11.00	Chevrolet

Engine Internal Dimensions

Displacement	Bore and Stroke	Rod Bearings	Main Bearings	Intake/Exhaust Valves
348	4.125x3.250	2.1990–2.2000	2.4980–2.4990	1.94/1.65 (1960–1961 340/350 hp 2.07/1.72)
409	4.312x3.500	2.1990–2.2000	2.4980–2.4990	2.07/1.72 (380/400/409/425 hp 2.19/1.73)
427	4.312x3.650	2.1990–2.2000	2.4980–2.4990	2.19/1.73

Block, Head, and Manifold Casting Numbers

Year	Engine	Casting Number
Engine Blocks		
1958	348	3732811, early
1958	348	3751872
1959–1961	348	3755011
1959–1961	348	3771705, truck, service block
1962–1965	348	3798962, truck, service block, has “X” on block
1963–1965	348	3857655, truck, has “X” on block
1961	409	3795623
1962	409	3788068
1963	409	3830814, has “X” on block
1964	409	3844422, has “X” on block
1965	409	3857656, has “X” on block
Cylinder Heads		
1958	348	3732791
1958	348	3759256
1959–1960	348	3758379
1960–1961	348	3767738
1960–1961	348	3781147, High Perf.
1962–1965	348	3819333, truck
1961	409	3795586, 340 hp
1962	409	3814690, 380/409 hp

Year	Engine	Casting Number
Cylinder Heads		
1963	409	3814690, 400/425 hp
1963–1965	409	3830817, 340 hp
1963	409	3837731, 430 hp
1964	409	3814690, 400/425 hp, through 11/12/63
1964	409	3852583, 400/425 hp
1962–1965	409	3819333, truck
Intake Manifolds		
1958–1961	348 4V	3749948
1958–1962	348 4V	3732757, 250 hp
1958–1959	348 4V	3780540, aluminum
1960–1961	348 4V	3753748, aluminum
1962–1965	348 4V	3844472, truck
1961	409 4V	3797776, aluminum
1962–1963	409 4V	3814678, 380/400 hp, aluminum
1962–1964	409 2x4V	3814881, 409/425 hp, aluminum
1963	409 2x4V	3830623, Z-11
1964–1965	409	3844465, 340 hp
1964–1965	409	3844463, 400 hp, aluminum
1962–1965	409 4V	3844472, truck

Block, Head, and Manifold Casting Numbers

Year	Engine	Casting Number
Exhaust Manifolds		
1958–1961	348	3732794 right, 3732793 left, 250/280 hp
1958	348	3732794 right, 3732793 left, 305/315 hp
1959–1961	348	3767584 right, 3767583 left, 305/315/320/335/340/350 hp
1961	409	3767584 right, 3767583 left
1962	409	3814682 right, 3814683 left, 380/409 hp, to 04/62
1962–1964	409	3822926 right, 3822925 left, 380/400/409/425/430 hp
1963–1964	409	3814682 right, 3814683 left, 340 hp
1965	409	3855162 right, 3855161 left, 340/400 hp

Intake ports of the 348 and 409 cid cylinder heads were similar to the Chevy small-block. Staggered valve placement is obvious on this photo. This head, #3819333, is for 1962–65 409 cid truck applications.

Engine Suffix Codes

Suffix Code	Engine	Equipment
1958		
F	348 cid 4V 250 hp	m/t
G	348 cid 4V 250 hp	PG a/t
H	348 cid 4V 250 hp	TG a/t
FA	348 cid 3x2V 280 hp	m/t
HA	348 cid 3x2V 280 hp	TG a/t
FD	348 cid 4V 305 hp	m/t
FB	348 cid 3x2V 315 hp	m/t
FC	348 cid 3x2V 315 hp	m/t, police
1959		
F	348 cid 4V 250 hp	m/t
H	348 cid 4V 250 hp	TG a/t
G	348 cid 4V 250 hp	PG a/t
FA	348 cid 3x2V 280 hp	m/t
GB	348 cid 3x2V 280 hp	PG a/t
HA	348 cid 3x2V 280 hp	TG a/t
FD	348 cid 4V 300 hp	m/t
GD	348 cid 4V 305 hp	PG a/t
FB	348 cid 3x2V 315 hp	m/t
GB	348 cid 3x2V 315 hp	PG a/t
FG	348 cid 4V 320 hp	m/t
FE	348 cid 3x2V 335 hp	m/t
1960		
F	348 cid 4V 250 hp	m/t
G	348 cid 4V 250 hp	PG a/t
H	348 cid 4V 250 hp	TG a/t
FA	348 cid 3x2V 280 hp	m/t
GB	348 cid 3x2V 280 hp	PG a/t
GD	348 cid 3x2V 280 hp	PG a/t
HA	348 cid 3x2V 280 hp	TG a/t
FE	348 cid 3x2V 320 hp	m/t
FG	348 cid 3x2V 320 hp	m/t
FH	348 cid 4V 335 hp	m/t
FJ	348 cid 4V 335 hp	m/t
1961		
F	348 cid 4V 250 hp	TG a/t
H	348 cid 4V 250 hp	m/t
FA	348 cid 3x2V 280 hp	3-spd m/t
HA	348 cid 3x2V 280 hp	TG a/t
FL	348 cid 4V 305 hp	m/t
GD	348 cid 4V 305 hp	PG a/t
GE	348 cid 3x2V 335 hp	PG a/t
FJ	348 cid 4V 340 hp	m/t
FH	348 cid 3x2V 350 hp	4-spd m/t
Q	409 cid 4V 360 hp	4-spd m/t
QA	409 cid 4V 360 hp	4-spd m/t
1962		
QA	409 cid 4V 380 hp	4-spd m/t
QB	409 cid 2x4V 409 hp	4-spd m/t
1963		
QG	409 cid 4V 340 hp	PG a/t
QC	409 cid 4V 340 hp	4-spd m/t
QA	409 cid 4V 400 hp	4-spd m/t
QB	409 cid 2x4V 425 hp	4-spd m/t
QM	427 cid 2x4V 430 hp	4-spd m/t
1964		
QC	409 cid 4V 340 hp	m/t
QQ	409 cid 4V 340 hp	4-spd m/t, TI
QG	409 cid 4V 340 hp	PG a/t
QR	409 cid 4V 340 hp	PG a/t, TI
QA	409 cid 4V 400 hp	4-spd m/t
QN	409 cid 4V 400 hp	4-spd m/t, TI
QB	409 cid 2x4V 425 hp	4-spd m/t
QP	409 cid 2x4V 425 hp	4-spd m/t, TI
1965		
JB	409 cid 4V 340 hp	4-spd m/t
JC	409 cid 4V 340 hp	4-spd m/t, TI
JE	409 cid 4V 340 hp	PG a/t
JF	409 cid 4V 340 hp	PG a/t, TI
JA	409 cid 4V 400 hp	4-spd m/t
JD	409 cid 4V 400 hp	4-spd m/t, TI

CHAPTER 7

CHEVROLET MARK IV BIG BLOCK

1965-1976

396, 402, 427, and 454

Chevrolet's second attempt at building a truly powerful big-block engine took shape in the form of the Mark IV engine series introduced in 1965. The previous W-series, with its odd cylinder heads, couldn't breathe, and a development program to get the engine to run better produced the Mark IV engine. The engine was used in the 1963 Daytona 500 race, where it qualified fastest, but mechanical problems kept it from finishing. Soon after the race, GM announced that it was pulling out of any direct factory racing participation or development. Still, the new design had shown potential, and it was eventually released on 1965 Chevrolet passenger cars and the Corvette.

As with the small-block, it's the cylinder heads that make the engine. Not only were the valves in the cylinder head staggered, but they were also angled (canted) on two planes, forming combustion chambers that resembled a semi-hemi arrangement. This meant that the port runners didn't have to make such sharp bends, and also the valves weren't shrouded as much because they tilted away from the combustion chamber walls. It all boiled down to a cylinder head that had ports and combustion chambers that could really flow and make power—not quite like a true hemi but a lot better than a wedge. It was a great design, and Ford used the same concept on the 429–460 big-blocks and the 351 Cleveland engines.

The heads that were first seen in the 1963 Daytona race were almost identical to the production cylinder heads. The first Turbo-Jet V-8 engine, as it was called by Chevrolet, was the 396 cid engine, which had a bore and stroke of 4.09x3.76 in. It was available in three power levels in 1965: 325-, 375-, and 425 hp. The higher horsepower engines had different cylinder heads than the 325 hp engine. The cylinder heads featured larger, rectangular ports and larger valves. These became known as the rectangular or big-port cylinder heads. The regular cylinder heads were called oval or small-port cylinder heads.

A 427 cid version of the big-block became available in 1966. This was easily accomplished by increasing the bore to 4.25 in., while the stroke remained the same at 3.76 in. Complementing the 396 cid engine in its three power levels (325-, 360-, and 375 hp) were 427 cid Turbo-Jets rated at 385-, 390-, and 425 hp.

Added in 1967 were more 427 cid V-8s, rated at 400-, 430-, and 435 hp. As the engines became better known through their option codes, it is the 1967 L88 that had particular significance for Chevrolet enthusiasts. This was an all-out high-performance version of the 427 cid engine that came with aluminum heads. It was purposely rated at only 430 hp, 5 hp less than the L71 435 hp engine, to discourage sales to unsuspecting owners who didn't really want a race engine in a street Corvette. You could also get aluminum cylinder heads on the L71 engine, thereby making the L71 an L89.

The 396 cid engines continued in the same three power levels as in 1966, although the 360 hp engine was downrated to 350 hp. The engine would be offered in these configurations through 1969.

It should be noted that the high-output 427 cid Turbo-Jet engines were available only in the Corvette. The Chevrolet passenger cars until 1967 could only be optioned out with the L36 385 hp engine. The L72, rated at 425 hp, was optional in 1968 and 1969, and a low-performance 427, the 335 hp LS1, was added to the passenger-car option list in 1969.

The 1968 and 1969 427 cid engine availability mirrored that of the 1967 model year. A lot has been written and said about the special ZL1 427 cid engine that was on the Corvette's option list in 1969. It was, in effect, an L88 with an aluminum block. Since this was a rather costly option at $4,718.35, only two engines were installed in the Corvette, although more were sold over the counter. Sixty-nine were installed in COPO Camaros.

Nineteen sixty-nine was the last year for the 427 cid engine—and the 396 cid engine as well. During the model year, the 396 cid engine's block was replaced with one that had a larger bore, 4.125 in. The result was 402 cid, yet the engine was still marketed as a 396 on Chevrolet Super Sport models (Nova, Monte Carlo, Camaro, and Chevelle). In other Chevrolet vehicles, the 402 was known as the Turbo-Jet 400, which shouldn't be confused with the 400 cid small-block, which was also introduced in 1970. It was known as the Turbo-Fire 400. The 402 cid big-block was removed from the option list after the 1972 model year.

In its last passenger-car permutation, the big-block engine was stroked to 4.00 in. in 1970 for 454 cid. It was designated LS4, LS5, and LS6. The most powerful was the LS6, rated at 450 hp in the 1970 Chevelle. In 1971 it was rated at 425 hp. The LS5, rated at 390 hp in 1970 and 365 hp in 1971, was available only for those two years, while the LS4, in declining output ratings, was available through the 1976 model year.

Light trucks were equipped with truck versions of the Turbo-Jet engines in 396-, 402-, and 454 cid displacements. Other configurations were used for heavier trucks and industrial applications.

396 cid

The 396 cid version of the big-block was available from 1965 to 1969. The engine made its debut in the 1965 Corvette. It had the L78 designation, and it was rated at 425 hp at 6,400 rpm, with 415ft-lb torque at 4,000 rpm. It came with the large-port, large-valve (2.19 in./1.72 in. intake/exhaust) cylinder heads, 11.0:1 compression ratio, four-bolt-main engine block, forged-steel crankshaft, solid-lifter camshaft, and an aluminum high-rise-type intake manifold with a Holley four-barrel carburetor. The same engine, as equipped in the Z16 Chevelle, was rated at 375 hp, and it had a hydraulic-lifter camshaft. The L78 produced during 1966–1969 used a solid-lifter camshaft.

The medium-performance L34 396 cid engine for 1966 was equipped with the four-bolt-main block, cast-iron crankshaft, small-port cylinder heads, 10.25:1 compression ratio, a higher lift hydraulic-lifter camshaft, cast-iron intake manifold, and Holley four-barrel carburetor. It was rated at 360 hp. From 1967 to 1969, it was rated at 350 hp at the same rpm ratings.

The low-performance 396 cid engine was the L35. It had the standard two-bolt-main engine block, cast-iron crankshaft, small-port cylinder heads, 10.25:1 compression ratio, a hydraulic-lifter camshaft, and cast-iron intake manifold with a Rochester Quadrajet carburetor for a 325 hp output.

An LS3 396 cid V-8 was optional on the 1969 full-size car line. It was strictly low performance, as it had a two-barrel carburetor.

402 cid

By increasing the 396's bore to 4.125 in., the 402 cid engine was created. This was done during the 1969 model year, so both 396 and 402 cid big-blocks were fitted that year. Option numbers (LS3, L34, L35, and L78) and power ratings were unchanged from those of the 396.

The L34, L35, and L78 continued to be available in 1970. There was also a limited run of the L78 equipped with aluminum cylinder heads; these were designated L89.

The 300 hp LS3 was also carried over into 1970 and made available on other Chevrolet car lines, including Chevelle. It was marketed as the Turbo-Jet 400. After the L34, L35, and L78 were dropped at the end of the 1970 model year, the LS3 was the only 402 cid engine left. It was dropped after the end of the 1972 model year.

427 cid

Certain numbers have a particular ring to them, and for Chevrolet enthusiasts the number 427 connotes high performance—lots of it. Just by looking at the hood emblems of a 427-equipped Corvette, you know that it's a serious performance car.

The first Mark IV 427 cid engine came out in 1966 on the Corvette and Chevrolet full-size car line. The L36 427 cid engine had a bore and stroke of 4.251x3.76 in. The L36 used the two-bolt-main bearing block, cast-iron crankshaft, hydraulic camshaft, small-port, small-valve cylinder heads, 10.25:1 compression ratio, cast-iron intake manifold (aluminum only on 1969 Corvette), and Rochester Quadrajet carburetor. It was rated at 390 hp. The L36 continued on the Corvette through the 1969 model year. The same engine, but rated at 5 hp less, was used on the full-size car line during 1967–1968 but returned to the 390 hp rating for 1969.

The LS5 version of the 454 cid big-block was available on the Chevelle. Small port heads and a Rochester Quadrajet carburetor made for 360hp.

Also released in 1966 was the more powerful L72. The L72 got the four-bolt-main engine block, forged crankshaft, large-port, large-valve cylinder heads, 11.0:1 compression ratio, solid-lifter camshaft, and an aluminum intake manifold with a Holley four-barrel carburetor. It was rated at 425 hp. The L72 was used in the Corvette only in 1966; it continued through 1969 on the full-size cars.

The L68 version was optional on Corvettes from 1967 to 1969. It was basically an L36 engine with a Tri-Power intake setup. It was rated at 400 hp.

Also optional on the 1967–1969 Corvette was the L71 427 cid V-8. It was similar to the 425 hp L72 engine, but it used the Tri-Power intake setup instead of a single four-barrel carburetor. It was rated at 435 hp.

The L89 version of the 427 cid engine was the L71 engine equipped with aluminum cylinder heads.

The most powerful 427 cid V-8 was the L88, even though it was rated at 430 hp. It had all the high-performance 427 components, plus aluminum cylinder heads. It came with an aluminum high-rise intake manifold and a Holley 850cfm carburetor.

The ZL1, available only during 1969 on the Corvette and Camaro, was an all-aluminum 427 cid engine.

The 427 cid V-8 you don't hear much about is the 1969 LS1. It used the two-bolt-main engine block, small-port, small-valve cylinder heads, 10.25:1 compression ratio, hydraulic camshaft, and cast-iron intake manifold with a Rochester Quadrajet carburetor. It was rated at 335 hp.

454 cid

With a bore of 4.251 in. and a stroke of 4.00 in., the 454 cid V-8 was the largest factory built big-block. Three versions of the engine were released—LS4, LS5, and LS6. The 454 was built from 1970 to 1976.

The LS4 was offered on the Chevrolet full-size car line. It was a low-performance engine with the two-bolt-main block, small-port cylinder heads, hydraulic camshaft, and a cast-iron intake manifold with a Rochester Quadrajet carburetor. It was rated at 345 hp at 4,400 rpm, with 500ft-lb torque at 3,000 rpm. The engine missed a year and then came back in 1972 with an SAE net rating of 270 hp. The LS4 was the only 454 cid big-block available during 1973–1976.

The LS5 was a medium-performance big-block. It used the two-bolt-main engine block, the small-port cylinder heads, a hydraulic camshaft, and a cast-iron intake manifold with a Rochester Quadrajet carburetor. Its power rating depended on which vehicle it was installed in. In the Corvette, it was rated at 390 hp in 1970 and 365 hp in 1971; in the Chevelle, it was rated at 360 hp in 1970 and 365 hp in 1971.

The LS6 was only available on the 1970 Chevelle and on the 1971 Corvette. The engine got the four-bolt-main engine block; the large-port, large-valve cylinder heads; a solid-lifter camshaft; and a low-rise aluminum intake manifold with a Holley four-barrel carburetor. The engine was rated at 450 hp in the Chevelle and 425 hp in the Corvette. The Chevelle version had cast-iron heads, while the Corvette version got aluminum cylinder heads.

There was also the stillborn LS7 for the 1970 Corvette. It was listed in factory literature, but the engine was never released. Initially, the engine was to have a Tri-Power intake, rated at 460 hp. Later, it was revised to a single 850cfm Holley four-barrel carburetor on an aluminum high-rise intake manifold for 465 hp output. In other respects, the LS7 was similar to the LS6 but with a more radical camshaft and open chamber aluminum cylinder heads.

Engine Blocks

There are three cast-iron blocks used with the Mark IV series engines. The standard passenger car block has two-bolt main-bearing caps in all five positions. The high-performance blocks have four-bolt main-bearing caps in the first four positions with thicker webbing and bulkheads.

The truck blocks have the four-bolt main-bearing caps, but the block's deck height is also higher, so they cannot readily interchange with passenger-car intake manifolds.

The all-aluminum ZL1 block is based on the passenger-car high-performance block patterns but is cast in aluminum. Cast-iron cylinder liners were shrunk-fit into the cylinder bores.

Cylinder Heads

It's the Mark IV's cylinder heads' featured canted valve heads that allowed the engine to breathe and thereby produce more power. All big-block heads use screw-in rocker arm studs, stamped steel rockers, and pushrod guide plates. There have been two basic cylinder head designs used on big-block Chevy engines.

The vast majority of factory cylinder heads have oval intake ports with valves that measure 2.06 in./1.72 in. intake/exhaust. These heads are the ones found on regular passenger-car applications, medium-performance applications, and trucks. These heads have the word "PASS" cast on the top of the cylinder head, under the valve cover. Truck versions have the word "TRUCK" cast on them.

High-performance cylinder heads have larger intake and exhaust ports. They are generally referred to as rectangular-port heads. Intake valve size on these cylinder heads is larger, measuring 2.19 in. These cylinder heads have the words "HI-PERF" cast on their top, underneath the valve cover.

There is also the question of open chamber and closed combustion chamber design. Most cylinder heads for 1960s and 1970s passenger-car applications, whether they are high performance or not, have the closed combustion chamber. The combustion chambers in these cylinder heads displace 110cc or less. However, Chevrolet found that enlarging the combustion chamber resulted in better engine breathing.

There is also quite a mystique surrounding the aluminum cylinder heads. The 1967 L88 and L89 aluminum cylinder heads (casting number 3904392) were copies of their cast-iron counterparts. They had closed combustion chambers, big ports, and the 2.19 in./1.72 in. intake/exhaust valves.

The 1968–1969 aluminum cylinder heads (casting number 3919842) also had the closed combustion chambers, but the exhaust valves were larger, measuring 1.84 in.

The 1969–1971 era (casting number 3946074) high-performance engines that used aluminum cylinder heads got heads with an open combustion chamber that displaced 118 cc. In addition, these heads also had larger 1.88 in. exhaust valves and round exhaust ports.

The only high-performance cast-iron heads that had the open combustion chambers were the 1971 cast-iron LS6 cylinder heads (casting numbers 3994025 and 3994026). The later small-port 454 cid cylinder heads had an open-chamber design as well. It should also be noted that many truck application cylinder heads had the larger open-combustion-chamber design, in conjunction with the small ports and valves.

Intake Manifolds

The great majority of passenger-car big-block Chevrolet V-8 engines were equipped with a cast-iron intake manifold and usually with a Rochester Quadrajet carburetor. High-performance engines were generally equipped with a high-rise aluminum intake manifold and a Holley carburetor. The 1970 high-performance 454s were equipped with low-rise intake manifolds.

The L71 and L89 engines were equipped with a Tri-Power Holley carburetor intake setup. The manifolds on these engines were cast in aluminum.

Exhaust Manifolds

The exhaust manifolds on the big-block Chevy followed industry practice, being made of cast iron. Although there were differences among the manifolds, they followed a similar design—four runners converging into a common outlet. The shape of the runners varied, as did the outlet size. The high-performance engines got manifolds with larger, freer-flowing runners and larger outlets.

Engine Identification

Chevrolet engine parts have various identification numbers and symbols on them. The best known are the casting number and date code. Both of these can be used to identify parts, and usually they are fairly conclusive. Each part will have a casting number

Big-block Chevy heads had either a PASS, TRUCK, HI-PER, or HI-PERF casting indicating usage. Although this is a truck application head with the smaller intake ports, it has the HI-PER casting. Note casting number location.

on it somewhere—on cylinder heads, it's under the valve cover; on intake manifolds, it can either be on the top or bottom; and on exhaust manifolds, it can be on either side. Chevrolet engine blocks have their casting numbers on the rear of the block, on the bellhousing flange.

In addition to the casting number, there will be a casting date code on the part. This code indicates the date and year the part was cast. Most Chevrolet engine blocks have this code on the top part of the bellhousing flange, but the number can be located elsewhere as well, such as on the side of the block.

Chevrolet often used the same casting number on a part that was used for several model years, so two parts can have the same casting number but different characteristics or features. Just because a part has the right casting number on it doesn't mean it is the correct part for your application.

Engine casting date codes consist of a letter and three or four digits. The letter indicates the month it was cast, with the letter A meaning January and L meaning December. The next two digits stand for the date of the month, and the last one or two digits stand for the last number or numbers of the model year. For example, B 228 could stand for February 22, 1968 (or 1958, 1978, or 1988). If you're looking at an exhaust manifold that came out of a 1968 Camaro, you can be pretty sure that the 8 in our example stands for 1968. Sometimes, Chevrolet used two numbers to designate the year, in which case the code for the previous example would read B 22 68. When two numbers are used for the year, they will be spaced slightly apart from the rest of the date code.

Each Chevrolet engine also has a number stamped on it to identify it and connect it with the car it is installed in. This number consists of the engine code and sometimes a part of the vehicle's VIN. The engine code consists of the Engine Plant Code, four digits indicating the date and month the engine was assembled, and the engine's Suffix Code. Engine plant codes are as follows: F = Flint Motor, V = Flint Engine, or T = Tonawanda. The four digits indicating date codes break down as follows: The first two numbers indicate the month and the other two the date. The Suffix Code indicates engine family, usage, and most of the time, transmission. Before 1970, this was a two-letter code. From 1970, this was a three-letter code. Suffix codes for these engines are listed in the Engine Suffix Code table.

This number is stamped on a pad on the passenger side of the engine block, just where the cylinder head and block meet. Also on the pad may be found the last eight digits of the car's VIN. This serves to tie in the installed engine with the chassis. From 1969, these numbers sometimes were also stamped on a pad near the oil filter, or they may just be stamped on the filter pad alone. However, most engines will have the number stamped on the front of the block, as indicated. As an example, the identification code T0422CRV would decode as follows: T = Tonawanda; 0422, April 22; CRV, 454 cid 450 hp with manual transmission.

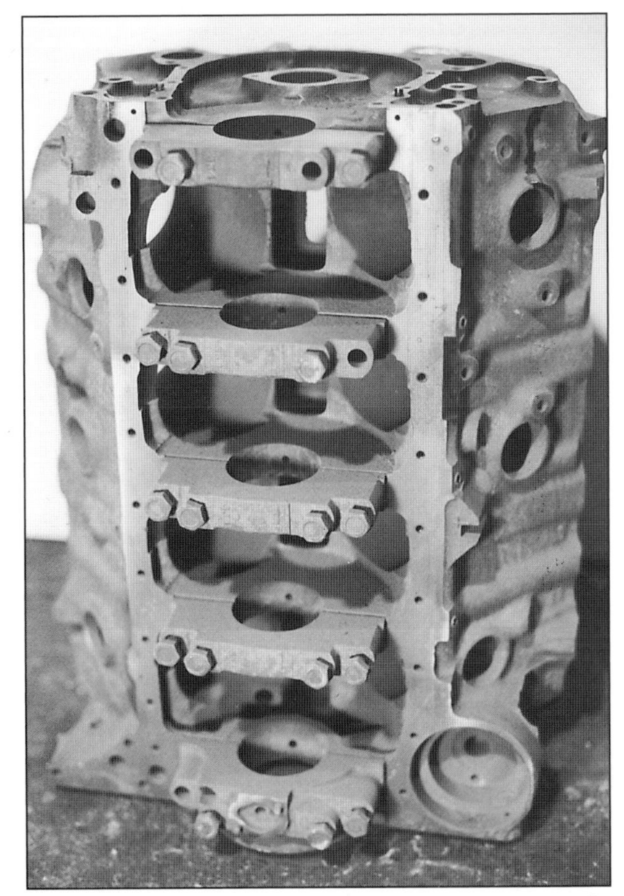

This is one of the reasons why the Chevy big-block has been such a popular engine for racing applications–the bottom end is very strong. This is a 427 cid truck block.

Keep in mind that the engine Suffix Codes are used over and over again. For example, the code CWT stands for a 1973 454 cid big-block V-8 rated at 275 hp and used on the 1973 Corvette. The same code was used on the 1974 version of the engine, again used on the Corvette, but rated at 270 hp. Some codes can even have five or more applications.

Most parts used on an engine should predate the assembly date code of the engine and should be within 30 days of engine assembly. There are exceptions, of course, such as parts cast for use at a later date or model year.

Engine Specifications

	Displacement	Carburetor	Horsepower	Torque	Compression Ratio	Notes
1965						
	396	4V	325@4,800	410@3,200	10.0	L35, Chevrolet
	396	4V	375@5,600	420@3,600	11.0	L78, Chevelle
	396	4V	425@6,400	415@3,600	11.0	L78, Corvette
1966						
	396	4V	325@4,800	410@3,200	10.25	L35, Chevrolet, Chevelle
	396	4V	360@5,600	420@3,600	10.25	L34, Chevelle
	396	4V	375@5,600	415@3,600	11.0	L78, Chevelle
	427	4V	390@5,200	460@3,600	10.25	L36, Corvette, Chevrolet
	427	4V	425@5,600	460@4,000	11.0	L72, Corvette, Chevrolet
1967						
	396	4V	325@4,800	410@3,200	10.25	L35, Chevrolet, Chevelle, Camaro

Engine Specifications

	Displacement	Carburetor	Horsepower	Torque	Compression Ratio	Notes
	396	4V	350@5,200	415@3,400	10.25	L34, Chevelle, Camaro
	396	4V	375@5,600	415@3,600	11.0	L78, Chevelle, Camaro
	427	4V	385@6,400	415@3,600	10.25	L36, Chevrolet
	427	4V	390@5,400	460@3,600	10.25	L36, Corvette
	427	3x2V	400@5,400	460@3,600	10.25	L68, Corvette
	427	4V	425@6,400	460@4,000	11.0	L72, Chevrolet
	427	4V	430@5,800	450@4,400	12.50	L88, Corvette
	427	3x2V	435@5,800	460@4,000	11.0	L71, Corvette
	427	3x2V	435@5,800	460@4,000	11.0	L89, Corvette, aluminum heads
1968						
	396	4V	310@4,800	400@3,200	10.25	light truck
	396	4V	325@4,800	410@3,200	10.25	L35, Chevrolet, Chevelle, Camaro
	396	4V	350@5,200	415@3,400	10.25	L34, Chevelle, Camaro, Chevy II
	396	4V	375@5,600	415@3,600	11.0	L78, Chevelle, Camaro, Chevy II
	427	4V	385@6,400	415@3,600	10.25	L36, Chevrolet
	427	4V	390@5,400	460@3,600	10.25	L36, Corvette
	427	3x2V	400@5,400	460@3,600	10.25	L68, Corvette
	427	4V	425@6,400	460@4,000	11.0	L72, Chevrolet
	427	4V	430@5,800	450@4,400	12.50	L88, Corvette
	427	3x2V	435@5,800	460@4,000	11.0	L71, Corvette
	427	3x2V	435@5,800	460@4,000	11.0	L89, Corvette, aluminum heads
1969						
	396	2V	265@4,800	400@2,800	9.0	LS3, Chevrolet
	396	4V	310@4,800	400@3,200	10.25	light truck
	396	4V	325@4,800	410@3,200	10.25	L35, Chevrolet, Chevelle, Camaro
	396	4V	350@5,200	415@3,400	10.25	L34, Chevelle, Camaro, Nova
	396	4V	375@5,600	415@3,600	11.0	L78, Chevelle, Camaro, Nova
	402	4V	325@4,800	410@3,200	10.25	L35, Chevrolet, Chevelle, Camaro
	402	4V	350@5,200	415@3,400	10.25	L34, Chevelle, Camaro, Nova
	402	4V	375@5,600	415@3,600	11.0	L78, Chevelle, Camaro, Nova
	427	4V	335@4,800	460@3,200	10.25	LS1, Chevrolet
	427	4V	390@5,400	460@3,600	10.25	L36, Corvette, Chevrolet
	427	3x2V	400@5,400	460@3,600	10.25	L68, Corvette
	427	4V	425@6,400	460@4,000	11.0	L72, Chevrolet, Camaro
	427	4V	430@5,800	450@4,400	12.00	L88, Corvette
	427	4V	430@5,800	450@4,400	12.00	ZL1, Corvette, Camaro, aluminum block/heads
	427	3x2V	435@5,800	460@4,000	11.0	L71, Corvette
	427	3x2V	435@5,800	460@4,000	11.0	L89, Corvette, aluminum heads
1970						
	402	4V	330@4,800	410@3,200	10.25	LS3, Chevelle, Camaro, Monte Carlo
	402	4V	350@5,200	415@3,400	10.25	L34, Chevelle, Camaro, Nova
	402	4V	375@5,600	415@3,600	11.0	L78, Chevelle, Camaro, Nova
	454	4V	345@4,400	500@3,000	10.25	LS3, Chevrolet
	454	4V	360@4,400	500@3,200	10.25	LS5, Chevelle, Monte Carlo
	454	4V	390@4,800	500@3,400	10.25	LS5, Corvette, Chevrolet
	454	4V	450@5,600	500@3,600	11.25	LS6, Chevelle
1971						
	402	4V	300@4,800	400@3,200	8.5	LS3, Chevelle, Camaro, Monte Carlo
	454	4V	365@4,800	465@3,200	8.5	LS5, Chevrolet, Chevelle, Monte Carlo
	454	4V	425@5,600	475@4,000	9.0	LS6, Corvette, Chevelle
1972						
	402	4V	240@4,400	345@3,200	8.5	LS3, Camaro, Chevelle, Monte Carlo
	454	4V	270@4,000	390@3,200	8.5	LS5, Chevrolet, Corvette, Chevelle, Monte Carlo
1973						
	454	4V	240@4,000	355@2,800	8.5	light truck
	454	4V	275@4,000	395@2,800	8.5	LS4, Chevrolet, Corvette, Chevelle, Monte Carlo
1974						
	454	4V	245@4,000	365@2,800	8.5	light truck

Displacement	Carburetor	Horsepower	Torque	Compression Ratio	Notes
454	4V	270@4,400	380@2,800		LS4, Chevrolet, Corvette, Chevelle, Monte Carlo
1975					
454	4V	245@4,000	355@3,000	8.5	light truck
454	4V	270@4,000	395@2,800	8.5	LS4, Chevrolet, Chevelle, Monte Carlo

Engine Internal Dimensions

Displacement	Bore and Stroke	Rod Bearings	Main Bearings	Intake/Exhaust Valves
396	4.094x3.760	2.1990–2.2000	2.7484–2.7490	2.06/1.72 (375 hp 2.19/1.72)
402	4.125x3.760	2.1990–2.2000	2.4980–2.4990	2.06/1.72 (375 hp 2.19/1.72*)
427	4.251x3.760	2.1990–2.2000	2.4980–2.4990	2.06x1.72 (425/430/435 hp 2.19/1.72*)
454	4.251x4.000	2.1990–2.2000	2.4980–2.4990	2.06x1.72 (425/450 hp 2.19/1.72*)

* 1.84 in. or 1.88 in. high performance heads only, other specs are the same.

Block, Head, and Manifold Casting Numbers

Year	Engine	Casting Number
Engine Blocks		
1965–1966	396	3855962, 360/375/425 hp
1966	396	3873858, 375 hp 4-bolt mains
1967	396	3902406, all 2- and 4-bolt mains
1966–1967	396	3855961, 325/360 hp
1968	396	3916323, all 2- and 4-bolt mains
1968–1969	396	3935440, all 2- and 4-bolt mains
1969	396/402	3955272, all 2- and 4-bolt mains
1968–1972	396/402	3968854, 3999290, light truck
1969–1972	396/402	3969854, all 2- and 4-bolt mains
1966–1967	427	3869942, 390/425 hp, 2- and 4-bolt mains
1967	427	3904351, all 2- and 4-bolt mains
1968	427	3916321, all 2- and 4-bolt mains
1968–1969	427	3935440, all 2- and 4-bolt mains
1969	427	3946052, 4-bolt mains, aluminum
1969	427	3955270, 3963512, all 2- and 4-bolt mains
1970–1971	454	3963512, all 2- and 4-bolt mains
1970–1972	454	3969854, all 2- and 4-bolt mains
1973–1975	454	3999289, pass. and light truck, 2-bolt mains
Cylinder Heads		
1965	396	3856208, 375 hp
1965	427	3856208, 425 hp
1966–1967	396	3873858, 375 hp
1966	427	3873858, 425 hp
1967	396	3904391, 375 hp
1967	427	3904391, 435 hp
1967	427	3904392, 430/435 hp, aluminum, 1.88 in. ex. valve
1967–1969	427	3919840, 425/435 hp

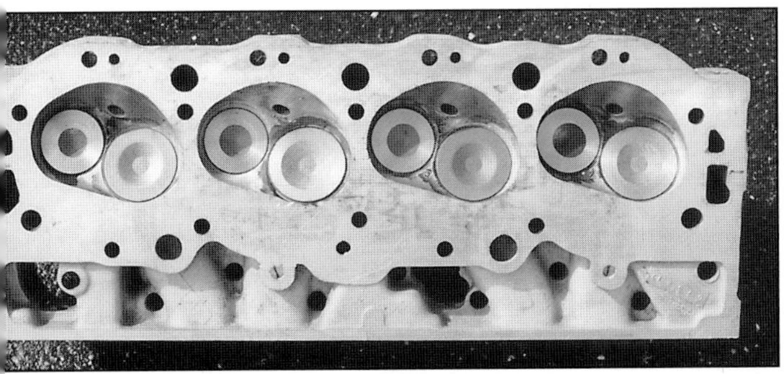

Open combustion chamber design was used on the 1969–71 high-performance big-block engines. There's hardly any room left for bigger valves. This head is cast in aluminum, #3946074.

Year	Engine	Casting Number
Cylinder Heads		
1966–1967	396	3909802, 325/350 hp
1966–1967	427	3909802, 385/390/400 hp
1968	396	3917215, 325/350 hp
1968	427	3917215, 390/400 hp
1968–1969	396	3919842, 375 hp, aluminum, 1.84 in. ex. valve
1968–1969	427	3919842, 430/435 hp, aluminum, 1.84 in. ex. valve
1968–1969	396	3931063, 325/350 hp
1968–1972	396/402	3931063, light truck
1969	427	3931063, 390/400 hp
1969	396	3933148, 265 hp
1968–1969	396	3965198, light truck
1970–1972	402	3933148, light truck
1969–1970	396/402	3946074, 375 hp, aluminum, 1.88 ex. valve
1969	427	3946074, 430/435 hp, aluminum, 1.88 ex. valve
1971	454	3946074, 425 hp, aluminum, 1.88 ex. valve
1970	402	3964290, 330/350 hp, light truck
1970	454	3964290, 390 hp
1970	396	3964291, 375 hp
1970	454	3964291, 450 hp
1971–1972	454	3993820
1971–1972	402	3993820, all
1972	402	3999241, 300/240 hp
1972	454	3999241, 270 hp
Intake Manifolds		
1965	396	3866948, 375/425 hp, aluminum
1965–1966	396	3856289, 325 hp
1966–1967	396	3866948, 325/350/360 hp
1966–1968	396	3883948, 325 hp
1966–1968	396	3885069, 375 hp, aluminum
1968	396	3919878, 375 hp, aluminum
1968–1969	396	3933163, 375 hp, aluminum
1969	396	3952900, 265 hp
1969	396	3931067, 325 hp
1970	402	3963569, 375 hp, aluminum
1970–1971	402	3955287, 300/330/350 hp
1972	402	6263753, 240 hp
1966–1967	427	3866948, 390 hp
1966–1968	427	3883948, 385/390 hp
1966–1968	427	3885069, 425 hp, aluminum
1967	427	3894382, 400 hp, aluminum
1967	427	3886093, 430 hp, aluminum
1967	427	3894374, 435 hp, aluminum

Block, Head, and Manifold Casting Numbers

Year	Engine	Casting Number
Intake Manifolds		
1968	427	3919849, 3937793, 390 hp, aluminum
1968	427	3919850, 400 hp, aluminum
1968	427	3919852, 435 hp, aluminum
1968	427	3919878, 425 hp, aluminum
1968–1969	427	3933163, 425 hp, aluminum
1968–1969	427	3933198, 430 hp, aluminum
1969	427	3931067, 335/390 hp
1969	427	3947801, 390 hp, aluminum
1969	427	3937795, 400 hp, aluminum
1969	427	3937797, 435 hp, aluminum
1970–1971	454	3955287, 360/365/390 hp
1970–1972	454	3963569, 425/450 hp, aluminum
1971–1972	454	3967474, 425 hp, aluminum
1972	454	6263753, 240/270 hp
1973	454	353015
1968–1969	396/427	6263818, 375/425 hp, aluminum
Exhaust Manifolds		
1965	396	3856306 right, 3857297 left, 325 hp
1965	396	3868874 right, 3869925 left, 375 hp
1965	396	3856302 right, 3856301 left, 425 hp
1966	396	3904399 right, 3883999 left, 325/360/375 hp
1966–1967	396	3884504 right, 3892307 left, 325 hp
1967–1970	396/402	3916178 right, 3909879 left, 325/350/375 hp
1966	427	3883828 right, 3883827 left, Chevrolet 425 hp
1966–1967	427	3884504 right, 3892307 left, 385/390 hp
1967–1969	427	3880828 right, 3880827 left, Corvette, 390/400/430/435 hp
1969	427	3916178 right, 3914613 left, Chevrolet, 335/390 hp
1969	427	3916178 right, 3909879 left, 427 COPO
1970–1971	454	3916178 right, 3909869 left, 360/365/390/425/450 hp
1970	454	3916178 right, 3969869 left, 390 hp
1971–1972	402	3989310 right, 3989343 left
1972–1974	454	3969869 right, 3939310 left, Corvette
1973–1975	454	353038 right, 329225 left
1973–1975	454	353038 right, 353030 left, police

Engine Suffix Codes

Suffix Code	Engine	Equipment	
1965 Corvette			
IF	396 cid 4V 425 hp6t	4-spd m/t, TI	
1965 Chevrolet			
IA	396 cid 4V 325 hp	m/t	
LF	396 cid 4V 325 hp	m/t	4-spd m/t
IC	396 cid 4V 325 hp	m/t	4-spd m/t, TI
IGH	396 cid 4V 325 hp	m/t	PG a/t
LB	396 cid 4V 325 hp	m/t	PG a/t

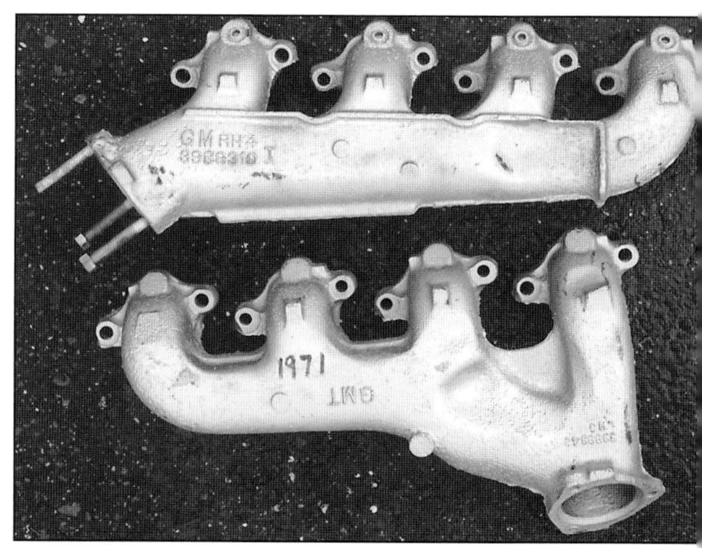

These exhaust manifolds are for 1971–72 402 and 454 engines. Top manifold, #3989310, has provision for the A.I.R. injection system. Bottom manifold, #3989343, does not.

Suffix Code	Engine	Equipment	
IGR	396 cid 4V 325 hp	m/t	PG a/t
II	396 cid 4V 325 hp	m/t	PG a/t TI
IV	396 cid 4V 325 hp	m/t	TH a/t
LC	396 cid 4V 325 hp	m/t	TH a/t
IW	396 cid 4V 325 hp	m/t	TH a/t, TI
IE	396 cid 4V 425 hp	4-spd m/t	
1965 Chevelle			
IX	396 cid 4V 375 hp	4-spd m/t	
IY	396 cid 4V 375 hp	4-spd m/t, COPO	
1966 Corvette			
IR	427 cid 4V 390 hp	PG a/t	
IL	427 cid 4V 390 hp	4-spd m/t	
IM	427 cid 4V 390 hp	4-spd m/t, A.I.R.	
IP	427 cid 4V 425 hp	4-spd m/t	
IK	427 cid 4V 425 hp	4-spd m/t	
1966 Chevrolet			
IA	396 cid 4V 325 hp	3- or 4-spd m/t, Holley	
IB	396 cid 4V 325 hp	3- or 4-spd m/t, A.I.R	
IG	396 cid 4V 325 hp	PG a/t	
IC	396 cid 4V 325 hp	PG a/t, A.I.R.	
IVR	396 cid 4V 325 hp	TH a/t, Rochester	
IN	396 cid 4V 325 hp	TH a/t, A.I.R.	
IVH	396 cid 4V 325 hp	TH a/t, Holley	
IH	427 cid 4V 390 hp	m/t	
IJ	427 cid 4V 390 hp	TH a/t	
II	427 cid 4V 390 hp	TH a/t, A.I.R.	
ID	427 cid 4V 425 hp	m/t	
IO	427 cid 4V 425 hp	TH a/t, A.I.R.	
1966 Chevelle			
ED	396 cid 4V 325 hp	4-spd m/t	
EH	396 cid 4V 325 hp	4-spd m/t, A.I.R.	
EK	396 cid 4V 325 hp	PG a/t	
EM	396 cid 4V 325 hp	PG a/t, A.I.R.	
EF	396 cid 4V 360 hp	4-spd m/t	
EJ	396 cid 4V 360 hp	4-spd m/t, A.I.R.	
EN	396 cid 4V 360 hp	PG a/t	
EL	396 cid 4V 360 hp	PG a/t, A.I.R.	
EG	396 cid 4V 375 hp	4-spd m/t	
1967 Corvette			
IQ	427 cid 4V 390 hp	PG a/t	

Suffix Code	Engine	Equipment
IR	427 cid 4V 390 hp	PG a/t, A.I.R.
IL	427 cid 4V 390 hp	4-spd m/t
IM	427 cid 4V 390 hp	4-spd m/t, A.I.R.
JD	427 cid 3x2V 400 hp	PG a/t
JG	427 cid 3x2V 400 hp	PG a/t, A.I.R.
JC	427 cid 3x2V 400 hp	4-spd m/t
JF	427 cid 3x2V 400 hp	4-spd m/t, A.I.R.
IT	427 cid 4V 430 hp	4-spd m/t
JE	427 cid 3x2V 435 hp	4-spd m/t
JA	427 cid 3x2V 435 hp	4-spd m/t, A.I.R.
IU	427 cid 3x2V 435 hp	4-spd m/t, aluminum heads
JH	427 cid 3x2V 435 hp	4-spd m/t, A.I.R., aluminum heads
1967 Chevrolet		
IA	396 cid 4V 325 hp	3- or 4-spd m/t
IB	396 cid 4V 325 hp	3- or 4-spd m/t, A.I.R.
IG	396 cid 4V 325 hp	PG a/t
IC	396 cid 4V 325 hp	PG a/t, A.I.R.
IV	396 cid 4V 325 hp	TH a/t
IN	396 cid 4V 325 hp	TH a/t, A.I.R.
IJ	427 cid 4V 390 hp	TH a/t
IO	427 cid 4V 390 hp	TH a/t, A.I.R.
IF	427 cid 4V 390 hp	TH a/t, A.I.R.
IS	427 cid 4V 390 hp	TH a/t
IH	427 cid 4V 390 hp	4-spd m/t
II	427 cid 4V 390 hp	4-spd m/t, A.I.R.
IX	427 cid 4V 390 hp	4-spd m/t, A.I.R
IE	427 cid 4V 390 hp	4-spd m/t
ID	427 cid 4V 425 hp	4-spd m/t
IK	427 cid 4V 425 hp	4-spd m/t, A.I.R
1967 Chevelle		
ED	396 cid 4V 325 hp	m/t
EH	396 cid 4V 325 hp	3- or 4-spd m/t, A.I.R.
ET	396 cid 4V 325 hp	TH a/t
EV	396 cid 4V 325 hp	TH a/t, A.I.R.
EK	396 cid 4V 325 hp	PG a/t
EM	396 cid 4V 325 hp	PG a/t, A.I.R.
EF	396 cid 4V 350 hp	4-spd m/t
EJ	396 cid 4V 350 hp	4-spd m/t, A.I.R.
EL	396 cid 4V 350 hp	PG a/t
EN	396 cid 4V 350 hp	PG a/t, A.I.R.
EU	396 cid 4V 350 hp	TH a/t
EW	396 cid 4V 350 hp	TH a/t, A.I.R.
EG	396 cid 4V 375 hp	4-spd m/t
EX	396 cid 4V 375 hp	4-spd m/t, A.I.R.
1967 Camaro		
MW	396 cid 4V 325 hp	m/t
MX	396 cid 4V 325 hp	3- or 4-spd m/t, A.I.R.
MY	396 cid 4V 325 hp	TH a/t
MZ	396 cid 4V 325 hp	TH a/t, A.I.R.
EI	396 cid 4V 350 hp	3- or 4-spd m/t
EY	396 cid 4V 350 hp	3- or 4-spd m/t, A.I.R.
EQ	396 cid 4V 350 hp	TH a/t
MQ	396 cid 4V 375 hp	4-spd m/t
MR	396 cid 4V 375 hp	4-spd m/t, A.I.R.
1968 Corvette		
IQ	427 cid 4V 390 hp	TH a/t
IL	427 cid 4V 390 hp	4-spd m/t
IO	427 cid 3x2V 400 hp	TH a/t
IM	427 cid 3x2V 400 hp	4-spd m/t
IT	427 cid 4V 430 hp	4-spd m/t
IR	427 cid 3x2V 435 hp	TH a/t
IU	427 cid 3x2V 435 hp	4-spd m/t

Suffix Code	Engine	Equipment
1968 Chevrolet		
IA	396 cid 4V 325 hp	m/t
IF	396 cid 4V 325 hp	m/t, h/d clutch, police
IK	396 cid 4V 325 hp	m/t, h/d clutch, police
IG, IN	396 cid 4V 325 hp	PG a/t
IV	396 cid 4V 325 hp	TH a/t
IE, IH	427 cid 4V 385 hp	m/t
IJ, IS	427 cid 4V 385 hp	TH a/t
IC	427 cid 4V 385 hp	m/t, police
IB	427 cid 4V 385 hp	TH a/t, police
ID	427 cid 4V 425 hp	4-spd m/t
1968 Chevy II		
MX	396 cid 4V 350 hp	3- or 4-spd m/t
MR	396 cid 4V 350 hp	TH a/t
MR	396 cid 4V 375 hp	4-spd m/t
1968 Chevelle		
ED	396 cid 4V 325 hp	3- or 4-spd m/t
EK	396 cid 4V 325 hp	PG a/t
ET	396 cid 4V 325 hp	TH a/t
EF	396 cid 4V 350 hp	3- or 4-spd m/t
EL	396 cid 4V 350 hp	PG a/t
EU	396 cid 4V 350 hp	TH a/t
EG	396 cid 4V 375 hp	4-spd m/t
1968 Camaro		
MW	396 cid 4V 325 hp	m/t or TH a/t
MY	396 cid 4V 325 hp	TH a/t
MX	396 cid 4V 350 hp	4-spd m/t
MR	396 cid 4V 350 hp	TH a/t
MQ	396 cid 4V 375 hp	4-spd m/t
MT	396 cid 4V 375 hp	4-spd m/t, aluminum heads
MV	427 cid 4V 425 hp	4-spd m/t, COPO
1968 C-10 Trucks		
XE	396 cid 4V 310 hp	m/t, A.I.R.
XF	396 cid 4V 310 hp	m/t
XG, XH	396 cid 4V 310 hp	3-spd m/t
XK	396 cid 4V 275 hp	m/t
XL, XM	396 cid 4V 275 hp	3-spd m/t
XN	396 cid 4V 275 hp	m/t
1968 C-20 Trucks		
XH	396 cid 4V 310 hp	3-spd m/t
XM	396 cid 4V 275 hp	3-spd m/t
XN	396 cid 4V 275 hp	m/t
1968 C-30 Trucks		
XF	396 cid 4V 310 hp	m/t
XN	396 cid 4V 275 hp	m/t
1969 Corvette		
LL	427 cid 4V 390 hp	TH a/t
MI	427 cid 4V 390 hp	TH a/t, TI
LM	427 cid 4V 390 hp	4-spd m/t
MH	427 cid 4V 390 hp	4-spd m/t, TI
LN	427 cid 3x2V 400 hp	TH a/t
MJ	427 cid 3x2V 400 hp	TH a/t, TI
LQ	427 cid 3x2V 400 hp	4-spd m/t
MK	427 cid 3x2V 400 hp	4-spd m/t, TI
MS	427 cid 4V 425 hp	4-spd m/t
LV	427 cid 4V 430 hp	TH a/t
LO	427 cid 4V 430 hp	4-spd m/t
MR	427 cid 4V 430 hp	4-spd m/t, TI
MG, ME	427 cid 4V 430 hp	4-spd m/t, ZL-1
LX	427 cid 3x2V 435 hp	TH a/t
LT	427 cid 3x2V 435 hp	4-spd m/t, h/d clutch
LR	427 cid 3x2V 435 hp	4-spd m/t
LW	427 cid 3x2V 435 hp	TH a/t, aluminum heads
LP, LU	427 cid 3x2V 435 hp	4-spd m/t, aluminum heads

Engine Suffix Codes

Suffix Code	Engine	Equipment
1969 Chevrolet		
JN	396 cid 4V 265 hp	m/t
JQ	396 cid 4V 265 hp	TH a/t
JP	396 cid 4V 265 hp	m/t
JO	396 cid 4V 265 hp	TH a/t
JR, JT	396 cid 4V 265 hp	m/t
LB	427 cid 4V 335 hp	m/t
LE	427 cid 4V 335 hp	TH a/t
LK	427 cid 4V 335 hp	m/t
LJ	427 cid 4V 335 hp	TH a/t
LY, MA	427 cid 4V 335 hp	m/t
LA	427 cid 4V 390 hp	3-spd m/t
LH	427 cid 4V 390 hp	4-spd m/t
MC	427 cid 4V 390 hp	4-spd m/t, h/d clutch
LG	427 cid 4V 390 hp	3-spd m/t, police
MB	427 cid 4V 390 hp	4spd m/t, h/d clutch
LC, LI	427 cid 4V 390 hp	TH a/t
LZ	427 cid 4V 390 hp	3-spd m/t, h/d clutch, police
LF	427 cid 4V 390 hp	TH a/t, police
LD	427 cid 4V 425 hp	4-spd m/t
MD	427 cid 4V 425 hp	4-spd m/t, h/d clutch
LS	427 cid 4V 425 hp	TH a/t
1969 Nova		
JI	396 cid 4V 350 hp	TH a/t
KF, JF	396 cid 4V 350 hp	m/t
KA	396 cid 4V 350 hp	m/t, h/d clutch
JL	396 cid 4V 375 hp	TH a/t
JH	396 cid 4V 375 hp	m/t
KC	396 cid 4V 375 hp	m/t, h/d clutch
1969 Chevelle		
JA	396 cid 4V 325 hp	m/t
JK	396 cid 4V 325 hp	TH a/t
JV	396 cid 4V 325 hp	m/t, h/d clutch
JC	396 cid 4V 350 hp	3- or 4-sp m/t
JE	396 cid 4V 350 hp	TH a/t
KB	396 cid 4V 350 hp	m/t, h/d clutch
JD	396 cid 4V 375 hp	4-spd m/t
KF	396 cid 4V 375 hp	TH a/t
KG	396 cid 4V 375 hp	4-spd m/t, aluminum heads
KH	396 cid 4V 375 hp	TH a/t, aluminum heads
KD	396 cid 4V 375 hp	m/t, h/d clutch
KI	396 cid 4V 375 hp	4-spd m/t, aluminum heads
CJA	402 cid 4V 325 hp	m/t
CJK	402 cid 4V 325 hp	TH a/t
CJV	402 cid 4V 325 hp	m/t, h/d clutch
CJC	402 cid 4V 350 hp	3- or 4-spd m/t
CJE	402 cid 4V 350 hp	TH a/t
CJD, CJF	402 cid 4V 375 hp	4-spd m/t
CKF	402 cid 4V 375 hp	TH a/t
MQ	427 cid 4V 425 hp	TH a/t, COPO 9562
MP	427 cid 4V 425 hp	4-spd m/t, COPO 9562
1969 Camaro		
JU	396 cid 4V 325 hp	m/t, h/d clutch
JB	396 cid 4V 325 hp	m/t
JG	396 cid 4V 325 hp	TH a/t
JF	396 cid 4V 350 hp	4-spd m/t
JI	396 cid 4V 350 hp	TH a/t
KA	396 cid 4V 350 hp	4-spd m/t
JH, KL	396 cid 4V 375 hp	4-spd m/t
KC	396 cid 4V 375 hp	4-spd m/t, h/d clutch
JJ	396 cid 4V 375 hp	4-spd m/t, aluminum heads
KE	396 cid 4V 375 hp	4-spd m/t, h/d clutch, aluminum heads
JL	396 cid 4V 375 hp	TH a/t
M	396 cid 4V 375 hp	TH a/t, aluminum heads
CJU	402 cid 4V 325 hp	m/t, h/d clutch
CJB	402 cid 4V 325 hp	m/t
CJG	402 cid 4V 325 hp	TH a/t
CJF	402 cid 4V 350 hp	4-spd m/t
CJI	402 cid 4V 350 hp	TH a/t
CJH	402 cid 4V 375 hp	4-spd m/t
CJL	402 cid 4V 375 hp	TH a/t
MO	427 cid 4V 425 hp	TH a/t, COPO 9561
MN	427 cid 4V 425 hp	4-spd m/t, COPO 9561
MM	427 cid 4V 430 hp	TH a/t, COPO 9560
ML	427 cid 4V 430 hp	4-spd m/t, COPO 9560
1969 C-10 Trucks		
YP, YQ	396 cid 4V 310 hp	TH a/t
YR	396 cid 4V 310 hp	m/t
1969 C-20 Trucks		
YP, YQ	396 cid 4V 310 hp	TH a/t
YR, YS	396 cid 4V 310 hp	m/t
1969 C-30 Trucks		
YP	396 cid 4V 310 hp	TH a/t, A.I.R.
YQ	396 cid 4V 310 hp	TH a/t
YR, YS	396 cid 4V 310 hp	m/t
1970 Corvette		
CGW	454 cid 4V 390 hp	TH
CRJ	454 cid 4V 390 hp	TH, TI
CZU	454 cid 4V 390 hp	4-spd m/t
CRI	454 cid 4V 390 hp	4-spd m/t, TI
CZN	454 cid 4V 465 hp	TH, aluminum heads, never produced
CZL	454 cid 4V 465 hp	4-spd m/t, aluminum heads, never produced
1970 Chevrolet		
CGS	454 cid 4V 345 hp	TH a/t, police, taxi
CGU	454 cid 4V 345 hp	TH a/t
CGT	454 cid 4V 390 hp	TH a/t, police, taxi
1970 Chevelle		
CKN, CKR, CKS	402 cid 4V 330 hp	4-spd m/t
CTX	402 cid 4V 350 hp	4-spd m/t
CTW	402 cid 4V 350 hp	TH a/t
CTZ	402 cid 4V 350 hp	4-spd m/t
CKO	402 cid 4V 375 hp	4-spd m/t
CTY	402 cid 4V 375 hp	TH a/t
CKT	402 cid 4V 375 hp	4-spd m/t, aluminum heads
CKP	402 cid 4V 375 hp	TH a/t, aluminum heads
CKQ	402 cid 4V 375 hp	4-spd m/t, h/d clutch
CKU	402 cid 4V 375 hp	4-spd m/t, aluminum heads
CRT, CRN	454 cid 4V 360 hp	4-spd m/t
CRQ	454 cid 4V 360 hp	TH a/t
CRV	454 cid 4V 450 hp	4-spd m/t
CRR	454 cid 4V 450 hp	TH a/t
CRS	454 cid 4V 450 hp	TH a/t, aluminum heads
1970 Nova		
CTX	402 cid 4V 350 hp	m/t
CTZ	402 cid 4V 350 hp	m/t, h/d clutch
CTW	402 cid 4V 350 hp	TH a/t
CKO	402 cid 4V 375 hp	m/t
CKQ	402 cid 4V 375 hp	m/t, h/d clutch
CTY	402 cid 4V 375 hp	TH 400 a/t

The top manifold, #3909880, is designed to fit 1967 Camaros while the bottom one, #3909879, fits a variety of 1967–70 applications.

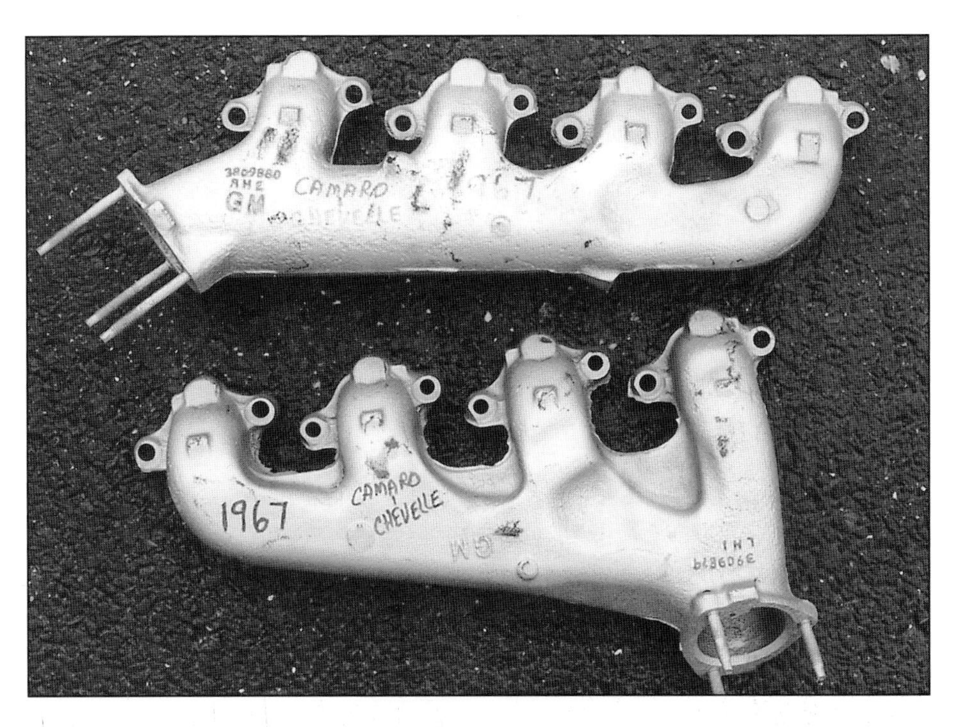

Suffix Code	Engine	Equipment
CKT	402 cid 4V 375 hp	m/t, aluminum heads
CKO	402 cid 4V 375 hp	m/t, h/d clutch
CKU	402 cid 4V 375 hp	m/t, h/d clutch, aluminum heads
1970 Camaro		
CTX	402 cid 4V 350 hp	4-spd m/t
CTW, CKO	402 cid 4V 350 hp	TH a/t
1970 Monte Carlo		
CKN, CKR, CKS	402 cid 4V 330 hp	4-spd m/t
CTX	402 cid 4V 350 hp	4-spd m/t
CTW	402 cid 4V 350 hp	TH a/t
CTZ	402 cid 4V 350 hp	4-spd m/t
CKO	402 cid 4V 375 hp	4-spd m/t
CTY	402 cid 4V 375 hp	TH a/t
CKT	402 cid 4V 375 hp	4-spd m/t, aluminum heads
CKP	402 cid 4V 375 hp	TH a/t, aluminum heads
CKQ	402 cid 4V 375 hp	4-spd m/t, h/d clutch
CKU	402 cid 4V 375 hp	4-spd m/t, aluminum heads
CRT, CRN	454 cid 4V 360 hp	4-spd m/t
CRQ	454 cid 4V 360 hp	TH a/t
1970 C-10 Trucks		
TBG	402 cid 4V 310 hp	TH a/t
TBH	402 cid 4V 310 hp	m/t
1970 C-20 Trucks		
TBH	402 cid 4V 310 hp	m/t
1970 C-30 Trucks		
TBG	402 cid 4V 310 hp	TH a/t
TBH	402 cid 4V 310 hp	m/t
1971 Corvette		
CPJ	454 cid 4V 365 hp	TH a/t
CPH	454 cid 4V 365 hp	m/t
CPX	454 cid 4V 425 hp	TH a/t, aluminum heads
CPW	454 cid 4V 425 hp	m/t, aluminum heads
1971 Chevrolet		
CLB	402 cid 4V 300 hp	TH a/t
CLR	402 cid 4V 300 hp	m/t
CLP	402 cid 4V 300 hp	TH a/t

Suffix Code	Engine	Equipment
CPG, CPD	454 cid 4V 365 hp	TH a/t
1971 Chevelle		
CLL	402 cid 4V 300 hp	m/t
CLS	402 cid 4V 300 hp	3-spd m/t, h/d
CLA	402 cid 4V 300 hp	m/t
CLB, CLP	402 cid 4V 300 hp	TH a/t
CLR	402 cid 4V 300 hp	m/t, police
CPA, CPG	454 cid 4V 365 hp	4-spd m/t
CPD	454 cid 4V 365 hp	TH a/t
CPP	454 cid 4V 425 hp	4-spd m/t
CPR, CPY, CPZ	454 cid 4V 425 hp	TH a/t
1971 Camaro		
CLA, CLB, CLC	402 cid 4V 300 hp	m/t
CLD	402 cid 4V 300 hp	TH a/t
1971 Monte Carlo		
CLL	402 cid 4V 300 hp	m/t
CLS	402 cid 4V 300 hp	3-spd m/t, h/d
CLA	402 cid 4V 300 hp	m/t
CLB, CLP	402 cid 4V 300 hp	TH a/t
CPA, CPG	454 cid 4V 365 hp	4-spd m/t
CPD	454 cid 4V 365 hp	TH a/t
1971 C-10 Trucks		
TKA	402 cid 4V 300 hp	m/t
TKB	402 cid 4V 300 hp	TH a/t
1971 C-20 Trucks		
TKA	402 cid 4V 300 hp	m/t
TKB	402 cid 4V 300 hp	TH a/t
1971 C-30 Trucks		
TKA	402 cid 4V 300 hp	m/t
TKB	402 cid 4V 300 hp	TH a/t
1972 Corvette		
CPJ	454 cid 4V 270 hp	TH a/t
CSS	454 cid 4V 270 hp	TH a/t, NB2
CPH	454 cid 4V 270 hp	m/t
CSR	454 cid 4V 270 hp	m/t, NB2
1972 Chevrolet		
CLR	402 cid 4V 210 hp	TH a/t, police
CTB	402 cid 4V 240 hp	TH a/t, A.I.R.
CTJ	402 cid 4V 240 hp	m/t, NB2, taxi, police

Engine Suffix Codes

Suffix Code	Engine	Equipment
CPD	454 cid 4V 270 hp	TH a/t, NB2
CRW	454 cid 4V 270 hp	TH a/t, A.I.R.
CRY	454 cid 4V 270 hp	TH a/t, taxi, police, A.I.R.
CPG	454 cid 4V 270 hp	TH a/t, police
1972 Chevelle		
CLA	402 cid 4V 240 hp	m/t
CLB	402 cid 4V 240 hp	TH a/t
CLS, CTA	402 cid 4V 240 hp	m/t
CTH	402 cid 4V 240 hp	3-spd m/t, h/d, A.I.R.
CTB	402 cid 4V 240 hp	TH a/t, A.I.R.
CTJ	402 cid 4V 240 hp	TH a/t, A.I.R., taxi, police
CPA	454 cid 4V 270 hp	m/t
CRX	454 cid 4V 270 hp	m/t, A.I.R.
CPD	454 cid 4V 270 hp	TH a/t
CRW	454 cid 4V 270 hp	TH a/t, A.I.R.
1972 Camaro		
CLA	402 cid 4V 240 hp	m/t
CTA	402 cid 4V 240 hp	m/t, A.I.R.
CLB	402 cid 4V 240 hp	TH a/t
CTB	402 cid 4V 240 hp	TH a/t, A.I.R.
1972 Monte Carlo		
CLA	402 cid 4V 240 hp	m/t
CLB	402 cid 4V 240 hp	TH a/t
CLS, CTA	402 cid 4V 240 hp	m/t
CTH	402 cid 4V 240 hp	3-spd m/t, h/d, A.I.R.
CTB	402 cid 4V 240 hp	TH a/t, A.I.R.
CPA	454 cid 4V 270 hp	m/t
CRX	454 cid 4V 270 hp	m/t, A.I.R.
CPD	454 cid 4V 270 hp	TH a/t
CRW	454 cid 4V 270 hp	TH a/t, A.I.R.

Suffix Code	Engine	Equipment
1972 C-10 Trucks		
TKA	402 cid 4V 210 hp	m/t
TKB	402 cid 4V 210 hp	TH a/t
TKM	402 cid 4V 210 hp	m/t
TLM	402 cid 4V 210 hp	TH a/t
1972 C-20 Trucks		
TKA	402 cid 4V 210 hp	m/t
TKB	402 cid 4V 210 hp	TH a/t
TKW	402 cid 4V 210 hp	m/t
TKX, TLM	402 cid 4V 210 hp	TH a/t
TKM	402 cid 4V 210 hp	m/t
1972 C-30 Trucks		
TKW	402 cid 4V 210 hp	m/t
TKX	402 cid 4V 210 hp	TH a/t
1973 Chevrolet		
CWD, CWL	454 cid 4V 215 hp	TH a/t
CWJ	454 cid 4V 215 hp	TH a/t, NB2, police
CWK	454 cid 4V 215 hp	TH a/t, police
CWD	454 cid 4V 245 hp	TH a/t, NB2
1973 Chevelle		
CWA	454 cid 4V 245 hp	4-spd m/t
CWC	454 cid 4V 245 hp	4-spd m/t, NB2
CWB	454 cid 4V 245 hp	TH a/t
CWD	454 cid 4V 245 hp	TH a/t, NB2
CWR	454 cid 4V 245 hp	m/t
1973 Monte Carlo		
CWA	454 cid 4V 245 hp	4-spd m/t
CWC	454 cid 4V 245 hp	4-spd m/t, NB2
CWB	454 cid 4V 245 hp	TH a/t
CWD	454 cid 4V 245 hp	TH a/t, NB2
CWR	454 cid 4V 245 hp	m/t

The first high-performance aluminum big-block intake manifold, #3866963, appeared on 1965 396 cid Corvette and Z-16 Chevelle applications. It accepts a Holley four-barrel carburetor.

Casting #3918852 fits the 1968 L71 Corvette engine. The three two-barrel setup is a good street system, as the engine runs primarily off of the smaller center carburetor. The larger outer carburetors kick in during full throttle acceleration.

Suffix Code	Engine	Equipment
1973 C-10 Trucks		
TRH	454 cid 4V 240 hp	TH400
TRL	454 cid 4V 240 hp	TH400, NB2
1973 C-20 Trucks		
TRA	454 cid 4V 240 hp	m/t, NB2
TRB	454 cid 4V 240 hp	TH400, NB2
TRH	454 cid 4V 240 hp	TH400
TRK	454 cid 4V 240 hp	TH400
TRL	454 cid 4V 240 hp	TH400, NB2
1973 C-30 Trucks		
TRA	454 cid 4V 240 hp	m/t, NB2
TRB	454 cid 4V 240 hp	TH400, NB2
TRJ	454 cid 4V 240 hp	m/t
TRK	454 cid 4V 240 hp	TH400
1974 Chevrolet		
CWU	454 cid 4V 235 hp	4-spd m/t
CWW	454 cid 4V 235 hp	TH a/t, police
CWY	454 cid 4V 235 hp	TH a/t, NB2, police
CXA	454 cid 4V 235 hp	TH a/t, NB2
CXB, CXU	454 cid 4V 235 hp	TH a/t
CXC	454 cid 4V 235 hp	TH a/t, NB2, police
CXT	454 cid 4V 235 hp	TH a/t, police
1974 Chevelle		
CWA	454 cid 4V 235 hp	4-spd m/t
CWD	454 cid 4V 235 hp	TH a/t, NB2
CWX	454 cid 4V 235 hp	TH a/t
CXM	454 cid 4V 235 hp	4-spd m/t
CXR	454 cid 4V 235 hp	TH a/t
CXS	454 cid 4V 235 hp	TH a/t, NB2
1974 Monte Carlo		
CWA	454 cid 4V 235 hp	4-spd m/t
CWD	454 cid 4V 235 hp	TH a/t, NB2
CWX, CXR	454 cid 4V 235 hp	TH a/t

Suffix Code	Engine	Equipment
CXM	454 cid 4V 235 hp	4-spd m/t
CXS	454 cid 4V 235 hp	TH a/t, NB2
1974 C-10 Trucks		
TRH	454 cid 4V 245 hp	TH400
TRL	454 cid 4V 245 hp	TH400, NB2
1974 C-20 Trucks		
TRJ, TRT	454 cid 4V 245 hp	m/t
TRW	454 cid 4V 245 hp	TH400
1974 C-30 Trucks		
TRJ	454 cid 4V 245 hp	m/t
TRW	454 cid 4V 245 hp	TH400
1975 Chevrolet		
CXX	454 cid 4V 215 hp	TH a/t, NB2
1975 Chevelle and Monte Carlo		
CXW	454 cid 4V 215 hp	TH a/t, NB2
1975 C-10 Trucks		
TRY	454 cid 4V 245 hp	exc. A.I.R., AT, A.I.R.
TSJ	454 cid 4V 245 hp	A.I.R.
TSM	454 cid 4V 245 hp	A.I.R., AT
TSK	454 cid 4V 245 hp	exc. NB2
TSL	454 cid 4V 245 hp	NB2
1975 C-20 Trucks		
TRZ	454 cid 4V 245 hp	m/t, NB2
TSA	454 cid 4V 245 hp	TH400, NB2
TSC	454 cid 4V 245 hp	m/t
TSD	454 cid 4V 245 hp	TH400
TSK	454 cid 4V 245 hp	exc. NB2
TSL	454 cid 4V 245 hp	NB2
1975 C-30 Trucks		
TRZ	454 cid 4V 245 hp	m/t, NB2
TSA	454 cid 4V 245 hp	TH400, NB2
TSC	454 cid 4V 245 hp	m/t
TSD	454 cid 4V 245 hp	TH400

CHAPTER 8

OLDSMOBILE

1949-1990

260, 303, 307, 324, 330, 350, 371, 394, 400, 403, 425 and 455

Nineteen forty-nine was an important year for automotive history. It was the year when Oldsmobile (and Cadillac) would both introduce ohv V-8 engines. The Oldsmobile Rocket V-8 engine had some interesting features that made the engine quite different from anything else offered in Detroit at the time. First, the engine's valves were located in the cylinder head, over the combustion chamber. The overhead valves were actuated by a camshaft that was located in the center of the engine, through a system of hydraulic lifters, pushrods, and shaft-mounted rocker arms. The Rocket V-8 also had an oversquare design with bore and stroke dimensions of 3.75x3.437 in.

The oversquare design meant less piston travel (and therefore less wear) when compared to the long-stroke flatheads. Another benefit of the new engine design was its capacity to use higher compression ratios; its better engine breathing through larger, more direct porting and valves; and a more efficient combustion chamber design. The designer of the engine, Charles Kettering, felt that the true potential of the engine wouldn't be realized until gasoline quality was good enough to allow 12:1 compression ratios. They did reach 10.5:1 by 1966.

The first Rocket V-8 displaced 303 cid, which was quite large for the time. It was rated at 135 hp with a 7.25:1 compression ratio. The engine was equipped with a single exhaust system and a two-barrel carburetor. The 135 hp engine would continue in this configuration through the 1951 model year. By 1953, a higher compression ratio had raised power to 150 and 165 hp. One unusual feature of the 303 cid engine was its main bearings. The first four had a 2.500 in. diameter; the fifth was larger, at 2.625 in.

In 1954, the Rocket V-8 was bored to 3.875 in. With the same stroke as the 303 cid engine it replaced, 3.437 in., it now displaced 324 cid. The 324 cid V-8 would be available through the 1956 model year, with a top horsepower rating of 240 hp on the four-barrel version in 1956. The 1956 324's cylinder heads had larger ports and valves as well.

The engine underwent another expansion in 1957. This time both bore and stroke were increased, as well as block deck height, to 4.00x3.688 in. for 371 cid. The 371's bottom end was modified as well. The crankshaft main-bearing journals were increased to 2.750 in., and all five main bearings were the same size. The engine was rated at 277 hp, but during the year a special version of the engine, code-named the J-2, was released. It featured a Tri-Power intake setup for 300 hp. The J-2 was also available in 1958, rated at 312 hp. The 371 cid engine, in two- and four-barrel form, was available through the 1960 model year.

Joining the 371 cid engine in 1959 was another bore and stroke combination of the Rocket V-8, 4.125x3.688 in. for 394 cid. There were also other internal changes to the engine, which were made on the 371 cid version as well. The crankshaft's main-bearing journals were increased again, this time to 3.000 in., and the rod journals were also bigger, at 2.500 in. In addition, the number of attaching bolts used on the cylinder head was increased from 18 to 22. In 1959, the 394 cid engine was rated at 315 hp; it would reach 345 hp by 1964, its last year of production.

Nineteen sixty-four marked the beginning of the "modern" era for the Oldsmobile V-8 engines, with the introduction of a new engine, the 330 cid small-block. The engine was still based on the same basic block casting, but there were many differences that make interchangeability between the older engines a moot point. These changes wouldn't all be in place until 1965, when the older 394 cid engine was finally replaced by the new 400 and 425 cid versions.

The modern-era Oldsmobile V-8 engines consisted of small-block and big-block engines. They weren't small- and big-block engines in the same sense as the Ford 289 cid V-8 was a small-block when compared to the Ford 428 cid V-8, but rather the terms were used to differentiate between smaller and larger displacement Oldsmobile engines. Both big- and small-block Oldsmobile engines looked the same at a casual glance. The big-blocks, though, were wider and taller. Small-block engines—those with a 260, 307, 330, 350, and 403 cid displacement, and produced from 1964 to 1990—had a block deck height of 9.33 in. Big-block engines—those with 400, 425, and 455 cid displacements produced from 1965 to 1976—had a taller deck height of 10.625 in.

There were also internal differences. Cylinder head port spacing and configuration was similar to the older engines, except that the cylinder heads used 10 bolts to attach them to the block. The intake manifold now sealed the lifter valley area (the older engines used a separate valley cover). Beginning in 1965, all Oldsmobile engines switched to stamped-steel rocker arms, which were oiled via tubular pushrods. Previous engines used shaft-mounted rockers. The small-block engines also had smaller rod and main-bearing specifications: 2.123 in./2.498 in.

Nineteen sixty-four was a transition year for the Rocket V-8. The 394 cid V-8s were available in 280-, 330-, and 345 hp variations, while the new 330 cid small-block could be had in 210- and 230 hp ratings with a two-barrel carburetor; a four-barrel was rated at 290 hp. A 310 hp version of the engine was introduced midyear for the new Cutlass 442.

Nineteen sixty-five saw the continuance of the 330 cid engine. The two-barrel version was rated at 250 hp, while a higher compression version of the same engine, 10.25:1 vs. 9.0:1, was rated at 260 hp. The four-barrel was rated at 315 hp.

Because the 394 cid engine was no longer available, two new big-blocks were introduced in 1965. The 400 cid engine, with a 4.00 in. bore and 3.975 in. stroke, was rated at 345 hp, and it was used exclusively on the 442 optioned Cutlass model. The larger 425 cid engine, with its 4.126 in. bore and 3.975 in. stroke, was available in 300 and 310 hp versions with a two-barrel carburetor, and in 360 and 370 hp versions with a four-barrel carburetor.

Five versions of the 330 cid small-block were available in 1966, rated from 250 to 320 hp. There were two version of the 442 400 cid engine—the four-barrel version was rated at 350 hp, while a Tri-Power version was rated at 360 hp. The Tri-Power engine was available only for 1966. The big 425 cid big-block was rated between 300 and 385 hp. The 385 hp version was used to power the new Toronado, and it was appropriately called the "Toronado Rocket."

Engine availability was the same for 1967. The exception was the withdrawal of the L69 400 cid Tri-Power engine and the addition of a 400 cid two-barrel Turnpike Cruiser engine for the 442. W-30 optioned 442 model engines had a functional ram-air system or "forced air," as Oldsmobile referred to it, and a more radical, hydraulic-lifter camshaft.

In 1968, the 330 cid engine was dropped and replaced by a bored version of the small-block V-8. Its larger, 4.057 in. bore and the same 3.385 in. stroke resulted in a 350 cid displacement. It was available in three flavors—250 hp, 310 hp, and as the Ram Rod 350, which put out 325 hp. The Ram Rod was part of the W-31 option package on the Cutlass, and the engine featured larger valves and hotter camshaft, over and above the regular four-barrel 350 cid engine.

The 400 cid big-block was still available in 1968, in 290–360 hp versions. The top dog Oldsmobile engine in 1968 was the new 455 cid Rocket V-8. With a bore of 4.126 in. and a stroke of 4.25 in., it was an undersquare engine, but it certainly generated a lot of torque. The most significant application of the engine was on the limited production Hurst/Olds, which was based on the 442. The 390 hp 455 cid Rocket V-8 was the largest in any American intermediate, and it wouldn't be until 1970 that Chevrolet, Buick, and Pontiac brought out similar-sized engines.

The basic Oldsmobile cylinder block design originated in 1949. All blocks were made with two-bolt main bearing caps. This is a late 1980s version. Configuration is the same as blocks produced in the 1960s and 1970s; however, the late blocks were lighter. Note thin oil pan railing and main bearing web area.

With minor rating changes, the 1968 engine lineup was essentially carried over for the 1969 model year. The 1970 engine lineup showed that the 400 cid V-8 had been dropped. Engine availability was limited to three 350 cid engines rated at 250-, 310-, and 325 hp. There were seven editions of the big 455 cid big-block, 310-, 320-, 365-, 370-, 375-, 390-, and 400 hp.

Nineteen seventy-one was the year that most American manufacturers detuned their engines to meet the beginning of increasingly stricter emission standards. Oldsmobile was no exception. The compression ratio was dropped to 8.5:1 across the board, which also reduced power output. The two Rocket 350 V-8s were rated at 240- and 260 hp, while the big 455s were rated at 280-, 320-, 340-, and 350 hp. These were all gross ratings (Oldsmobile rated the engines using the more realistic SAE net method, and that lowered horsepower even more). The reality, though, was that most of the power figures issued by Detroit manufacturers during the 1950s and 1960s, especially on the high-performance engines, were pretty suspect anyway.

Nineteen seventy-two saw further erosion in power output. The two 350 cid Rocket V-8s were rated at 160- and 180 hp; the Rocket 455 was available in 225-, 250-, 270-, and 300 hp ratings.

From 1972 on, these two engines would lose any of the high-performance capabilities they had, at least in the 1960s context. The 455 cid V-8 would finally be dropped in 1976; the 350 cid engine would continue on until 1985, and it would end up being used by other GM divisions. It would also be converted to a diesel in 1977.

A 260 cid variation of the small-block was introduced in 1975. The engine had a bore and stroke of 3.50x3.385 in., which amounted to a debored 350. It was rated at 110 hp.

A 307 cid variation was available from 1980 to 1990 and at the other end of the scale, a larger small-block, displacing 403 cid, was introduced in 1976. It had the largest bore of any Oldsmobile V-8 engine, 4.351 in. and a stroke of 3.385 in. It put out 185 hp and the engine lasted through the 1979 model year.

260 cid

The 260 cid Olds V-8 was a smog-era engine. It had a bore and stroke of 3.50x3.385 in. and used a hydraulic camshaft, cast-iron crankshaft, small-port and small-valve cylinder heads, forged-steel connecting rods, cast-aluminum pistons, and cast-iron intake (later engines had aluminum intakes) and exhaust manifolds. It was rated at 110 hp in 1975, and the engine remained in production until 1981.

There was also a 260 cid diesel version of the engine, available from 1979 to 81. It was rated at 90 hp.

303 cid

The first Rocket V-8 of 1949 had a bore and stroke of 3.75x3.437 in. and displaced 303 cid. It used a forged-steel crankshaft, forged-steel connecting rods, cast-aluminum pistons, a two-barrel cast-iron intake manifold, and cast-iron exhaust manifolds. The ohv cylinder heads featured wedge combustion chambers, and the valves themselves measured 1.75 in. intake and 1.4375 in. exhaust. An unusual feature of the engine was that the crankshaft's main-bearing journals measured 2.5000 in. on the first four positions and 2.625 in. at the number five position. The 1949 Rocket V-8 was rated at 135 hp, and the engine was in service through the 1953 model year.

307 cid

The 307 cid Oldsmobile engine was introduced in 1980. It had a bore and stroke of 3.800x3.385 in. and had all the low-performance internal components that one would expect—cast pistons,

The casting number on 1965 and later blocks can be found on the front of the engine on this pad. The 1980s blocks also included a designation showing the engine size in liters, such as 5.0L on this block.

crankshaft, small ports and valves, single exhaust system, and so forth, but it did come with a four-barrel intake manifold and carburetor. The engine got hydraulic roller lifters in 1985.

324 cid

The 324 cid configuration of the Rocket V-8 was introduced in 1954 and was in service through the 1956 model year. It had a bore and stroke of 3.875x3.437 in. and was similar to the 303 cid Rocket, except in displacement. In the years it was in service, the engine was available in two power outputs—with either a two-barrel or four-barrel carburetor. The 1956 engine got cylinder heads with larger valves and larger ports.

330 cid

This was the first "small-block" Oldsmobile V-8, introduced in 1964. It was also the first expression of the revamped V-8 Oldsmobile engine, and it featured many improvements over the previous Rocket V-8s, including redesigned cylinder heads. The V-8 had a bore and stroke of 3.398x3.385 in. and a forged-steel crankshaft. Because of its lower, 9.330 in. deck height, the 330 cid Rocket was considered a small-block. The highest output 330 cid Rocket was the one used on the 1965 442 Cutlass. With a four-barrel carburetor and a stronger hydraulic camshaft, it was rated at 315 hp.

The 1964–1965 engines generally used shaft-mounted rocker arms; 1966–1967 engines got stamped-steel rocker arms with bridged pivots, which were oiled through the tubular pushrods.

350 cid

The 350 cid small-block engine was introduced in 1968. It had a bore and stroke of 4.057x3.385 in. Initially, the 350 cid V-8 was used, in various configurations, as the optional V-8 engine on the Oldsmobile intermediates. Later, it was also used on the full-size cars, as the small standard V-8. In the 1970s, the 350 became one of the "big" engines. The hot version of the 350 cid V-8 was the one used on the 1968–1970 W-31 option package. It was called the Ram Rod 350 in 1968, and with its four-barrel carburetor, higher performance hydraulic-lifter camshaft, larger valve cylinder heads, and forced-air induction, it was rated at 325 hp.

The output of the engine, like that of all other Oldsmobile engines, gradually declined through the 1970s.

The Oldsmobile 350 cid V-8 also had the honor of being the first GM engine, along with the Cadillac 500 cid V-8, to use a modern computer-controlled EFI system. The EFI engine was used in Cadillac automobiles. The system used a two-barrel throttle body on a cast-iron intake manifold, which was a modified two-barrel carburetor intake, along with eight fuel injectors. The injectors would inject fuel in two groups, first the numbers 1, 2, 7, and 8 cylinders, and then the numbers 3, 4, 5, and 6 cylinders. The engine was rated at a mild 180 hp.

The Oldsmobile 350 was also chosen for conversion to diesel specifications. The engine was introduced in 1977 and initially proved unreliable. Unfortunately, by the time GM got around to fixing the problems, the diesel's reputation couldn't have been worse. The early production engines were almost guaranteed to fail. Most of the 350 diesels were rated at 120 hp.

371 cid

The 1957 371 cid configuration was the second displacement increase for the Rocket V-8. It was basically a bored and stroked 371 cid engine, as it had 4.00x3.688 in. dimensions. It had all the usual Rocket V-8 features: two-bolt-main engine block, forged-steel crankshaft and connecting rods, cast-iron manifolds, and a hydraulic-lifter camshaft.

The most interesting version of the engine was the so-called J-2. The J-2 was introduced in 1957 and its claim to fame was its Tri-Power intake system. The engine was rated at 300 hp in 1957 and 312 hp in 1958.

394 cid

This was the largest displacement of the original Rocket V-8, with its bore and stroke of 4.125x3.688 in. Besides redesigned cylinder heads, the engine also used a larger journal crankshaft, with mains measuring 3.000 in. and rods 2.500 in. It was available in two- and four-barrel versions, and the highest output rating on the engine, 345 hp, was available from 1962 to 1964.

400 cid

This was the first of the new big-block Oldsmobile engines introduced in 1965. The 400 cid V-8 had a bore and stroke 4.00x3.975 in. The engine was considered a big-block because it had a taller deck height than the small-block Oldsmobile engines, 10.625 in. vs. 9.330 in. This made the 400 cid Rocket and other big-blocks 2 in. wider. The 400 cid configuration was used exclusively on the 1965–1967 Cutlass with the 442 option package, the 1968–1969 442 model, and on the 1968–1969 Vista-Cruiser station wagons. The engines used at this time were generally similar, with detail differences. The 1965–1967 engines were equipped with forged-steel crankshafts; 1968–1969 engines generally came with a cast crankshaft. Although all engines no longer used shaft-mounted rockers, there are differences between the 1965–1966 engines and the later ones (see Cylinder Head section). With the exception of the Turnpike Cruiser 442 engine, which was fitted with a two-barrel carburetor, and the 360 hp Tri-Power, all other 400 cid Rockets were equipped with a four-barrel carburetor. The regular 400 cid engines got cylinder heads with 2.00 in./1.625 in. intake/exhaust valves; 400 cid engines that were part of the W-30 package got larger 2.07 in. intake valves and a higher performance hydraulic camshaft.

403 cid

The 403 cid V-8 was introduced in 1976. In spite of its large displacement, the engine used the low block, so it was considered a small-block engine. It wasn't much of a high-performance engine, as most were rated at 185 hp. The 403 got a cast-iron crankshaft, a lightened engine block, cast-iron manifolds, and a hydraulic camshaft. The engine was used on other GM division cars, including on Pontiac's Trans Am.

425 cid

This engine replaced the 394 cid engine on Oldsmobile's full-size cars during 1965–1967. It had a 4.125 in. bore and 3.975 in. stroke.

The engine followed a configuration similar to that of the 400 cid engine. All used a forged-steel crankshaft, a four-barrel carburetor, cast-iron exhaust and intake manifolds, and a hydraulic-lifter camshaft. The Toronado engines were set up to produce more power; they had cylinder heads with larger intake valves, 2.07 in. vs. 2.00 in.

455 cid

The largest displacement Rocket V-8 was introduced in 1968 when the big block's stroke was increased to 4.25 in., with the bore remaining at 4.126 in. This big motor was known for its torque producing capabilities, which made it an excellent street engine. A small, undetermined number were produced with forged-steel crankshafts; otherwise the 455s had cast-iron or nodular iron crankshafts. Connecting rods were forged steel, and pistons were cast aluminum. Most of the engines were also equipped with a cast-iron four-barrel intake manifold. The exception was the 1970–1972 W-30 optioned cars, which had aluminum intake manifolds.

The 455 cid Rocket was the powerplant of choice for Oldsmobile's 1968–1969 big cars; Hurst used a 390 hp (1968) and 380 hp (1969) version of the engine on the Hurst/Olds. In 1970, the 455 cid engine was the standard 442 engine, as the 400 cid engine had been dropped.

The higher output versions of the engine had larger intake valves (2.07 in. vs. 2.00 in.), as well as several bottom-end modifications, such as a windage tray. The engine was dropped after the 1976 model year.

Engine Blocks

There have been quite a few engine blocks used over the years on the Rocket V-8. All Oldsmobile engine blocks were made from cast iron, with 4.625 in. bore centers, and all used two-bolt main-bearing caps. Some can be differentiated from others, especially the early blocks, by the size of their main-bearing journals, head bolt configuration, deck height size, and hydraulic-lifter angle and lifter diameter. Of course, bore size also helps identify them. The 303- and 324 cid blocks had a 2.500 in. main-bearing journal, except for the fifth journal, which measured 2.625 in. All 1957–1958 371 cid blocks had 2.750 in. diameter journals, and all five journals were this size. The 1956 and later blocks also had a taller deck height.

The main-bearing journals on 1959–1964 371- and 394 cid blocks were increased to 3.000 in., and because the cylinder heads were different, there were 22 bolts used to attach the cylinder heads to the block.

Starting in 1964, the engine series was divided into small and big blocks. The "big block" description was used on the 400-, 425-, and 455 cid engines, which used a taller engine block, with a deck height measuring 10.625 in. vs. 9.330 in. on the small-block engines. Ten 7/16 in. head bolts held the cylinder head down on the small-blocks; 1/2 in. bolts were used on the big-blocks. The 1977–1979 350-350 Diesel-403 cid engines also were equipped with the 1/2 in. bolts.

The 1965–1967 blocks also have different lifter diameters and cam bank angles. The 1965 400 cid blocks and 1965–1966 425 cid blocks (except those used on the 1966 Toronado) have a 45-degree cam bank angle (that is, the angle that the lifter bores have in relation to the camshaft). All other engines have a 39-degree angle. The 1966–1967 400 cid engines and 425 cid Toronado engines use larger, 0.921 in. diameter lifters. All other engines use 0.842 in. diameter lifters.

Most small-block engine blocks dating from 1977 on, except for the diesel block, have much lighter "windowed" bulkheads to support the main caps.

Cylinder Heads

Again, there has been quite a variation of cylinder heads for the Oldsmobile V-8, and these should be divided into two sets—1949–1964 cylinder heads and 1964–later.

The early cylinder heads used shaft-mounted rocker arms to open and close the valves. The intake ports were rectangular. The two outer exhaust ports were round, and the center two ports merged into one large oval outlet. Valve sizes on the 1949–1955 engines measured 1.75 in./1.4375 in. intake/exhaust. Nineteen fifty-six and later cylinder heads had larger intake ports and valves of 1.875 in./1.562 in. intake/exhaust. As mentioned in the Block section, 1959–1964 cylinder heads used 22 mounting bolts.

In 1964, the cylinder heads were redesigned. Port configuration was similar to the older heads in that the intakes were still rectangular, but the exhaust ports, while still in the same position, were also rectangular. There was also a recessed divider in the center two ports, whose length varied on some of the high-performance applications. Generally, the divider was the cause of a horsepower decrease on all engines because it did not extend all the way to the port flange.

Intake port size also varied. Big-block cylinder heads had taller and wider intake ports, about 3/8 in. bigger when compared to the 330-, 350-, 403 cid small-block cylinder heads. The 260- and later 307- and 350 cid cylinder heads had even smaller ports.

Valve sizes also varied. The regular production 330- and 350 cid engines got 1.875 in./1.562 in. intake/exhaust valves. The performance W-31 350 cid engines had 1.995 in./1.625 in. intake/exhaust valves. Big-block valve sizes were 2.00 in./1.625 in. intake/exhaust, but high-performance and higher output variants had 2.072 in. intake valves.

Valve actuation also changed with the 1964 and later engines. Instead of rocker shafts, all Oldsmobile engines used stamped-steel fulcrum-type rocker arms. With the exception of some 1965 400–425 cid heads that used a three-piece design similar to Chevrolet's small-block rocker setup, the rockers were paired and held in place by an aluminum or steel bridge.

Intake Manifolds

There hasn't been a great variety of Oldsmobile intake systems. They used either two- or four-barrel cast-iron intake manifolds, with several exceptions. The 1957 J-2 engine used a Tri-Power system, as did the 1966 L69 400 cid engine. Nineteen sixty-five and later four-barrel intake manifolds were all designed to accept the Rochester Quadrajet carburetor. The only exceptions are the 1965 400–425 cid big-blocks, which used a Carter AFB carburetor. There were several high-performance aluminum intake manifolds. The 1970–1972 W-30 455 cid engines had them, as did the 1970 W-31 350 cid engines. Oldsmobile started to use aluminum on the 260-, 307-, and 350 cid engine intake manifolds in the late 1970s in order to save weight. These aren't considered to be performance manifolds.

Exhaust Manifolds

The Rocket V-8 engines were equipped with both single and dual exhaust systems. The exhaust manifolds were made of cast iron and differed in terms of outlet size and direction, depending on application. Toronado exhaust manifolds were made specifically for the Toronado and therefore do not readily interchange with other applications. The same is generally true with 1965 and later big- and small-block engines. The 1969–1972 exhaust manifolds have an exhaust divider in the center port, which improves output; 1967 and earlier engines do not have a divider.

Engine Identification

The Oldsmobile part identification system included casting numbers and date codes that indicated when a part was cast or manufactured. All 1949–1964 engine blocks had their casting number located on the right rear side of the block. All 1965 and later blocks had the casting number located on the horizontal shelf behind the water pump, to the left of the oil fill tube. Besides the casting number, there was a large letter or a number code in front of the casting number. The letter or number code was about 1-1/2 in. tall. A letter indicated a big-block engine, while a number indicated a small-block. There was also a one- to three-digit number on the block near the distributor. This number indicated the day of the year the block was cast, 1–365.

Casting numbers were also used on cylinder heads and intake and exhaust manifolds. Pre-1964 cylinder heads usually had the casting number under the valve cover area. Location varied on early intake and exhaust manifolds. The large letter or number code system was also used on cylinder heads and manifolds on the later engines. Late heads usually had a six-digit casting number located around the middle valve cover bolt, three digits on either side, so that the casting number was visible with the valve cover in place. Some heads had the number under the valve cover area, too. The last three digits of the casting number were also repeated on the underside of the head.

Late exhaust manifolds usually had the casting number in the center area, with the large letter or number code over the front exhaust port and sometimes over the rear port. All 1968–1972 exhaust manifolds also had a divider in the center two ports (which improved flow). Intake manifolds usually had the casting number on top of the manifold on one of the intake runners.

There was also additional information used on engines, which was typically stamped, rather than cast. This usually included an assembly date code (meaning when the engine was put together), a production sequence number (which was, in effect, a serial number for the engine), and depending on the year, the vehicle's VIN. The vehicle's VIN is especially important from a collector's point of view, as it served to connect a particular engine with a specific vehicle. From 1968 on, Oldsmobile included a portion of the vehicle's VIN on the engine.

Engines from 1949 to 1957 had a production sequence number stamped on the left side of the block on a pad. It did not identify the engine. From 1958 to 1964, the engine number was stamped on the cylinder head, over the left center exhaust port. Small-block engines from 1961 to 1967 had their number stamped on a pad in front of the right cylinder head.

Beginning in 1958, Oldsmobile started to stamp a prefix in front of the production number. The prefix identified the engine. Some engines also used a suffix at the end of the production number. All of these are listed here. Let's take a look at an example: X001005 stands for the fifth 1966 260 hp 330 cid V-8. X001001L stands for the fifth 1966 250 hp 330 cid V-8.

Oldsmobile switched to a more informative numbering system in 1968. The information was stamped on a vertical pad on the left front side of the block, where the cylinder head meets the block. A typical number is 39M156781. It can be decoded as follows: 3 = Oldsmobile, 9 = model year (1969), M = plant code, 156781 = the last six digits of the vehicle's VIN.

The engine production number was still used, but it, too, was changed somewhat. Its location was moved to the oil fill tube, and the first digit of the number was the last number of the model year. There were no prefixes or suffixes. Instead, a decal, with a two-letter engine code, also listed here, was placed on the oil fill tube.

Listed here are Oldsmobile engine numbers and codes. The numbers shown for 1949–1958 are the starting engine numbers. From 1959 through 1967, only the prefix and suffix letters are listed. From 1968–1975, the engine codes are listed.

Engine Production Sequence Numbers and Codes

Code	Engine	Notes
1949		
8A1001 and up	303 cid	
1950		
A-194001 and up	303 cid	an added H indicates a/t
1951		
8C-1001 and up	303 cid	an added B indicates m/t
1952		
R-1001 and up	303 cid	
1953		
R-215001 and up	303 cid	
1954		
V-1001 and up	324.3 cid	
1955		
V-400001 and up	324.3 cid	
1956		
V-1000001 and up	324.3 cid	
1957		
A-001001 and up	371 cid	
1958		
B-001001 and up	371 cid	
1959		
C	371 cid	
D	394 cid	
1960		
CE	371	export
C	371 cid 240 hp	Dynamic 88
CH	371 cid 260 hp	Dynamic 88
DE	394	export
D	394 cid 315 hp	Super 88, 98
DE	394	export
1961		
F	394 cid 250 hp	
G	394 cid 275/325/330 hp	
1962		
FE	394 cid	export
FL	394 cid 260 hp	
F	394 cid 280 hp	
G	394 cid 330 hp	
GS	394 cid 345 hp	
1963		
HE	394 cid	export
HL	394 cid 260 hp	
H	394 cid 280 hp	
J	394 cid 330 hp	
JS	394 cid 345 hp	
1964		
TH	330 cid	export
TE	330 cid	export
T	330 cid 230 hp	
TK	330 cid 245 hp	
HE	394 cid	export
HL	394 cid 260 hp	
H	394 cid 280 hp	
J	394 cid 330 hp	
JS	394 cid 345 hp	
1965		
TE	330 cid	export
UE	330 cid	export
UH	330 cid	export
T	330 cid 250 hp	F-85, Cutlass
UL	330 cid 250 hp	Jetstar 88
U	330 cid 260 hp	Jetstar 88
TG	330 cid 315 hp	F-85, Cutlass
UG	330 cid 315 hp	Jetstar 88
V	400 cid 345 hp	442
ME	425 cid	export
NE	425 cid	export
ML	425 cid 300 hp	

Date code on late Oldsmobile cylinder blocks is located near the distributor.

Code	Engine	Notes
M	425 cid 310 hp	
N	425 cid 360 hp	
NS	425 cid 370 hp	
1966		
WE	330 cid	export
UE	330 cid	export
XE	330 cid	export
XH	330 cid	export
WH	330 cid	export
W	330 cid 250 hp	F-85, Cutlass
WL	330 cid 310 hp	F-85, Cutlass
WG	330 cid 320 hp	F-85, Cutlass
XL	330 cid 250 hp	Jetstar 88
X	330 cid 260 hp	Jetstar 88
V	400 cid 350/360 hp	442
ME	425 cid	export
NE	425 cid	export
ML	425 cid 300 hp	
M	425 cid 310 hp	
N	425 cid 365 hp	
NS	425 cid 375 hp	
NT	425 cid 385 hp	
1967		
WE	330 cid 250 hp	F-85, Cutlass, Vista Cruiser
W	330 cid 260 hp	F-85, Cutlass, Vista Cruiser
WG	330 cid 320 hp	F-85, Cutlass
XE	330 cid 250 hp	Delmont 88
X	330 cid 260 hp	Delmont 88
XG	330 cid 320 hp	Delmont 88
V	400 cid 350 hp	442
PE	425 cid	export
RE	425 cid	export
PL	425 cid 300 hp	
P	425 cid 310 hp	

Code	Engine	Notes
R	425 cid 365 hp	
RS	425 cid 375 hp	
RT	425 cid 385 hp	
1968		
QK	350 cid	m/t, export
QC	350 cid	a/t, export
QY	350 cid	m/t, export
QO	350 cid	a/t, export
QI	350 cid 250 hp	m/t
QA	350 cid 250 hp	a/t
QB	350 cid 250 hp	a/t, a/c
TL	350 cid 250 hp	m/t, Delmont 88
TB	350 cid 250 hp	a/t, Delmont 88
TD	350 cid 250 hp	a/t, Delmont 88
TN	350 cid 310 hp	a/t, Delmont 88
QV	350 cid 310 hp	m/t
QN	350 cid 310 hp	a/t
QP	350 cid 310 hp	a/t, a/c
QX	350 cid 325 hp	m/t, W31
QL	400 cid 290 hp	a/t
QR	400 cid 325 hp	a/t
QS	400 cid 325 hp	a/t, a/c
QW	400 cid 350 hp	m/t
QU	400 cid 360 hp	m/t, W30
QT	400 cid 360 hp	a/t, W30
UJ	455 cid 310 hp	m/t
UC	455 cid 310 hp	a/t
UD	455 cid 310 hp	a/t
UA	455 cid 320 hp	a/t
UB	455 cid 320 hp	a/t
UN	455 cid 365 hp	a/t
UO	455 cid 365 hp	a/t
US	455 cid 375 hp	a/t
UT	455 cid 375 hp	a/t
UV	455 cid 375 hp	a/t
QE	455 cid 390 hp	a/t, Hurst/Olds

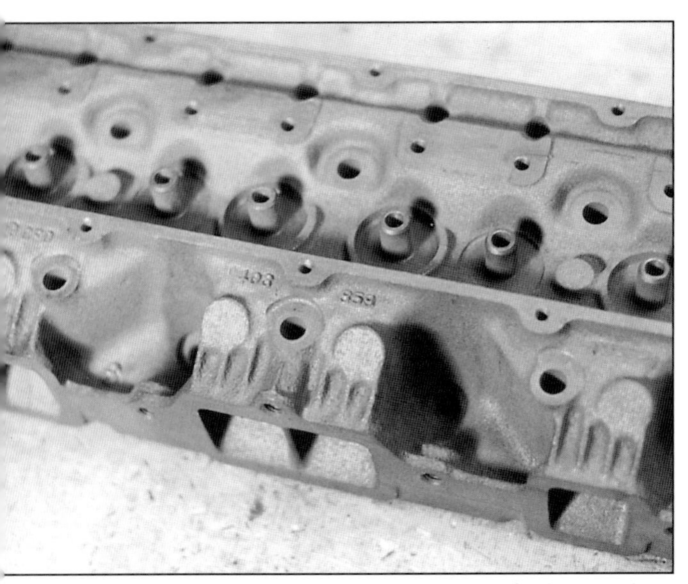

The cylinder head casting number can be found on top of both center exhaust ports on 1965 and later Oldsmobile heads.

Engine Production Sequence Numbers and Codes

Code	Engine	Notes
UW	455 cid 400 hp	a/t
1969		
QK	350 cid	m/t, export
QC	350 cid	a/t, export
QY	350 cid	m/t, export
QO	350 cid	a/t, export
QI	350 cid 250 hp	m/t
QA	350 cid 250 hp	a/t
QB	350 cid 250 hp	a/t, a/c
QJ	350 cid 250 hp	a/t, a/c
TL	350 cid 250 hp	m/t
TB	350 cid 250 hp	a/t
TD	350 cid 250 hp	a/t
QV	350 cid 310 hp	m/t
QN	350 cid 310 hp	a/t
QP	350 cid 310 hp	a/t, a/c
QX	350 cid 325 hp	m/t, W31
QD	350 cid 325 hp	a/t, W31
QR	400 cid 325 hp	a/t
QS	400 cid 325 hp	a/t, a/c
QW	400 cid 350 hp	m/t
QL	400 cid 350 hp	a/t, W32
QU	400 cid 360 hp	m/t, W30
QT	400 cid 360 hp	a/t, W30
UJ	455 cid 310 hp	m/t
UC	455 cid 310 hp	a/t
UD	455 cid 310 hp	a/t
UA	455 cid 320 hp	a/t
UB	455 cid 320 hp	a/t
UN	455 cid 365 hp	a/t
UO	455 cid 365 hp	a/t
US	455 cid 375 hp	a/t
UT	455 cid 375 hp	a/t
UV	455 cid 375 hp	a/t
UW	455 cid 375 hp	a/t
QE	455 cid 380 hp	a/t, Hurst/Olds
1970		
QA	350 cid 250 hp	a/t
QI	350 cid 250 hp	m/t
QJ	350 cid 250 hp	a/t
TC	350 cid 250 hp	a/t
TD	350 cid 250 hp	a/t
TL	350 cid 250 hp	m/t
QV	350 cid 310 hp	m/t
QN	350 cid 310 hp	a/t
QP	350 cid 310 hp	a/t, a/c
QX	350 cid 325 hp	m/t
QD	350 cid 325 hp	a/t
TY	455 cid 320 hp	a/t
TX	455 cid 320 hp	a/t, a/c
TU	455 cid 365 hp	m/t
TW	455 cid 365 hp	a/t
TV	455 cid 365 hp	a/t, a/c
TS	455 cid 370 hp	m/t, W30
TT	455 cid 370 hp	a/t, W30
US	455 cid 375 hp	a/t
UL	455 cid 390 hp	a/t
UV	455 cid 400 hp	a/t
UW	455 cid 400 hp	a/t
1971		
QI	350 cid 240 hp	m/t
QA	350 cid 240 hp	a/t
QJ	350 cid 240 hp	a/t, a/c
TC	350 cid 240 hp	a/t
TD	350 cid 240 hp	a/t
TE	350 cid 240 hp	m/t
QB	350 cid 260 hp	m/t
QO	350 cid 260 hp	m/t
QN	350 cid 260 hp	a/t
QP	350 cid 260 hp	a/t, a/c
TY	455 cid 280 hp	a/t
TX	455 cid 280 hp	a/t, a/c
UC	455 cid 280 hp	a/t
UD	455 cid 280 hp	a/t
UE	455 cid 280 hp	m/t
TQ	455 cid 320 hp	a/t
TP	455 cid 320 hp	a/t, a/c
TW	455 cid 320 hp	a/t
TV	455 cid 320 hp	a/t
UN	455 cid 320 hp	a/t
UO	455 cid 320 hp	a/t
TU	455 cid 340 hp	m/t
TA	455 cid 340 hp	m/t
TN	455 cid 340 hp	m/t, h/d clutch
TW	455 cid 340 hp	a/t
TV	455 cid 340 hp	a/t, a/c
TS	455 cid 350 hp	m/t, W30
TB	455 cid 350 hp	m/t, W30, h/d clutch
TT	455 cid 350 hp	a/t, W30
TT	455 cid 350 hp	a/t, W30, a/c
US	455 cid 350 hp	a/t
UT	455 cid 350 hp	a/t
1972		
QA	350 cid 160/175 hp	m/t
QB	350 cid 160/175 hp	a/t
QC	350 cid 160/l75 hp	a/t, a/c
QN	350 cid l75 hp	a/t
QD	350 cid 180/200 hp	m/t
QE	350 cid 180/200 hp	m/t
QJ	350 cid 180/200 hp	a/t
QK	350 cid 180/200 hp	a/t, a/c
QP	350 cid 180 hp	a/t
US	455 cid 225 hp	a/t
UT	455 cid 225 hp	a/t
UA	455 cid 250 hp	a/t

This is the performance intake manifold for the 1970 W-30 455 cid Olds. While it flows better than other stock intake manifolds, it leaves much to be desired for it to be considered a true high-performance intake manifold. It would make more power if it was taller and had larger runner volume.

Code	Engine	Notes
UB	455 cid 250 hp	a/t, a/c
UU	455 cid 265 hp	a/t
UV	455 cid 265 hp	a/t
UD	455 cid 270 hp	m/t
UE	455 cid 270 hp	m/t, h/d clutch
UL	455 cid 300 hp	m/t, W30
UN	455 cid 300 hp	m/t, W30, h/d clutch
UO	455 cid 300 hp	a/t, W30

Casting number and date code are easily visible on Oldsmobile exhaust manifolds. The letter code ("W" and "Z") is located on the front exhaust runner.

Code	Engine	Notes
1973		
QN, QO, QP	350 cid 160 hp	a/t
QQ, QS, QT	350 cid 160 hp	a/t
QA, QB	350 cid 180 hp	a/t
QJ, QK	350 cid 180 hp	a/t
QU, QV	350 cid 180 hp	a/t
QC, QD	350 cid 180 hp	m/t
QE, QL	350 cid 180 hp	m/t
UA, UB, US	455 cid 225 hp	a/t
UD	455 cid 225 hp	m/t
UT, UU, UV	455 cid 225 hp	a/t

Engine	Code
1974	
350 cid 180 hp	QO, QU, QW, TB, TC, TL, TO
455 cid 210 hp	VA, VB, VC, VD, VL, VO, VP, UA, UC, UD, UL, UN, UP, UR, UO, UV, UX
1975	
455 cid 190 hp	UB, UE, UP, UC, UD, VB, VC, VE, VP

Engine Specifications

	Displacement	Carburetor	Horsepower	Torque	Compression Ratio	Notes
1949						
	303	2V	135@3,600	263@1,800	7.25	
1950						
	303	2V	135@3,600	263@1,800	7.25	
1951						
	303	2V	135@3,600	263@1,800	7.50	
1952						
	303	2V	145@3,600	280@1,800	7.50	
	303	4V	160@3,600	283@1,800	7.50	
1953						
	303	2V	150@3,600	280@1,800	7.50	
	303	4V	165@3,600	284@1,800	7.50	
1954						
	324	2V	170@4,000	300@2,000	8.25	
	324	4V	185@4,000	300@2,000	8.25	
1955						
	324	2V	185@4,000	320@2,000	8.50	

Engine Specifications

	Displacement	Carburetor	Horsepower	Torque	Compression Ratio	Notes
	324	2V	202@4,000	332@2,400	8.50	
1956						
	324	2V	230@4,000	340@2,400	9.25	
	324	4V	240@4,000	350@2,800	9.25	
1957						
	371	4V	277@4,400	400@2,800	9.50	
	371	3x2V	300@4,600	415@2,800	10.0	
1958						
	371	2V	265@4,400	390@2,400	10.0	
	371	4V	305@4,600	410@2,800	10.0	
	371	3x2V	312@4,600	415@2,800	10.0	
1959						
	371	2V	270@4,600	390@2,400	9.75	
	371	4V	300@4,600	410@2,800	9.75	
	394	4V	315@4,600	435@2,800	9.75	
1960						
	371	2V	240@4,600	375@2,400	8.75	
	394	4V	315@4,600	435@2,800	9.75	
1961						
	394	2V	250@4,200	405@2,400	8.75	88
	394	2V	275@4,600	415@2,400	10.0	88
	394	4V	325@4,600	435@2,800	10.0	88, 98
	394	4V	330@4,600	440@2,800	10.25	Starfire
1962						
	394	2V	280@4,400	430@2,400	10.25	88
	394	4V	330@4,600	440@2,800	10.25	88, 98
	394	4V	345@4,600	440@3,200	10.50	Starfire
1963						
	394	2V	280@4,400	430@2,400	10.25	88
	394	4V	330@4,600	440@2,800	10.25	88, 98
	394	4V	345@4,600	440@3,200	10.50	Starfire, 98
1964						
	330	2V	230@4,400	325@2,400	9.0	F-85, 88
	330	2V	245@4,600	345@3,200	10.25	F-85, Vista Cruiser, Cutlass
	330	4V	290@4,800	355@2,800	10.25	F-85, Vista Cruiser
	330	4V	310@5,200	360@3,600	10.25	442, F-85, Cutlass, Vista Cruiser
	394	2V	260@4,400	410@2,400	8.75	88
	394	2V	280@4,400	430@2,400	10.25	88
	394	4V	330@4,600	440@2,800	10.25	88, 98
	394	4V	345@4,600	440@3,200	10.50	Jetstar, Starfire, 88, 98
1965						
	330	2V	250@4,800	335@2,400	9.0	F-85, 88, Vista Cruiser, Cutlass
	330	2V	260@4,800	355@3,200	10.25	Jetstar 88
	330	4V	315@5,200	360@3,600	10.25	Jetstar 88 Vista Cruiser, Cutlass
	400	4V	345@4,800	440@3,200	10.25	Cutlass 442
	425	2V	300@4,400	430@2,400	9.0	Dynamic 88, Delta 88
	425	2V	310@4,400	450@2,400	10.25	Dynamic 88, Delta 88
	425	4V	360@4,800	470@2,400	10.25	Ninety-Eight, Dynamic 88, Delta 88
	425	4V	370@4,800	470@3,200	10.50	Starfire, Jetstar, Ninety-Eight, Delta 88
1966						
	330	2V	250@4,800	335@2,400	9.0	Jetstar 88, F-85
	330	2V	260@4,800	355@3,200	10.25	Jetstar 88
	330	4V	310@4,800	360@2,800	9.0	Vista Cruiser, Cutlass, F-85
	330	4V	320@5,200	360@2,800	10.25	Vista Cruiser, Cutlass, F-85
	400	4V	350@5,200	440@3,600	10.50	442
	400	3x2V	365@5,000	440@3,600	10.50	442, Cutlass, F-85
	425	2V	300@4,400	430@2,400	9.0	Delta 88, Ninety-Eight
	425	2V	310@4,400	450@2,400	10.25	Delta 88, Dynamic 88
	425	4V	365@4,800	470@3,200	10.25	Delta 88, Dynamic 88, Ninety-Eight
	425	4V	375@4,800	470@3,200	10.50	Delta 88, Ninety-Eight, Starfire
	425	4V	385@4,800	475@3,200	10.50	Toronado

	Displacement	Carburetor	Horsepower	Torque	Compression Ratio	Notes
1967						
	330	2V	250@4,800	335@2,400	9.0	F-85, Vista Cruiser, Cutlass, Delmont 88
	330	2V	260@4,800	355@3,200	10.25	Delmont 88
	330	2V	310@4,800	360@2,800	9.0	F-85, Vista Cruiser, Cutlass, Cutlass Supreme
	330	4V	320@5,200	360@2,800	10.25	F-85, Vista Cruiser, Cutlass, Cutlass Supreme, Delmont 88
	400	2V	300@4,600	425@3,000	10.50	442
	400	4V	350@5,200	440@3,600	10.50	442
	425	2V	300@4,400	430@2,400	9.0	Delmont 88, Delta 88
	425	2V	310@4,400	450@2,400	10.25	Delmont 88, Delta 88
	425	4V	365@4,800	470@3,200	10.25	Delmont 88, Delta 88, Ninety-Eight
	425	4V	375@4,800	470@3,200	10.50	Delmont 88, Delta 88, Ninety-Eight
	425	4V	385@4,800	475@3,200	10.50	Toronado
1968						
	350	2V	250@4,400	355@2,600	9.0	Cutlass, F-85, Cutlass Supreme, Custom Vista Cruiser, Delmont 88
	350	4V	310@4,800	390@3,200	10.25	Cutlass, F-85, Cutlass Supreme, Vista Cruiser, Delmont 88
	400	2V	290@4,600	425@2,400	9.0	442, Custom Vista Cruiser
	400	4V	325@4,800	440@3,200	10.50	442, Custom Vista Cruiser
	400	4V	350@4,800	440@3,600	10.50	442
	400	4V	360@5,400	440@3,600	10.50	442
	455	2V	310@4,200	490@2,400	9.0	Delmont 88, Delta 88
	455	2V	320@4,200	500@2,400	9.0	Delmont 88, Delta 88
	455	4V	365@4,800	410@3,000	10.25	Delmont 88, Delta 88, Ninety-Eight
	455	4V	375@4,800	510@3,000	10.25	Toronado
	455	4V	390@5,000	500@3,000	10.25	Hurst/Olds
	455	4V	400@4,800	500@3,200	10.25	Toronado
1969						
	350	2V	250@4,400	355@2,600	9.0	Vista Cruiser, Cutlass Supreme, Cutlass, F-85
	350	4V	310@4,800	390@3,200	10.25	Vista Cruiser, Cutlass Supreme
	350	4V	325@5,400	390@3,200	10.50	442, Cutlass, F-85
	400	4V	325@4,600	440@3,000	10.50	Vista Cruiser, 442
	400	4V	350@4,800	440@3,200	10.50	442
	400	4V	360@5,400	440@3,600	10.50	442
	455	2V	310@4,200	490@2,400	9.0	Delta 88
	455	4V	365@4,600	510@3,000	10.25	Delta 88, Ninety-Eight
	455	4V	375@4,600	510@3,000	10.25	Toronado
	455	4V	380@5,000	500@3,000	10.25	Delta 88, Hurst/Olds
	455	4V	400@4,800	500@3,200	10.25	Toronado
1970						
	350	2V	250@4,400	355@2,600	9.0	Delta 88, Royale, Vista Cruiser, Cutlass Supreme
	350	4V	310@4,800	390@3,200	10.25	Delta 88, Royale, VistaCruiser, Cutlass Supreme
	350	4V	325@5,400	390@3,200	10.50	Cutlass, F-85
	455	2V	320@4,200	500@2,400	9.0	Cutlass Supreme
	455	4V	365@5,000	500@3,200	10.50	442, Ninety-Eight, Delta 88, Royale, Vista Cruiser, Cutlass Supreme
	455	4V	370@5,200	500@3,600	10.50	442
	455	4V	375@4,600	510@3,000	10.25	Toronado
	455	4V	390@5,000	500@3,000	10.25	Delta 88, Royale
	455	4V	400@4,800	500@3,200	10.25	Toronado
1971						
	350	2V	240@4,200	350@2,400	8.50	Cutlass, F-85, Cutlass Supreme, Delta 88
	350	4V	260@4,600	360@3,200	8.50	Cutlass, F-85, Cutlass Supreme
	455	2V	280@4,000	445@2,000	8.50	Vista Cruiser, Delta 88
	455	4V	320@4,400	460@2,800	8.50	Vista Cruiser, Ninety-Eight
	455	4V	340@4,600	460@3,200	8.50	442

Engine Specifications

	Displacement	Carburetor	Horsepower	Torque	Compression Ratio	Notes
	455	4V	350@4,700	460@3,200	8.50	442
	455	4V	350@4,400	465@2,800	8.50	Toronado
1972						
	350	2V	160@4,000	275@2,400	8.50	Cutlass, Cutlass Supreme, F-85, Vista Cruiser, Delta 88
	350	4V	180@4,000	275@2,800	8.50	Cutlass, F-85, Vista-Cruiser, Delta 88
	455	4V	225@3,600	360@2,600	8.50	Cutlass Supreme, Delta 88, Ninety-Eight
	455	4V	250@4,200	370@2,800	8.50	Toronado
	455	4V	270@4,400	370@3,200	8.50	Cutlass Supreme, Vista Cruiser, Cutlass, F-85
	455	4V	300@4,700	410@3,200	8.50	Cutlass Supreme, Cutlass, F-85
1973						
	350	2V	160@3,800	275@2,400	8.50	Cutlass, Cutlass Supreme, Delta 88
	350	4V	180@4,000	275@2,800	8.50	Cutlass, Cutlass Supreme, Delta 88
	455	4V	225@3,600	360@2,600	8.50	Ninety-Eight, Delta 88
	455	4V	250@4,000	375@2,800	8.50	Toronado
	455	4V	270@4,200	370@3,200	8.50	Cutlass, Cutlass Supreme
1974						
	350	4V	180@3,800	275@2,800	8.50	Cutlass, Cutlass Supreme, Delta 88
	350	4V	200@4,200	300@3,200	8.50	Cutlass, Delta 88
	455	4V	210@3,600	350@2,400	8.50	Custom Cruiser, Ninety Eight
	455	4V	230@3,800	370@2,800	8.50	Toronado
	455	4V	275@4,200	370@3,200	8.50	Cutlass, Cutlass Supreme
1975						
	350	4V	170@3,800	275@2,400	8.50	Cutlass, Cutlass Supreme, Delta 88
	455	4V	190@3,600	350@2,400	8.50	Cutlass Supreme, Ninety-Eight, Custom Cruiser
	455	4V	215@3,600	370@2,400	8.50	Toronado

Engine Internal Dimensions

Displacement	Bore and Stroke	Rod Bearings	Main Bearings	Intake/Exhaust Valves
303	3.750x3.437	2.249–2.250	2.498–2.499*	1.75/1.44
324	3.875x3.437	2.249–2.250	2.498–2.499*	1.75/1.44
330	3.938x3.385	2.000	2.495	1.875/1.562
350	4.057x3.385	2.1238–2.1248	2.4988–2.4998	1.875/1.562****
371	4.000x3.688	2.249–2.250	2.748–2.749**	1.875/1.562
394	4.125x3.688	2.4992–2.5002	2.999–3.000	1.875/1.562
400	4.000x3.975	2.4988–2.5003	2.9993–3.0003	2.00/1.625***
425	4.126x3.975	2.4988–2.5003	2.9993–3.0003	2.00/1.625***
455	4.125x4.250	2.4988–2.5003	2.9993–3.0003	2.00/1.625***

* The fifth main bearing: 2.623–2.624
** 1959–1960 had 2.999–3.000 in. journals
*** High-performance engines (generally) had 2.072 in. intake valves
**** See Cylinder Head specs

Block, Head, and Manifold Casting Numbers

Year	Engine	Casting Number
Engine Blocks		
1949–1953	303	555614
1954–1956	324	568922
1964	330	381917, 381917A, Code 1
1965	330	381917, Code 2
1968–1970	350	395558, Code 2
1973–1974	350	395558
1957–1959	371	568922, 573562
1959–1963	394	574534, 578135, 582813
1964	394	585786
1965	400	389298, Code B
1966–1967	400	390925, Code E
1968–1969	400	396026, Code G
1965	425	381917, 386525, Code A
1966–1967	425	389244, Code D
1968–1972	455	396021, Code F
1972–1975	455	396021 Code Fa
Cylinder Heads		
1949–1950	303	555643, 560905
1951	303	559988
1952–1953	303	563372, 561370
1954	324	564350
1955	324	566185
1956	324	567321
1964	330	385101, 1.875/1.562 valves, Code 1
1965	330	394189 (part no.), 1.875/1.562 valves, Code 2

Year	Engine	Casting Number
Cylinder Heads		
1966	330	389394, Code 3, 1.875/1.562 valves
1967	330	394497, Code 4, 1.875/1.562 valves
1968–1969	350	397742, Code 5, 1.875/1.562 valves
1970	350	403859, Code 6, 1.875/1.562 valves; W-31, 1.995/1.562 valves
1971	350	409147, Code 7, 1.875/1.562 valves; W-31, 1.995/1.625 valves
1972	350	409147, Code 7a, 1.875/1.562 valves
1973–1976	350	411929, Code 8, 1.875/1.562 valves
1957–1958	371	569137, 571870
1959–1960	371/394	573305, 513350
1961	394	577608
1962–1964	394	583832
1965	400/425	383821, Code A
1965	400/425	383821, late 1965 Code B
1966	400/425	389395, Code B
1967–1969	400/425	394548, Code C
1968–1969	400	400370, Code D
1968–1970	455	403686, Code E
1970	455	404438, W-30, 2.072/1.625 valves, Code F
1971	455	409100, W-30, Code G
1971	455	409160, 2.072/1.625 valves, Code H
1972	455	409100, W-30, Code Ga
1973–1976	455	411783, Code J
1973–1976	455	413191, Code K, Ka
Intake Manifolds		
1949–1950	303 2V	556714, 557709
1951–1953	303 2V	560676
1951–1953	303 4V	561779
1954–1955	324 2V	564266
1954–1955	324 4V	567672
1964	330 2V	387491
1965	330 2V	381920
1966–1967	330 2V	391135
1966–1967	330 4V	390327
1968	350 2V	398583
1968–1969	350 4V	398663
1973	350 4V	411863
1974	350 4V	411990
1974–1975	350 4V	411880, Code 16
1957	371 4V	569301
1957–1958	371 3x2V	571898, casting 5771145
1959–1960	394 2V	573387
1959–1960	394 4V	587503
1965	400 4V	384439, Code B
1966–1967	400/455 4V	390390, Code E
1966	400 3x2V	393238, Code F
1969	400 4V	398662, 398664
1967	425 2V	391136
1967	425 4V	397357, Code G
1967	400/425 4V	387958
1968–1969	400/455 4V	398662, Code J
1968–1969	455 4V	398664, Toronado Code K
1969	455 4V	405233, H/O

Year	Engine	Casting Number
Intake Manifolds		
1970	455 4V	406115, W-30, aluminum
1970–1971	455 2V	407566
1970–1972	455 4V	404521, Code L
1970–1972	455 4V	407567, m/t, Code R
1971–1972	455 4V	407570, W-30, aluminum, Code A
1972	455 4V	410448, m/t, Code U
1972	455 4V	404522, 407569, m/t
1971	455 2V	388625, Code H
1973	455 4V	412753
1973–1976	455 4V	412493, Toronado, Code X
1973–1974	455 4V	411990, Code Y
1973–1976	455 4V	413111, Code Y
1973–1974	455 4V	231890, marine, hearse, ambulance
Exhaust Manifolds		
1949–1953	303	561270 right, 561751 left
1954–1955	324	563300 right, 563296 left
1956	324	563300 right, 567569 left
1964–1967	330	398704 left, 393383 left
1965–1967	330	381921 right, 380145 left
1968–1970	350	381921 right, 380001 left
1970	350	411961 left
1971–1973	350	398704 right
1973–1974	350	411962 right, 411961 left, X body
1974	350	398704, A, B
1957–1958	371	568926 right, 568677 left
1959–1960	371/394	573324 right, 573325 left
1961–1962	394	579278 right, 579279 left
1963–1964	394	587510 right, 587193 left, single exhaust
1963–1964	394	587510 right, 587793 left, dual exhaust
1965–1966	425	384784 right, 384785 left, single exhaust
1965–1966	425	384784 right, 393233 left (part no.)
1965–1967	425	398708 right, 406199 left
1965–1967	400	389268 Code W, right, 389269 Code X, left
1967–1969	425/455	398708 Code T right, 384785 Code A, left
1968	455	398708 Code T right, 398706 Code R, left
1968	400	398706 right, 412287 left, 442, Cutlass, H/O
1969	400	402294 right, 4122287 left
1968–1970	455	384895 right, Code S, full-size cars
1969–1974	455	402295 left, Code W, 442, W30, Cutlass, H/O
1969–1972	455	402294 right, Code Z, Cutlass, 442, W30, H/O
1972	455	411230 right
1972	455	411961 left
1971–1974	455	412287 left, Code Z, 442, W30
1973–1974	455	411970 right, Code H; 407103 left, Code J, Toronado
1971–1975	455	407103 left, Toronado

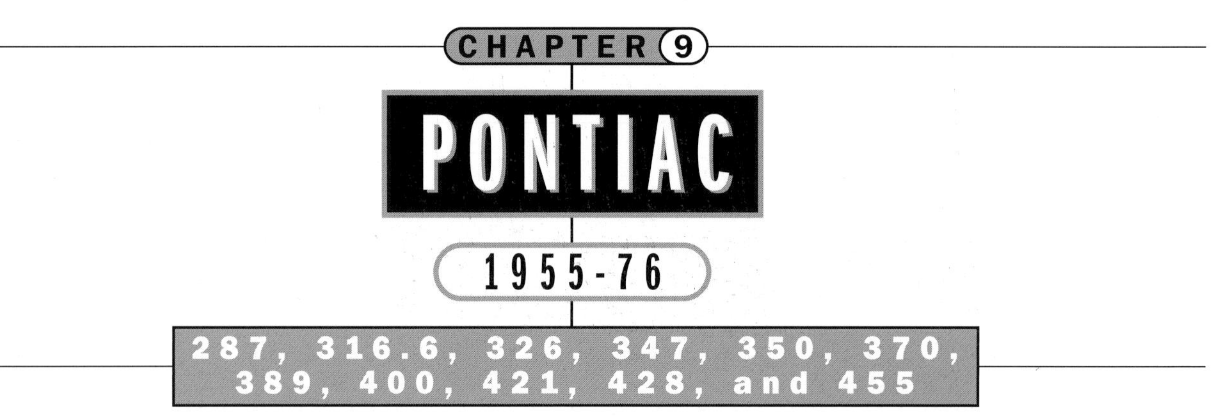

Pontiac, along with Chevrolet, was the last GM division to introduce a modern ohv V-8 engine, in 1955. There were actually quite a few similarities between the Pontiac and Chevy engines. Both engines had the same bore, 3.25 in., while the Pontiac had a 0.25 in. more stroke (3.25 in.), for 287 cid. Both engines used stamped-steel rocker arms (Pontiac had actually originated the concept back in 1948, but it seems that Chevrolet has gotten all the credit). The Pontiac was about 2 in. taller and about 75lb heavier. Beyond that, there were a number of differences that set the engines apart.

The Pontiac's wedge-shaped combustion chambers were fully machined because it was easier with machined combustion chambers to equalize the compression ratio between cylinders, and it also helped eliminate hot spots that cause pre-ignition. Oiling to the rockers was not through hollow pushrods as it was with later engines; each ball pivot was lubricated by an oil passage that ran the length of the cylinder head. The gallery was fed by a passage from a camshaft journal. In 1961, Pontiac started to follow Chevrolet's practice of using hollow pushrods, and by 1965 all Pontiac V-8 engines used pushrod-oiled rocker arms.

The valve guides on the 1955 engines were removable; after 1955, removable valve guides were not used. Pontiac also used a windage tray from the very beginning, which helped control oil aeration.

Internally, the Pontiac V-8 typically used a cast-iron crank, forged-steel connecting rods, and cast-aluminum pistons. From 1963 on, most engines, except for some of the high-performance versions, used cast rods. The Pontiac cylinder head ports were also somewhat different from Chevrolet's, although the basic location layout was similar. The Pontiac had descent flowing intake ports, but the stock exhaust ports were somewhat restrictive (necessitated by engine and chassis clearance considerations), which is why Pontiac engines were equipped with a dual-pattern camshaft. The exhaust valve's duration was longer than the intake valve's, which means that Pontiac engineers allowed the exhaust valve to stay open longer to compensate for the exhaust port restriction.

The 1955 Pontiac Strato-Streak 287 cid engine was rated at 173-, 180-, and 200 hp. In 1956, the engine's bore was opened up to 3.9375 in. for 316.6 cid. There were five versions, with power ratings from 192 hp to 285 hp. The 285 hp Strato-Streak engine had 10.0:1 compression and two four-barrel carburetors.

The 316.6 cid engine lasted for only one year. For 1957, Pontiac again adjusted the engine's bore and stroke, to 3.9375x3.562 in. for 347 cid. The top engine put out 317 hp with a 10.0:1 compression ratio. The 290- and 317 hp engines were the first to use a Tri-Power intake setup, which used three two-barrel carburetors. These engines were certified for use in NASCAR racing. It was also in 1957 that Pontiac released a FI version of the 347 cid V-8 for use in the new Bonneville model. It is generally agreed that the Pontiac's system was more refined than the one used on the Corvette, but poor sales and high cost forced Pontiac to withdraw FI as an option by 1959.

For 1958, the engine was bored out to 4.0625 in. while the stroke remained at 3.652 in. The result was 370 cid. The hot NASCAR engines were called "Tempest," while the high-performance street engines became the Trophy series. The 1958 engine featured numerous internal improvements, including redesigned rings, enlarged exhaust ports, freer-flowing exhaust manifolds, and valve covers that were designed to seal better.

Nineteen fifty-nine saw the engine's stroke increased to 3.75 in. for the familiar 389 cid. The 389 cid displacement was available through the 1966 model year, in various configurations and power outputs. Nineteen fifty-nine was also the first year for Super Duty (SD) engines. Pontiac used the SD term on the 389- and on later 421- and 455 cid engines. The 1959–1962 SD 389 cid engines were built with forged-steel crankshafts, forged-steel connecting rods, and four-bolt-main engine blocks. The SD engines and the complementary parts program were intended for race use, but because of NASCAR and NHRA rules, the engines had to be available for sale in street production vehicles. Very few cars were so equipped.

In 1961 the Pontiac V-8 underwent another transformation. It was bored and stroked to 4.094x4.000 in. for 421 cid. The 421 cid engine was part of the SD series and was available only on an over-the-counter basis. Besides the new bore and stroke, the engine had larger main-bearing journals on the crankshaft, measuring 3.250 in. (previous engines were 3.000 in.), and used a complementary engine block with larger main-bearing journal caps. Most of these blocks were also fitted with four-bolt main-bearing caps on the numbers 2, 3, and 4 positions. The top horsepower street 421 cid engines from 1963 to 1966 were designated HO, for high output. These engines were equipped with cast Armasteel (nodular iron) crankshafts. The high point for the racing SD 421s, as far as NASCAR racing goes, came during 1961 and 1962. During the 1961 season, Pontiac won 30 races, and in 1962, 22.

The big 389- and 421 cid engines were too much engine for the smaller Tempest, so in 1963 another engine variation was released. The 326 cid Pontiac had a 3.78 in. bore and 3.750 in. stroke for an actual displacement of 336 cid. From 1964 on, the engine's bore was reduced to 3.7187 in., which resulted in a true 326 cid. The 326 cid engine was in production through the 1967 model year with the lowest power rating being 250 hp and the highest being 285 hp. By adjusting the bore to 3.88 in. in 1968, the 326 cid engine became a 350 cid. The 350 cid V-8 was available through the 1977 model year.

Going back to the big engines, the 400 cid V-8 came into being in 1967; it was based on the small-bearing engine block,

This high-performance block was designed for use on the 303 cid Trans Am engine. Note extra ribbing in the lifter area and chamfered cylinder bores. *Pontiac Motor Division*

and it was an outgrowth of the 389 cid engine. It had a 4.12 in. bore and 3.75 in. stroke. The hot dog 400 cid V-8s were all designated "Ram Air." The 400 cid engine lasted through the 1979 model year.

The 421 cid engine was replaced by the 428 cid V-8 in 1967, and it lasted through the 1969 model year. It had a bore of 4.12 in. and a stroke of 4.00 in.

All of GM's engines got major displacement increases in 1970. Buick and Oldsmobile engines hit 455 cid, Chevrolet's big-block displaced 454 cid, Cadillac went to 500 cid, and Pontiac's V-8 reached 455 cid, with an undersquare 4.15 in. bore and 4.21 in. stroke. The big 455 cid engine stayed in production through the 1976 model year, and one of Pontiac's best engines, the Super Duty 455, was based on the 455.

There were two more engines based on the Pontiac V-8 block. The 301 cid version was available from 1977-81. The best known of these was the turbocharged version used on the 1980–1981 Firebird. The last appearance of the Pontiac V-8 engine was the small 265 cid version (4.3l) available in 1981.

Today, when it comes to high-performance Pontiac engines, the emphasis is mostly on the late-1960s Ram Air series engines. The fact that the early SD engines were used in many stock car and drag racing wins in the late 1950s and early 1960s is now pretty much forgotten—except by die-hard Pontiac enthusiasts. The fact that Pontiac had developed hemi heads for the engine and that it even had a double overhead cam 421 in 1963 is also forgotten. Pontiac was a force to be reckoned with, but that all stopped when GM decided to pull out of all racing activities in 1963. It seems that Pontiac followed that edict fairly closely, while Chevrolet managed to maintain a credible racing presence through several "back-door" operations (such as those of Jim Hall and Roger Penske). Pontiac made some half-hearted attempts in the late 1960s and early 1970s, for example, with the 303 cid Trans Am engine and the Ram Air V engines, but they were all characterized by being too little and too late.

287 cid

The original Pontiac V-8 was introduced in 1955 in three power ratings, 173-, 180-, and 200 hp. The engine was equipped with a forged-steel crankshaft, forged rods, cast-aluminum pistons, and cast-iron intake and exhaust manifolds. The 200 hp engine was equipped with a four-barrel carburetor. All engines were equipped with a hydraulic-lifter camshaft.

316.6 cid

The 316.6 was introduced in 1956, replacing the 287 cid V-8. Like the 287 cid engine, the 316.6 featured a forged-steel crankshaft, forged-steel rods, and cast-aluminum pistons. The cylinder heads did not use removable valve guides. The regular production engines were rated at 205- and 227 hp. The big development in 1956 was the release of the special 285 hp version of the Strato-Streak V-8. The engine was equipped with a dual four-barrel intake setup and a modified valvetrain that featured a hotter hydraulic-lifter camshaft, special lifters, and valve springs. This engine was the first of many high-performance Pontiac engines to come.

326 cid

The 326 cid Pontiac, with its 3.72 in. bore and 3.75 in. stroke, served as the base V-8 engine on various Pontiac cars from 1963 to 1967. Interestingly, the 1963 version had a larger, 3.78 in. bore for 336 cid. During this period, the two-barrel version was rated at 250 hp; the four-barrel version, which also included dual exhausts, was rated at 260-, 280-, and 285 hp. The engine was otherwise a low-performance engine, with cast-iron intake and exhaust manifolds, a two-bolt-main engine block, and cast-iron connecting rods and crankshaft.

The 285 hp version became known as the 326 HO on the 1967 Firebird.

347 cid

In 1957, a 347 cid displacement was arrived at by increasing the Strato-Streak's stroke to 3.5625 in.; the bore remained at 3.9375 in. The 347 cid engines were all equipped with forged-steel crankshafts, forged-steel rods, cast-aluminum pistons, and hydraulic-lifter camshafts.

Most Pontiac 347s were rated between 227- and 270 hp, but 1957 saw the release of several high-performance variants, the 290- and 317 hp versions, which both used the Tri-Power intake setup for the first time. These Tri-Power engines were certified for use in NASCAR racers.

Also new was the FI 347 for use in the Bonneville. The engine used the same Rochester FI system as Chevrolet used on the Corvette, but there were detail differences. The FI engine was not rated by Pontiac, but best estimates indicated power output was around 295 hp.

350 cid

The 350 cid Pontiac was in service from 1968 to 1977. The two-barrel versions of the engine were rated between 155- and 265 hp; the four-barrel versions were rated between 165- and 330 hp. Except for the 1968–1969 four-barrel versions (which were rated between 320- and 330 hp), the 350 cid V-8 was another low-performance motor. The 1968–1969 four-barrel Firebird 350 was known as the 350 HO. The engine also had the distinction of powering the last GTO, the 1974, and it was rated at 200 hp SAE net.

370 cid

The 370 cid was the result of a 4.0625 in. bore and 3.5625 in. stroke in 1958. Lasting only one year, 370 cid engines were available in many configurations. The most significant, as usual, were the high-performance variants. The Tri-Power engine was rated at 300 hp, while the NASCAR-certified version put out 330 hp. There was also a single four-barrel version that used the Carter AFB carburetor for 315 hp.

The Bonneville was available with carbureted engines in 1958, but the FI, rated at 310 hp, was also available. It is believed that about 200 Bonnevilles were so equipped. The system was discontinued after the model year because of high cost and lack of performance. The FI system, though, was used in various drag racing events with better success.

389 cid

The 389 cid V-8, introduced in 1959, seemed to be a good size for Pontiac. The engine remained in production through the 1966 model year, and it is one of the most recognized. The engine had a bore of 4.0625 in. and a stroke of 3.75 in. and was built in a great variety of configurations. Regular production engines were equipped with cast-iron intake manifolds with either a two- or four-barrel carburetor, a hydraulic-lifter camshaft, forged connecting rods (cast for 1963–1966 engines), cast-aluminum pistons, and cast-iron exhaust manifolds.

High-performance Trophy engines were available from 1959 to 1962; the highest output engines were those with the Tri-Power intake setup.

There were also the SD engines built during 1959–1962. These engines were specifically made for NHRA or NASCAR racing but were also available on street cars. These engines used four-bolt-main engine blocks, forged-steel crankshafts, forged-steel connecting rods, and forged-aluminum pistons. Induction systems were either a single four-barrel carburetor or the Tri-Power setup. All 1960–1963 SD engines also used a mechanical-lifter camshaft.

400 cid

The 400 cid V-8 replaced the 389 cid engine in 1967, and Pontiac kept the engine in service until 1979. The 400 had a bore of 4.12 in. and a stroke of 3.75 in. The regular production 400 cid engines were available in two- and four-barrel-carburetor form, and all were equipped with cast internal components—rods, pistons, crankshaft. The engines that stand out are the Ram Air series, and we'll look at each individually.

RAM AIR: The first Ram Air 400 cid engine was used on the 1967 GTO and Firebird. The Ram Air engine had a hotter hydraulic-lifter camshaft, freer-flowing exhaust manifolds, a Quadrajet four-barrel carburetor (that wouldn't open all the way, which is how Pontiac limited horsepower), and a functional ram-air induction system, which was the reason the engine was called "Ram Air." In the Firebird, the engine was rated at 325 hp; in the GTO it was rated at 360 hp. In other respects, the Ram Air 400 was similar to the regular production engines. The engine was fitted with chrome valve covers, air cleaner, and oil filler cap.

RAM AIR II: The Ram Air II engine replaced the Ram Air engine during the 1968 model year. The main differences between it and the previous Ram Air engine were new cylinder heads (that featured round exhaust ports) and a four-bolt-main engine block. The engine was rated at 340 hp on the Firebird and 366 hp on the GTO.

RAM AIR III: This engine replaced the Ram Air II in 1969. It was essentially the same engine, but it used the regular "D" exhaust-port cylinder heads. It was rated at 335 hp on the Firebird and 366 hp on the GTO.

RAM AIR IV: The Ram Air IV was the highest-rated production version of the 400 cid engine. Added to the Ram Air III engine were forged aluminum pistons, an aluminum intake manifold, the round exhaust-port cylinder heads, 1.65:1 ratio rocker arms, and a stronger camshaft. It was rated 345 hp on the Firebird and 370 hp on the GTO.

RAM AIR V: Although 89 engines were made and there were plans to have the engine used on the 1970 Firebird and GTO, the engine never made it into regular production. The main difference between this engine and other Pontiacs was the special Tunnel-Port cylinder heads. These were similar to the design used at Ford—large round intake ports gave the fuel mixture a direct shot to the combustion chamber. The pushrods went through the center of each port in a hollow sleeve, and unlike most Pontiac engines, the Ram Air V used a mechanical-lifter camshaft. The engine used a matching aluminum intake manifold and Holley four-barrel carburetor. The engine block was a four-bolt-main unit that had special ribbing in the lifter bore, and the motor also used forged-steel connecting rods with special capscrews. These rods were pretty hefty, but they were the engine's Achilles heel, as they had a tendency to let go. The tunnel-port heads were also a bit too much for the engine because the engine would have had to be revved up to a ridiculously high rpm to take advantage of the port size.

421 cid

The 1961–1966 421 cid engine was essentially a bored and stroked 389. The bore was increased to 4.094 in. while the stroke went up to 4.00 in. In addition, the 421 cid engine used an engine block that had larger, 3.250 in. main-bearing journals and four-bolt main-bearing caps. The SD 421s, as with the SD 389s, were race engines set up for use on the drag strips or on the NASCAR tracks. The SD 421s were built with forged-steel crankshafts and rods and used either single four-barrel carburetion systems for the stock car engines or dual-quad systems for engines destined to be used on the drag strip.

The high-performance street 421 cid engines didn't go into service until the 1963 model year (although there were a few 1962 Grand Prix equipped with the 421 SD).

In top street trim, the hot 421s were the 421 HOs. From 1963 to 1966, all these engines came with Tri-Power and were rated at 370 hp (1963–1964) and 376 hp (1965–1966). Tri-Power was also used on the non-HO 421 cid engines, for 350 hp in 1964 and 356 hp in 1965–1966. The single four-barrel 421s, with 320- and 338 hp, were regular passenger-car engines.

428 cid

The 428 cid V-8 was available on full-size Pontiac cars and the Grand Prix between 1967 and 1969. A 4.12 in. bore and a 4.00 in. stroke resulted in 428 cid. These big motors got the four-bolt-main blocks (except several of the 1969 360 hp engines), along with the cast crankshafts, rods, and pistons. All were equipped with a four-barrel carburetor and a dual exhaust system. The 1967 engines were available with either a 360- or 376 hp output, 1968 engines were available in either 375- or 390 hp, and the 1969s in either 360-, 370-, or 390 hp configurations.

455 cid

The biggest factory Pontiac V-8 was the 455 cid engine of 1970–1976. The 455 cid engine had a 4.15 in. bore and a 4.21 in. stroke. Besides the Pontiac 455, the only other American V-8s with longer-stroke-than-bore dimensions were the Oldsmobile 455- and the Buick 350 cid engines. Cadillac's 500 cid V-8 was also undersquare, but only by 0.004 in.

An undersquare engine has the tendency to produce quite a bit of low-end torque. That was certainly true for the 455, but this engine also had the distinction of producing quite a bit of horsepower as well. The best example is the 1973–1974 455 SD. The

455 SD was rated at 290 hp—not bad, considering the emission constraints of the time. This was 20 hp more than the comparable Chevrolet 454 cid big-block, which had the advantage of a shorter stroke and the canted-valve cylinder heads.

The higher-output 455 cid engines were usually equipped with the four-bolt-main engine block; the low-horsepower engines and all engines after 1973 (except the 455 SD) were all equipped with the two-bolt-main block. Most, but not all, 455s came with a Rochester Quadrajet carburetor mounted on a cast-iron intake manifold.

In its first year of production, the 455 cid engine was available with either 360- or 370 hp versions. The 360 hp engine was available on big Pontiac cars and on the Grand Prix. The optional engine on these cars was rated at 370 hp. The 370 hp engine was downrated to 360 hp when installed on the GTO, and there was no difference in power output when the GTO was equipped with Ram Air induction. All engines got the four-bolt-main bottom end.

The 1971 engines featured lowered horsepower rating due to a decrease in compression ratio. The top engine, the 455 HO, was rated at 335 hp gross and 310 hp SAE net. The HO was also equipped with an aluminum intake manifold and round-exhaust-port cylinder heads.

Nineteen seventy-two saw further erosion in output; the 455 HO was rated at 300 hp gross but did include the new GM HEI electronic ignition system.

For 1973, Pontiac surprised the automotive world with the introduction of the 310 hp 455 SD engine. Available only on the Firebird, the engine got a specially strengthened four-bolt-main engine block with provision for a dry-sump oiling system, forged-steel connecting rods, and forged-aluminum pistons. The crankshaft was cast from nodular iron. The cylinder heads featured round exhaust ports, and the induction system consisted of a cast-iron intake manifold with a Rochester Quadrajet carburetor. Late in the model year, due to changing emission requirements, the 455 SD was downrated to 290 hp, and this was the version that reached production. The engine was carried over into 1974, and it was the last gasp for 1960s-style performance at Pontiac.

For 1975 and 1976, the 455's compression ratio was further reduced to 7.6:1, resulting in a 200 hp output.

Engine Blocks

Pontiac engines have used two basic block castings. All Pontiac V-8s, except for the 421-, 428-, and 455 cid blocks, have 3.000 in. main-bearing journals, and these blocks were equipped with either two- or four-bolt main-bearing caps. All SD engines, most HOs, and the Ram Air II and V engines all used four-bolt blocks. The 421-, 428-, and 455 cid blocks have 3.250 in.-diameter main-bearing journals, and almost all of these engines are fitted with four-bolt-main caps. Those that don't often have the extra two bolt holes in the block.

There are several ways to identify Pontiac blocks. The simplest way is to see how many freeze plugs there are on each side of the block. The 1966 and earlier blocks have two freeze plugs on each side. If there are side motor-mount holes, the block is a 1959–1966. If there aren't any, the block is of 1955–1958 vintage. If the block has three freeze plugs per side, then it is a 1967 or later block. If the block has two motor-mount holes, then it is a 1967–1969. If it has three or five, it is a 1970 or later block.

Cylinder Heads

There has been quite a variety of cylinder heads for the Pontiac V-8. That is normal, considering the fact that the engine was in production for over 25 years. Some generalities can be made, however.

All production Pontiac cylinder heads were cast iron and all used individual stamped-steel rocker arms. Most heads were equipped with screw-in rocker arm studs. All Pontiac cylinder heads had machined combustion chambers. All 1968 and later cylinder heads have an open combustion chamber type, while 1967 and earlier chambers are closed. Cylinder heads that had round exhaust ports also had a rounded combustion chamber.

Intake ports were a rectangular shape, except on the Ram Air V heads, which had large, round intake ports. Exhaust port configuration has also followed the same general shape. The exhaust ports are "D" shaped. The only deviation is the round-port cylinder heads used on the 400 cid Ram Air II, Ram Air IV, and the 1971–1974 455 HO and SD engines.

Beginning with several 1964 engines (330-, 389-, 350-, 370-, 421 hp) all engines have their rocker arms lubricated by hollow pushrods, which are fed oil by the hydraulic lifters. Previous cylinder heads had an oil passage running the length of the cylinder head and fed oil through a camshaft bearing. All engines except the 1960–1963 SD and 1969–1970 Ram Air IV used rockers with 1.50:1 ratio. The other engines used rockers with a 1.65:1 ratio.

Intake Manifolds

Most Pontiac engines built over the years were equipped with cast-iron intake manifolds with either a two- or four-barrel carburetor. High-performance engines, such as the early SD engines, were equipped with aluminum single four-barrel, dual four-barrel, or Tri-Power intake manifolds. Later performance engines, such as the Ram Air IV and 455 HO, were also equipped with aluminum single four-barrel intake manifolds.

Exhaust Manifolds

Pontiac V-8 engines used conventional cast-iron exhaust manifolds in various shapes and with various size outlets. High-performance manifolds had larger and freer-flowing passages. Round-exhaust-port manifolds will not interchange with the standard "D" port manifolds.

One anomaly regarding factory exhaust manifolds are those for most 1971–1972 engines. The cylinder heads on these engines are not drilled and tapped for the outside two bolts of the exhaust manifold because the exhaust manifolds for these years do not have those two holes.

Engine Identification

As with all other auto manufacturers, Pontiac used casting numbers and date codes to identify all major engine components. And as with most other manufacturers, there are only "general" rules that apply—meaning there are exceptions. This boils down to something like this: All parts have identification numbers on them, except the ones that don't.

Pontiac engine blocks have a casting number and date code on the right side of the block. Blocks cast during the 1964 model year (except for the 421 cid blocks) and later have this number located on the distributor pad. The date code uses a letter code for the month (A–L) followed by two or three digits that stand for the date of the month and the last digit of the year. An example would be B229, which decodes to February 22, 1969. The exception to the rule is when the letter M was used to designate December for 1967 models.

The same system was used on cylinder heads and manifolds—a casting number and a date are usually found on these parts, but not always. On cylinder heads, in addition to the regular casting number, Pontiac also cast the last two (but not always the last two) digits of the casting number on top of the center exhaust ports (but they can appear elsewhere as well).

Pontiac also took care not only to identify the engine through various codes but also to stamp the vehicle's VIN on the block as well. From 1955, the vehicle's VIN was stamped on the right front

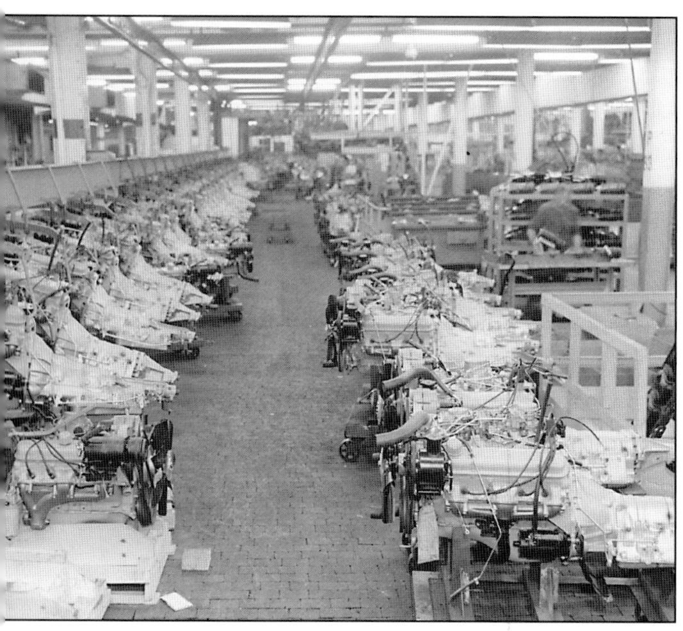

Pontiac engines ready for installation at a Pontiac assembly plant, circa 1965. *Pontiac Motor Division*

side of the block. In 1968, as with other GM divisions, an enhanced number was used along with the VIN. The number started with 2 for Pontiac, followed by a model-year digit, a plant code, and the vehicle's VIN.

Beginning with the 1959 model year, Pontiac added an engine/transmission code (listed in the tables) and a six- or seven-digit engine production sequence number. The engine/transmission code was at first located on a decal on the right valve cover, but during the 1959 model year, Pontiac started stamping the code on the block itself. Before 1964, there were additional codes stamped on the block to identify what transmission the vehicle was equipped with. In 1965, Pontiac used a two-letter coding system to identify the engine/transmission combination the vehicle was fitted with. Generally, codes beginning with a "W" are manual transmission cars, "Y" or "Z" are automatics, and "X" codes can be either.

Engine Codes

The following are the engine/transmission codes used from 1959 to 1975 on Pontiac V-8 engines. Engines from 1955–1958 were stamped with just the vehicle's VIN.

Code	Engine	Notes
1955–1958		
Engine ID is vehicle VIN		
1959		
531936	389 cid 215 hp	m/t
ET	389 cid 215 hp	m/t
ES	389 cid 215 hp	m/t
ER	389 cid 215 hp	a/t
D	389 cid 245 hp	m/t
531912	389 cid 245 hp	m/t
DT	389 cid 245 hp	m/t
532969	389 cid 245 hp	m/t, export
N	389 cid 245 hp	m/t, export
532968	389 cid 245 hp	a/t
J	389 cid 245 hp	a/t
532970	389 cid 245 hp	a/t, export
K	389 cid 245 hp	a/t, export
532971	389 cid 260 hp	a/t
F	389 cid 260 hp	a/t
531913	389 cid 260 hp	m/t
H	389 cid 260 hp	m/t
532973	389 cid 260 hp	a/t, export
L	389 cid 260 hp	a/t, export
532974	389 cid 260 hp	a/t, export
M	389 cid 260 hp	a/t, export
A	389 cid 280 hp	a/t
532972	389 cid 300 hp	m/t, police
FP	389 cid 300 hp	m/t, police
B	389 cid 300 hp	a/t
532976	389 cid 300 hp	a/t, police
BP	389 cid 300 hp	a/t, police
532979	389 cid 315 hp	m/t
G	389 cid 315 hp	m/t
C	389 cid 315 hp	a/t
532977	389 cid 330 hp	m/t
AL	389 cid 330 hp	m/t
53978	389 cid 345 hp	a/t
AK	389 cid 345 hp	a/t
532981	389 cid 345 hp	m/t
AN	389 cid 345 hp	m/t
532982	389 cid 345 hp	a/t
AM	389 cid 345 hp	a/t
1960		
A2	389 cid 215 hp	m/t
G4	389 cid 215 hp	m/t
R2	389 cid 215 hp	m/t, export
E3	389 cid 230 hp	a/t
J1	389 cid 230 hp	a/t, export
K1	389 cid 230 hp	a/t, export
B2	389 cid 235 hp	m/t
H4	389 cid 235 hp	m/t
L1	389 cid 281 hp	a/t, export
N1	389 cid 281 hp	a/t, export
Al	389 cid 283 hp	a/t
P4	389 cid 303 hp	m/t, police
Bl	389 cid 303 hp	a/t
P1	389 cid 303 hp	a/t, police
C4	389 cid 318 hp	m/t
C1	389 cid 318 hp	a/t
F4	389 cid 333 hp	m/t
Fl	389 cid 333 hp	a/t
M4	389 cid 348 hp	m/t
C1	389 cid 348 hp	a/t
C1	389 cid 348 hp	m/t, SD
C1	389 cid 363 hp	m/t, SD
1961		
A2, A4	389 cid 215 hp	m/t
G4	389 cid 215 hp	m/t, h/d clutch
E3	389 cid 230 hp	a/t
W3	389 cid 230 hp	a/t, a/c
J1	389 cid 230 hp	a/t, export
K1	389 cid 230 hp	a/t, export
E7	389 cid 230 hp	a/t
W7	389 cid 230 hp	a/t, a/c
B2	389 cid 235 hp	m/t
B4	389 cid 235 hp	m/t
H4	389 cid 235 hp	m/t, h/d clutch
R2	389 cid 240 hp	m/t, export
R4	389 cid 240 hp	m/t, export
K5	389 cid 257 hp	a/t, export
Q5	389 cid 257 hp	a/t, export

Code	Engine	Notes
AI	389 cid 267 hp	a/t
S1	389 cid 267 hp	a/t, a/c
LB	389 cid 276 hp	a/t, export
NB	389 cid 276 hp	a/t, export
A5	389 cid 283 hp	a/t
S5	389 cid 283 hp	a/t
BF	389 cid 287 hp	a/t
TF	389 cid 287 hp	a/t, a/c
P4	389 cid 303 hp	m/t, police, h/d lifters
P6	389 cid 303 hp	m/t, police, h/d lifters
PO	389 cid 303 hp	a/t, police, h/d lifters
P9	389 cid 303 hp	a/t, police, h/d lifters
BB	389 cid 303 hp	a/t
TB	389 cid 303 hp	a/t, a/c
C4, C6, C8, RC4, RC6, RC8, CD, CE RCD, RCE	389 cid 318 hp	m/t
CO, RCO, I9, R19	389 cid 318 hp	a/t
F4, F6, F8,	389 cid 333 hp	m/t
FD, FE, FO, U9	389 cid 333 hp	m/t
M4, M6, M8 RM4, RM6, RM8 MD, ME, RMD, RME	389 cid 348 hp	m/t
MO, RMO, V9, RV9	389 cid 348 hp	a/t
*	389 cid 368 hp	m/t, 4V or 3x2V, SD
*	421 cid 373 hp	m/t, 2x4V, SD

* over-the-counter

1962

Code	Engine	Notes
OIA	389 cid 215 hp	m/t
03B	389 cid 215 hp	m/t
20L	389 cid 230 hp	a/t
21L	389 cid 230 hp	a/t, a/c
40R	389 cid 230 hp	a/t
41R	389 cid 230 hp	a/t, a/c
02B	389 cid 235 hp	m/t
04B	389 cid 235 hp	m/t, h/d clutch
23H	389 cid 240 hp	a/t
05A	389 cid 239 hp	m/t, export
44M	389 cid 257 hp	a/t, export
15H	389 cid 267 hp	a/t
17H	389 cid 267 hp	a/t, a/c
45P	389 cid 276 hp	a/t, export
35M	389 cid 283 hp	a/t
37M	389 cid 283 hp	a/t, a/c
06B	389 cid 303 hp	m/t
16K	389 cid 303 hp	a/t
16KJ	389 cid 303 hp	a/t
36P	389 cid 303 hp	a/t
38P	389 cid 303 hp	a/t, a/c
39N	389 cid 303 hp	a/t, h/d lifters
IOB	389 cid 318 hp	m/t
27J	389 cid 318 hp	a/t
49N	389 cid 318 hp	a/t
29J, 29K	421 cid 320 hp	a/t
08B	389 cid 333 hp	m/t
25J	389 cid 333 hp	a/t
47N	389 cid 333 hp	a/t
11B	389 cid 348 hp	m/t
28J	389 cid 348 hp	a/t

Code	Engine	Notes
50N	389 cid 348 hp	a/t
12B	389 cid 385 hp	m/t, SD
12T	389 cid 385 hp	m/t, SD
13B	421 cid 405 hp	m/t, SD
13U, 13BU	421 cid 405 hp	m/t, SD

1963

Code	Engine	Notes
O1A	389 cid 215 hp	m/t
03B	389 cid 215 hp	m/t, h/d clutch
20L	389 cid 230 hp	a/t
21L	389 cid 230 hp	a/t, a/c
40R	389 cid 230 hp	a/t, a/c
41R	389 cid 230 hp	a/t, a/c
02B	389 cid 235 hp	m/t
04B	389 cid 235 hp	a/t, h/d clutch
23H	389 cid 240 hp	a/t, export
05A	389 cid 239 hp	m/t, export
44M	389 cid 257 hp	a/t, export
15H	389 cid 267 hp	a/t
17H	389 cid 267 hp	a/t, a/c
45P	389 cid 276 hp	a/t, export
35M	389 cid 283 hp	a/t
37M	389 cid 283 hp	a/t, a/c
06B	389 cid 303 hp	m/t
16K	389 cid 303 hp	a/t
18K	389 cid 303 hp	a/t, a/c
36P	389 cid 303 hp	a/t
38P	389 cid 303 hp	a/t, a/c
39N	389 cid 303 hp	a/t, h/d lifters
07B	389 cid 313 hp	a/t
26-6	389 cid 313 hp	a/t
48N	389 cid 313 hp	a/t
22B	421 cid 320 hp	m/t
34J	421 cid 320 hp	a/t
43N	421 cid 320 hp	a/t
08B	421 cid 353 hp	m/t, 421 HO
25G	421 cid 353 hp	a/t, 421 HO
47Q	421 cid 353 hp	a/t, 421 HO
11B	421 cid 370 hp	m/t, 421 HO
28G	421 cid 370 hp	a/t, 421 HO
50Q	421 cid 370 hp	a/t, 421 HO
12-5, 12U, 125T	421 cid 390 hp	m/t, SD
13-5,13U, 135U	421 cid 405 hp	m/t, SD
24U	421 cid 410 hp	m/t, SD

1963 Tempest

Code	Engine	Notes
68X	326 cid 250 hp	m/t
690	326 cid 250 hp	a/t
71X	326 cid 260 hp	m/t
600	326 cid 260 hp	a/t
70X	326 cid 280 hp	m/t
590	326 cid 280 hp	a/t
75-9	421 cid 405 hp	m/t, SS

1964 Pontiac

Code	Engine	Notes
01A	389 cid 215 hp	m/t
02B	389 cid 215 hp	m/t, h/d trans
03A	389 cid	a/t, export
04L	389 cid 230 hp	a/t
05L	389 cid 230 hp	a/t, a/c
08R	389 cid 230 hp	a/t
09R	389 cid 230 hp	a/t, a/c
22B	389 cid 235 hp	m/t, h/d trans
11H	389 cid 267 hp	a/t
12H	389 cid 267 hp	a/t, a/c
13L	389 cid	a/t, export
10A	389 cid 283 hp	m/t
17M	389 cid 283 hp	a/t

Engine Codes

Code	Engine	Notes
18M	389 cid 283 hp	a/t, a/c
19R	389 cid	a/t, export
25K	389 cid 303 hp	a/t
26K	389 cid 303 hp	a/t, a/c
27P	389 cid 303 hp	a/t
28P	389 cid 303 hp	a/t, a/c
29N	389 cid 306 hp	a/t
30R	389 cid	a/t
23B	389 cid 306 hp	m/t
32B	389 cid 330 hp	m/t
33-6	389 cid 330 hp	a/t
34N	389 cid 330 hp	a/t
35B	421 cid 320 hp	m/t
38S	421 cid 320 hp	a/t
43N	421 cid 320 hp	a/t
44B	421 cid 350 hp	m/t
475S	421 cid 350 hp	a/t
49N	421 cid 350 hp	a/t
458B	421 cid 370 hp	m/t, 421 HO
46G, 50Q	421 cid 370 hp	a/t, 421 HO
1964 Tempest		
925	326 cid 250 hp	m/t
960	326 cid 250 hp	a/t
945	326 cid 280 hp	m/t, 326 HO
971	326 cid 280 hp	a/t, 326 HO
78X	389 cid 325 hp	m/t, GTO
79J	389 cid 325 hp	a/t, GTO
76X	389 cid 348 hp	m/t, GTO
77J	389 cid 348 hp	a/t, GTO
1965 Pontiac		
WA, XA	389 cid 256 hp	m/t
WB	389 cid 256 hp	m/t, h/d clutch
YB	389 cid 256 hp	a/t, a/c
XB	389 cid 256 hp	a/t, a/c
WC	389 cid 290 hp	m/t, h/d clutch
WD	389 cid	m/t
YC	389 cid 290 hp	a/t, a/c
YD	389 cid 290 hp	a/t, a/c
XC	389 cid	a/t
YE	389 cid 325 hp	a/t
YF	389 cid 325 hp	a/t
WE	389 cid 333 hp	m/t
WF	389 cid 338 hp	m/t
YG	389 cid 338 hp	a/t
WG	421 cid 338 hp	m/t
YH	421 cid 338 hp	a/t
WH	421 cid 356 hp	m/t
YJ	421 cid 356 hp	a/t
WJ	421 cid 376 hp	m/t, 421 HO
YK	421 cid 376 hp	a/t, 421 HO
1965 Tempest, GTO		
WP	326 cid 250 hp	m/t
YN	326 cid 250 hp	a/t
WR	326 cid 285 hp	m/t
YP	326 cid 285 hp	a/t
WT	389 cid 335 hp	m/t
YS	389 cid 335 hp	a/t
WS	389 cid 360 hp	m/t
YR	389 cid 360 hp	a/t
1966 Pontiac		
WA	389 cid 256 hp	m/t
WB	389 cid 256 hp	m/t
XA	389 cid	m/t

Code	Engine	Notes
YA	389 cid 256 hp	a/t, a/c
WC	389 cid 290 hp	m/t
YU	389 cid 290 hp	a/t, a/c
YC	389 cid 290 hp	a/t, a/c
YD	389 cid 290 hp	a/t, a/c, A.I.R.
XB	389 cid	m/t, a/c
YV	389 cid 290 hp	a/t, a/c
YW, YE	389 cid 325 hp	a/t
YF, YX	389 cid 325 hp	a/t
XC	389 cid	a/t
WE	389 cid 333 hp	a/t
YL	389 cid 333 hp	m/t
YH	421 cid 338 hp	a/t
YZ	421 cid 350 hp	a/t
WH	421 cid 356 hp	m/t
YJ	421 cid 356 hp	a/t
WJ	421 cid 376 hp	m/t, 421 HO
YM, YK	421 cid 376 hp	a/t, 421 HO
1966 Tempest, GTO		
WP	326 cid 250 hp	m/t
WX	326 cid 250 hp	m/t, A.I.R.
YN	326 cid 250 hp	a/t
XF	326 cid 250 hp	a/t, A.I.R.
WR	326 cid 285 hp	m/t
YP	326 cid 285 hp	a/t
XG	326 cid 285 hp	a/t, A.I.R.
WW	389 cid 335 hp	m/t, A.I.R.
WT	389 cid 335 hp	m/t
YS	389 cid 335 hp	a/t
XE	389 cid 335 hp	a/t, A.I.R.
WS	389 cid 360 hp	m/t
WV	389 cid 360 hp	m/t, A.I.R.
YR	389 cid 360 hp	a/t
XS	389 cid 360 hp	m/t
1967 Pontiac		
XA	400 cid 260 hp	m/t
XB	400 cid 260 hp	a/t
WA, WB	400 cid 265 hp	m/t
WM, WM	400 cid 265 hp	m/t, A.I.R.
YA	400 cid 265 hp	a/t
YB	400 cid 265 hp	a/t, A.I.R.
YC, XV	400 cid 290 hp	a/t
YD	400 cid 290 hp	a/t, a/c
XU	400 cid 290 hp	a/t, a/c
YU	400 cid 290 hp	a/t, A.I.R.
YV	400 cid 290 hp	a/t, a/c
XC	400 cid 293 hp	a/t, A.I.R.
YE, XW	400 cid 325 hp	a/t
YF, XX	400 cid 325 hp	a/t, a/c
YX,	400 cid 325 hp	a/t, A.I.R., a/c
WD, XT	400 cid 333 hp	m/t, A.I.R.
WE, WY	400 cid 333 hp	m/t
XY	400 cid 350 hp	m/t, A.I.R.
XZ	400 cid 350 hp	m/t
YL	400 cid 350 hp	a/t, A.I.R.
XH	400 cid 350 hp	a/t
XJ, WF	400 cid 350 hp	a/t, a/c
WG	428 cid 360 hp	m/t
YY	428 cid 360 hp	m/t, A.I.R.
YH, Y2	428 cid 360 hp	a/t
XD	428 cid 360 hp	a/t, A.I.R.
WJ	428 cid 376 hp	m/t
XK	428 cid 376 hp	m/t, A.I.R.
YK	428 cid 376 hp	a/t

Code	Engine	Notes
Y3	428 cid 376 hp	a/t
YK	428 cid 376 hp	a/t, A.I.R.
1967 Tempest, GTO		
WP	326 cid 250 hp	m/t
WX	326 cid 250 hp	m/t, A.I.R.
YN	326 cid 250 hp	a/t
XF	326 cid 250 hp	a/t, A.I.R.
WR	326 cid 285 hp	m/t
XR	326 cid 285 hp	m/t, A.I.R.
YP	326 cid 285 hp	a/t
XG	326 cid 285 hp	a/t, A.I.R.
XM	400 cid 255 hp	a/t
XL	400 cid 255 hp	a/t, A.I.R.
WT	400 cid 335 hp	m/t
WW	400 cid 335 hp	m/t, A.I.R.
YS	400 cid 335 hp	a/t
WS	400 cid 360 hp	m/t
WV	400 cid 360 hp	m/t, A.I.R.
YZ	400 cid 360 hp	a/t
XS	400 cid 360 hp	m/t
YR	400 cid 360 hp	m/t, A.I.R.
XP	400 cid 360 hp	a/t
XP	400 cid 360 hp	a/t
1967 Firebird		
WC	326 cid 250 hp	m/t
WH	326 cid 250 hp	m/t, A.I.R.
YJ	326 cid 250 hp	a/t
XI	326 cid 250 hp	a/t, A.I.R.
WK	326 cid 285 hp	m/t
WO	326 cid 285 hp	m/t, A.I.R.
YM	326 cid 285 hp	a/t
XO	326 cid 285 hp	a/t, A.I.R.
WZ	400 cid 325 hp	m/t
WU	400 cid 325 hp	m/t, A.I.R.
YT	400 cid 325 hp	a/t
WQ	400 cid 325 hp	m/t, A.I.R.
XN	400 cid 325 hp	a/t
WI	400 cid 325 hp	m/t

Code	Engine	Notes
1968 Pontiac		
YA, XA	400 cid 265 hp	a/t
WA	400 cid 290 hp	m/t
WB	400 cid 290 hp	m/t
YC, ZR	400 cid 290 hp	a/t
YE, YF	400 cid 340 hp	a/t
XZ	400 cid 350 hp	m/t
XH	400 cid 350 hp	a/t
WG	428 cid 375 hp	m/t
YH	428 cid 375 hp	a/t
WJ	428 cid 390 hp	m/t
YK	428 cid 390 hp	a/t
1968 Tempest, GTO		
WD	350 cid 265 hp	m/t
YN	350 cid 265 hp	a/t
WR	350 cid 320 hp	m/t
YP	350 cid 320 hp	a/t
XM	400 cid 265 hp	a/t
WT	400 cid 350 hp	m/t
YS	400 cid 350 hp	a/t
WS	400 cid 360 hp	m/t, 400 HO
YZ	400 cid 360 hp	a/t, 400 HO
XS	400 cid 360 hp	m/t, Ram Air I
XP	400 cid 360 hp	a/t, Ram Air I
WY	400 cid 366 hp	m/t, Ram Air II
XW	400 cid 366 hp	a/t, Ram Air II
1968 Firebird		
WC	350 cid 265 hp	m/t
YJ	350 cid 265 hp	a/t
WK	350 cid 320 hp	m/t
YM	350 cid 320 hp	a/t
WZ	400 cid 330 hp	m/t
YT	400 cid 330 hp	a/t
WQ	400 cid 335 hp	m/t, 400 HO
YW	400 cid 335 hp	a/t, 400 HO
WI	400 cid 335 hp	m/t, Ram Air I
XN	400 cid 335 hp	a/t, Ram Air I
WU	400 cid 340 hp	m/t, Ram Air II

Exhaust port side of a 4X Pontiac cylinder head. The head identification code (4X) is generally located on top of the center two ports; however, the location does vary. Exhaust port configuration is a weak point on the Pontiac head, as the exhaust must make a 135-degree turn to exit. Note lack of outer exhaust manifold bolt holes.

Engine Codes

Code	Engine	Notes
XT	400 cid 340 hp	a/t, Ram Air II
1969 Pontiac		
YA, YB	400 cid 265 hp	a/t
YF	400 cid 265 hp	a/t, Grand Prix
WA, WD	400 cid 290 hp	m/t
WB, WE	400 cid 290 hp	m/t
YC, YD	400 cid 290 hp	a/t
XZ	400 cid 340 hp	a/t, Bonneville
WX	400 cid 350 hp	m/t, Grand Prix
XH	400 cid 350 hp	a/t, Grand Prix
YL, YH	428 cid 360 hp	a/t
WG	428 cid 360 hp	m/t
XK, XE	428 cid 360 hp	a/t, police
XJ	428 cid 360 hp	a/t, police
WJ	428 cid 390 hp	m/t, police
YK	428 cid 390 hp	a/t
WF	428 cid 370 hp	m/t, Grand Prix
XF	428 cid 370 hp	a/t, Grand Prix
WL	428 cid 390 hp	m/t, Grand Prix
XG	428 cid 390 hp	a/t, Grand Prix
1969 Tempest, GTO		
WP, WU	350 cid 265 hp	m/t
XR, XS,	350 cid 265 hp	a/t
YN, YU	350 cid 265 hp	a/t
WV	350 cid 330 hp	m/t
XU	350 cid 330 hp	a/t
XM, XX	400 cid 265 hp	a/t
WT	400 cid 350 hp	m/t
YS	400 cid 350 hp	a/t
WS	400 cid 366 hp	m/t, Ram Air III
YZ	400 cid 366 hp	a/t, Ram Air III
WW	400 cid 370 hp	m/t, Ram Air IV
XP	400 cid 370 hp	a/t, Ram Air IV
1969 Firebird		
WC, WM	350 cid 265 hp	m/t
XL, XB	350 cid 265 hp	a/t
YJ, YE	350 cid 265 hp	a/t
WN	350 cid 325 hp	m/t, 350 HO
XC	350 cid 325 hp	a/t, 350 HO
WZ	400 cid 330 hp	m/t
YT	400 cid 330 hp	a/t
WQ	400 cid 335 hp	m/t, Ram Air III
YW	400 cid 335 hp	a/t, Ram Air III
WH	400 cid 345 hp	m/t, Ram Air IV
XN	400 cid 345 hp	a/t, Ram Air IV
1970 Pontiac		
W7	350 cid 255 hp	m/t
X7	350 cid 255 hp	a/t
WE	400 cid 290 hp	m/t
YD	400 cid 290 hp	a/t
YB	400 cid 265 hp	a/t, Grand Prix
XZ	400 cid 330 hp	a/t
WX	400 cid 350 hp	m/t, Grand prix
XH	400 cid 350 hp	a/t, Grand Prix
YH	455 cid 360 hp	a/t
WG	455 cid 370 hp	m/t, Grand Prix
XF	455 cid 370 hp	a/t, Grand Prix
1970 Tempest, GTO		
WU	350 cid 255 hp	m/t
YU	350 cid 255 hp	a/t
XX	400 cid 265 hp	a/t
XV	400 cid 330 hp	a/t
WT	400 cid 350 hp	m/t

This exhaust manifold from a 1972 400 cid engine shows the missing outer bolts. The manifold will eventually leak.

Code	Engine	Notes
YS	400 cid 350 hp	a/t
WS	400 cid 366 hp	m/t, Ram Air III
YZ	400 cid 366 hp	a/t, Ram Air III
WW	400 cid 370 hp	m/t, Ram Air IV
XP	400 cid 370 hp	a/t, Ram Air IV
WA	455 cid 360 hp	m/t
YA	455 cid 360 hp	a/t
1970 Firebird		
WU	350 cid 255 hp	m/t
YU	350 cid 255 hp	a/t
XX	400 cid 265 hp	a/t
WT	400 cid 330 hp	m/t
YS	400 cid 330 hp	a/t
WS	400 cid 345 hp	m/t, Ram Air III
YZ	400 cid 345 hp	a/t, Ram Air III
WW	400 cid 370 hp	m/t, Ram Air IV
XP	400 cid 370 hp	a/t, Ram Air IV
1971 Pontiac		
WR	350 cid 250 hp	m/t
YU, XP	350 cid 250 hp	a/t
WS	400 cid 265 hp	m/t
XX	400 cid 265 hp	a/t
YS	400 cid 300 hp	a/t
WT	400 cid 300 hp	m/t, Grand Prix
WK	400 cid 300 hp	m/t, Grand Prix
WG	455 cid 280 hp	m/t
YA, YG	455 cid 280 hp	a/t
WJ	455 cid 325 hp	m/t
YE	455 cid 325 hp	a/t
YC	455 cid 325 hp	a/t, Grand Prix
1971 Le Mans, Tempest, GTO		
WR, WU	350 cid 250 hp	m/t
YU, YN, XR	350 cid 250 hp	a/t
XX	400 cid 265 hp	a/t
WT, WK	400 cid 300 hp	m/t
YS	400 cid 300 hp	a/t
YC	455 cid 325 hp	a/t
WL, WC	455 cid 335 hp	m/t
YE	455 cid 335 hp	a/t
1971 Firebird		
WR, WU	350 cid 250 hp	m/t
YU, XR	350 cid 250 hp	a/t
WT, WK	400 cid 300 hp	m/t
YS	400 cid 300 hp	a/t
XX	400 cid 265 hp	a/t
YC	455 cid 325 hp	a/t

Code	Engine	Notes
WL, WC	455 cid 335 hp	m/t
YE	455 cid 335 hp	a/t
1972 Pontiac		
YV	350 cid 175 hp	a/t, Ventura
WR	350 cid 175 hp	m/t
YR	350 cid 175 hp	a/t
YX, YZ, ZX	400 cid 200 hp	a/t
WS, WK	400 cid 250 hp	m/t
YS, YT	400 cid 250 hp	a/t
YH	455 cid 200 hp	a/t
YC, YA, ZH	455 cid 250 hp	a/t
WM	455 cid 300 hp	m/t
YB	455 cid 300 hp	a/t
1972 Le Mans		
WR	350 cid 175 hp	m/t
YR	350 cid 175 hp	a/t
YX, YZ, ZX	400 cid 200 hp	a/t
WS, WK	400 cid 250 hp	m/t
YS, YT, YC	400 cid 250 hp	a/t
WM, YB	455 cid 300 hp	m/t
1972 Firebird		
WR, YR	350 cid 175 hp	m/t
YX, YZ	400 cid 200 hp	a/t
WS, WK	400 cid 250 hp	m/t
YS	400 cid 250 hp	a/t
WM	455 cid 300 hp	m/t
YB	455 cid 300 hp	a/t
WD	455 cid 300 hp	m/t
YE	455 cid 300 hp	a/t
1973 Pontiac		
Y7	350 cid 150 hp	a/t
YV	350 cid 150 hp	a/t, Ventura
ZR, ZT, ZV	350 cid 150 hp	a/t
ZK, YZ	400 cid 170 hp	a/t
XV	350 cid 175 hp	m/t, Ventura
YP, Y4, Y1	400 cid 185 hp	a/t
ZN	400 cid 200 hp	a/t
YT, YN, Y3	400 cid 230 hp	a/t

Code	Engine	Notes
XK	400 cid 230 hp	a/t
YA, YK, YC, YD	455 cid 250 hp	a/t
X7, XE, XL, XM	455 cid 250 hp	a/t
ZA, ZC	455 cid 250 hp	a/t
1973 Le Mans		
Y2, YL, YR	350 cid 150 hp	a/t
ZR, ZT	350 cid 150 hp	a/t
YZ, ZK, ZX, ZC	400 cid 170 hp	a/t
XR	350 cid 175 hp	m/t
YP, YX	400 cid 185 hp	a/t
YT, XK	400 cid 230 hp	a/t
WP, WK, WS	400 cid 230 hp	m/t
Y6, YF, YG	400 cid 230 hp	m/t
Y3, YN, YS, YY	400 cid 230 hp	a/t
ZS	400 cid 230 hp	a/t
X5, XN, XX	400 cid 230 hp	a/t
YA, YC, YD, YK	455 cid 250 hp	a/t
X7, XE, XL, XM	455 cid 250 hp	a/t
ZA, ZC	455 cid 250 hp	a/t
1973 Firebird		
YL, YR	350 cid 150 hp	a/t
ZR, ZT	350 cid 150 hp	a/t
XR	350 cid 175 hp	m/t
ZK, ZX, YZ	400 cid 170 hp	a/t
YX	400 cid 185 hp	a/t
WK, WP	400 cid 230 hp	m/t
Y6, YG	400 cid 230 hp	m/t
Y3, YS, XN	400 cid 230 hp	a/t
YD, YK	455 cid 250 hp	a/t
X7, XM	455 cid 250 hp	a/t
WT, WW	455 cid 250 hp	m/t
YA, YC	455 cid 250 hp	a/t

The left arrow indicates the date code on this 1970 block. The arrow on the right points to the block casting number.

Engine Codes

Code	Engine	Notes
XE, XL	455 cid 250 hp	a/t
1974 Pontiac		
WB	350 cid 155 hp	m/t, Ventura
YB	350 cid 155 hp	a/t, Ventura
ZB	350 cid 155/170 hp	a/t
AA	350 cid 155 hp	a/t
WP	350 cid 200 hp	m/t, Ventura, GTO
YP	350 cid 200 hp	a/t, Ventura, GTO
YS	350 cid 200 hp	a/t, Ventura, GTO
ZP	350 cid 200 hp	a/t, Ventura, GTO
YF, YH, YJ, YK	400 cid 190 hp	a/t
AD, AH, ZD	400 cid 190 hp	a/t
YL, YM, YT, YZ	400 cid 200 hp	a/t
A3, AT	400 cid 200 hp	a/t
Y3	400 cid 225 hp	m/t
Y4, Y6, Y9	455 cid 250 hp	a/t
A4, AU	455 cid 250 hp	a/t
Z4, Z6	455 cid 250 hp	a/t
YX, YY	455 cid 250 hp	a/t
ZU, ZW, ZX	455 cid 250 hp	a/t
YR, YU	455 cid 250 hp	a/t
1974 Le Mans		
WA	350 cid 155 hp	m/t
YA, YC	350 cid 155 hp	a/t
ZA	350 cid 155/170 hp	a/t
AA	350 cid 155 hp	a/t
WN	350 cid 170 hp	m/t
YN	350 cid 170 hp	a/t
YF, YH	400 cid 190 hp	a/t
AD, AH	400 cid 190 hp	a/t
ZD, ZH	400 cid 190 hp	a/t
ZJ, ZK	400 cid 190 hp	a/t
YL, YM	400 cid 200 hp	a/t
A3, AT	400 cid 200 hp	a/t
YT, YZ	400 cid 200 hp	a/t
ZS, ZT	400 cid 200 hp	a/t
Y3, WT, WR	400 cid 225 hp	m/t
Y9, YU, YW	455 cid 250 hp	a/t
A4, AU	455 cid 250 hp	a/t
Z4, ZU, ZW	455 cid 250 hp	a/t
YX, YY	455 cid 250 hp	a/t
1974 Firebird		
WA	350 cid 155 hp	m/t
YA	350 cid 155 hp	a/t
ZA	350 cid 155/170 hp	a/t
AA	350 cid 155 hp	a/t
WN	350 cid 170 hp	m/t
YN	350 cid 170 hp	a/t
YF, YH	400 cid 190 hp	a/t
AD, AH	400 cid 190 hp	a/t
ZJ, ZK	400 cid 190 hp	a/t
YL, YM	400 cid 200 hp	a/t
A3, AT	400 cid 200 hp	a/t
YT, YZ	400 cid 200 hp	a/t
ZS, ZT	400 cid 200 hp	a/t
Y3, WT, WR	400 cid 225 hp	m/t
Y9, YY, YW	455 cid 250 hp	a/t
A4, AU	455 cid 250 hp	a/t
Z4, ZU, ZW	455 cid 250 hp	a/t
W8, Y8	455 cid 290 hp	m/t
1975 Pontiac		
YH	400 cid 170 hp	a/t
YT, YM, ZT	400 cid 185 hp	a/t
YU, YW	455 cid 200 hp	a/t
ZU, ZW	455 cid 200 hp	a/t
1975 Le Mans		
YA	350 cid 155 hp	a/t
ZP	350 cid 175 hp	a/t
YH	400 cid 170 hp	a/t
YT, ZT	400 cid 185 hp	a/t
YW, ZU	455 cid 200 hp	a/t
1975 Firebird		
YB	350 cid 155 hp	a/t
YN, ZP	350 cid 175 hp	m/t
WT, YS	400 cid 185 hp	m/t
WX	455 cid 200 hp	m/t

Engine Specifications

	Displacement	Carburetor	Horsepower	Torque	Compression Ratio	Notes
1955						
	287	2V	173@4,600	260@2,400	7.4	m/t
	287	2V	180@4,600	264@2,400	8.0	
	287	4V	200@4,800	264@2,600	8.0	
1956						
	316.6	2V	192@4,400	297@2,400	7.9	m/t
	316.6	2V	205@4,600	294@2,600	8.9	
	316.6	4V	216@4,800	315@2,800	8.9	m/t
	316.6	4V	227@4,800	312@3,000	8.9	
	316.6	2x4V	285@5100	330@2,600	10.0	Strato-Streak
1957						
	347	2V	227@4,600	333@2,300	8.5	
	347	4V	244@4,400	344@2,400	8.5	m/t
	347	4V	252@4,600	354@2,400	10.0	
	347	4V	270@4,800	359@2,800	10.0	
	347	3x2V	290@5,000	NA	10.0	NASCAR
	347	FI	295@5,000	NA	10.25	
	347	3x2V	317@5,200	NA	10.0	NASCAR
1958						
	370	2V	240@4,500	354@2,600	8.6	

	Displacement	Carburetor	Horsepower	Torque	Compression Ratio	Notes
	370	4V	255@4,500	360@2,600	8.6	m/t
	370	2V	270@4,600	388@2,800	10.0	
	370	4V	285@4,600	395@2,800	10.0	
	370	3x2V	300@4,600	400@3,000	10.5	
	370	FI	310@4,800	400@3,400	10.5	
	370	4V	315@5,000	NA	10.5	NASCAR
	370	3x2V	330@5,200	NA	10.5	NASCAR
1959						
	389	2V	215@3,600	390@2,000	8.6	
	389	2V	245@4,200	392@2,000	8.6	m/t
	389	4V	260@4,200	400@2,800	8.6	m/t
	389	2V	280@4,400	407@2,800	10.0	
	389	4V	300@4,600	420@2,800	10.0	
	389	3x2V	315@4,800	425@3,200	10.0	
	389	4V	330@4,800	420@2,800	10.0	SD
	389	3x2V	345@4,800	425@3,200	10.0	SD
1960						
	389	2V	215@3,600	390@2,000	8.6	
	389	2V	230@3,600	390@2,000	8.6	
	389	4V	235@3,600	402@2,800	8.6	
	389	4V	283@4,400	413@2,800	10.25	
	389	4V	303@3,600	390@2,000	10.25	
	389	3x2V	318@4,600	430@3,200	10.75	
	389	4V	333@4,800	425@2,800	10.75	
	389	3x2V	348@4,800	425@3,200	10.75	SD
	389	3x2V	363@4,800	425@3,200	10.75	SD (over the counter)
1961						
	389	2V	215@3,600	390@2,000	8.6	
	389	2V	230@3,600	390@2,000	8.6	
	389	4V	235@3,600	402@2,800	8.6	
	389	4V	287@4,400	417@2,400	10.25	
	389	4V	303@4,600	390@2,000	10.25	
	389	3x2V	318@4,600	430@3,200	10.75	
	389	4V	333@4,800	425@2,800	10.75	
	389	3x2V	348@4,800	425@3,200	10.75	
	389	3x2V/4V	368@4,800	425@3,200	10.75	SD (over the counter)
	421	2x4V	373@5,400	NA	11.00	SD (over the counter)
1962						
	215	4V	190@4,800	240@3,200	10.25	Tempest
	389	2V	215@3,600	390@2,000	8.6	
	389	2V	230@3,600	390@2,000	8.6	
	389	4V	235@3,600	402@2,800	8.6	
	389	4V	240@3,600	402@2,800	7.8	
	389	4V	267@4,200	405@2,400	10.25	
	389	4V	283@4,400	413@2,800	10.25	
	389	4V	303@4,600	390@2,000	10.25	
	389	3x2V	318@4,600	430@3,200	10.75	
	389	4V	333@4,800	425@2,800	10.75	
	389	3x2V	348@4,800	425@3,200	10.75	
	389	4V	385@5,200	333@4,800	10.75	SD, Catalina 2dr
	421	4V	320@4,000	455@2,800	10.75	
	421	2x4V	405@5,600	425@4,400	11.00	SD, Catalina 2dr
1963						
	336	2V	260@4,800	362@2,800	10.25	Tempest (called a 326)
	336	4V	280@4,800	355@3,200	10.25	Tempest (called a 326)
	389	2V	215@3,600	390@2,000	8.6	
	389	2V	230@3,600	390@2,000	8.6	
	389	4V	235@3,600	402@2,800	8.6	
	389	4V	267@4,200	405@2,400	10.25	
	389	4V	283@4,400	413@2,800	10.25	
	389	4V	303@4,600	390@2,000	10.25	
	389	3x2V	313@4,600	430@3,200	10.25	
	421	4V	320@4,000	455@2,800	10.75	

Engine Specifications

	Displacement	Carburetor	Horsepower	Torque	Compression Ratio	Notes
	421	4V	353@5,000	460@3,000	10.75	HO
	421	3x2V	370@5,200	460@3,800	10.75	HO
	421	4V	390@5,800	425@3,600	12.00	SD, Catalina 2dr
	421	2x4V	405@5,600	425@4,400	12.00	SD, Catalina 2dr, Tempest
	421	2x4V	410@5,600	435@4,400	13.00	SD, Catalina 2dr
1964						
	326	2V	260@4,800	362@2,800	10.25	Tempest
	326	4V	280@4,800	355@3,200	10.25	Tempest
	389	2V	215@3,600	390@2,000	8.6	Pontiac
	389	2V	230@3,600	390@2,000	8.6	Pontiac
	389	4V	235@3,600	402@2,800	8.6	Pontiac
	389	4V	267@4,200	405@2,400	10.50	Pontiac
	389	4V	283@4,400	413@2,800	10.50	Pontiac
	389	4V	303@4,600	390@2,000	10.50	Pontiac
	389	4V	283@4,400	413@2,800	10.50	Pontiac
	389	4V	306@4,600	390@2,000	10.50	Grand Prix
	389	4V	325@4,800	428@3,200	10.75	Tempest
	389	4V	330@4,600	430@3,200	10.75	Pontiac
	389	3x2V	348@4,900	428@3,600	10.75	Tempest
	421	4V	320@4,000	455@2,800	10.75	Pontiac
	421	3x2V	350@4,600	460@3,000	10.75	Pontiac
	421	3x2V	370@5,200	460@3,800	10.75	Pontiac, HO
1965						
	326	2V	250@4,600	333@2,800	8.6	Tempest
	326	4V	285@5,000	359@3,200	10.50	Tempest
	389	2V	256@4,600	388@2,400	8.6	Pontiac
	389	4V	290@4,600	418@2,400	10.50	Pontiac
	389	4V	325@4,800	429@3,200	10.50	Pontiac
	389	4V	333@5,000	429@3,200	10.50	Pontiac
	389	4V	335@5,000	431@3,200	10.75	Tempest
	389	3x2V	338@5,000	432@3,200	10.75	Pontiac
	389	3x2V	360@5,200	424@3,600	10.75	Tempest
	421	4V	338@4,600	459@2,800	10.50	Pontiac
	421	3x2V	356@4,800	459@3,200	10.75	Pontiac, HO
	421	3x2V	376@5,000	461@3,600	10.75	Pontiac, HO
1966						
	326	2V	250@4,600	333@2,800	9.2	Tempest
	326	4V	285@5,000	359@3,200	10.50	Tempest
	389	2V	256@4,600	388@2,400	8.6	Pontiac
	389	4V	290@4,600	418@2,400	10.50	Pontiac
	389	4V	325@4,800	429@3,200	10.50	Pontiac
	389	4V	333@5,000	429@3,200	10.50	Pontiac
	389	4V	335@5,000	431@3,200	10.75	GTO
	389	3x2V	360@5,200	424@3,600	10.75	GTO
	421	4V	338@4,600	459@2,800	10.50	Pontiac
	421	4V	350@4,600	459@2,800	10.50	Pontiac
	421	3x2V	356@4,800	459@3,200	10.75	Pontiac
	421	3x2V	376@5,000	461@3,600	10.75	Pontiac, HO
1967						
	326	2V	250@4,600	333@2,800	9.2	Tempest, Firebird
	326	4V	285@5,000	359@3,200	10.50	Tempest, Firebird
	400	2V	255@4,400	397@2,400	8.6	GTO
	400	2V	260@4,800	445@2,900	8.6	Pontiac
	400	2V	265@4,600	397@2,400	8.6	Pontiac
	400	4V	290@4,600	428@2,500	10.50	Pontiac
	400	4V	325@4,800	445@2,900	10.50	Pontiac (10.75 c/r Firebird)
	400	4V	333@5,000	445@3,000	10.50	Pontiac
	400	4V	335@4,600	459@2,800	10.75	GTO
	400	4V	350@4,800	440@3,000	10.50	Pontiac
	400	4V	360@5,100	438@3,600	10.75	GTO
	421	4V	360@4,600	472@3,200	10.50	Pontiac
	421	4V	376@5,100	462@3,400	10.75	Pontiac

	Displacement	Carburetor	Horsepower	Torque	Compression Ratio	Notes
1968						
	350	2V	265@4,600	355@2,800	9.2	Tempest, Firebird
	350	4V	320@5100	380@3,200	10.50	HO, Tempest, Firebird
	400	2V	265@4,600	397@2,400	8.6	Pontiac, Tempest
	400	4V	290@4,600	428@2,500	10.50	Pontiac
	400	4V	330@4,800	445@2,900	10.75	Firebird
	400	4V	335@5,000	445@3,400	10.75	Firebird, HO/Ram Air I
	400	4V	340@4,800	445@2,900	10.50	Firebird, Ram Air II
	400	4V	350@5,000	445@3,000	10.75	Pontiac
	400	4V	360@5,100	445@3,600	10.75	GTO, HO/Ram Air I
	400	4V	366@5,400	445@3,600	10.75	GTO, Ram Air II
	428	4V	375@4,800	472@3,200	10.75	Pontiac
	428	4V	390@5,200	465@3,400	10.75	Pontiac
1969						
	350	2V	265@4,600	355@2,800	9.2	Tempest, Firebird
	350	4V	320@5,100	380@3,200	10.50	HO, Tempest, Firebird
	400	2V	265@4,600	397@2,400	8.6	Pontiac, Tempest, GTO
	400	4V	290@4,600	428@2,500	10.50	Pontiac
	400	4V	330@4,800	430@3,300	10.75	Firebird, Tempest (10.5 C.R.)
	400	4V	335@5,000	430@3,400	10.75	Firebird, Ram Air III
	400	4V	340@4,800	445@2,900	10.75	Pontiac
	400	4V	345@5,400	430@3,700	10.50	Firebird, Ram Air IV
	400	4V	350@5,000	445@3,000	10.75	Pontiac (10.5 c/r), GTO
	400	4V	360@5,100	445@3,600	10.75	GTO, HO/Ram Air I
	400	4V	366@5,400	445@3,600	10.75	GTO, Ram Air III
	400	4V	370@ 5,500	445@3,900	10.75	GTO, Ram Air IV
	428	4V	360@4,600	472@3,200	10.50	Pontiac
	428	4V	370@4,800	472@3,200	10.75	Pontiac
	428	4V	390@5,200	465@3,400	10.75	Pontiac
1970						
	350	2V	255@4,600	355@2,800	8.8	Tempest, Firebird
	400	2V	265@4,600	397@2,400	8.8	Pontiac, Tempest, GTO, Firebird
	400	4V	290@4,600	428@2,500	10.00	Pontiac
	400	4V	330@4,800	430@3,300	10.00	Pontiac, Firebird, Tempest
	400	4V	345@5,400	430@3,700	10.50	Firebird, Ram Air III
	400	4V	350@5,000	445@3,000	10.25	Pontiac, GTO
	400	4V	366@5,400	445@3,600	10.75	GTO, Ram Air III
	400	4V	370@5,500	445@3,900	10.75	GTO, Firebird, Ram Air IV
	455	4V	360@4,300	500@2,700	10.00	Pontiac, GTO
	455	4V	370@4,600	500@3,100	10.25	Pontiac
1971						
	307	2V	200@4,600	300@2,400	8.5	Ventura (Chevrolet V-8)
	350	2V	250@4,400	350@2,400	8.0	Pontiac, Le Mans, Firebird
	400	2V	265@4,600	397@2,400	8.2	Pontiac, Le Mans, Firebird
	400	4V	300@4,800	400@3,600	8.2	Pontiac, Grand Prix, Le Mans, GTO, Firebird
	455	4V	280@4,400	455@2,000	8.2	Pontiac, GTO, Grand Prix
	455	4V	325@4,400	455@3,200	8.2	Pontiac, GTO, Firebird, Le Mans
	455	4V	335@4,800	480@3,600	8.4	Pontiac, GTO, Firebird, HO
1972						
	307	2V	130@4,400	230@2,400	8.5	Ventura (Chevrolet V-8)
	350	2V	175@4,400	275@2,000	8.0	Pontiac, Le Mans, Firebird, Ventura
	400	2V	200@4,000	295@2,800	8.2	Pontiac, Le Mans, Firebird
	400	4V	250@4,400	325@3,200	8.2	Pontiac, Grand Prix, Le Mans, GTO
	455	4V	250@4,400	455@2,000	8.2	Pontiac, GTO, Grand Prix
	455	4V	300@4,400	455@3,200	8.4	Firebird
1973						
	350	2V	150@4,400	275@2,000	7.6	Pontiac, Le Mans, Firebird, Ventura
	350	2V	175@4,400	275@2,000	7.6	Le Mans, Firebird, Ventura
	400	2V	170@3,600	320@2,000	8.0	Pontiac, Le Mans, Firebird

Engine Specifications

	Displacement	Carburetor	Horsepower	Torque	Compression Ratio	Notes
	400	2V	185@4,000	320@2,400	8.0	Pontiac, Le Mans, Firebird
	400	4V	200@4,000	310@2,400	8.0	Pontiac
	400	4V	230@4,400	325@3,200	8.0	Pontiac, GTO, Le Mans, Firebird, Grand Prix
	455	4V	250@4,000	370@2,800	8.0	Pontiac, GTO, Le Mans, Grand Prix, Firebird
	455	4V	290@4,000	395@3,200	8.4	Firebird, SD
1974						
	350	2V	155@4,400	275@2,000	7.6	Le Mans, Firebird, Ventura
	350	2V	170@4,400	275@2,000	7.6	Le Mans, Firebird, Ventura
	350	2V	200@4,400	295@2,800	7.6	GTO
	400	2V	190@4,000	330@2,400	8.0	Pontiac, Le Mans, Firebird
	400	4V	200@4,000	320@2,400	8.0	Pontiac, Le Mans, Firebird, Grand Prix
	400	4V	225@4,000	330@2,800	8.0	Pontiac, Le Mans, Firebird, Grand Prix
	455	4V	250@4,000	380@2,800	8.0	Pontiac, Le Mans, Grand Prix, Firebird
	455	4V	290@4,000	395@3,200	8.4	Firebird, SD
1975						
	350	2V	155@4,000	275@2,000	7.6	Le Mans, Firebird, Ventura
	350	2V	175@4,000	280@2,000	7.6	Le Mans, Firebird, Ventura
	400	2V	170@4,000	315@2,000	7.6	Pontiac, Le Mans, Firebird
	400	4V	185@3,600	315@2,000	7.6	Pontiac, Le Mans, Firebird
	455	4V	200@3,500	355@2,400	7.6	Pontiac, Le Mans, Firebird, Grand Prix, HO

Engine Internal Dimensions

Displacement	Bore and Stroke	Rod Bearings	Main Bearings	Intake/Exhaust Valves
287	3.750x3.250	2.2488–2.2498	2.498–2.499	1.72/1.50
316.6	3.9375x3.250	2.2488–2.2498	2.498–2.499	1.72/1.50
326*	3.7187x3.750	2.250	3.000	1.88/1.60
347	3.9375x3.562	2.2488–2.2498	2.623–2.624	1.88/1.60
350	3.8750x3.750	2.250	3.000	1.96/1.66
370	4.0625x3.562	2.2488–2.2498	2.623–2.624	1.88/1.60
389	4.0625x3.750	2.2488–2.2498	2.998–2.999	1.88/1.60, 1965–1966 1.96/1.66 (1959–1960 SD 1.92/1.66, 1961–1962 SD 2.02/1.76)
400	4.1200x3.750	2.250	3.000	2.11/1.77(1973-up 2.11/1.66)
421	4.0937x4.000	2.250	3.250	1.96/1.66 (exc. 320 hp 421 1.92/1.66; 1962–1963 SD 2.02/1.76)
428	4.1200x4.000	2.250	3.250	2.11/1.77
455	4.1510x4.210	2.250	3.250	2.11/1.77 (1973-up 2.11/1.66 exc. SD 2.11/1.77)

* For 1963, 3.780x3.750 for 336 cid

Block, Head, and Manifold Casting Numbers

Year	Engine	Casting Number
Engine Blocks		
1955	287	518037
1956	316.6	521560
1957	347	523293
1958	370	528456
1959	389	532000
1960	389	536387
1961	389/421	538181
1962	389	538181, 542346
1962	421	538181, SD
1963	326	538211
1963	389	543680
1963	421	544988
1964	326	9773153
1964	389	9773155

Year	Engine	Casting Number
Engine Blocks		
1964	421	9773157
1965	389	9778789
1965	421	9778791
1966	326	9778840
1966	389	9778789
1966	421	9778791, 9782611
1967	326	9786339
1967	400	9786133
1967	428	9786135
1968–1969	350	9790079
1968–1969	400	9790071
1968	400	9792506, Ram Air
1968–1969	428	9792968
1969	400	9792506, Ram Air IV

Most Pontiac engines were equipped with a two-barrel intake manifold, which provided good economy and good low-end torque. This manifold is for the 1972 engines.

Year	Engine	Casting Number
Engine Blocks		
1969	303	546313
1969	400	9792968
1970	350	9799916
1970	400	9799914
1970	400	9799914, Ram Air III
1970	400	979991, Ram Air IV
1970	400	481708, Ram Air V
1970	455	9799140
1971–1972	350	481990
1971–1974	400	481988
1971	455	483677, 485428, HO
1972	455	485426
1972	366	212
1973–1974	350	488986
1973–1974	455	485428
1973–1974	455	132, SD
1975	350	488986, 500810
1975	400	488986, 500557
1975–1976	455	500813
Cylinder Heads		
1955	287	518024
1956	316.6	522010
1957	347	523298, 524852 (FI)
1958	370	528511, XX528511XX (FI)
1959	389	531395
1960	389	536109, 535461 (SD)
1961	389	538177
1961	389/421	540306, SD
1962	389/421	540306, 544127, SD
1962	389	538177
1963	326	543797, 250 hp
1963	326	546232, 9772652, 260/280 hp
1963	389	543796, 215/230/235 hp
1963	389	543797, 267/283/303/313 hp
1963	421	543797, 320 hp
1963	421	9770716, 353/370 hp
1963	421	544127, 9771980, SD
1964	326	9773345, 250 hp
1964	326	9773395, 280 hp
1964	389	543796, 215/230/235 hp

Year	Engine	Casting Number
Cylinder Heads		
1964	389	9773345, 267/283/303/306 hp
1964	389	9770716, 325/330/348 hp
1964	421	9773345, 320 hp
1964	421	9770716, 350/370 hp
1965	326	62, 250 hp
1965	326	22, 285 hp
1965	389	75, 256 hp
1965	389	76, 290/325/333 hp
1965	389	77, 335/338/360 hp
1965	421	76, 338 hp
1965	421	77, 356/376 hp
1966	326	094, 250 hp
1966	326	095, 285 hp
1966	389	091, 256 hp
1966	389	092, 290/325/333 hp
1966	389	093, 335/360 hp
1966	421	092, 338/350 hp
1966	421	093, 356/376 hp
1967	326	140, 250 hp
1967	326	141, 285 hp
1967	400	142, 255/260/265 hp
1967	400	143, 061, 290/325/333 hp
1967	400	670, 9787671, 187, 350 hp
1967	400	670, 325/335/360 hp
1967	400	670, 97, 997, 325/360 hp, Ram Air
1967	428	670, 9787671
1968	350	17, 265 hp
1968	350	18, 320 hp
1968	400	14, 265 hp
1968	400	15, 290/340 hp
1968	400	16, 62, 330/350/360 hp
1968	400	31, 335/360 hp
1968	400	96, 340/366 hp
1968	428	16, 216, 62
1969	350	47, 265 hp
1969	350	48, 325 hp
1969	400	45, 265 hp
1969	400	46, 290 hp
1969	400	16, 62, 340 hp

Block, Head, and Manifold Casting Numbers

Year	Engine	Casting Number
Cylinder Heads		
1969	400	16, 62, 330/335/340/350/366 hp
1969	400	722, 345/370 hp
1969	400	44, Ram Air V
1969	428	16, 46, 360 hp
1969	428	62, 370 hp
1969	428	16, 62, 390 hp
1970	350	11, 47, 255 hp
1970	400	11, 47, 265 hp
1970	400	16, 290 hp
1970	400	16, 330 hp, Pontiac, Tempest
1970	400	12, 330 hp, m/t
1970	400	13, 330 hp, a/t
1970	400	12, 345 hp
1970	400	13, 350 hp
1970	400	12, 350 hp, GTO, m/t
1970	400	13, 350 hp, GTO, a/t
1970	400	12, 366 hp
1970	400	614, 370 hp
1970	455	15, 360 hp, Pontiac
1970	455	64, 260/370 hp, GTO, Grand Prix
1971	350	94
1971	400	99, 265 hp
1971	400	96, 330 hp
1971	455	98, 280 hp
1971	455	66, 325 hp
1971	455	197, 335 hp
1972	350	7H1
1972	400	7J2, 200 hp
1972	400	7K3, 250 hp
1972	455	7L4, 200 hp
1972	455	7M5, 7M5, 250 hp
1972	455	7F6, 300 hp
1973	350/400	46, 4C, 150/170/175/185 hp
1973	400	4X, 4C, 200 hp
1973	400	4X, 230 hp
1973	455	4X, 215/250 hp
1973	455	16, 485216, 290 hp
1974	350	46, 4C, 155/170 hp
1974	350	46, 200 hp
1974	400	46, 4C, 175/190 hp
1974	400	4X, 4C, 4H, 200 hp
1974	400	4X, 4C 225 hp, a/t
1974	400	4X, 225 hp, m/t
1974	455	4X, 215/250 hp
1974	455	16, 290 hp
1975	350/400	5C, 6X
1975	455	51, 6H
Intake Manifolds		
1955	287 2V	521510
1955	287 4V	521512
1956	316.6 2V	521570
1956	316.6 4V	521571
1956	316.6 2x4V	523554
1963	326 2V	9770263
1963	326 4V	9770264
1964	326 2V	9770263
1964	326 4V	9770264
1965	326 2V	9778817
1965	326 4V	9778816

Year	Engine	Casting Number
Intake Manifolds		
1966	326 2V	9782894
1966	326 4V	9782896
1967	326 2V	9784438
1967	326 4V	9782896, 9782896 (Quadrajet)
1957	347 2V	523813
1957	347 4V	523814
1957	347 3x2V	528533
1968	350 2V	9790418, 9784233 (late)
1968	350 4V	9790140, 9794234 (late)
1969	350 2V	9784233
1969	350 4V	9794234
1971	350 2V	481732
1972	350 2V	485911
1973	350 2V	492292
1974	350 2V	495104
1974	350 4V	495106
1975	350 2V	496142
1975	350 4V	496140
1958	370 2V	528577
1958	370 4V	528577
1958	370 3x2V	529571
1959	389 2V	534318, 532119
1959	389 4V	532120
1959	389 3x2V	532422
1960	389 2V	536517
1960	389 4V	536518, 535482 (SD)
1960	389 4V	535889, SD, aluminum
1960	389 3x2V	536194, 5355552 (SD)
1961	389 2V	538201
1961	389 4V	535889, SD, aluminum
1961	389 3x2V	538202
1961	389 3x2V	540510, SD, aluminum
1962	389 2V	541474
1962	389 4V	541475
1962	389 4V	544128, SD, aluminum
1962	389 3x2V	541690, SD
1963	389 2V	9770263
1963	389 4V	9770264
1963	389 3x2V	9770275
1964	389 2V	9770263
1964	389 4V	9770264
1964	389 3x2V	9775088
1965	389 2V	9778817
1965	389 4V	9778816
1965	389 3x2V	9778818
1966	389 2V	9782894
1966	389 4V	9782895
1966	389 3x2V	9782898
1967	389 2V	9784438
1967	389 4V	9782896, 9782896 (Quadrajet)
1968	400 2V	9790418, 9784233 (late)
1968	400 4V	9790140, 9794234 (late)
1969	400 2V	9784233
1969	400 4V	9794234
1969	400 4V	9796614, Ram Air IV
1970	400 2V	9799067
1970	400 4V	9799068
1970	400 4V	9799084, Ram Air IV, aluminum
1970	400 4V	545288, Ram Air V, aluminum
1971	400 2V	481732
1971	400 4V	481733

High-performance Pontiac engines were equipped with a stronger, four-bolt main bearing cap block.

Year	Engine	Casting Number
Intake Manifolds		
1972	400 2V	485911
1972	400 4V	485912
1973	400 2V	492292
1973	400 4V	485912, 492744, 494282
1974	400 2V	495104
1974	400 4V	495106
1975	400 2V	496142
1975	400 4V	496140
1961	421 2x4V	542991, SD, aluminum
1962–1964	421 4V	544128, SD, aluminum
1962	421 2x4V	9770319, 9770859, SD, aluminum
1963	421 4V	9770274
1963	421 3x2V	9770275
1963	421 2x4V	9772598, 9772598, SD, aluminum
1964	421 4V	9770264
1964	421 3x2V	9775088
1965	421 4V	9778816
1965	421 3x2V	9778817
1966	421 4V	9782896
1966	421 3x2V	9782898
1967	428 4V	9782896, 9782896 (Quadrajet)
1968	428 4V	9790140, 9794234 (late)
1969	428 4V	9794234
1970	455 4V	9799068
1971	455 4V	481733

Year	Engine	Casting Number
Intake Manifolds		
1972	455 2V	485911
1972	455 4V	485912
1972	455 4V	488945, HO, aluminum
1973	455 4V	485912, 492744, 494282
1973	455 4V	494405, 494419, 485640 (aluminum), SD
1974	455 4V	495106
1974	455 4V	495107
1975	455 4V	496140
Exhaust Manifolds		
1955	287	518091 right, 518089 left
1956	316.6	521624 right, 521630 left
1957	347	523537 right, 523539 left
1957	347	524883 right, 523539 left, FI
1958	370	528595 right, 528598 left
1958	370	530374 right, 530965 left, FI
1959	389	537508 right, 532312 left
1960	389	537508 right, 532312 left
1961	389	537508 right, 538238 left
1962	389	537508 right, 538238 left
1963	389/421	9779325 right, 5445470 left
1963–1964	421	545106 right, 537455 left, HO
1964	389/421	9779325 right, 5445470 left
1965	389/421	9779325 right, 9779033 left
1965–1966	421	9779493 right, 9779595 left, HO
1966	389/421	9779325 right, 9779033 left
1967	350/400/428	9779325 right, 9779495 left
1967	428	9779493 right, 9779595 left, HO
1967	400	9779493 right, 9779495 left, Firebird Ram Air
1967	400	9777641 right, 9777646 left, GTO Ram Air
1968	350/400/428	9779325 right, 9779033 left
1968	400	9777641 right, 9791637 left, GTO Ram Air
1968	400	9794033 right, 9794035 left, GTO Ram Air II
1968	400	9794036 right, 9794038 left, Firebird Ram Air II
1969	350/400/428	9797073 right, 9779495 left
1969	400	9797072 right, 9779495 left, GTO Ram Air
1969	400	9797075 right, 9794035 left, GTO Ram Air IV
1969	400	9797074 right, 9797038 left, Firebird Ram Air IV
1970	350/400/455	490142 right, 490144 left
1970	400	9799720 right, 478140 left, 400 Ram Air III
1970	400	9799721 right, 478141 left, 400 Ram Air IV
1971–1972	455	9799721 right, 478141 left, HO
1971–1974	350/400 455	490142 right, 490143 left
1973–1974	455	490802 right, 490803 left, SD
1975	350/400/455	4999623 right, 495986 left

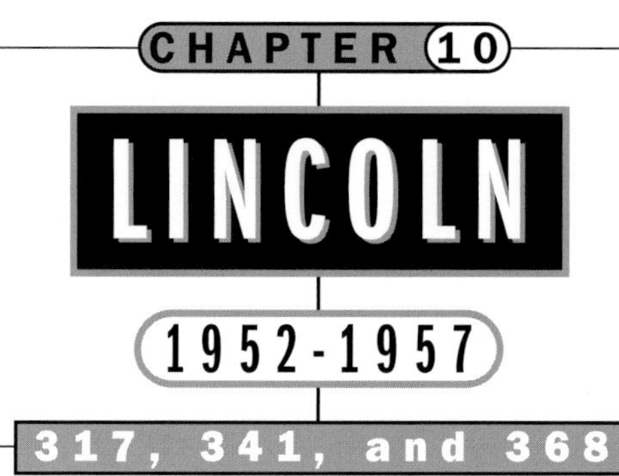

Ford's first modern American production ohv V-8 engine was the 317 cid (actual displacement was 317.5 cid) V-8, and it was installed on the 1952 Lincoln. The 1952–1957 Lincoln V-8s were of the "Y-block" design.

The name *Y-block* was used to show that the engine, when seen from the end, resembled a *Y* rather than the *V* of the flathead. The reason for this was the lowered block skirts, which extended below the centerline of the crankshaft. There was a lot of hoopla at the time that these lowered skirts gave better support to the main-bearing caps. This extra skirting doesn't touch the caps, though. If they don't touch, they can't add any extra support.

The Lincoln 317 cid V-8 had a compression ratio of 7.5:1. It was rated at 160 hp, which was only 4 hp more than the 1951 336 cid "InVincible 8" flathead V-8 it replaced. While the old flathead had an undersquare bore and stroke of 3.50x4.25 in., however, the new Lincoln V-8 had an oversquare measurement of 3.80x3.50 in. The oversquare design meant less piston travel (and therefore less wear) when compared to the long stroke flathead.

Another benefit of the new engine design was the possibility of using higher compression ratios, better engine breathing through larger, more direct porting, a more efficient combustion chamber design, better engine cooling, and integral valve guides. Integral valve guides, besides being less costly to produce, allowed the valve running temperature to be reduced by 100 degrees, as the heat flowed through the head casting more efficiently. (With removable guides, the heat from the valve stem has to travel through two dissimilar metals, and the joint between the two acts as a barrier, slowing the transfer of heat to the cylinder head casting.) When the guide is finally worn, the fit can be restored by using valves with thicker stems. The guides can also be drilled for bronze inserts, or replaceable guides can be installed.

The horsepower race was in full swing in the 1950s. In response, the Lincoln V-8 was increased in displacement to 341 cid in 1955, and then again in 1956, to 368 cid. At 368 cid, the Lincoln V-8 had reached its limits regarding displacement, while at the same time the Lincoln cars kept getting bigger and heavier. This was also compounded by the fact that other manufacturers' engines put out more power than the Lincoln V-8. The engine was retired and replaced by the new MEL series in 1958.

Still, the Lincoln V-8 had its moment of glory. During 1952, 1953, and 1954 the Lincoln dominated the annual Pan American race held in Mexico. At that time, the race was as well known as the Indy 500 or the Le Mans endurance race. The big Lincolns, with their superior chassis (the first to use ball-joints on the front suspension), were faster in the corners, and the cars were able to hit 125–130mph on the straights with a 3:31 rear axle ratio.

317 cid

The 317 cid Lincoln used a cast nodular iron crankshaft with 2.62 in. main-bearing journals and 2.249 in. rod journals. The main and rod bearing journals were slightly smaller than those of the flathead it replaced, but whereas the flathead used three main bearings, the Lincoln 317's crank was supported by five.

The output of the 1953 version of the 317 cid engine was increased by 45 hp (205 hp at 4,200 rpm). This was achieved through an increased compression ratio (to 8.0:1), larger intake valves measuring 2.00 in., an improved Holley four-barrel carburetor, a higher lift camshaft, a dual-diaphragm distributor with centrifugal mechanical advance, and freer-flowing exhaust and intake manifolds.

The 1954 engine, although it did not produce any more horsepower, nevertheless benefited from numerous improvements. These included a single-diaphragm full-vacuum distributor, redesigned hydraulic lifters, and a larger air cleaner. Also, the Holley carburetor, for the first time, got vacuum-controlled secondary venturi operation. The 317 was discontinued at the end of the 1954 model year.

341 cid

For 1955, the Lincoln V-8's bore was increased to 3.94 in. for a resultant 341 cid. With the increased compression ratio of 8.5:1, horsepower was upped to 225 hp at 4,400 rpm with an impressive 332ft-lb torque at 2,500 rpm. The 341 was discontinued at the end of the model year.

368 cid

In 1956, the Lincoln V-8 was bored and stroked to 4.00x3.66 in. for a displacement of 368 cid. Once again, the compression ratio was upped, this time to 9.0:1. Output went up substantially, to 285 hp at 4,600 rpm and torque to 402ft-lb at 3,000 rpm. Engine improvements included a redesigned carburetor, larger exhaust valves measuring 1.64 in., new exhaust manifolds, a larger fuel pump, and a dual-diaphragm distributor. The valve covers and air cleaner were also now painted black instead of gold. Lincoln was trying to play catch-up ball with competing makes, such as Chrysler and Cadillac, whose engines had more power than Lincoln's.

In its last year, 1957, the Lincoln V-8 was basically a carryover, but there were improvements. Pistons and combustion chambers were redesigned for a resultant 10.0:1 compression ratio, a new Carter four-barrel carburetor was used (along with a new Paper-Pak air cleaner), and the distributor this time used centrifugal and vacuum advance. The exhaust manifolds were also revised for better flow, and the oil filter was changed from a replaceable element to a spin-on, throw-away filter. These modifications gave 300 hp at 4,800 rpm and 415ft-lb torque at 3,000 rpm.

Engine Blocks

All Lincoln engines in this chapter used the same basic engine block. Because it was designed prior to the time of thin-wall castings, it is very heavy for its size and displacement. As mentioned earlier, its claim to fame was the lowered side skirts, which Ford continued to use on the FE series big-blocks introduced in 1958.

One advantage of the thick-wall design was that the Lincoln V-8s could be bored to larger sizes without fear of cutting through to the water jackets.

Cylinder Heads

Only one cylinder head was available on the first 317 cid Lincoln of 1952. It yielded a 7.5:1 compression ratio. Intake valve size was 1.80 in. with the exhaust valve measuring 1.51 in. Intake valve size was increased to 2.00 in. in 1953.

Although the Lincoln V-8 was basically an enlarged Y-block, there was one major difference in cylinder head porting. While the Y-blocks used an arrangement that put one intake port over another, the Lincoln V-8 used a conventional side-by-side setup.

Intake Manifolds

Intake manifolds on the Lincoln were all made of cast iron and used a four-barrel carburetor, except for the 1952 engine, which came with a two-barrel.

Exhaust Manifolds

All Lincoln engines used conventional cast-iron exhaust manifolds that exited at the rear of the engine.

Engine Identification

Lincoln's method of identifying engine parts follows typical industry procedures. Each part generally has a casting number cast onto it consisting of letters and numbers in a particular order. Let's look at a typical part number, in this case, ECU-6049-B, which is the cylinder head for the 1957 368 cid engine. It breaks down as follows:

ECU: engine ID code, ECU = 368 cid

6049: these four numbers are a subgroup; for example, Lincoln cylinder head numbers are numbered 6049; intake manifolds are 9424, camshafts 6250, etc.

B: is an application suffix code. For example, on a camshaft, the letter A might stand for a high-performance solid-lifter cam, while the letter B might stand for a two-barrel engine hydraulic cam.

Casting numbers are similar to part numbers; however, there are major differences. Usually, the subgroup numbers will not actually be used on the part itself, but indicated in the parts book, if listed at all. Sometimes, however, the subgroup number is on the part itself, and sometimes the casting number is the same as the part number.

Date codes are also used. A typical date code might be 7 B 16-. The 7 indicates the last digit of the year, in this case 1957. The B indicates the month of February (letters range from A for January to M for December [I is not used]). The 16 indicates the day of the month.

Depending on the part you're looking at, the date code is probably as important as the casting number itself, especially if you're trying to determine origin. Parts installed in a Lincoln vehicle have to have been cast or manufactured before the car itself was built. This can be up to 30 days or more and still be considered original. On parts that were manufactured, the date codes are stamped on the part, rather than cast.

As for engine identification in relation to the vehicle it was installed in, there wasn't any on the 317-, 341-, or 368 cid V-8s. Lincoln did not assign any special serial number or engine code to the engine itself until 1970. Lincoln did not start using VIN ID codes until 1958, with the introduction of the MEL engine series. There was no engine or VIN identification in connection with the 1952–1957 series Lincoln engines.

Engine Specifications

	Displacement	Carburetor	Horsepower	Torque	Compression Ratio
1952					
	317	2V	160@3,900	284@1,800	7.50
1953					
	317	4V	205@4,200	305@2,300	8.00
1954					
	317	4V	205@4,200	305@2,300	8.00
1955					
	341	4V	225@4,400	332@2,500	8.5
1956					
	368	4V	285@4,600	402@3,000	9.0
1957					
	368	4V	300@4,800	415@3,000	10.1

Engine Internal Dimensions

Displacement	Bore and Stroke	Rod Bearings	Main Bearings	Intake/Exhaust Valves
317	3.800x3.500	2.248–2.249	2.6235–2.6243	1.80/1.51 (1953 2.00/1.51)
341	3.9375x3.500	2.248–2.249	2.6235–2.6243	2.00/1.51
368	4.000x3.660	2.248–2.249	2.6235–2.6243	2.00/1.64

Block, Head, and Manifold Part and Casting Numbers

Year	Engine	Part or Casting Number
Engine Blocks		
1952–1953	317	EAD-6010-D
1954	317	EAD-6020-F
1955	341	EBJ-6010-B
1956	368	ECU-6010-A
1957	368	ECU-6010-C, casting ECU6015
Cylinder Heads		
1952	317	EAD-6049-C
1953–1954	317	EAD-6049-D, EAD-6049-F
1955	341	EBJ-6049-E
1956	368	ECU-6049-B
1957	368	ECU-6049-B
Intake Manifolds		
1952	317	EAD-9424-B
1953–1955	317/341	EBJ-9424-B
1956	368	ECU-9424-A
1957	368	ECU-9424-E
Exhaust Manifolds		
1952–1954	317	EAD-9431-C left, EAD-9430-C right (internal thermostat), EAD-9430-D right (external thermostat)
1955	341	EBJ-9431-A left, EBJ-9430-1A right
1956	368	ECU-9431-A left (Lincoln), ECV-9430-A left (Continental), ECU-9430-1A right (Lincoln), ECV-9431-1A right (Continental)
1957	368	ECU-9431-A left (Lincoln), ECV-9430-A left (Continental), ECU-9430-1A right (Lincoln), ECV-9431-1A right (Continental)

Lincoln VIN ID Code Guide

Lincoln did not assign a VIN ID code for any of the engines installed in 1952–1957 Lincoln vehicles.

CHAPTER 11

FORD, MERCURY AND EDSEL Y-BLOCK

1954-1964

239, 256, 272, 292 and 312

After a 22-year reign, Ford's famous flathead V-8 engine was finally put out to pasture and replaced by the "new" Y-Block V-8 engine in 1954. Actually, it wasn't Ford's first modern ohv V-8 engine; the Y-block engine design was first used on the 1952 Lincoln (and some trucks as well), and it displaced 317 cid. But as far as the Ford Division goes, the 1954 introduction of the 239 cid ohv Y-block was a big step forward.

The name Y-block was used to describe the engine because, when seen from the end, the block resembled a "Y" rather than a "V." The reason for this was the lowered block skirts, which extended below the centerline of the crankshaft. There was a lot of hoopla at the time that these lowered skirts gave better support to the main bearings, but they actually didn't. Unfortunately, this extra skirting doesn't touch the caps, and because it doesn't touch, it can't add any extra support.

The real reason for extending the skirt on the block was so the wings to which the transmission housing was mounted had more support. Without the wings, there wouldn't be any way to mount the transmission. This was one of the problems with the old flathead V-8. The bottom of the transmission was attached to the oil pan—not a very good way to support the transmission. The wings at the side of the Y-block, along with the upper mounting points, provided excellent support.

Ford's first ohv Y-block had the same displacement, 239 cid, and compression ratio, 7.2:1, as the flathead it replaced. It was rated at 130 hp, which was 20 hp more than the 1953 239 cid flathead. While the flathead had a bore and stroke of 3.187x3.750 in., however, the Y-block had an oversquare measurement of 3.50x3.10 in. Like the Lincoln V-8, the 239 used integral valve guides.

By today's standards, the Y-block had some interesting, if not peculiar, characteristics. Most notable is the intake port arrangement on the cylinder heads. One port was situated on top of the other. The thinking was that this configuration gave better mixture distribution, as it promoted turbulence at the sharp corners of the manifold. Engines with a single exhaust system built during 1954–1956 used a crossover pipe that linked the left and right manifolds. The crossover pipe ran over the top front of the engine, making it easy to burn yourself, if you weren't careful.

Another unusual characteristic was the use of a small oil passage that fed the rocker shafts. Oil for the rockers went through this passage from the block deck and through the heads. Because it was small, the passage was prone to clogging, which led to rocker failure. There were numerous aftermarket kits available that tapped into an oil passageway in the block and directed the oil through copper tubing to the rocker shafts.

The Y-block was also a very heavy engine, especially in relation to its physical size and power output. It was built before the days of thin-wall casting techniques. The complete engine with all accessories weighed in at about 660lb. This was actually a fairly light engine for the time.

Mercury, though, got a different version of the Y-block, and it was only for 1954. This Y-block got a 3.62 in. bore and a stroke of 3.10 in., for a 256 cid and 161 hp.

In 1955, the Y-block's bore and stroke were increased so that the engine yielded 272 and 292 cid. The stroke was increased from 3.10 to 3.30 in. on both engines, while the bore was increased to 3.625 in. for the 272 cid version and 3.75 in. for the 292 cid version. The 272 cid engine was used on Ford passenger cars, while the 292 was targeted for the new Thunderbird.

Nineteen fifty-six saw the addition of another bore-and-stroke combination, the biggest yet. This version, thanks to its 3.80 in. bore and 3.44 in. stroke, displaced 312 cid. The 272-, 292-, and 312 cid engines, in various configurations, were offered in 1956 and again in 1957.

Ford introduced a new engine family in 1958, the FE series. It just wasn't practical to expand the Y-block series, so all but the 292 were dropped, though the 312 cid engine was used on some Mercury models through 1961. The 292 cid Y-block was offered on Ford passenger cars and trucks until 1962; the 292 was also used on 1959 and 1960 Edsels.

As was the case in the 1960s, Ford and the other auto manufacturers in the 1950s were engaged in a horsepower race. The marketing people at Ford believed that winning races was an effective way of giving their cars a youthful image. Chevrolet came out with FI for its small-block V-8, and Ford countered with the Paxton supercharger on the 312 cid engine. With the Paxton pumping out a constant 5–6psi manifold boost, mid-range and upper-end horsepower were increased. The street version of the engine was rated at 300 hp at 4,800 rpm. With some minor tweaks, the engine pumped out an honest 340 hp on Ford's stock-car racers. And the stockers were untouchable, winning race after race and setting track records.

The Y-block had a very short life span of only nine years. It was in essence a stopgap engine, as it didn't have anywhere near the potential of Chevy's small-block V-8, introduced in 1955. The small-block Ford engines that eventually replaced the Y-block weighed 200lb less and had superior porting and manifolding. They became the mainstay of Ford's racing efforts in the 1960s.

The truck versions of the Y-block V-8 used beefier crank and rod forgings. These were interchangeable with those of the passenger car engines. Truck Y-block engines were available until 1964.

239 cid

The 239 cid Y-block used a cast nodular iron crankshaft with 2.50 in. main-bearing journals and 2.188 in. rod journals. A hydraulic camshaft and 7.2:1 cast-aluminum pistons combined to yield 130 hp with a two-barrel carburetor. Cast iron was the material of choice for the intake and exhaust manifolds. The engine was available only for the 1954 model year on both Ford passenger cars and Ford light trucks.

A 1956 312 cid Y-block V-8 in a Thunderbird. This is the 245hp single four-barrel version.

256 cid

With a 3.62 in. bore and 3.10 in. stroke, the 256 cid displacement Y-block engine was used only on Mercury cars during the 1954 model year. Save for the displacement increase and higher compression ratio of 7.5:1, the 256 cid V-8 was practically identical to the 239 cid Ford version, though the 256 put out more power, 161 hp at 4,400 rpm.

272 cid

In 1955, the Y-block's stroke was increased from 3.10- to 3.30 in. and the bore was increased to 3.625 in. to create the 272 cid version. The 272 cid engine was used exclusively on Ford passenger cars and trucks.

There were two versions of the engine available in 1955. The two-barrel engine with a 7.6:1 compression ratio was rated at 162 hp. The four-barrel engine had an 8.5:1 compression ratio and more power, too, at 182 hp.

Both 1956 versions of the 272 cid Y-block were equipped with a two-barrel carburetor. Manual transmission cars had engines with an 8.0:1 compression ratio for 173 hp; automatics had a higher ratio, 8.4:1, for 176 hp.

In its last year, 1957, the 272 cid V-8 was rated at 190 hp, with a two-barrel carburetor and an 8.6:1 compression ratio.

The 162 hp version of the engine was used on Ford light trucks in 1955. In 1956, the 176 hp engine was used, but in the Courier with a manual transmission it was rated at 173 hp, and in the F-series version it was rated at 167 hp. The 1957 Courier 272 cid V-8 was rated at 190 hp while the F-series version was rated at 171 hp. In 1958, the 272 was used only on the F-series trucks and was unchanged from the engine's 1957 configuration.

292 cid

Also introduced in 1955, the 292 cid Y-block had a bore and stroke of 3.75x3.30 in. and a compression ratio of 8.1:1, for a 193 hp output on manual transmission cars and 8.5:1 for 198 hp on automatic transmission cars. Both engines used a four-barrel carburetor. The 292 was used on the then-new 1955 Thunderbird and on the Mercury Montclair.

Both 1956 editions of the engine had 1/10 of a point less compression ratio. Even so, they were rated slightly higher, at 200- and 202 hp. The 1957 engines got a higher compression ratio of 9.0:1, but they were both equipped only with a two-barrel carburetor, for 212- and 206 hp, respectively.

The engine continued to see service in Ford passenger cars through the 1962 model year, with steadily lower power ratings. It was used on the 1959–1960 Edsel Ranger, and it was also optional on 1961 Mercury cars.

The 292 cid Y-block had a longer run as a truck engine. It was used on the Ford Courier from 1956 to 1960, with power ratings of 202-, 212-, 205-, 200-, and 185 hp, respectively; it became optional on 1959–1960 F-series trucks, with a 181 hp rating; and from 1961 to 1964 it was again optional on the F-series trucks, with a 160 hp output. All truck engines used a solid-lifter camshaft and a two-barrel carburetor.

312 cid

The biggest Y-blocks were those that had a bore and stroke of 3.80x3.44 in. and a displacement of 312 cid. There were two versions available in 1956. Manual transmission cars had a 312 cid engine that was rated at 215 hp with an 8.4:1 compression ratio. Automatics were rated at 225 hp with a 9.0:1 compression ratio. Both engines used a four-barrel carburetor and had dual exhausts.

Nineteen fifty-seven was the high point for the 312 cid Y-block. The automatic version was rated at 245 hp with a 9.0:1 compression ratio. A dual four-barrel intake setup was optional, for a 265 hp output. The Paxton supercharged version was rated at 300 hp.

The engine was basically retired after 1957, but it was used on the 1958 Mercury Medalist (rated at 235 hp) and on the 1959 Mercury Monterey (rated at 210 hp). It was last used on the 1960 Mercury Monterey, rated at 205 hp.

Engine Blocks

As mentioned earlier, Y-block engine blocks were designed prior to the time of thin-wall casting, and their claim to fame was the lowered side skirts, which Ford continued to use on the FE-series big-blocks introduced in 1958.

One advantage of the thick-wall design was that the Y-blocks could be bored to larger sizes without fear of cutting through to the water jackets. For example, the 272 cid version, with its stock bore of 3.625 in., could be overbored to 3.830 in., which is 0.030 in. over the 312's stock bore.

There is some difference in cam bearing sizes used on the Y-blocks. Early 1954 engines got a camshaft with 1/8 in. larger bearings than did late 1954—and all other Y-block—engines. Late 1954 and 1955 camshafts had holes in the center cam journal to direct oil flow to the rockers. In 1955, a groove replaced the holes, requiring a different center cam bearing. The grooved camshafts will work with 1954–1955 blocks as long as matching bearings are also used. The camshafts on all Y-block engines were the mechanical variety, requiring periodic lash adjustment.

Cylinder Heads

Only one cylinder head was available on the first 239 cid Y-block of 1954. It yielded a 7.2:1 compression ratio. Intake valve size was 1.647 in. Exhaust valve size was 1.51 in. All subsequent cylinder heads featured different intake valve sizes, but all Y-block heads came with the same 1.51 in. exhaust valves.

With the introduction of the 272- and 292 cid versions of the Y-block in 1955 came three different cylinder heads. The only difference between them was combustion chamber size, which yielded different compression ratios depending on the engine. Intake valve size was increased to 1.78 in.

In 1956, the 312 cid version was added to the lineup, and cylinder head choices expanded to four. In a move to simplify matters for 1957, Ford cut down the number of heads to one. Compression ratio changes were then made through the use of different pistons. The only exception to this was the cylinder head used on the supercharged 312 cid engine, which had a larger combustion chamber to reduce the compression ratio of the engine. In addition, the heads got revised water jacket cores in order to provide additional support over the cylinder area. This was done to reduce the possibility of blown head gaskets. Intake valve size was increased once again in 1957, this time to 1.925 in. Ports were also enlarged in 1957 for better flow.

The heads used in 1958 and 1959 were the same as those used in 1957. For 1960–1962, the intake valve size was reduced to 1.647 in., and ports were smaller as well. This was done to improve fuel economy.

The standard rocker arm ratio on the Y-blocks was 1.43:1. The only deviation from this was on the 1956–1957 engines, which got 1.54:1 ratio rockers.

Intake Manifolds

The great majority of Y-blocks came with a two-barrel cast-iron intake manifold. The 239 cid engine came only with a two-barrel intake. The 1955 and 1956 engines were built with either a two- or four-barrel intake manifold. The best four-barrel intake is the 1957 part number B7A-9424-B, as it has the largest ports. Besides these, a special dual four-barrel intake was available only for 1957. Approximately 2,100 312 cid engines were equipped with the dual four-barrel setup (part number B7A-9424-D). Besides the supercharged version, this was the hottest Y-block variant. The consensus of the hot-rodding set was that this carb and intake setup was a bit much for the engine. Various aluminum aftermarket manifolds were available for the Y-block V-8s. One of the best was the Edelbrock Tri-Power intake, which used stock Ford two-barrel carburetors. The optimum configuration with this manifold is to use progressive linkage so that only the center carburetor is used for normal driving. The outboard carburetors are engaged only at full throttle. Ford used both Holley and Ford four-barrel carburetors.

Exhaust Manifolds

The Y-block was equipped with both single and dual exhaust systems. The 1954 engine came with only a single exhaust system. The single exhaust systems on 1955 and 1956 engines used a crossover pipe that connected left and right manifolds. The crossover pipe was located in front of the engine.

The Y-block dual exhaust system used conventional exhaust manifolds that angled down at the rear of the engine. The 1957 312 cid engines used exhaust manifolds that had a larger diameter rear opening, and these are considered the best of the stock manifolds.

Engine Identification

Ford's method of identifying engine parts follows typical industry procedures in that each part had a number cast onto it. On Y-blocks, that number consists of letters and numbers in a particular order. Let's look at a typical part number, in this case, B5A9-9425-D, which is the intake manifold for the 1955 292ci engine. It breaks down as follows:

B: this letter indicates the decade—B is 1950–1959.

5: this number indicates the year of the decade—5 would be 1955 in our example.

A9: this is a Ford car line number

9425: these four numbers are a subgroup—for example, Ford cylinder head numbers are numbered 6049; intake manifolds are 9425, camshafts 6250, etc.

D: is an application suffix code. On a camshaft, for example, the letter A might stand for a high-performance solid-lifter cam, while the letter B might be for a two-barrel engine hydraulic cam.

The intake port arrangement on the Y-block was definitely out of the ordinary. This positioning was supposed to add turbulence to the fuel mixture and the end result would be better throttle response.

Casting numbers are similar to part numbers, but there are major differences. Usually, the subgroup numbers will not actually be used on the part itself, but they will be indicated in the parts book, if the casting number is listed at all. However, sometimes the subgroup number is on the part itself, and sometimes the casting number is the same as the part number.

Date codes were also used. A typical date code might be 9 B 16-. The 9 indicates the last digit of the year, in the case of the Y-block it would be 1959. The B indicates the month, ranging from A for January to M for December (I is not used), in this case February. The 16 indicates the day of the month.

Depending on the part you're looking at, the date code is probably as important as the casting number itself, especially if you're trying to determine originality. Parts installed in a Ford vehicle have to have been cast or manufactured before the car itself was built. The difference can be up to 30 days or more and still be considered original. On parts that were manufactured, the date codes are stamped on the part, rather than cast.

In this era, Ford didn't stamp the vehicles' VIN on the engine, so there's no way to determine if a particular engine is original equipment in a particular car. You can tell what engine type is supposed to be in a given car, though, because a code in the VIN gives this information. On 1954–1959 models, the engine code was the first letter of the vehicle's VIN. Beginning in 1960, the code was in the fifth position, and it remained in that position until 1981. Ford used the codes over and over, so the same code can denote different engines in different years. The codes are listed in the tables.

It's not the same for Mercury, though, with the Y-block engines. Mercury used a different VIN identification system, which did not include a digit for the engine until 1958. Some sources have indicated that the block casting letters are the engine code, but this is incorrect.

Engine Specifications

	Displacement	Carburetor	Horsepower	Torque	Compression Ratio	Notes
1954						
	239	2V	130@4,200	214@1,800	7.20	cars, trucks
	256	2V	161@4,400	238@2,000	7.50	Mercury
1955						
	272	2V	162@4,200	258@2,200	7.60	cars, trucks
	272	4V	182@4,400	268@2,600	8.50	cars

Engine Specifications

	Displacement	Carburetor	Horsepower	Torque	Compression Ratio	Notes
	292	4V	188@4,400	272@2,500	7.60	m/t, Mercury
	292	4V	193@4,400	280@2,600	8.10	m/t, cars, T-Bird
	292	4V	198@4,400	286@2,500	8.50	a/t, cars, T-Bird, Mercury
1956						
	272	2V	167@4,400	260@2,400	8.00	m/t, cars, trucks
	272	2V	173@4,400	260@2,400	8.00	m/t, cars, trucks
	272	4V	176@4,400	264@2,600	8.50	a/t, cars, trucks
	292	4V	200@4,600	285@2,600	8.00	m/t, cars
	292	4V	202@4,400	289@2,600	8.40	a/t, cars, T-Bird
	312	4V	210@4,600	312@2,600	8.00	Mercury
	312	4V	215@4,600	317@2,600	8.40	m/t, cars, T-Bird, Mercury
	312	4V	225@4,600	324@2,600	8.40	a/t, cars, T-Bird, Mercury
1957						
	272	2V	171@4,400	260@2,400	8.00	trucks
	272	2V	190@4,500	270@2,700	8.60	cars, trucks
	292	4V	212@4,600	297@2,700	9.00	cars, T-Bird
	292	4V	206@4,500	297@2,700	9.00	m/t, cars
	312	4V	245@4,500	332@3,200	9.70	a/t, cars, T-Bird
	312	4V	255@4,600	340@2,600	9.70	Mercury
	312	2x4V	265@4,800	336@3,400	9.70	m/t, cars, T-Bird
	312	super-charged 4V	300 hp	NA	8.30	m/t, cars, T-Bird
1958						
	272	2V	171@4,400	260@2,400	8.00	trucks
	272	2V	190@4,500	270@2,700	8.60	trucks
	292	2V	205@4,500	295@2,400	8.80	cars
	312	4V	235@4,500	332@3,200	9.70	Mercury
1959						
	292	2V	186@4,200	292@2,200	8.80	trucks
	292	2V	200@4,400	285@2,400	8.80	cars
	312	4V	210@4,400	325@2,200	9.60	Mercury
1960						
	292	2V	171@4,200	292@2,200	8.80	trucks
	292	2V	185@4,200	292@2,200	8.80	cars
	312	2V	205@4,000	328@2,100	9.70	cars, Mercury
1961						
	292	2V	160@4,000	279@2,200	8.80	trucks
	292	2V	175@4,200	279@2,200	8.80	cars, Mercury
1962						
	292	2V	160@4,000	279@2,200	8.80	trucks
	292	2V	170@4,200	279@2,200	8.80	cars
1963						
	292	2V	160@4,000	279@2,200	8.80	trucks
1964						
	292	2V	160@4,000	279@2,200	8.80	trucks

Engine Internal Dimensions

Displacement	Bore and Stroke	Rod Bearings	Main Bearings	Intake/Exhaust Valves
239	3.500x3.100	2.188–2.189	2.4984–2.4988	1.647/1.510
256	3.6250x3.100	2.188–2.189	2.4984–2.4988	1.647/1.510
272	3.6250x3.300	2.188–2.189	2.4984–2.4988	1.780/1.510 (1957–1960 1.925/1.510)
292	3.7500x3.100	2.188–2.189	2.4984–2.4988	1.780/1.510 (1957–1960 1.925/1.510, 1960–1962 1.647/1.510)
312	3.8000x3.440	2.188–2.189	2.6235–2.6243	1.925/1.510 (1957–1960 1.925/1.510)

Block, Head, and Manifold Part and Casting Numbers

Year	Engine	Part or Casting Number
Engine Blocks		
1954	239	EBU-6010-E, casting EBU6015
1954	256	EBY-6010-E, casting EBY6015
1955	272	B5A-6010-C, casting ECG6015
1955	292	B5A-6010-A, casting ECK6015, ECL6015
1956	272	B6A-6010-D, casting ECG6015, KBY6015

Block, Head, and Manifold Part and Casting Numbers

Year	Engine	Part or Casting Number
1956	292	B6A-6010-B, casting ECK6015
1956	312	B6A-6010-C, casting ECZ6015
1957	272	B6A-6010-D, casting ECG6015, KBY6015
1957	292	B6A-6010-B, casting EDB6015
1957	312	B6A-6010-C, casting ECZ6015
1958	292	B9AE6015, casting EDB6015
1958	312	B6A-6010-C, casting ECZ6015
1959	292	B6A-6010-B, casting EDB6015
1959	312	B6A-6010-C, casting ECZ6015
1960	292	B6A-6010-B, casting EDB6015
1960	312	B6A-6010-C, casting ECZ6015
1961–1962	292	B6A-6010-B, casting EDB6015
Cylinder Heads		
1954	239	B4A-6049-G, casting EBU-F, EBU-G
1955	272 162 hp	B5A-6049-D, casting ECL-A
1955	292 193 hp	B5A-6049-H, casting ECG-B; B5A-6049-D, casting ECG-D
1955	272 182 hp	B5A-6049-G, casting ECG-A
1955	292 198 hp	B5A-6049-A, casting ECL-B; B5A-6049-B, casting ECL-C
1956	272 173 hp	B6A-6049-M, casting ECZ-C, ECG-T

Year	Engine	Part or Casting Number
Cylinder Heads		
1956	292 202 hp	B6A-6049-M, casting ECZ-C, ECG-T
1956	312 225 hp	B6A-6049-M, casting ECZ-C, ECG-T
1956	272 176 hp	B6A-6049-N, casting ECG-H, ECG-R
1956	292 200 hp	B6A-6049-P, casting ECZ-B, EDB-B
1956	312 215 hp	B6A-6049-P, casting ECZ-B, EDB-B
1957	272 171 hp	casting ECR
1957	272 190 hp	B7A-6049-A, casting ECZ-E, 5752113
1957	292 206 hp	B7A-6049-D, casting ECZ-F
1957	292 212 hp	B7A-6049-D, casting ECZ-F
1957	312 245 hp	B7A-6049-D, casting ECZ-F
1957	312 265 hp	B7A-6049-D, casting ECZ-F
1957	312 300 hp	B7A-6049-E, casting EDB-D, EDB-E
1958	292	B7A-6049-A, casting ECZ-E, 5752113
1958	312	B7A-6049-A, casting ECZ-E, 5752113, B8TZ-6049-D
1959	292	B7A-6049-A, casting ECZ-E, ECZ-C 5752113
1959	312	B8TZ-6049-D
1960	292	C0AZ-6049-A, casting ECZ-C, C0AE-6090-A, 0ACE-6090-A
1960	312	C0TZ-6049-A
1960–1962	292	truck casting C0TE-6090-B, C1TE-6090-D

This is a stock cast-iron four-barrel carburetor intake manifold for the 292 cid and 312 cid engines.

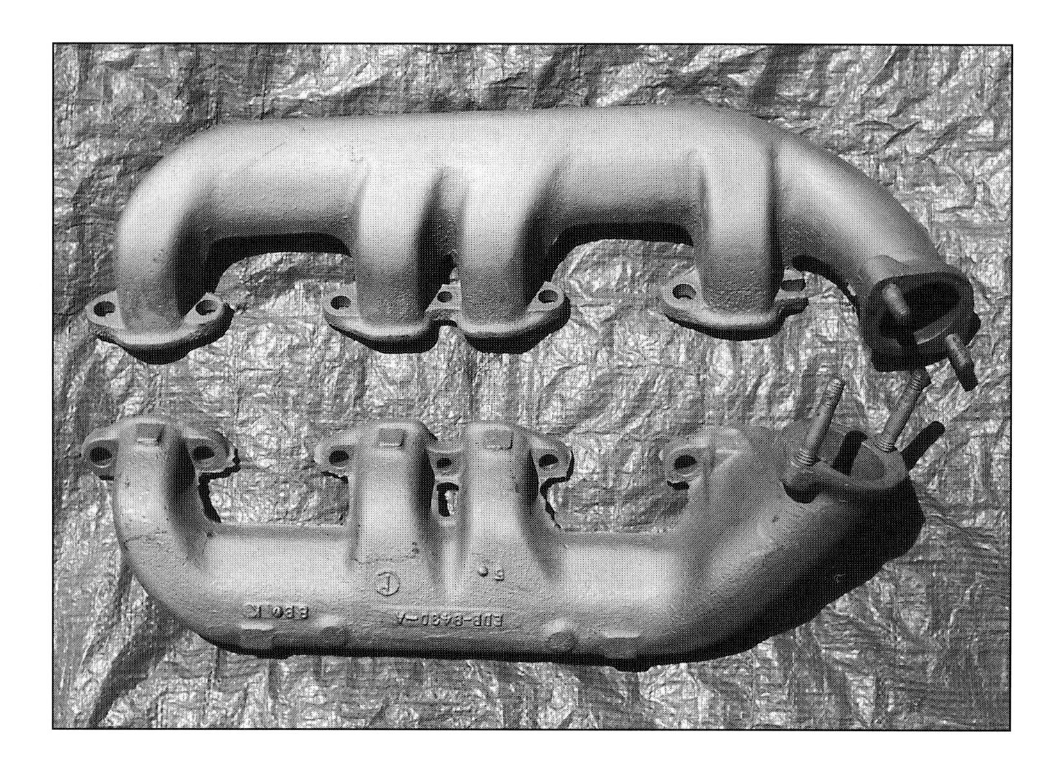

These exhaust manifolds typify the overall design of Y-block exhaust manifolds. They are designed to go above the exhaust ports in order to clear the car's chassis. These are Thunderbird units, EDB-9430-A and EDB-9431-A.

Block, Head, and Manifold Part and Casting Numbers

Year	Engine	Part or Casting Number
Cylinder Heads		
1961	292	C0AZ-6049-A, casting C0AE-6090-A, ECZ-C, 0ACE-6090-A
1962	292	C1AZ-6049-A, casting C0AE-6090-A,ECZ-C, 0ACE-6090-A
1963–1964	292	truck casting C1TE-6090-D
Intake Manifolds		
1954	2V	EBU-9425-D
1955	2V	B5A9-9425-E, B6C-9425-B
1955	4V	B5A9-9425-D
1956	2V	B6A9-9425-C, B6C-9425-B
1956	4V	B6A9-9425-B
1957	2V	B9A-9424-B, B6C-9425-B
1957	4V	B7A-9424-B
1957	2x4V	B7A-9424-C
1957	supercharged	B7A-9424-B, casting ECG-9421-D
1958	2V	B9A-9424-B
1958	4V	B7A-9424-B
1959	2V	B9A-9424-B
1959	4V	B7A-9424-B
1960	2V	C0AE-9425-F
1961	2V	C0AE-9425-F
1962	2V	C0AE-9425-F
Exhaust Manifolds		
1954	all	B4A-9430-B right, B4A-9431-A left
1955–1956	all	B5A-9430-B right, B5A-9430-1B left, single exhaust; B5A-9430-C, B5A-9431-C, left, dual exhaust, Ford car; B5S-9431-D, left, dual exhaust, T-Bird and Interceptor, 292 cid; B6A-9431-A, left, dual exhaust, T-Bird and Interceptor, 312 cid
1957–1958	all	B7S-9431-A left, B7S-9430-A right
1959–1964	all	C2AZ-9430-A right, C2AZ-9431-A left

VIN Identification Codes

Code	Year	Engine
B	1957	272 190 hp
C	1957	292 206/212 hp
C	1958	292 205 hp
C	1959	292 299 hp
D	1957	312 245 hp
E	1957	312 270/285 hp
F	1957	312 300/340 hp
L	1958	312 255 hp
M	1955	272 182 hp
M	1956	292 200/202 hp
P	1954	256 160 hp
P	1955	292 193/198/205 hp
P	1956	312 215/225 hp
P	1959	312 210 hp
P	1960	312 205 hp
T	1960–1962	292, export
U	1954	239 130 hp
U	1955	272 162 hp
U	1956	252 173/176 hp
W	1960	292 185 hp
W	1961	292 175 hp
W	1962	292 170 hp

CHAPTER 12

FORD MEL SERIES

1958-1968

383, 410, 430, and 462

Model year 1958 saw the introduction of two engine families at Ford Motor Company. The FE-series V-8s were for use on Ford passenger cars and trucks and on the new Edsel, thus the F (Ford) E (Edsel) designation. Another engine series, the MEL engine family, was for use on Mercury, Edsel, and Lincoln cars, thus the M (Mercury) E (Edsel) L (Lincoln) designation. It seems that it would have been easier to use just one of the two engine families for all Ford-made cars, but why simplify when you can complicate? Actually, this is what happened anyway. With the exception of the Lincoln MEL V-8, Ford abandoned the MEL engines at the end of the 1960 model year. This was because the American public became concerned with fuel economy, and the big, heavy MEL engines were not very fuel efficient. The Lincoln version lasted until 1968.

The MEL engines were a second-generation Y-block-type design, meaning the deep side skirts, first used on the 1952–1957 Lincoln V-8s, were retained. The MEL series was an oversquare design that was available in three displacements in 1958—383-, 410-, and 430 cid. The 383 had a 4.30x3.30 in. bore and stroke, while the 410 cid and 430 cid versions were 4.20x3.70 in. and 4.30x3.70 in., respectively. The 410 was available for only one year, on 1958 Edsel Corsair and Citation models. The 383- and 430 cid engines were used on 1958–1960 Mercury cars, while the Lincoln used the 430 from 1958 to 1965.

In 1966, the MEL 430 cid engine was bored and stroked to 4.38x3.83 in., which resulted in 462 cid. The extra cubic inches were needed to power the heavier, redesigned 1966 Lincolns, and it also enabled Lincoln to advertise that it had the largest V-8 engine of any American passenger car. The 462 was scheduled to be retired by the end on the 1967 model year, but several thousand of these engines remained unsold, so the 462 was available on the 1968 Lincoln, along with the new 460 cid "385" series V-8 that was officially introduced in 1968.

In terms of high performance, the MEL engines were not very popular. They weren't around long enough, and the aftermarket parts that were available were few and expensive. Still, engine stroker kits, camshaft kits, and intake manifolds were available. Edelbrock, Weiand, and Offenhauser offered six- and eight-carburetor log-type manifolds, and Weiand even offered a setup to accept a GMC 6-71 blower.

383 cid

The 383 cid engine had a 4.30x3.30 in. bore and stroke and it was available only on 1958–1960 Mercury cars. The Marauder 312, as it was called, was rated at 312 hp and the Marauder 330 was rated at 330 hp for 1958; both engines had Holley four-barrel carburetors. The 1959 engine was rated at 322 hp. The last time the engine was used was on the 1960 Mercury Monterey and Commuter. The Marauder V-8 was rated at 280 hp with its two-barrel carburetor and 8.5:1 compression ratio.

410 cid

This particular bore and stroke combination of 4.20x3.70 in. was used exclusively by 1958 Edsel Corsair and Citation models. The E-475 engine was named for its 475ft-lb torque output. The engine had a 10.5:1 compression ratio, a Holley four-barrel carburetor, dual exhausts, and a hydraulic-lifter camshaft.

430 cid

This MEL engine was in production the longest. For most of the time it was in production it had the distinction of being the largest cubic displacement engine of any American V-8 engine. In its Super Marauder guise, the engine also boasted the highest advertised horsepower rating in 1958—400 hp. The engine also had the proper hot-rodding appeal, as it was equipped with a triple two-barrel intake setup.

The 430 cid engine was used by Mercury during 1958–1960. The 1958 engine was offered in three versions (360-, 375-, or 400 hp). The 1959–1960 versions were slightly detuned to produce 345 hp. This was done through a compression ratio reduction to 10.5:1 and use of a two-barrel carburetor.

The Lincoln 430 cid MEL engine in 1958 generated 375 hp at 4,800 rpm and 490ft-lb torque at 3,100 rpm. The compression ratio was 10.5:1. The engine in 1959 was basically unchanged; however, compression ratio dropped to 10.0:1 for a reduced output of 350 hp at 4,400 rpm. Maximum torque remained the same, but it was generated at 300 rpm less. The 1960 version got a milder camshaft, but the biggest change was the use of a two-barrel carburetor, a Carter ABD. This reduced output further, to 315 hp.

The 430 cid MEL engine was modified in 1963. New pistons raised the compression ratio to 10.1:1 and the use of a four-barrel carburetor returned. Horsepower was upped to 320, while torque output remained the same. The engine would remain in this form through the 1965 model year.

462 cid

In its last configuration, the 1966–1968 Lincoln MEL engine was rated at 340 hp. It had a 4.38 in. bore and 3.83 in. stroke, for a displacement of 462 cid. As with the 430 cid engine it replaced, the 462 used a four-barrel carburetor, dual exhausts, and a hydraulic-lifter camshaft.

Engine Blocks

All MEL Y-block engines used the same basic engine block. Because they were designed prior to the time of thin-wall castings, they are very heavy, considering their size and cubic-inch displacement. That shouldn't be a surprise because the MEL series was designed for use on larger, heavier cars. Maximum overbore on the 430 cid blocks is only 0.030 in. Racers at the time were using aftermarket stroker kits to increase stroke by 0.625 in., which resulted in 504 cid.

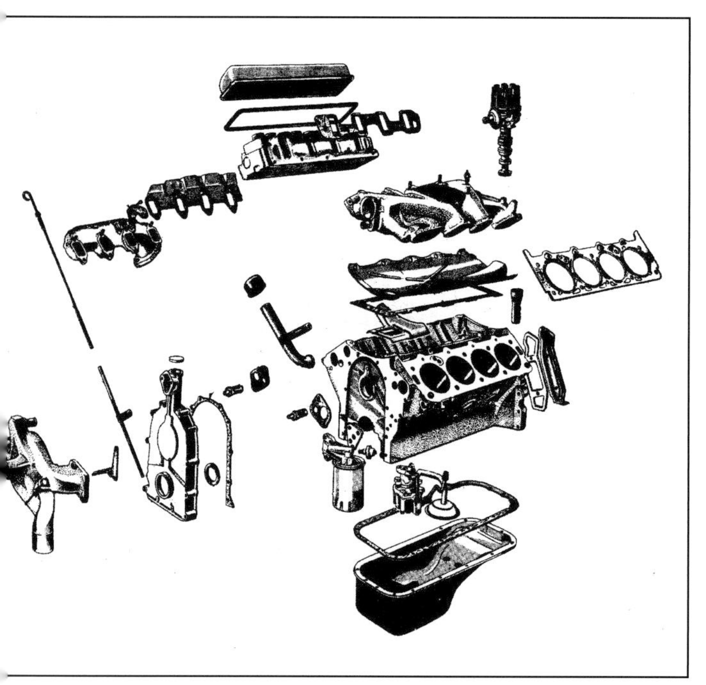

The MEL series was conventional Ford "Y" block design. Porting was similar to the FE series engines. The biggest difference from other Ford engines of that era were the cylinder heads. *Ford Motor Company*

Cylinder Heads

The MEL series engines were built with unique cylinder heads. The heads, which featured larger ports and valves than the previous Lincoln V-8s, were flat. The cylinder head and block deck were milled at a 10-degree angle, which resulted in a wedge-shaped combustion chamber in the block. The big advantage of this type of design is that the same head can be used on all engines (compression ratio can be adjusted through the use of different pistons). The cylinder heads used intake/exhaust valves of 2.09 in./1.78 in., and shaft-mounted rocker arms actuated the valves.

Intake Manifolds

The MEL engines were available with either a two-barrel or four-barrel cast-iron intake manifold. The 1963 430 cid engine has the distinction of having the carburetor's primary two bores located in the center of the manifold. The only exception was the aluminum 3x2V intake used on the 1958 Super Marauder engine.

Exhaust Manifolds

The MEL engines were equipped with both single and dual exhaust systems. The conventionally designed exhaust manifolds were made of cast iron.

Engine Identification

Ford's method of identifying engine parts follows typical industry procedures in that each part generally has a number cast onto it, and with Ford, that number consists of letters and numbers in a particular order. Let's look at a typical part number, in this case, C6VY-6010-A, which is the cylinder head for the 1966 462ci engine. It breaks down as follows:

C: this letter indicates the decade—B is 1950–1959, C is 1960–1969, D is 1970–1979.

6: this number indicates the year of the decade—6 would be 1966 in our example.

VY: this is a Ford car line number.

6010: these four numbers are a subgroup—for example, Ford cylinder head numbers are numbered 6010; intake manifolds are 9424, camshafts 6250, etc.

A: is an application suffix code. On a camshaft, for example, the letter A might stand for a high-performance solid-lifter cam, while the letter B might be for a two-barrel engine hydraulic cam.

Casting numbers are similar to part numbers, but there are major differences. Usually, the subgroup numbers will not actually be used on the part itself, but they will be indicated in the parts book, if the casting number is listed at all. However, the subgroup number is sometimes on the part itself, and sometimes the casting number is the same as the part number.

Date codes were also used. A typical date code is 9 B 16-. The 9 indicates the last digit of the year, which in this case would be 1959. The B indicates the month, with B standing for February (the month code ranges from A for January to M for December, with I not used). The 16 indicates the day of the month.

Depending on the part you're looking at, the date code is probably as important as the casting number itself, especially if you're trying to determine originality. For a car to be considered original, the parts installed in it have to have been cast or manufactured before the car itself was built. This can be up to 30 days or more and still be considered original. On parts that were manufactured, the date codes are stamped on the part, rather than cast.

In this era, Ford didn't stamp the vehicle's VIN on the engine, so there's no way to determine if a particular engine is original equipment in a particular car. You can tell what engine type is supposed to be in a given car, though, because a code in the VIN gives this information. On 1954–1959 models, the engine code was the first letter of the vehicle's VIN. Beginning in 1960, the code was in the fifth position, and it remained in that position until 1981. Ford used the codes over and over, so the same code can denote different engines in different years. The codes are listed in the tables.

The engines did have an "engine code," as some manuals indicate. But it was just a glorified date code that indicated date of manufacture, plant, and inspector's identification. It was located on the left front of the block by the cylinder head.

Engine Specifications

	Displacement	Carburetor	Horsepower	Torque	Compression Ratio	Notes
1958						
	383	4V	312@4,600	405@2,900	10.5	Mercury
	383	4V	330@4,800	425@3,000	10.5	Mercury
	410	4V	345@4,600	475@2,600	10.5	Edsel
	430	4V	360@4,600	480@3,000	10.5	Edsel
	430	4V	375@4,800	490@3,100	10.5	Lincoln
	430	3x2V	400@5,200	500@3,200	10.5	Mercury
1959						
	383	4V	322@4,600	420@2,800	10.0	Mercury
	430	4V	345@4,400	480@2,800	10.0	Mercury
	430	4V	350@4,800	490@3,100	10.10	T-Bird

Displacement		Carburetor	Horsepower	Torque	Compression Ratio	Notes
	430	4V	375@4,800	490@3,100	10.5	Lincoln
1960						
	383	2V	280@4,200	405@2,200	8.5	Mercury
	430	4V	310@4,100	460@2,200	10.0	Mercury
	430	2V	315@4,100	465@2,200	10.0	Lincoln
	430	4V	350@4,800	490@3,100	10.10	T-Bird
1961						
	430	2V	315@4,100	465@2,200	10.0	Lincoln
1962						
	430	2V	315@4,100	465@2,200	10.0	Lincoln
1963						
	430	4V	320@4,600	465@2,600	10.0	Lincoln
1964						
	430	4V	320@4,600	465@2,600	10.1	Lincoln
1965						
	430	4V	320@4,600	465@2,600	10.1	Lincoln
1966–1968						
	462	4V	340@4,600	485@2,800	10.25	Lincoln

Engine Internal Dimensions

Displacement	Bore and Stroke	Rod Bearings	Main Bearings	Intake/Exhaust Valves
383	4.300x3.660	2.599–2.600	2.8994–2.9003	2.09/1.78
410	4.2031x3.703	2.599–2.600	2.8994–2.9003	2.09/1.78
430	4.300x3.700	2.599–2.600	2.8994–2.9003	2.09/1.78
462	4.380x3.830	2.599–2.600	2.8994–2.9003	2.09/1.78

Block, Head, and Manifold Part and Casting Numbers

Year	Engine	Part or Casting Number
Engine Blocks		
1958–1960	383, 430	COME-6010-A, casting EDG6015, 5751091
1958	410	B8KY-6010-B, casting EDG6015
1961–1965	430	C4VY-6010-A, casting EDJ6015
1966–1968	462	C6VY-6010-A
Cylinder Heads		
1958–1960	all	casting EDG6090, EDJ6090 (430 cid)
1961–1962	430	C1VY-6049-A
1963–1965	430	C3VY-6049-A (before 06/01/64), C3VY 6049-C (after 05/31/64)
1966	462 w/ A.I.R.	C6VY-6049-A (before 11/22/65), C6VY 6049-D (after 11/21/65)
1966	462 w/o A.I.R.	C6VY-6049-C
1967	462 w/ A.I.R.	C6VY-6049-D
1967	462 w/o A.I.R.	C6VY-6049-C
1968	462 w/ A.I.R.	C6VY-6049-D
Intake Manifolds		
1958–1959	410/430 4V	C1JE-9424-A
1958	430 3x2V	PB8M-9424-A
1959	383 2V	PB9M-9424-A
1959	383/430 4V	C1JE-9424-A
1960	430 4V	C1JE-9424-A
1961–1962	430 2V	C1VE-9424-C
1963–1965	430 4V	C3VY-9424-B
1966–1968	462 4V	C6VY-9424-A

Year	Engine	Part or Casting Number
Exhaust Manifolds		
1958	383/410/430	EDG-9430-A right, B9ME 9431-A left
1959–1960	383/430	B8LY-9430-A right, B9ME 9431-A left
1966	430	C6VE-9430-A right, C6VE 9431-C left
1958–1968	430/462	B8LY-9430-A right, C6VY 9431-B left

VIN Identification Codes

Code	Year	Engine
E	1960	383, export
E	1960	430, export
G	1966–1968	462 340 hp
H	1958	430 375 hp
H	1959	430 350 hp
H	1960	430 315 hp
H	1961–1962	430 300 hp
H	1963	430 320 hp
J	1958	430 400 hp
K	1958	430 360 hp
K	1960–1962	430, export
L	1959	430 345 hp
M	1958–1959	383 312/322/330 hp
M	1960	430 310 hp
N	1959–1960	383 280 hp
N	1964–1965	430 320 hp
X	1958	410 345 hp
7	1963–1965	430, export
7	1967–1968	462, export

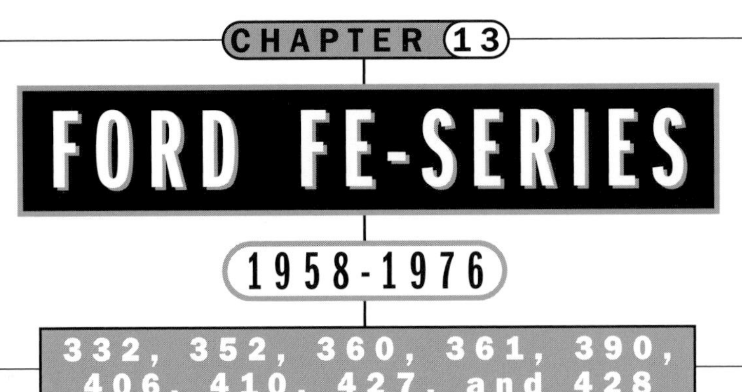

The FE series is probably Ford's best-known engine series of the 1960s and was used in practically every Ford and Mercury passenger car and truck. It was also one of Ford's best engines when it came to high-performance street applications and, of course, in racing. FEs were used on practically every one of Ford's racing endeavors—most notably in the Le Mans-winning Ford GT endurance race cars.

The FE series engines were made in many displacements—332-, 352-, 361-, 390-, 391-, 406-, 410-, 427-, and 428 cid—and the engines were used in passenger cars from 1958 to 1971, while truck usage began in 1958 and ended in 1976. The F stands for Ford and the E for Edsel, as the engines were originally slated for use in Ford and Edsel cars.

Like the Y-block ohv engines that preceded them, the FE series engines were an oversquare design, with the bore being larger than stroke. They, too, were of Y-block design, as the lowered block skirts extended below the centerline of the crankshaft. This was supposed to provide additional support for the main bearings. As we shall see, a few of these engines did make use of the lowered skirts to support the bearings, but it is open to debate as to whether the lowered skirts did anything for all other FE-series engines. Like the Y-blocks, the FE-series engines were of the "thick-wall" design, meaning they were on the heavy side.

An interesting feature of the FE-series engines is the rather large intake manifold they all use, which resulted in a comparatively narrow head casting. Because the head is so narrow, the pushrods have to go through the intake manifold. On the other hand, replacing the typical stock cast-iron intake manifold with a factory or aftermarket aluminum intake does result in a substantial reduction in engine weight.

The first FE series engines were 332- and 352 cid on 1958 Ford and Thunderbird. There was also the oddball 361, which was used only on 1958–1959 Edsel cars and later on some light trucks, though with the "360" designation. Because of the great variety of FE-series engines, we'll look at each displacement separately.

332 cid

This was the first FE-series engine, and it was available only on the Ford line of cars during 1958–1959. The 332 had a bore and stroke of 4.00x3.30 in. and a compression ratio of 9.5:1. The 332 had a cast-iron crankshaft and forged-steel connecting rods. The two-barrel version was rated at 240 hp, and the four-barrel version (Holley or Ford carb) at 265 hp. All 332s came with a mechanical camshaft, which necessitated the use of adjustable rocker arms. Combustion chambers were machined, at least during part of the model year (see the 352 cid engine section that follows).

The engine was available again on 1959 Ford cars and on the Courier truck, but only with the two-barrel carburetor. The compression ratio was reduced to 8.9:1, which resulted in 225 hp. The engine was also available on the 1959 Edsel Corsair, and it was known as the Express V-8.

352 cid

By simply increasing the stroke of the 332 cid engine to 3.50 in., the result was 352 cid. This was the standard (and only) engine available on the 1958 Thunderbird. With a four-barrel carburetor, it was rated at 300 hp. Compression ratio was 10.2:1. As with the 332 cid version, the FE 352 used a cast-iron crank, forged-steel rods, a mechanical-lifter camshaft, and had machined combustion chambers. Interestingly, the previous year's supercharged Y-block 312 cid V-8 was also rated at 300 hp, but there was a big difference in performance. The 352 was obviously overrated, while the 312 was underrated.

During the 1958 model year, the machined combustion-chamber heads were replaced with heads that used cast chambers. The reason for the machined combustion chambers was to reduce possible hot spots and therefore pre-ignition. However, the quality of available premium gas in 1958 was inconsistent, so it was decided to replace the machined chambers with cast chambers. This had the effect of reducing compression ratio to 9.6:1 on the 352. These later heads were also cheaper to manufacture.

Besides being the standard engine on the 1959 Thunderbird, the 352 cid V-8 was also optional on 1959-model Ford cars. Even with the compression ratio drop to 9.6:1, the engine was still rated at 300 hp. It was equipped with a four-barrel carburetor.

As the 332 cid engine was dropped for 1960, a two-barrel version of the 352 cid engine took its place on the option list on the Ford line. It was rated at 235 hp. The 300 hp 352 cid was carried over on the 1960 Thunderbird. The Ford and Edsel versions, however, had a torque rating that was 1ft-lb more than that of the T-Bird engine, at 381ft-lb. In its highest output configuration, the High Performance (HP) 352 of 1960 was rated at 360 hp at 6,000 rpm with 380ft-lb torque at 3,400 rpm. The engine used an aluminum intake manifold.

From 1961 to 1963, the 352 cid FE was available only with a two-barrel intake. Its horsepower was 220. Nineteen sixty-one was the first year that 352 cid saw service in Mercury cars and 1962 was the last. Prior to 1961, Mercury used the MEL and Y-block V-8s.

During 1964–1966, the 352 cid was promoted to four-barrel status. Power went up, to 250 hp. Compression ratio was 9.3:1.

The 352 cid engine also saw service in the 1958–1960 Ford Courier. The four-barrel version used during 1958–1960 was rated at 300 hp. The 1960 two-barrel version was rated at 220 hp. The engine was also used on Ford F-series pickups and Econoline vans between 1965 and 1967. With a two-barrel carburetor, the 352 cid engine was rated at 208 hp.

The High Performance 406 cid engine replaced the HP 390 as the top performance Ford engine in 1962. The engine used the same block and also the same three two-barrel Holley carburetor setup for 405hp. The single four-barrel version was rated at 385hp.

360 cid and 361 cid

The 361 cid version of the FE series was available in cars only on the 1958–1959 Edsel line. It was basically a bored 352, as its bore and stroke were 4.0469x3.500 in. The 1958 engine, with its 10.5:1 compression ratio, Ford four-barrel carburetor, and hydraulic-lifter camshaft, was rated at 303 hp.

The 1959 engine had the same horsepower ratings, but featured a 9.6:1 compression ratio due to the switch-over to cylinder heads with cast combustion chambers.

The engine was also used on Ford trucks from 1968 to 1976. On light trucks, it was designated a 360 cid engine. Not built for high performance, these engines had lower compression ratios, usually around 8.5:1, and featured heavy-duty internal componentry. The engine was rated at 215 hp with a two-barrel carburetor from 1968 to 1971; from 1971 to 1976 it was rated at 196 hp.

The 361 cid FT (Ford Truck) engine shared the same internal dimensions, but used heavy-duty parts and a forged-steel crank shaft. The 361 cid engine was used on medium and heavy-duty trucks.

390 cid

When the 352 cid engine was bored and stroked to 4.05x3.78 in., it resulted in the 390 cid engine, introduced in 1961. This particular FE displacement lasted until 1971 on Ford passenger car applications and until 1976 in trucks.

The 1961 390 cid V-8 came in three flavors. The regular 390, with its 9.6:1 compression ratio, Ford four-barrel carburetor, hydraulic camshaft, and dual exhausts, was rated at 300 hp. The 300 hp version was available through 1965. The compression ratio was upped to 10.0:1 on the 1964–1965 engines. The 300 hp workhorse of 1961–1965 got a little more compression in 1966, 10.5:1, and was uprated to 315 hp. It was an optional engine on Ford and Mercury cars through 1968.

More interesting were the HP 390s that were also introduced in 1961. These engines used a different block from other FE engines. The block had thicker main-bearing webs and caps and additional reinforcing ribs for bottom-end strength. The oil passages in the block were enlarged, and a pressure relief valve was located in an extra boss cast between the fourth and fifth bulkheads, below the main oil gallery. Placing the oil pressure relief valve at the end of the oiling system ensured that there was sufficient oil pressure throughout the system. The valve was set to go off at 75 psi. The pressure relief valve on the oil pump was retained, but it was designed to limit pressure on cold starts. The valve was set at 105 psi. HP 390 cid blocks can be identified by the letters HP that are cast on the right side of the block, on the back of the block and in the lifter gallery.

The HP 390s came with mechanical-lifter camshafts and adjustable rocker arms. These rockers had a 1.76:1 ratio, while hydraulic-cammed engines got 1.73:1 ratio rockers. The cylinder heads on these engines also had smaller combustion chambers (59.7–62.2cc vs. 69cc for the regular heads), stronger rod bolts (which measured 13/32 in. vs. 3/8 in.), and special flat-top pistons. Although the crankshafts were cast iron, as on the regular FE engines, the cranks had a 1/8 in. groove on the main journals for improved oiling.

The single four-barrel engine was rated at 375 hp at 6,000 rpm and 427ft-lb torque at 3,400 rpm. Compression ratio was 10.6:1 and the intake manifold was cast in aluminum. A strong engine, the HP 375 hp 390 cid was also available in 1962.

The strongest 390 cid engine was rated at 401 hp. This, incidentally, was the highest factory horsepower rating for the 390 cid V-8s. The increase in power was due to the three two-barrel carburetors on an aluminum intake, which had a combined flow rating of 860cfm. This engine was also available in 1962.

A detuned version of the three-two-barrel 390 cid engine was made available on the 1962–1963 Thunderbird. A milder cam and a lower compression ratio (10.5:1) accounted for the power decrease to 340 hp at 5,000 rpm. Torque was the same as for the 401 hp version, but it came in at 200 rpm lower.

Another variant of the 390 cid engine was introduced in 1962 and was available through 1965. This was the 330 hp Police Interceptor (PI) engine. It was first used on Mercury cars in 1962 and then used on Ford cars in 1963. It came with dual exhausts, four-barrel intake manifold and carburetor (Holley or Ford), and mechanical-lifter camshaft.

Finally, there was the 390 GT engine. The engine was available from 1966 to 1969. The 1966 version was rated at 335 hp at 4,800 rpm, the 1967 and 1969 versions were rated at 320 hp at 4,800 rpm, and the 1968 at 325 hp at 4,800 rpm. All 390 GT engines came with dual exhausts, a hydraulic-lifter camshaft, 10.5:1 compression ratio (11.0:1 for the 1966 engine), and a Holley 600cfm carburetor (Ford carburetor on the 1969).

Besides these, there were also several two-barrel carburetor 390s available during 1966–1971.

Ford began using the 390 cid engine in light trucks in 1968. The engine changed little over the time it was used. From 1968 to 1971, it was rated at 255 hp with a two-barrel carburetor. From 1972 to 1976, the two-barrel version was rated at 201 hp. A four-barrel engine was added in 1974, rated at 215 hp, and it was carried over to 1976, the engine's last year of production.

406 cid

In 1962, Ford increased the 390's bore by 0.080 in., from 4.05 to 4.13 in., to create the 406 cid engine, which replaced the HP 390 as the premier Ford performance engine. It was a transition engine from the HP 390 cid V-8 to the more potent 427 cid V-8s.

The 406 cid engine used the same type of engine block as the HP 390 cid V-8, with its stronger bottom end and revised oil galleries. These engines also used two-bolt main-bearing caps. A small number of late-1963 engines had cross-bolted main caps in the numbers 2, 3, and 4 positions. The caps used on these engines were wider and were made to accept bolts that go through the side of the block. In this way, the cross-bolt caps made the most of the FE engine's Y-block side skirts to increase bottom-end strength.

The cylinder heads on the 406 cid engines used larger valves—2.09 in. intake and 1.66 in. exhaust—and the 406 had the 1.76 ratio adjustable rockers. Compression ratio was higher, too, at 11.4:1, although some sources indicate that the 405 hp version had a 12.1:1 compression ratio in 1963.

As was the HP 390s, the 406 cid V-8 was available in two versions. The single four-barrel version used an aluminum intake manifold with a 600cfm Holley Carburetor and was rated at 385 hp. The other version used the triple two-barrel Holley intake setup (840cfm) for an output of 405 hp.

410 cid

If you take the 390 cid engine and increase its stroke by 0.20 in., from 3.78 to 3.98 in., the result would be 410 cid. The 410 cid was used only on 1966 and 1967 Mercury cars.

The cylinder heads used on the 410 were the same heads used on the regular 390 cid engines, which came with 2.04 in. intake and 1.57 in. exhaust valves, actuated by hydraulic-lifter camshaft. A cast-iron intake manifold with a Ford carburetor was used for a 330 hp output.

427 cid

Just as for Chevrolet enthusiasts, the number 427 has a certain "magic" about it for Ford enthusiasts. At 425 hp, the 427 was the most powerful engine in stock form ever fitted to a Ford passenger car, and it was available from 1964 to 1968 on certain Ford passenger cars. In terms of how it fits in with the rest of the FE engine family, the 427 was a bored HP 390. With its 4.23x3.78 in. bore and stroke, the 427 cid engine was more oversquare than the 390- or the 406 cid engines and thus more conducive to high-rpm power output.

The 427 was built in three versions, Low Riser (LR), Medium Riser (MR), and High Riser (HR), but they were not built in that order. The LR was available in 1963, 1964, and 1968; the MR during 1965–1967; and the HR in 1964–1965. Adding to this variety is the single-overhead-camshaft (SOHC) 427, which we'll look at separately, and the Tunnel Port (TP) 427. The LR, MR, and HR were used to describe the intake manifold height of the 427 cid engine family. The HR engine, with its taller intake manifold, was 2–3 in. taller than the regular 427 cid engine, which was then referred to as the LR. The MR was essentially an HR engine fitted with cylinder heads with shorter intake ports than the HR's.

427 Low Riser

The 427 cid LR became available in late 1963 and continued on through the 1964 model year. It used the same type of engine block as the HP 390 and 406 cid engines, a cast-iron crankshaft, a solid-lifter camshaft, and cylinder heads that had 2.04 in. intake and 1.66 in. exhaust valves; the 1964 engines got heads with larger intake valves measuring 2.09 in. (These heads, incidentally, were the same heads that would later be used on the 428 Cobra Jet [CJ] V-8). A small number of 1963–1964 LR engines had cross-bolted main caps in the numbers 2, 3, and 4 positions. The caps used on these engines were wider and were made to accept bolts that go through the side of the block. In this way, the cross-bolt caps made the most of the FE engine's Y-block side skirts to increase bottom-end strength.

The LR was available with two intake setups. The single Holley four-barrel version was rated at 410 hp. The dual four-barrel setup was rated at 425 hp. Both intake manifolds on these engines were cast in aluminum. Compression ratio was 11.5:1 on both engines.

The LR surfaced again for a short time on 1968 Mercury Cougars and Ford Mustangs. Although it was still an LR in design, there were considerable differences between this version and the earlier ones. The engine block was the better "side-oiler" block

The 428 Cobra Jet engine powered Ford's hot street cars during 1968–70.

used on all 1965–1967 427 cid engines. The side-oiler block had a different oiling system than other FE-series blocks, and the main oil gallery was on the lower left side of the engine. Unlike other 427 cid engines, the 1968 LR engine used a hydraulic camshaft, so additional oil galleries were added to the block. The cylinder heads used the same size valves as the earlier LRs. Only one version was made, rated at 390 hp. Compression was 10.9:1, and the engine used a single 650cfm Holley four-barrel carburetor.

427 Medium Riser

The MR was available from 1965 to 1967. One of the problems with the HR 427 cid engine was that the tall cylinder intake ports and intake manifold made it necessary for whatever car used the engine to have a bubble-type hood or a large hood scoop. The MR remedied that situation because its cylinder head intake ports were 0.38 in. lower. The intake ports measured 1.34x2.34 in. while the HR's ports were 1.34x2.72 in.

Actually, the MR's port dimensions weren't anything really new, being the same as on the 1960–1962 HP 352 and 390 cid engines. The same heads were later used on the 1968–1970 428 CJ engines, but with smaller valves. The difference between these heads and all the others is that the MR heads used much larger valves, 2.195 in. intake and 1.73 in. exhaust. Because the valves were larger and spaced farther apart, they required wider rocker-shaft stands, part number C5AE-6531-A. The combustion chambers on the MR were also quite large, 88–91cc, and they were also fully machined.

The MR was also equipped with a forged-steel crankshaft and special cap-screw connecting rods. Like the LR and HR, the MR came with a mechanical-lifter camshaft. The MR also benefited from the better side-oiler engine block. The side-oiler block had a different oiling system than other FE-series blocks (the main oil gallery was on the lower left side of the engine). In addition, all MR engines used the cross-bolt main-bearing caps in the numbers 2, 3, and 4 positions.

The MR, in spite of its better porting and larger valves, was rated the same as the 1963–1964 LRs: 410- and 425 hp.

427 High Riser

The HR 427 was first made available during 1964. The name "High Riser" is derived from the special cylinder heads and accompanying intake manifold used on the engine. The HR cylinder head, C4AE-6049-F, had the tallest rectangular ports of any FE-series cylinder head, measuring 2.72x1.34 in. Valve size was also larger than those of the LR, 2.195 in./1.73 in. intake/exhaust. The taller ports and tall intake manifold were designed to give the intake air-fuel mixture a better entry angle into the combustion chamber. This they did, and power was boosted in the 5,000–7,000 rpm range.

It used the same type of engine block as the HP 390 and 406 cid engines, a cast-iron crankshaft, a solid-lifter camshaft, and all HRs had the cross-bolted main-bearing caps. The HR engines used wider rockershaft stands (due to the larger valves) and also special shorter rockershaft pedestals. There were two intake manifolds available for the HR, a single and a dual four-barrel aluminum intake manifold. These do not interchange with any other FE-series engine.

427 Tunnel Port

Introduced in 1967, the 427 TP cylinder heads were another over-the-counter option. The cylinder heads had the largest intake ports and valves of any 427 cid FE-series wedge head. The round ports were positioned to give the most direct path to the intake valves, rather than curving around the pushrods, as with other FE-series heads. The pushrods operated through a tube in the center of each port. Three intake systems were made for the Tunnel-Port—a single four-barrel single plane and two dual four-barrel carburetor setups (one a single plane and the other a dual plane). These manifolds fit only Tunnel-Port heads.

Besides the larger ports, the Tunnel-Port head used the same machined combustion chamber design as the MR, along with the same rockershafts. Intake valves were larger, measuring 2.25 in., and the exhausts were 1.73 in. The heads were Domestic Special Order parts. You could buy a complete engine with these heads, under part number C70E-6007-T-361A, or just the heads under part number C8AX-6049-A. The intake manifolds were sold separately.

In other respects, the Tunnel-Port engines were just like the MRs.

427 cid SOHC

This is the ultimate configuration of the FE-series big-block engine. The 427 SOHC (or "Cammer") was designed to be used in Ford stock cars to compete against Chrysler's 426 Hemi engine. For various reasons, it was never used in stock car races, but the engine eventually found itself in various Ford race cars and in some street cars as well. The engine was never offered as an option on any Ford passenger car or truck but was available as an over-the-counter option.

What made the Cammer different was the cast-aluminum cylinder heads that used fully machined hemispherical combustion chambers. Why hemi heads? Hemi heads provide considerably more upper-end breathing, and therefore more power, than a comparable wedge-chamber design. With very few exceptions, most engines produced today, especially the overhead-cam, multi-valve engines, have hemi combustion chambers, or a variation thereof.

The intake ports of the heads were round and large; the exhaust ports were "D" shaped. Valves measured 2.25 in. intake and 1.90 in. exhaust. The stainless-steel valves were made with either tulip or flat heads. Interestingly, these valves also fit the Boss 429 cylinder heads as well.

Although the left and right heads were cast from the same pattern, they were not interchangeable after they were machined. Another peculiarity is that the right head has six cam bearings while the left head uses five. Obviously, the cams themselves are not interchangeable, either. Connecting the two camshafts is a very long, 6ft timing chain. The Cammer uses intake manifolds specifically made for it; the two most common are single four-barrel and dual four-barrel setups. The engine was rated at 615 hp with a single four-barrel Holley carburetor. The heads are capped off by two distinctive aluminum rocker covers.

The rest of the engine, the short-block, was very similar to the one used on the MR engine: The side-oiler, cross-bolted block was used, but there were enough differences that the block was not directly interchangeable with other wedge engine blocks. The main difference is that two bosses were cast into the back of each cylinder bank. These were drilled to allow oil to drain back to the oil pan from each head. In addition, the block's original front two cam bearings were used. The other three were blocked off, but the fourth bearing had a modified backside to allow oil to flow to the right cylinder head. The crankshaft was forged steel, and the rods were the special Le Mans-type capscrew rods. Naturally, the Cammer uses unique pop-up pistons.

The engine was never used in factory stock car racers. Most of its race successes were on the drag strip, especially in blown fuel dragsters. The engine was available from Ford between 1965 and 1968.

428 cid

The largest permutation of the FE-series engine was the 428 cid engine. Depending on your outlook, the 428 cid V-8 was a bored and stroked 390 cid V-8, or a stroked 406 cid, or a bored 410 cid V-8. Whichever way you look at it, its bore and stroke was 4.13x3.98 in.

The 428 cid engine was introduced in 1966, in two configurations. The regular 428 cid used the standard FE-series block with a cast-iron crankshaft, forged-steel connecting rods, a single four-barrel carburetor, and a cast-iron intake manifold. Power output was 345 hp. Compression ratio was 10.5:1. The cylinder heads were the regular production FE series cylinder heads, with 2.04 in. intake and 1.57 in. exhaust valves.

The more powerful Police Interceptor (PI) version was rated at 360 hp. It used an aluminum intake manifold, a hotter camshaft, and stronger connecting rods with thicker rod bolts.

The regular 428 cid engine was used on Ford passenger cars until 1969. In high-performance applications, the 428 CJ took its place in late 1968.

There was also a special 428 cid application for use on 1967–1968 Shelby Mustangs. The 1967 version used a dual four-barrel intake setup. Curiously, the engine was rated at 355 hp, 5 hp less than the PI it was based on. The 1968 version's horsepower went up to 360 hp, even though it was equipped only with a single Holley four-barrel carburetor mounted on an aluminum intake manifold.

428 Cobra Jet and Super Cobra Jet

This was the hot 428 cid engine. It was introduced late in the 1968 model year on the Mustang, Cougar, and Shelby Mustang. There wasn't really anything new here, just a recombination of existing parts from Ford's parts bin.

The engine block used on the 428 CJ engine was basically a standard FE-series block—meaning it wasn't a side-oiler and it didn't have the cross-bolted bottom end—but the 428 CJ engine block had a higher iron nodularity, as did the cast-iron crankshaft. The connecting rods were the PI type. The intake manifold was a cast-iron copy of the aluminum intake manifold used on the 360 hp PI 428. The carburetor was a Holley 735cfm four-barrel. The camshaft was the same one used on the 1968 390 GT engine. The cylinder heads were also similar to the ones used on the 427 cid LR engine, in that they used the same size valves, 2.09 in. intake and 1.66 in. exhaust. The intake port openings, though, were the same as those used on the 427 MR, measuring 2.34x1.34 in. The combustion chambers were as cast.

The result was 335 hp at 5,200 rpm and 440ft-lb torque at 3,400 rpm. These advertised power figures were obviously underrated, but so were most of Ford's other higher output FE-series engines. In fact, most high-performance Detroit engines of the late 1960s were generally misrepresented.

There was yet another FE-series variant, the 428 Super Cobra Jet (SCJ). Although the SCJ was identical in power output rating the CJ, the SCJ was given several internal modifications designed to make the engine more durable. It had the same Le Mans-type capscrew rods used on the 427 cid MR engine but with a different part number, C9ZZ-6200-A. The rods used shorter capscrews designed to clear the block. The SCJ was also externally balanced. It seems that if Ford was really serious about durability, it would have also included the side-oiler 427 block, or at least the HP 390 cid block, with the SCJ. All 428 SCJ cars were equipped with an external engine oil cooler, which is an easy way to identify an SCJ. The engine tags on SCJs had the codes 422S, 423S, 424S, or 425S stamped on them while the regular CJs were stamped either 418S, 419S, 420S, or 421S.

Shelby FE-Series Engines

Carroll Shelby used the 427 cid and 428 cid FE-series engines in the Shelby Cobra and Shelby GT500 Mustangs. The Cobra generally used the 427 cid MR V-8. The Shelby GT500 Mustangs got the 428 cid PI V-8 fitted with the dual four-barrel intake setup for 1967 and a single four-barrel version for 1968. The 1967–1968 Shelby big-block engines were fitted with distinctive Shelby air cleaners and valve covers.

Engine Blocks

There were three versions of the FE-series engine block. All engines, with the exception of the HP 390-, 406-, and 427 cid engines, used the standard block. The standard block has the stock two-bolt-main caps and a relatively restrictive oiling system. In this design, the main bearings were the last to receive oil, and the internal oil passages were small, with sharp bends at the corners.

The 1961–1963 HP 390 and 406 and 1963–1964 427 cid engines used a different block. It had stronger bottom-end webbing and an oil system that used larger, less-restrictive oil passages. It also had a pressure relief valve located at the end of the main oil passage. All these engines used mechanical lifters, so there was no provision for lifter oil passages. The 390 cid blocks had the letters "HP" on the right front side of the block, behind the flywheel and inside the lifter gallery. Some 406s and 427s built prior to 1965 also had the cross-bolted main-bearing cap bolts.

The best FE-series block was used on 1965–1968 427 engines, including the 427 SOHC. This was the side-oiler block. Besides the cross-bolted bottom end, the block had a different oiling system. The main gallery was on the lower left side of the block, hence the term "side-oiler." The critical main bearings were supplied with oil directly from this side oil passage. With the exception of the 1968 block, the side-oiler blocks did not have provisions for using a hydraulic-lifter camshaft.

Cylinder Heads

If anything, it's the various cylinder-head combinations that have given the FE-series its reputation for complexity. Ford used the engine in many applications—from trucks to high-performance street cars to all-out race cars. By using different cylinder heads, Ford was able to tailor the FE engine for a particular application. The cylinder heads are the single most important component in the power-making ability of an engine. With the exception of the SOHC 427, all FE-series engines had a wedge-type combustion-chamber design with inline valves.

All FE-series engines, except the 406, 427, and 428 CJ/SCJ engines, came with 2.04 in. intake and 1.57 in. exhaust valves. The 406, 427 LR (and the 1968 427), and 428 CJ/SCJ engines came with a larger 2.09 in. intake and 1.66 in. exhaust valves. All MR and HR heads had 2.19 in. intakes and 1.72 in. exhaust valves. The TP heads got even larger intakes—2.25 in.—but used the 1.72 in. MR and HR exhaust valves. The 427 SOHC engine came with unique 2.25 in. intakes and 1.90 in. exhausts.

With the exception of the 427 SOHC engine, all FE-series engines had the same size exhaust ports: 1.84x1.28 in. Excepting the 427 Tunnel-Port and 427 SOHC, all FE engines had intake ports of the same width, 1.34 in. The differences, therefore, lie in the port height. The vast majority of engines had the "standard" size intake port height of 1.93 in. These include the 332, 352, 361, 390, 406, 410, 427 LR (and 1968 427), and 428 cid engines. The HP 352 and 390, 427 MR, and 428 CJ/SCJ had taller ports, measuring 2.34 in. The 427 HR had even taller ports, measuring 2.72 in. The 427 Tunnel-Port and SOHC engines had unique rounded intake ports, and the 427 SOHC had its own "D"-shaped exhaust ports.

Combustion chamber size was also varied, but that hasn't really added to the confusion.

With the exception of the 427 SOHC and some 427 MRs, all cylinder heads were cast iron. The exceptions were cast of aluminum.

Intake Manifolds

There is no question that Ford spent a lot of research dollars on intake manifold design. The result was a great variety of intake manifolds—something for every application on the street and on the race track (see the tables).

The vast majority of FE-series engines were equipped with cast-iron intake manifolds with either a two-barrel or four-barrel bolt pattern. The stock cast-iron intake manifolds were big, heavy pieces of iron.

Just about every FE-series displacement was at one time the high-performance Ford engine. Accordingly, these high-performance versions were always equipped with an aluminum intake manifold. The HP 352-, 390-, and 406 cid engines had a dual-plane aluminum intake manifold with a single four-barrel carburetor. Some HP 390- and 406 cid engines also came with a triple two-barrel Holley carburetor intake system, which looked pretty good and also provided a good balance between power and fuel economy. The 428 CJ/SCJ came with a cast-iron copy of the aluminum 428 PI intake, although the first 50 preproduction 428 CJ Mustangs were equipped with the aluminum manifold.

The engine that had the most cylinder head combinations also had the most intake manifolds made for it. This was the 427 cid engine. All 427 cid engines were equipped with aluminum intake manifolds. The LR could have been had with either a single four-barrel or dual four-barrel intake system. The same went for the MR, for which single-plane manifolds were also available. The "sidewinder" single four-barrel intake for the MR had the carburetor offset to the left, thereby equalizing the length of the runners. This was the manifold developed for the 427 cid powered Mark II Le Mans winning GT-40s. Only two manifolds were made for the HR, a dual-plane single four-barrel and a dual-plane dual four-barrel unit.

There were three intake manifold castings made for the 427 cid TP: a single-plane single four-barrel and two dual four-barrel intakes—one a single plane and the other a dual plane.

The 427 SOHC was equipped with any number of factory intakes, from a single four-barrel to the usual (for 427s) dual four-barrel system.

There were also many aftermarket manifolds available from the usual suppliers—Edelbrock, Weiand, and Offenhauser.

Exhaust Manifolds

All FE-series engines were equipped with cast-iron exhaust manifolds. These were entirely conventional in nature, exiting toward

If you've seen the exhaust ports of one FE series cylinder head, you've seen them all. They all have the same size port dimension. This particular one is a 427 Tunnel Port head.

the back of the engine. As a general rule, cars with four-barrel carburetors were equipped with a dual exhaust system, and cars with two-barrel carburetor were equipped with a single exhaust system.

The factory higher performance engines, such as the HP 390-, 406-, and 427 cid engines, came with rather elaborate manifolds that were certainly free flowing, in the context of cast-iron exhaust manifolds. These castings are rare today. The 428 CJ/SCJ engines were also equipped with better flowing exhaust manifolds than other passenger car FE engines.

In general, all FE-series exhaust manifolds will fit any FE-series heads. There is an exception, though; the 1966–1968 390- and 1968 427 cid engines had a different bolt pattern, while the 428 CJ heads had both patterns.

Engine Identification

Ford's method of identifying engine parts follows typical industry procedures in that each part has a casting number cast onto it, and for Fords, that number consists of letters and numbers in a particular order. Let's look at a typical part number—in this case, C8OZ-6049-K, which is the cylinder head for the 1968 428 CJ engine. It breaks down as follows:

C: this indicates the decade (B is 1950–1959, C is 1960–1969, D is 1970–1979);

8: this indicates the year of the decade (8 would be 1968 in our example);

OZ: this indicates the car line;

6049: a subgroup number (for example, all Ford cylinder heads are numbered 6049, intake manifolds are 9424, camshafts 6250, and so on);

K: this is an application suffix code (for example, on a camshaft, the letter A might stand for a high-performance solid-lifter cam, while the letter B might be for a two-barrel engine with hydraulic cam). The various codes and suffixes are listed in the tables.

Casting numbers are similar to part numbers, but there are major differences. Usually, the subgroup numbers were not used in the number cast on the part itself, but they will be indicated in the parts book, if the casting number is listed at all. Sometimes, however, the subgroup number is on the part itself, and sometimes the casting number is the same as the part number.

Date codes were also used. A typical date code might be as follows: 9 B 16: the 9 indicates the last digit of the year (in this case it could be 1959 or 1969); the B indicates the month, in this case February (the months were coded A for January through M for December, but I was not used); the 16 indicates the day of the month.

Depending on the part you're looking at, the date code is probably as important as the casting number itself, especially if you're trying to determine originality. To be considered original, parts installed in a Ford vehicle have to have been cast or manufactured before the car itself was built. This can be up to 30 days or more and still be considered original. On parts that were manufactured, the date codes were stamped on the part, rather than cast.

There wasn't any engine identification in relation to the vehicle it was installed in until 1970, when Ford began stamping the car's VIN on the block, on the left rear side of the block, just below the cylinder head. On pre-1970 Fords, you can't determine if a particular engine is original equipment in a particular car. Ford did assign an engine code for use in the vehicle's VIN. In this way, you can at least tell by looking at a VIN what engine the car was built with. On 1954–1959 models, the engine code was the first digit of the vehicle's VIN. Beginning in 1960, the code was in the fifth position, and it remained in that position until 1981. Ford used the codes over and over, the same code standing for different engines. These codes are listed in the tables.

There was an engine identification code stamped on engines from 1960 to 1964, but this code consisted of just the date the engine was built, the engine plant, and an inspector's identification code. It was located on the left front side of the engine. It didn't tie the engine in with the car.

From 1964, Ford placed a small metal tag (which was usually attached to the coil hold-down bolt) that included information about the engine. Most of these codes are included in the tables. These tags were easily lost, so they are often missing from engines today.

The 427 Tunnel Port head had much larger, rounded intake ports. But where are the tubes that the pushrods go through, you may ask? They are in the intake manifold as the intake forms the rest of the cylinder head. The exhaust ports on the Tunnel Port were the same as all other FE series engines.

Engine Specifications

	Displacement	Carburetor	Horsepower	Torque	Compression Ratio	Notes
1958						
	332	4V	265@4,600	360@2,800	9.5	Ford
	352	4V	300@4,600	395@2,800	10.2	Ford, T-Bird
1959						
	332	2V	225@4,600	325@2,200	8.9	Ford, Edsel
	352	4V	300@4,600	395@2,800	10.2	Ford, T-Bird
1960						
	352	4V	235@4,400	350@2,400	8.9	Ford
	352	4V	300@4,600	380@2,800	9.6	Ford, Edsel, T-Bird
	352	4V	360@6,000	380@3,400	10.6	Ford
1961						
	352	2V	220@4,400	376@2,400	8.9	Ford
	390	4V	300@4,600	427@2,800	9.6	Ford, T-Bird
	390	4V	330@5,000	427@3,200	9.6	Ford, PI
	390	4V	375@6,000	427@3,400	10.6	Ford
	390	3x2V	401@6,000	430@3,500	10.6	Ford
1962						
	352	2V	220@4,400	376@2,400	8.9	Ford
	390	4V	300@4,600	427@2,800	9.6	Ford, T-Bird
	390	4V	330@5,000	427@3,200	9.6	Ford, PI
	390	3x2V	340@6,000	430@3,500	10.6	Ford, T-Bird
	390	4V	375@6,000	427@3,400	10.6	Ford
	390	3x2V	401@6,000	430@3,500	10.6	Ford
	406	4V	385@5,800	444@3,400	11.4	Ford
	406	3x2V	405@5,800	448@3,500	11.4	Ford
1963						
	352	2V	220@4,400	376@2,400	8.9	Ford
	390	2V	250@4,400	378@2,400	8.9	Mercury
	390	4V	300@4,600	427@2,800	9.6	Ford, Mercury, T-Bird
	390	4V	330@5,000	427@3,200	9.6	Ford, Mercury, PI
	406	4V	385@5,800	444@3,400	11.4	Ford, Mercury
	406	3x2V	405@5,800	448@3,500	12.1	Ford, Mercury
	427	4V	410@5,600	476@3,400	11.6	Ford, Mercury, LR
	427	2x4V	425@6,000	480@3,700	12.0	Ford, Mercury, LR
1964						
	352	4V	250@4,400	352@2,800	9.3	Ford

Displacement	Carburetor	Horsepower	Torque	Compression Ratio	Notes
390	2V	250@4,400	378@2,400	8.9	Mercury
390	2V	266@4,600	378@2,400	9.4	Mercury
390	4V	300@4,600	427@2,800	11.0	Ford, Mercury, T-Bird
390	4V	330@5,000	427@3,200	10.1	Ford, Mercury, PI
427	4V	410@5,600	476@3,400	11.6	Ford, Mercury, LR
427	2x4V	425@6,000	480@3,700	11.6	Ford, Fairlane, Mercury, LR
1965					
352	4V	208@4,000	310@2,800	8.4	trucks
352	4V	250@4,400	352@2,800	9.3	Ford
390	2V	250@4,400	378@2,400	8.9	Mercury
390	2V	266@4,600	378@2,400	9.4	Mercury
390	4V	300@4,600	427@2,800	11.0	Ford, Mercury, T-Bird
427	4V	410@5,600	476@3,400	11.6	Ford, Mercury, MR
427	2x4V	425@6,000	480@3,700	11.6	Ford, Mercury, MR
427	4V	615@7,000	515@3,800	13.0	SOHC
1966					
352	4V	208@4,000	310@2,800	8.4	trucks
352	4V	250@4,400	352@2,800	9.3	Ford
390	2V	275@4,400	401@2,600	9.5	Ford, Fairlane, Mercury, Comet
390	4V	315@4,600	427@2,800	10.5	Ford, T-Bird
410	4V	330@4,600	444@2,800	10.5	Mercury
427	4V	410@5,600	476@3,400	11.6	Ford, Mercury, MR
427	2x4V	425@6,000	480@3,700	11.6	Ford, Mercury, MR
428	4V	345@4,600	462@2,800	10.5	Ford, Mercury, T-Bird
428	4V	360@5,400	459@3,200	10.5	Ford, Mercury, PI
1967					
352	4V	208@4,000	310@2,800	8.4	trucks
390	2V	270@4,400	401@2,600	9.5	Ford, Fairlane, Mercury, Comet
390	4V	315@4,600	427@2,800	10.5	Ford, T-Bird
390	4V	320@4,600	427@3,200	10.5	Mustang, Fairlane, Cyclone GT, Cougar, GT
410	4V	330@4,600	444@2,800	10.5	Mercury
427	4V	410@5,600	476@3,400	11.6	Ford, Mercury, MR
427	2x4V	425@6,000	480@3,700	11.6	Ford, Mercury, MR
428	4V	345@4,600	462@2,800	10.5	Ford, Mercury, S-55, T-Bird
428	4V	360@5,400	459@3,200	10.5	Ford, Mercury, PI
428	2x4V	355@5,400	420@3,200	10.5	Shelby Mustang GT500
1968					
360	2V	215@4,400	327@2,400	8.4	trucks
390	2V	255@4,400	376@2,600	8.6	trucks
390	2V	265@4,400	401@2,600	9.5	Ford, Fairlane, Torino, Mercury
390	2V	280@4,600	427@2,800	10.5	Ford
390	4V	315@4,600	427@2,800	10.5	T-Bird, Mercury
390	4V	325@4,800	427@2,800	10.5	Mustang, Fairlane, Cyclone GT, Cougar GT
427	4V	390@5,600	460@3,200	10.9	Mustang, Cougar, LR
428	4V	335@5,200	440@3,400	10.6	Mustang, Cougar, Shelby GT500 KR, CJ
428	4V	340@4,600	462@2,800	10.5	Ford, Mercury
428	4V	360@5,400	459@3,200	10.5	Ford, Mercury, PI
428	4V	360@5,400	420@3,200	10.5	Shelby, Cobra GT500
1969					
360	2V	215@4,400	327@2,400	8.4	trucks
390	2V	255@4,400	376@2,600	8.6	trucks
390	2V	265@4,400	401@2,600	9.5	Ford, Mercury
390	2V	280@4,600	427@2,800	10.5	Mercury
390	4V	320@4,800	427@3,200	10.5	Mustang, Fairlane, Torino, Montego, Cyclone GT, Cougar GT
428	4V	335@5,200	440@3,400	10.6	Mustang, Cougar, Fairlane, Torino, Cyclone, Cougar, CJ, SCJ
1970					
360	2V	215@4,400	327@2,400	8.4	trucks

Engine Specifications

	Displacement	Carburetor	Horsepower	Torque	Compression Ratio	Notes
	390	2V	255@4,400	376@2,600	8.6	trucks
	390	2V	265@4,400	401@2,600	9.5	Ford, Mercury
	428	4V	335@5,200	440@3,400	10.6	Mustang, Cougar, Fairlane, Torino, Cyclone, Cougar, CJ, SCJ
1971						
	390	2V	255@4,400	376@2,600	9.0	Ford, Mercury
	360	2V	215@4,400	327@2,400	8.4	trucks
	390	2V	255@4,400	376@2,600	8.6	trucks
1972						
	360	2V	196@4,000	327@2,400	8.4	trucks
	390	2V	201@4,000	376@2,600	8.6	trucks
1973						
	360	2V	196@4,000	327@2,400	8.4	trucks
	390	2V	201@4,000	376@2,600	8.6	trucks
1974						
	360	2V	196@4,000	327@2,400	8.4	trucks
	390	2V	201@4,000	376@2,600	8.6	trucks
1975						
	360	2V	196@4,000	327@2,400	8.4	trucks
	390	2V	201@4,000	376@2,600	8.6	trucks

Engine Internal Dimensions

Displacement	Bore and Stroke	Rod Bearings	Main Bearings	Intake/Exhaust Valves
332	4.000x3.300	2.4380–2.4388	2.7484–2.7492	2.04/1.57
352	4.002x3.500	2.4380–2.4388	2.7484–2.7492	2.04/1.57
360	4.047x3.500	2.4380–2.4388	2.7484–2.7492	2.04/1.57
361	4.047x3.500	2.4380–2.4388	2.7484–2.7492	2.04/1.57
390	4.052x3.784	2.4380–2.4388	2.7484–2.7492	2.04/1.57
406	4.130x3.784	2.4380–2.4388	2.7484–2.7492	2.09/1.66
410	4.054x3.980	2.4380–2.4388	2.7484–2.7492	2.04/1.57
427	4.232x3.784	2.4380–2.4388	2.7484–2.7492	2.09/1.66 LR, 2.195x1.733 MR, 2.195x1.733 HR, 2.25x1.733 TP, 2.25x1.90 SOHC
428	4.132x3.980	2.4380–2.4388	2.7484–2.7492	2.04/1.57 (2.09/1.65-CJ)

Block, Head, and Manifold Part and Casting Numbers

Year	Engine	Part or Casting Number
Engine Blocks		
1958	332	casting EDC, EDG
1958	332	casting 575063
1958–1959	332	casting 5751091
1959	332	casting B9AE-B
1958	352	casting EDC
1958–1959	352	C3AZ-6010-B, casting EDG6015, 751091
1959–1960	352	casting B9AE-B
1960	352	High Performance COAZ-6010B,casting EDC-B, EDC-C
1961–1962	352	C2AE-6010, casting C1AE-G
1963	352	casting C3AE-A, C3AE-F
1964	352	casting C3AE-G, C4AE-A
1965	352	casting C5AE-C
1963–1967	352	C5AE-6010-A
1966	352	casting C6TE-C, C6TE-L
1966–1967	352	casting C6ME-A
1967	352	casting C6ME-A
1968–1976	360	truck, casting C6ME, C6ME-A, C8AE-A, C8AE-C, C8AE-E
1973–1976	360	truck, casting D3TE, D3TE-1, D3TE-AC, D3TE-HA, D3TE-AC

A popular intake manifold was the three two-barrel setup. It provided a boost in power, good fuel economy, and it looked pretty good, too. This unit fits all FE series engines except the High Riser, Tunnel Port, and 427 SOHC engines.

Year	Engine	Part or Casting Number
Engine Blocks		
1968–1976	360	truck, service block, casting D7TE-BA
1958	361	casting 58
1959	361	casting 59
1961	390	High Performance C2AZ-6010-B, casting C1AE-V, C1AE-BC
1962	390	High Performance C2AZ-6010-B, casting C2AE-BE, C2AE-BR, C2AE-BS
1961–1962	390	C1AE-6010-AD, casting C1AE-C, C1AE-G
1962	390	casting C2SE
1963	390	casting C3SE-A
1963	390	Police Interceptor C3AZ-6010-S, casting C3AE-KY, C3ME-B
1964	390	Police Interceptor C3AZ-6010-S, casting C4AE-F
1965	390	Police Interceptor C3AZ-6010-Y, casting C5AE-B
1964	390	casting C4AE-D
1965	390	casting C3AE-AY, C5AE-A
1966–1976	390	casting C6ME, C6ME-A
1968–1976	390	casting C8AE-A, C8AE-C, C8AE-E
1973–1976	390	casting D3TE, D3TE-1, D3TE-AC, D3TE-HA
1974–1976	390	casting D4TE-AC
1961–1976	390	Service Block casting D7TE-BA
1962	406	casting C2AE-J, C2AE-K, C2AE-V
1962–1963	406	casting C2AE-BD w/cross bolts
1962–1963	406	casting C3AE-D, C3AE-C w/o cross bolts
1966–1967	410	casting C6ME, C6ME-A
1963	427	C3AZ-6010-AK, casting C3AE-M, C3AE-AB
1964	427	casting C4AE, C4AE-A
1965	427	casting C3AE-Z, C5AE-A, C5AE-E
1965	427	Side-oiler, casting 5AE-D, C5AE-D
1965–1966	427	Side-oiler to 12-9-65, casting C5AE-H, C6AE-B
1965–1966	427	Side-oiler, casting 6AE-C, C6AE-C
1966	427	Side-oiler, casting C6AE-B
1966–1967	427	Side-oiler, casting C6AE-D
1967	427	Side-oiler, casting C7AE-A
1966–1968	427	Irrigation, casting C5JE-D, C7JE-E
1968	427	Marine, casting C6JE-B, C7JE-A
1968	427	Side-oiler, C8AZ-6010-B, casting C8AE-B, C8AE-H, C8AE-A
1966	428	Police Interceptor, casting C6AE-B, C6AE-F
1966–1967	428	C6AZ-6010-A, casting C6AE-A
1966–1970	428	casting C6ME, C6ME-A
1967–1970	428	casting C7ME, C7ME-A
1968–1970	428	C6AZ-6010-F, casting C8ME
Cylinder Heads		
1958	332/352	casting EDC, EDC-E
1958–1959	332/352/361	B9AZ-6049-G, casting 5752142, 5752143
1960-61	352	High Performance COAE-6049-C, casting COAE-6090-D
1960	352	COAZ-6049-G, casting COAE-6090-C
1961	352	casting C1SE A
1961–1963	352	casting C1AE A
1962–1963	352	C2SZ-6049-B, casting C2SE-6090-B
1964–1965	352	casting C4AE, C4AE-G
1966	352	C6AZ-6049-A, casting C6TE-B, C6TE-G, C6AE-AA
1966	352	casting C6AE-D w/Thermactor
1966	352	casting C6AE-R, R, C6AE-J, C6AE-RVL
1966–1967	352	C6AZ-6049-A, casting C6AE-AB
1967	352	casting C7AE-A
1968	360	casting C8AE-B
1968	360	casting C9AE-A, C8AE-H , w/Thermactor
1972–1976	360	casting D2TE-AA, D3TE, D3TE-B, D3TE-C, D3TE-E, D3TE-F
1961	390	casting C1SE-A
1960–1961	390	High Performance COAE-6049-C, casting COAE 6090-D
1962	390	High Performance COAE-6049-C, casting COAE 6090-D, early 1962
1962	390	High Performance, casting C2SE-6090-A, late 1962
1962–1963	390	High Performance, casting C2SE-6090-A, T-Bird 3x2V
1963	390	High Performance, casting C4SE-6090-A,
1961–1963	390	casting C1AE-A
1962–1963	390	C2SZ-6049-B, casting C2SE-6090-B

Block, Head, and Manifold Part and Casting Numbers

Year	Engine	Part or Casting Number
Cylinder Heads		
1964–1965	390	casting C4AE, C4AE-G
1966	390	C6AZ-6049-A, casting C6TE-B, C6TE-G, C6AE R,
1966	390	casting C6AE-D w/Thermactor
1966	390	casting C6OE-6090 H, Fairlane, Comet, w/Thermactor
1966–1967	390	casting C6OE-AB, Fairlane, Mustang, Cougar, Comet, w/Thermactor
1966–1967	390	C6AZ-6049-A, casting C6AE-AB
1966–1967	390	casting C6OE-Y, C6OE-AC, Fairlane GT
1966–1967	390	casting C6OE-AA, C7AE-A, Fairlane, Comet
1967	390	casting C7AE-A
1968	390	casting C8OE-A, Comet, Cougar, Fairlane, Mustang, w/Thermactor
1968	390	casting C9AE-A, C8AE-H , w/Thermactor
1968	390	casting C8AE-B
1972–1976	390	casting D2TE-AA, D3TE, D3TE-B, D3TE-C, D3TE-E, D3TE-F
1968	390	casting C9AE-A, C8AE-H , w/Thermactor
1968	390	casting C6AE-L, C6AE-U, Mercury 390 4V, 2V w/high compression
1969	390	casting C8OE-F, w/Thermactor
1969	390	casting C8OE-XX
1972–1976	390	casting D3TE-D, D5AE, w/Thermactor
1962	406	C2AZ-6049-A, casting C2SE-6090-B, to 01-29-62
1962–1963	406	C2AZ-6049-B, casting C2SE-6090-C, 01/29/62 to 12-17-63
1963	406	C3AZ-6049-H, casting C3AE-6090-C after 12/17/62
1966	410	casting C6TE-B, C6TE-G, C6AE-AA
1966	410	casting C6AE-D w/Thermactor
1967	410	casting C7AE-A
1963	427	Low Riser, C3AE-6049-D, casting C3AE-6090-D to 03/15/63, C3AE-6049-G, casting C3AE-6090-G after 03/15/63
1964–1965	427	Low Riser, C3AZ-6049-K, casting C3AE-6090-J
1963	427	High Riser, casting C3AE-6090-F
1964	427	High Riser, casting C4AE-6090-F
1965–1967	427	Medium Riser, C5AE-6049-G, casting C5AE-6090-F
1966–1967	427	Medium Riser C5AZ-6049-C, casting C5AE-6090-R
1968	427	Tunnel Port C8AX-6049-A, casting C7OE-6090-K, C8AX
1968	427	Low Riser, casting C8AE-6090-J, C8AE-N, Fairlane, Montego
1968	427	Low Riser, casting C8WE-6090-A, C8AE-N, Mustang, Cougar
1966	428	casting C6TE-B, C6TE-G, C6AE-AA
1966	428	casting C6AE-D w/Thermactor
1967	428	casting C7AE-A
1966–1967	428	C6AZ-6049-A, casting C6AE-AB
1968–1969	428	C8AZ-6049-B, casting C8AE-B
1968	428	C8AZ-6049-A, casting C9AE-A, C8AE-H , w/Thermactor
1966–1967	428	Police Interceptor, casting C6AE-AA, w/Thermactor
1968–1970	428	Police Interceptor, C8AZ-6049-N casting C8AE-F, w/Thermactor
1968	428	Cobra Jet, C8OZ-6049-F, C8OZ-6049-K, casting C8OE-6090-H
1968–1970	428	Cobra Jet, Super Cobra Jet, casting C8OE-6090-N
Intake Manifolds		
1958–1961	332/352 2V	C1AE-9424-A
1958–1961	332/352 4V	C1AE-9424-B
1962–1963	352 2V	C3AZ-9424-F, w/ 1/4 in. temp. sender
1962–1963	352 4V	C3AZ-9424-E, w/ 1/4 in. temp. sender
1963–1964	352 4V	C4AZ-9424-B, w/ 1/8 in. temp. sender
1965–1966	352 4V	C5AZ-9424-D, C5AZ-9424-M, w/ 1/8 in. temp. sender
1965–1966	352 2V	C5AZ-9424-L, trucks
1965–1967	352 2V	C5AZ-9424-L
1973	360 2V	D3TZ-9424-A, trucks
1961–1963	390 3x2V	C1AE-9424-E, C3AZ-9424-D, aluminum
1961–1963	390 4V	C1AE-9424-C, C3AZ-9424-C, aluminum
1963	390 3x2V	C3SZ-9424-A, aluminum, T-Bird
1962–1963	390 2V	C3AZ-9424-F, w/ 1/4 in. temp. sender
1962–1963	390 4V	C3AZ-9424-E, w/ 1/4 in. temp. sender
1963–1964	390 4V	C4AZ-9424-B, w/ 1/8 in. temp. sender, casting C4SE-9425-A
1965–1966	390 4V	C5AZ-9424-D, C5AZ-9424-M, w/ 1/8 in. temp. sender
1966	390 2V	C6AZ-9424-D
1966–1967	390 4V	C6AZ-9424-K, C6AZ-9424-N casting C5AE-9425-C

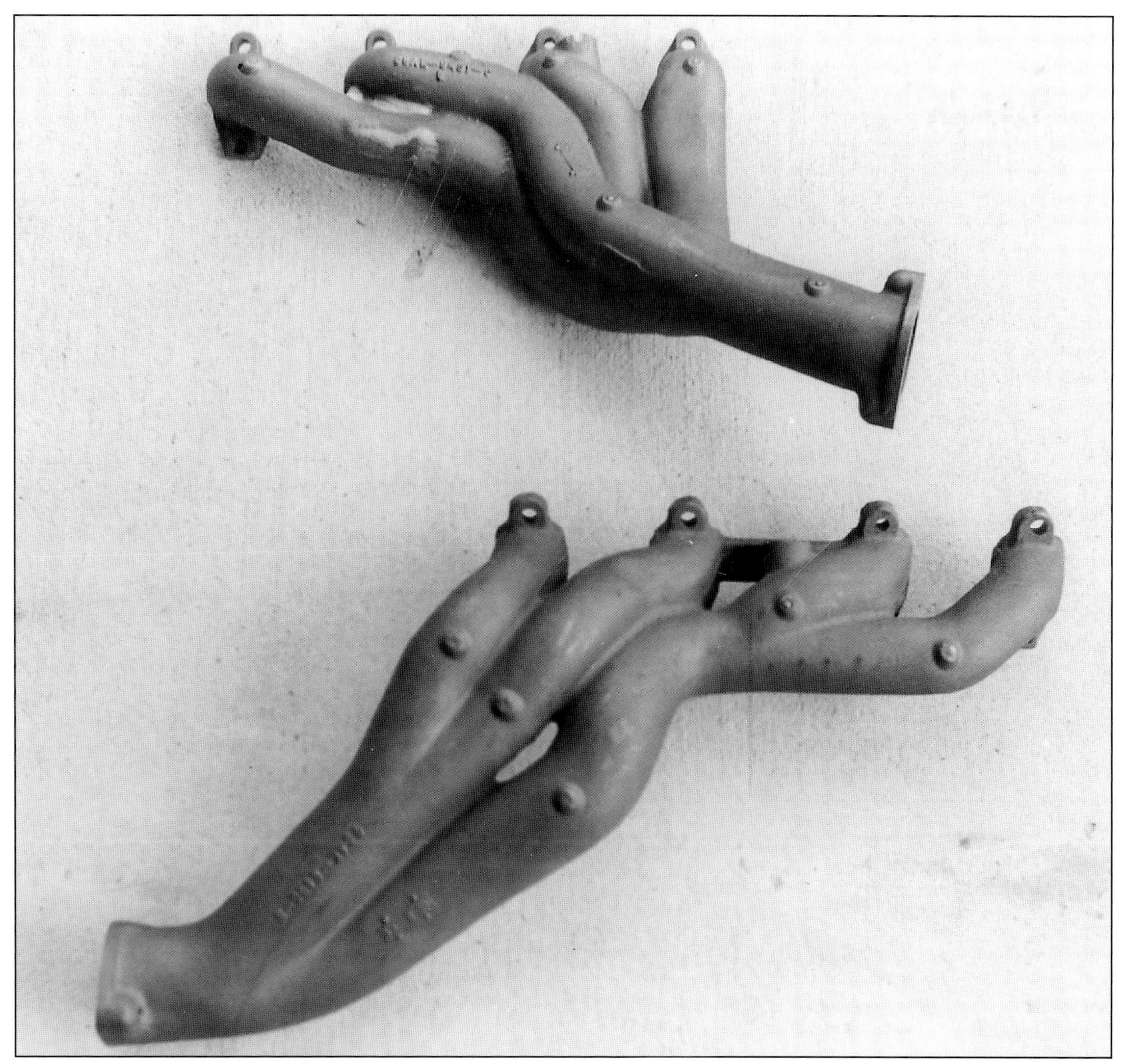

Ford made some interesting exhaust manifold castings for the FE. These were made to fit the High Performance 390 cid, 406 cid, and 427 cid engines. Obviously from the unequal length school of thought, these were about as free-flowing as could be in the cast iron context, given the confines of the engine compartment.

Year	Engine	Part or Casting Number
Intake Manifolds		
1968–1970	390 2V	C9AZ-9424-E
1968	390 4V	C8AZ-9424-C, casting C7AF-9425-F
1974–1975	390 4V	D4TZ-9424-B, truck
1975–1976	390 4V	D5TZ-9424-L, truck
1962–1963	406 4V	C1AE-9424-C, C3AZ-9424-C, aluminum
1961–1963	406 3x2V	C1AE-9424-E, C3AZ-9424-D, aluminum
1962–1963	406 2x4V	C3AZ-9424-L, aluminum, casting C3AE-9425-J
1963–1964	427 4V	C3AZ-9424-J, aluminum, LR
1963–1965	427 2x4V	C5AZ-9424-C, aluminum, LR
1963–1964	427 4V	C4AE-9425-G, aluminum, HR
1963–1965	427 2x4V	C4AE-9425-F, aluminum, HR

Year	Engine	Part or Casting Number
Intake Manifolds		
1966–1967	427 4V	C6AZ-9424-L, C6AZ-9424-M, aluminum, MR "Sidewinder"
1966–1967	427 2x4V	C5AZ-9424-F, C5AZ-9424-G, aluminum, MR dual-plane, casting C6OA-9425-A
1966–1967	427 2x4V	C8AX-9424-A, aluminum, MR single-plane, casting C72X-9425-A
1967	427 4V	C8AX-9424-B, TP, aluminum, single plane
1967	427 2x4V	C7OE-9424-A, TP, aluminum, single plane
1967	427 2x4V	C7OE-9424-B, TP, aluminum, dual plane

This is a typical head casting number location for the FE series cylinder head.

Block, Head, and Manifold Part and Casting Numbers

Year	Engine	Part or Casting Number
Intake Manifolds		
1968	427 4V	C6AZ-9424-H
1968	428 4V	C8AZ-9424-C
1966–1968	428 4V	C6AZ-9424-H, PI, aluminum
1969	428 4V	C6AZ-9424-H, PI
1968–1970	428 4V	C80Z-9424-B, CJ, casting C80E-9425-C
Exhaust Manifolds		
1958–1959	332/352	B8S9-9430-A right, B8S9-9431-A left
1960	352	C3AZ-9430-A right,C3AZ-9431-A left, HP
1960–1962	352	C3SZ-9430-A right, C2AZ-9431-B left
1963	352	C3AZ-9430-A right, C3AZ-9431-D left
1963–1965	352	C5SZ-9430-A right, C3AZ-9431-D left
1965–1966	352	C5TZ-9430A right, C5TZ-9431-A left, trucks
1966–1967	352	D0TZ-9430-A right, C5TZ-9431-A left, trucks
1968–1973	360	D0TZ-9430-A right, C8TZ-9431-B left, trucks
1975	360	D0TZ-9430-A right, D5TZ-9431-C left, trucks
1975	360	D0TZ-9430-A right, D5TZ-9431-B left, trucks
1963	390 3x2V	C3SZ-9430-A right, C2AZ-9431-B left
1961–1962	390	C3SZ-9430-A right, C2AZ-9431-B left
1961	390	C3AZ-9430-A right, C3AZ-9431-A left, HP
1962	390	C3AZ-9430-E right, C3AZ-9431-E left
1962–1964	390	C3AZ-9430-E right, C3AZ-9431-E left, PI
1963–1965	390	C3AZ-9430-A right, C3AZ-9431-D left
1967	390-4V	C6AZ-9430-A right, C3AZ-9431-D left
1966	390	C60Z-9430-A right, C60Z-9431-A left, Comet, Fairlane
1967–1968	390	C60Z-9430-A right, C70Z-9431-A left, Mustang, Cougar, Comet, Fairlane
1966–1967	390	C6AZ-9430-A right, C3AZ-9431-D left, Ford, Mercury
1968	390	C8AZ-9430-A right, C8AZ-9431-A left, to 09/15/67, Ford, Mercury

Year	Engine	Part or Casting Number
Exhaust Manifolds		
1968–1969	390	C9OZ-9430-B right, C7OZ-9431-A left, after 12/15/68, Mustang, Cougar, Fairlane, Comet
1968–1973	390	D0TZ-9430-A right, C8TZ-9431-B left, trucks
1975	390	D0TZ-9430-A right, D5TZ-9431-C left, trucks
1966–1967	428	C6AZ-9430-A right, C3AZ-9431-D left, Ford, Mercury
1962–1963	406	C3AZ-9430-E right, C3AZ-9431-E left, to 11/22/62
1962–1963	406	C3AZ-9430-C right, C3AZ-9431-F left, after 11/22/62
1963–1964	427	C3AZ-9430-E right, C3AZ-9431-E left
1966–1967	428	C6AZ-9430-A right, C3AZ-9431-D left, Ford, Mercury
1966–1967	410	C6AZ-9430-A right, C3AZ-9431-D left, Mercury
1968	427	C7OZ-9430-C right, C7OZ-9431-A left, Comet, Fairlane
1968	427	C7OZ-9430-A right, C7OZ-9431-A left, Mustang, Cougar
1968	428	C8OZ-9430-A right, C8OZ-9431-A left, Mustang, Cougar, Fairlane, Comet
1968	428	C8AZ-9430-A right, C8AZ-9431-A left, to 09/15/67, Ford, Mercury
1968–1970	428CJ	C9OZ-9430-C right, C8OZ-9431-B left

VIN Identification Codes

Code	Year	Engine
B	1958	332 240 hp
B	1959	332 225 hp
B	1962–1963	405 385 hp
G	1958	332 265 hp
G	1960	390, export
G	1962–1963	406 405 hp
H	1958–1959	352 300 hp
H	1964–1967	390 266/270 hp
M	1962–1963	390 340/401 hp
M	1966–1967	410 330 hp, Mercury
P	1961–1966	390 330 hp, PI
P	1967–1970	428 360 hp, PI
Q	1961–1962	390 375 hp
Q	1963–1964	427 410 hp
Q	1966–1969	428 345 hp (1967 355 hp Shelby, 1968 360 hp Shelby)
Q	1968–1970	428 335 hp, CJ (non-Ram Air)
R	1961–1962	390, export
R	1963–1967	427 425 hp, LR, MR, HR (1966 480/505 hp and Shelby)
R	1968–1970	428 335 hp, CJ w/Ram Air
S	1966	390 335 hp, GT
S	1967	390 320 hp, GT
S	1968	390 325 hp, GT
S	1969	390 320 hp, GT
W	1958–1959	361 303 hp
W	1968	427 390 hp
X	1960–1963	352 220 hp
X	1964–1966	352 250 hp
X	1967–1969	390 280 hp
X	1970	390 270 hp
Y	1960	352 300/360 hp
Y	1966–1969	390 265 hp
Z	1961–1962	390 375/401 hp
Z	1962–1964	390 300 hp
Z	1966–1968	390 315 hp
8	1966–1968	428, export
9	1963	390, export

Engine-Tag Identification Codes

Code	Engine	VIN Code
310	390 2V	Y
311	390 2V	Y
312	390 2V	Y
313	390 4V	Z
315	390 4V	Z
316	390 2V	H, Y
317	390 2V	X
318	390GT 4V	S
319	390GT 4V	S
321	390GT 4V	S
322	390GT 4V	S
324	390GT 4V	S
341	390 4V	Z
343	390 4V	Z
348	390 4V	P
349	390 4V	P
350	427 4V	W
353	427 2x4V	R
357	390 4V	Z
359	427 4V	W
359J	427 SOHC 2x4V	D
360	427 4V	W
361B	427 2x4V	W
361J	427 2x4V	R
362	427 2x4V	R
363	427 SOHC 4V	L
364	427 4V	W
382	390GT 4V	S
383	390GT 4V	S
384	390GT 4V	S
385	390GT 4V	S
386	390GT 4V	S
400	428CJ 4V	Q
401	428CJ 4V	Q
404	428 4V	P
405	428 4V	P
407	428CJ 4V	R
408	428CJ 4V	R
410	428CJ 4V	Q
418	428CJ 4V	R
419	428CJ 4V	R
420	428CJ 4V	R
421	428CJ 4V	R
422	428CJ/SCJ 4V	R
423	428CJ/SCJ 4V	R
424	428CJ/SCJ 4V	R
425	428CJ/SCJ 4V	R
426	428CJ/SCJ 4V	R

CHAPTER 14

FORD 90-DEGREE

1964-UP

221, 260, 289, 302 and 351 Windsor

Ford's 90-degree V-8, otherwise known as its small-block V-8, was first introduced in 1962 for use in the new Ford Fairlane and Mercury Meteor intermediates. It was quite a departure from previous Ford engines. For one thing it was small—only 20 in. wide across the exhaust manifolds, excluding flanges. For comparison, the small-block Chevy at that time measured 27 in. across. Besides its compact size, the small-block Ford was light. The complete engine, including all accessories, bellhousing, and clutch, weighed less than 475lb. The 239 cid Y-block engine introduced in 1954 weighed 200lb more.

The small-block Ford engine was released in two displacements. The smallest, which displaced 221 cid, had a bore and stroke of 3.50x2.87 in. With an 8.7:1 compression ratio, power output was rated at 143 hp at 4,500 rpm and 217ft-lb torque at 2,200 rpm. The 260 cid version had a bore and stroke of 3.80x2.87 in. With the same compression ratio, power output was 164 hp. These small V-8s were perfectly suited for use in smaller American cars.

The reason for the engine's smaller dimensions was so that it would fit into a smaller car, such as the Fairlane. Compact cars such as the AMC Rambler and many foreign makes became very popular in the late 1950s as an increasingly larger segment of the car-buying public grew interested in economical transportation. The small-block Ford was designed to provide relatively economical operation, along with a modicum of power.

To save weight, Ford used thin-wall casting techniques, first seen on the 1960 Falcon six-cylinder engine. This enabled the engineers to design an engine in which wall thickness could be tightly controlled, thereby eliminating excessively thick (and heavy) sections of the engine. All modern-era Ford V-8 engines up to this time had been of the Y-block design, but Ford's new small-block lacked the Y-block's skirts extending below the centerline of the crankshaft. By not having this lowered skirt area, the small-block Ford was lighter and did not sacrifice anything in the way of bottom-end strength, even with the stock two-bolt main-bearing caps. In fact, all engines in the 90-degree family had two-bolt main-bearing caps. The only exception was the Boss 302, which used four-bolt-main caps.

As with other Ford engines, the small-block was oversquare, meaning that the bore was larger than the stroke.

The small-block used a cast nodular crankshaft, which weighed only 37lb, with forged-steel connecting rods. The pistons were conventional cast aluminum. The small-block also used a hydraulic-lifter camshaft, but in another departure from previous Ford engines, the engine used individually mounted cast-iron rocker arms, similar to the design used on the Chevrolet small-block V-8s. These were cheaper, lighter, and simpler to manufacture than the previously used shaft-mounted rockers. Rocker ratio was 1.6:1.

The cylinder heads were typical wedge design with valves measuring 1.59 in./1.39 in. intake/exhaust on the 221 cid, and 1.67 in./1.45 in. on the 260 cid. In the intake department, the 221 and 260 cid engines used a cast-iron two-barrel intake manifold and carburetor.

The small-block was enlarged in 1964. By increasing the bore to 4.00 in., the small-block displaced 289 cid. In this form, the small-block powered practically every Ford vehicle.

There were two major changes made to the small-block during its life. In mid-1965, Ford switched to a six-bolt bellhousing, from the previous five-bolt unit. The six-bolt bellhousing was designed to accept a larger, 11 in. clutch and the Ford "top-loader" manual transmission. Engines built after February 1966 got different rocker arms. Previously, all small-blocks used conventional slotted rockers with a ball-and-stud pivot. These were replaced with "rail" rockers on all subsequent engines, except the 289 cid HP engine and Boss 302. The rail rockers have a tab on either side of the rocker tip that fits over the valve stem and thus keeps it aligned.

The next change occurred in 1968. By increasing the 289's bore to 3.00 in., the engine displaced 302 cid. This was the practical displacement limit for the engine, given its dimensions. By the 1980s the small-block 302 became the "big" engine in most Ford vehicles and it was the engine that powered the 5.0l Mustangs. The engine is still in production today, in Ford trucks.

In 1969, Ford raised the deck height by 1.275 in. This made it possible to install a crankshaft that had 0.50 in. greater stroke. The resultant displacement was 351 cid. The engine became known as the 351 Windsor (351W), because it was made at Ford's Windsor engine plant. The 351W is still in production today, powering Ford's full-size vans.

The last, and probably most interesting, permutation of the small-block was the Boss 302 of 1969–1970. Strictly a high-performance engine, the Boss 302 combined the best of the 90-degree small-block engine family with the cylinder heads of the 335 engine family, also known as the Cleveland engine. The engine was used in a limited-production Mustang, the 1969–1970 Boss 302 and also on the Mercury Cougar Eliminator of 1970.

221 cid

With the possible exception of the 255 cid version of the small-block built during 1980–1982, the 221 cid version of the series is probably the rarest 90-degree small-block engine. It was available for only two years, 1962–1963. It had a bore and stroke of 3.50x2.87 in. and with an 8.7:1 compression ratio, power output was rated at 143 hp. That's only 7 hp more than the largest six-cylinder engine that Ford had at the time. There is nothing, besides its being the first and smallest engine in the 90-degree engine family, to make it outstanding.

260 cid

As the 221 cid engine was obviously not living up to expectations people had at its release, a larger, more powerful version was

This is an original Trans Am Boss 302 race engine. Although it's difficult to see, the engine is equipped with a Bud Moore mini-plenum intake manifold.

added later in the 1962 model year to complement Ford's engine option list. The 221 cid V-8 just wasn't making enough power. The Fairlane, while it might have been "small" by American standards, was still a hefty car for just 221 cid. With a wider bore, 3.80 in., and the same stroke as the 221 cid engine, the 260 cid small-block put out 164 horsepower, an improvement over its predecessor.

Although the intake and exhaust ports were left unchanged, the 260 cid benefited from larger intake/exhaust valves, 1.67 in./1.45 in. Again, the 260 cid engine had a pretty nondescript hydraulic camshaft, an 8.7:1 compression ratio, and a two-barrel cast-iron intake manifold and carburetor. Still, it was the 260 cid V-8 that showed the potential of the engine. It was small, compact, and had the ability to rev. Carroll Shelby used the 260 in his original Cobra, and because of its small size, Sunbeam (an English manufacturer) used the engine in its Tiger sports car.

289 cid

Now here was an engine! Ford once again increased the small-block's bore, this time to 4.00 in., in 1964, with the stroke remaining the same as the 260's: 2.87 in. It was the engine of choice in Ford's new Mustang, but it was also available in most of Ford's other cars.

The basic 289 cid V-8 was rated at 200 hp at 4,400 rpm, with 282ft-lb torque at 2,400 rpm. Like all the previous small-blocks, the 200 hp 289 cid engine used a two-barrel Ford carburetor, hydraulic camshaft, and a single exhaust system. The 200 hp V-8 was available through the 1967 model year, and in 1968 basically the same engine, though downrated to 195 hp, was available as well. The engine was designed to provide good, economical, reliable transportation.

By adding dual exhausts, a four-barrel cast-iron intake manifold and carburetor, and raising the compression ratio to 9.0:1, output on the 289 cid V-8 hit 210 hp. This version was available only for a short time in 1964 until it was replaced by a more powerful 225 hp version. The 225 hp engine used a larger four-barrel carburetor, and the compression ratio was raised to 10.0:1. The engine would be available in this configuration through the 1967 model year.

289 High Performance

In HP (High Performance) variation, the 289 cid V-8 showed its true potential. Carburetion and camshaft changes allowed the engine to rev higher and therefore produce the kind of power it was meant to. The HP 289 cid engine was available from 1964 to 1967.

The engine block had a higher nodularity content (something that you can't easily verify, but it does have larger two-bolt main caps, something you can see). The crankshaft was also slightly different than that of other small-blocks; it had an additional counterweight on the front for better high- rpm balancing. Connecting rods were stronger than those on the plain Jane 289s. The beefier rods used thicker, 3/8 in. rod bolts, as opposed to the regular ones that measure 5/16 in.

The cylinder heads had the same size ports and valves as the regular production heads. They were equipped with screw-in rocker studs, necessary for use with the mechanical-lifter camshaft that enabled the HP 289 to rev to 6,000 rpm and above. Complementing the mechanical-lifter camshaft was a dual-point distributor. The engine was equipped with a performance damper in order to reduce vibrations and flexing at high rpm. The engine was also fitted with the cast-iron four-barrel intake manifold and a Ford 480cfm four-barrel carburetor. The cast-iron exhaust manifolds on the HP 289 were freer flowing than those of the regular 289s.

With these modifications, the HP 289 pumped out 271 hp at 6,000 rpm with 312ft-lb torque at 3,400 rpm.

302 cid

The small-block's stroke was increased to 3.00 in. in 1968 for a 302 cid, which was, coincidentally, the same as Chevy's Z28 small-block. Besides the stroke change, there were no internal changes to the engine. The 302 cid used a cast-iron crank, forged rods, cast pistons, a hydraulic camshaft, and either a two- or four-barrel cast-iron intake manifold. As before, there were two versions of the small-block for 1968. The two-barrel, single-exhaust motor was rated at 210 hp, and the four-barrel, dual-exhaust, higher-compression motor put out 230 hp. There were no high-performance 302s for 1968, save for the TP 302, which was never released for sale.

From 1969 to 1983, the non-Boss 302 cid engine was available only with a two-barrel carburetor. During 1969–1973, it served as the base V-8 engine for most of Ford's vehicles. As the decade wore on, the 302's power output got lower and lower, hitting a laughably low of 122 hp by 1975! The problem was that the 302 (and all Detroit V-8s) were hobbled by increasingly stringent emission controls. EGR valves, catalytic converters, retarded timing, higher engine temperatures, unleaded gasoline, and the like were used to control emissions. The emission-control technology was in its infancy, and the engineers weren't able to both control emissions and maintain a reasonable level of power. The 302 cid V-8, as can be seen by its output figures, suffered greatly. It wasn't until the mid-1980s, with the wider use of EFI and advanced electronic controls, that the engine was able to produce power once again.

Tunnel Port 302

During the 1960s, Ford produced a number of interesting variations on the small-block. One that got quite a bit of attention, but was never available on any street car, was the TP (Tunnel Port) 302. Actually, there was one "official" street Mustang with the TP V-8—this was a Mustang lent to *Car and Driver* magazine for use in a road test against a 1968 Z/28 Camaro.

The thinking behind the 302 TP was similar to that of the 427 TP engine. By having the pushrods fit inside a sleeve, the intake port could be enlarged, thereby increasing the quantity of fuel-air mixture that the heads could flow by giving a more direct shot to the intake valve. The valves on the engine were 2.12 in. intake and 1.54 in. exhaust. The street version of the engine came with two 540cfm Holley four-barrel carburetors.

Two versions of the engine were made. One used conventional adjustable rockers for the Trans Am race series, while the NASCAR versions used shaft-mounted rockers. Ford never did produce enough engines for use on street cars for homologation purposes, which is why the SCCA insisted that Ford build the required number of Boss 302 Mustangs in 1969.

Ford released the raised-deck small-block in 1969. More commonly known as the 351 Windsor, this engine is installed in a Mercury. These engine are still in production today in Ford light trucks.

The problem with the TP heads is that the ports were too large, given the metallurgy and valve-train technology of the day. In order to produce the power it was designed to, the TP had to be revved up to 8,000–9,000 rpm. This was beyond the safe limit for the 302's bottom end and oiling system. Plus, the engine was put together by Ford Engine and Foundry, and not by the race teams themselves. Toward the end of the season, the race teams asked Ford if they could switch back to the older 289 engines. The 289s didn't put out as much power, but they were a lot more reliable.

Boss 302

This is the highest-performance version of Ford's 90-degree V-8 family. It was available for only two model years, 1969 and 1970, on a special Mustang Boss 302 Sportsroof model and in 1970 on the Mercury Cougar Eliminator. The engine was built so Ford could use it in SCCA's Trans Am Series. Unlike the unreliable TP 302 used in the 1968 series, Ford was forced to actually make the engine available on street cars, and the Mustang model chosen for it was also called Boss 302. The rules required that at least 1,000 Mustangs had to be built with this engine. Production exceeded this amount with 1,628 in 1969, a total surpassed by the 7,013 built in 1970. A total of 450 1970 Cougar Eliminators were also Boss 302-equipped.

The major difference between the Boss 302 and other small-block engines was the cylinder heads. The Boss 302 heads were an entirely different design. The standard small-block heads, with their small ports and valves, were adequate for passenger car use but entirely inadequate for track use. That is why the TP 302 was brought into being as a stopgap measure until the Boss 302 engine became available. The cylinder heads were actually almost the same as those that were to be used on Ford's new 335 (Cleveland) engine family in 1970, and because the new 335 engine series used the same bore spacing and head bolt pattern as the 90-degree V-8 engine family, the heads physically fit the small-block engine block. All that had to be done was to modify the cylinder heads' water passages to work with the small-block.

Whereas the regular small-block engines had their valves arranged in a straight line, the valves on the Boss 302 were canted, just like those introduced on Chevrolet's big-block V-8 in 1965. Canting the valves allows for larger valves and more efficient port design, which results in better engine breathing.

The ports of the Boss 302 cylinder heads were truly gargantuan (in the Ford tradition) when compared to the regular small-block heads. The valves were also much larger, 2.23 in./1.71 in. intake/exhaust. These were much too big for street use, considering the small displacement of the engine. The 1970 Boss 302 heads came with slightly smaller intake valves, 2.19 in. The same heads, with different water passages, were used on the 1970–1974 351C engines with four-barrel carburetors.

Besides the larger ports and valves, the Boss 302 heads used threaded rocker arm studs, pushrod guide plates, and stamped-steel sled-fulcrum rockers, as the engine came with a mechanical-lifter camshaft.

The Boss 302 was rated at 290 hp, the same rating as the Chevy Z/28 302 and Chrysler's 340 cid small-block with triple two-barrel carburetors.

The block used on the Boss 302 was a special 302 block. Unlike regular production 302 blocks, the Boss 302 block came with four-bolt main-bearing caps and can be identified from the outside by their screw-in freeze plugs. The Boss 302 was also equipped with a much stronger forged-steel crankshaft. The 1969 versions were cross-drilled, while the 1970 engines (except for some early ones) were not. The Boss 302 forged-steel connecting rods were similar to the 289 HP rods, but used different 3/8 in. bolts. The racing Boss 302s used even better connecting rods. The major weak point of the street Boss 302 engine was the forged-aluminum pistons. These did not have strong enough side skirts, which result in cracking and even breaking. The stock compression ratio was 10.5:1.

A dual-plane single four-barrel aluminum intake manifold and a Holley 780cfm carburetor were used on all street Boss 302 engines. There were several manifolds that Ford made for race use, the most famous being the Cross Boss setup. It was used only in one race because there were problems with the special Ford Autolite inline carburetors.

The Boss 302 intake manifold does not interchange with any regular small-block manifolds; it is made to be used only with the Boss 302 heads. The same applies for the exhaust manifolds. These were fairly efficient, as far as cast-iron exhaust manifolds go, but will not fit other small-block heads.

351 Windsor

The small-block engine, because of its inherent compact size, had reached its practical displacement limit with the introduction of the 302 cid engine in 1968. There were two problems that faced Ford engineers. First, because of its 4.00 in. bore spacing, there just wasn't any room left in the block for a bore increase. And you couldn't increase the 302's stroke without having the crankshaft hit the piston skirts. The least-expensive solution was to increase displacement by adding 1.275 in. to the small-block's deck height so that a crank with a 1/2 in. greater stroke could be used. While they were at it, they strengthened the block with heavier cylinder walls and bulkheads around the mains. At the same time, the crank's main and rod bearings were made larger (increasing to 3.000 in. and 2.2486 in., respectively) to handle the 351's greater torque output.

The 351 cid V-8 was still part of the 90-degree engine family, but it had very little interchangeability with other small-block engines. In fact, the only part that is a direct interchange between the 351W and other small-block engines is the camshaft. However, the 351 has a different firing order, 1-3-7-2-6-5-4-8, so the distributor must be rewired should a camshaft from the small-blocks be used. The 351 required the use of longer connecting rods, a wider intake manifold, longer pushrods, and, of course, a different crankshaft. The engine was referred to as the 351W (for Windsor, the plant where the engines were built). This was done to differentiate it from the new 1970 351C (for Cleveland), a medium-block engine in Ford's 335 engine family—an entirely different engine family from the 90-degree engine series.

Although few other parts would interchange between the 351W and the other small-blocks, the 351's cylinder heads can be made to fit the other small-blocks, despite detail differences (the 351 cid heads use larger diameter [1/2 in.] cylinder head bolts and the water passages are different). The 351W heads used the so-called GT-40 combustion chamber design, with larger valves of 1.84 in./1.54 in. intake/exhaust. The ports on the 351W heads are also slightly larger than those on the regular 302 cid heads.

Ford started using the same heads on both the 302 and 351W in 1977 (with the 351s using larger, 1/2 in. head bolts). The valves used on both engines were the 302's size—1.78 in./1.45 in. intake/exhaust.

Shelby Small-Blocks

Carroll Shelby used the small-block V-8 in his Cobra and on the Shelby Mustangs. The 260 cid V-8 was used in approximately 75 Cobras, while the rest of the small-block-powered cars came with the 289 cid V-8.

The 1965–1966 Shelby Mustangs were equipped with a special 306 hp version of the 289 cid HP motor. Shelby took over from where Ford left off. The engine got an aluminum Cobra High Rise intake manifold with a 715cfm Holley four-barrel carburetor, special Tri-Y steel tube headers, a larger Cobra aluminum oil pan, and the distinctive Cobra aluminum valve covers. The engine was rated at 306 hp at 6,000 rpm with 329ft-lb torque at 4,200 rpm. In 1966, the Shelby Mustang was optionally available with the Ford automatic transmission. The carburetor on these cars was a Ford 600cfm unit.

A small number of 289 cid Shelby Mustangs were equipped with the Paxton supercharger from 1966 through 1968. The power output of these engines was 390 hp, according to a July 1966 *Car Life* magazine road test.

The 1968 GT350 Shelby Mustangs were fitted with the four-barrel version of the 302 cid V-8. Unlike the highly modified HP 289s, the 302 was stock Ford, but it did have the Cobra High Rise intake manifold and a 600cfm Holley four-barrel carburetor. It was rated at 20 hp more (250 hp) than the regular 302 cid V-8. It also came with the Cobra valve covers and air cleaner.

The 1969–1970 Shelby GT350 Mustangs were all equipped with the 351W engine. It was identical to the regular production four-barrel version, but it did get a Shelby aluminum intake manifold and valve covers. The manifold was probably worth at least 20 horsepower, but the engine was still rated the same 290 hp, as was the stock engine.

Engine Blocks

Most of the 90-degree engine family used the same basic engine block, but there were a few variations. During the middle of the 1965 model year, Ford switched to a six-bolt bellhousing design from the previous five-bolt. Thus, all 221- and 260 cid versions of the small-block have blocks that will accept only the five-bolt bellhousing; all 302 and 351 Windsor engines have the six-bolt pattern. The 289 cid engines can be of either the five- or six-bolt pattern, and that applies to the HP 289 cid block as well.

The very best of the 90-degree blocks was the Boss 302 block (see the Boss 302 section). The second best was the 289 cid HP block. Cast of higher nodular iron, the HP 289 had thicker main-bearing caps. The regular 302 block's cylinder bores were different from the others, in that they protruded farther out at the bottom of the cylinder in order to give extra support to the pistons. The 351W block was taller and wider than the other small-blocks, but it was still of the two-bolt-main variety. In addition, the 351 Windsor used larger main and connecting rod bearings than other small-block engines did.

You can get a pretty good idea how compact the small-block Ford is by looking at the block. This is a 302 version as the cylinders extend slightly below the bottom of the block–there sure isn't much room for overboring. Main caps also look a little on the lightweight side, yet the engine isn't known for bottom-end problems.

Late 302 short-block. The engine, save for electronic controls and fuel injection, has remained basically unchanged for almost 30 years.

Cylinder Heads

There were three basic cylinder heads for the small-block Ford: the regular production 221/260/289/302 heads, the 351W heads, and the Boss 302 heads. Within each group there are minor variations in terms of port, valve, and combustion-chamber sizes and shapes, and whether or not they were matched for air injection emission systems.

The heads with the smallest ports, valves, and combustion chambers were those of the 221 cid V-8. Valves measured 1.59 in./1.39 in. intake/exhaust. The 260 cidV-8 used heads with the same size ports and valves, but with combustion chambers that were larger.

The 289 cid engines had larger ports and valves. The 1963–1964 heads had valves measuring 1.67 in./1.45 in. intake/exhaust; later 289s and all 302s got larger, 1.78 in. intake valves. The 351W got heads with still larger ports and valves, 1.84 in./1.54 in. intake/exhaust. There were various combustion-chamber sizes used on these, and after 1977, the 351W engines used heads that had the same size ports and valves as the regular 302 engines.

As stated earlier, engines built after February 1966 (except the HP 289 and 302 Boss) were equipped with Ford's rail rocker arms, as opposed to the previously conventional ball-and-stud rockers used on earlier heads. The HP 289 cid engines all came with screw-in rocker studs and conventional rockers, and the heads also had slotted pushrod guide holes. All other small-block engines had larger round pushrod holes because the rail rockers were used to keep proper rocker arm alignment. The Boss 302 heads were completely different from any used on the small-block engines; see the Boss 302 section.

Intake Manifolds

The majority of Ford small-block V-8s came with a cast-iron two-barrel carburetor intake manifold. Higher output 289-, 302-, and 351 cid engines came with a cast-iron four-barrel intake and four-barrel carburetor. No factory Ford passenger car came with an aluminum intake manifold.

Shelby versions of the small-block were all equipped with aluminum intake manifolds, and there was a great variety of Ford high-performance aluminum intakes available over the counter. These were marketed under the Ford, Cobra, and Shelby brands.

The 351 cid Windsor engine was available with either two- or four-barrel cast-iron intakes; the 1969–1970 Shelby 351s came with an aluminum four-barrel intake.

The TP and Boss 302 engines used intake manifolds that were unique to those engines and will not fit any other small-block engine.

Exhaust Manifolds

The typical small-block came with cast-iron exhaust manifolds that exited at the rear of the block. They are known to crack. The HP 289 engines came with freer-flowing exhaust manifolds. Boss 302 exhaust manifolds will only fit Boss 302 or 351C four-barrel engines.

Engine Identification

Ford's method of identifying engine parts follows typical industry procedures in that each part has a casting number cast onto it, and for Fords, that number consists of letters and numbers in a particular order. Let's look at a typical part number, in this case, C8OZ-6049-E, which is the cylinder head for a 1968 289 cid engine. It breaks down as follows:

C: this indicates the decade (B is 1950–1959, C is 1960–1969, D is 1970–1979);

8: this indicates the year of the decade (8 would be 1968 in our example);

OZ: this indicates the car line

6049: a subgroup number (all Ford cylinder heads are numbered 6049, intake manifolds are 9424, camshafts 6250, and so on);

E: this is an application suffix code (for example, on a camshaft, the letter A might stand for a high-performance solid-lifter cam, while the letter B might be for a two-barrel engine with hydraulic cam). The various codes and suffixes are listed in the tables.

Casting numbers are similar to part numbers, but there are major differences. Usually, the subgroup numbers were not used in the number cast on the part itself, but they will be indicated in the parts book, if the casting number is listed at all. Sometimes the subgroup number is on the part itself, however, and sometimes the casting number is the same as the part number.

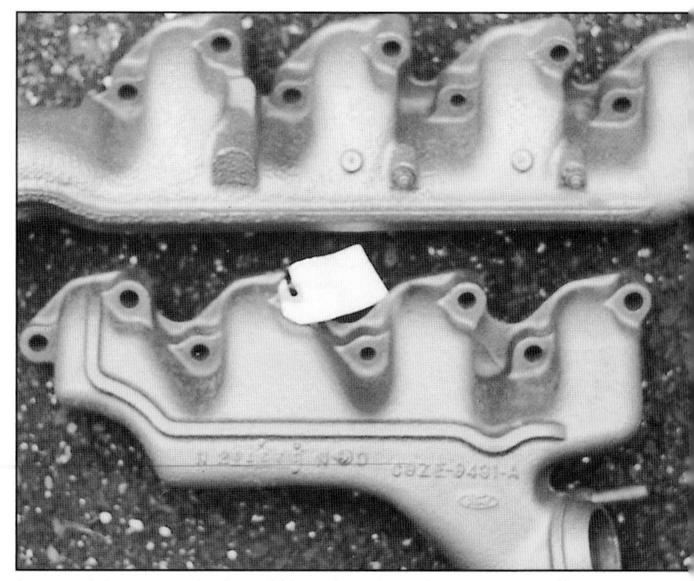

As you might expect, the Boss 302 engine came with completely different exhaust manifolds than other small block engines. Casting number and date code are visible on the left manifold.

Date codes were also used. A typical date code might be as follows: 9 B 16, where the 9 indicates the last digit of the year (in this case it could be 1959 or 1969); the B indicates the month, in this case February (the months were coded A for January through M for December, but I was not used); the 16 indicates the day of the month.

Depending on the part you're looking at, the date code is probably as important as the casting number itself, especially ifyou're trying to determine originality. To be considered original, parts installed in a Ford vehicle have to have been cast or manufactured before the car itself was built. This can be up to 30 days or more and still be considered original. On parts that were manufactured, the date codes were stamped on the part, rather than cast.

There wasn't any engine identification in relation to the vehicle it was installed in until 1970, when Ford began stamping the car's VIN on the left rear side of the block just below the cylinder head. On pre-1970 Fords, you can't determine if a particular engine is original equipment in a particular car. The only exceptions were the Boss 302 engines. The car's VIN was stamped on the engine block itself, thereby tying the engine to the chassis it was installed in. Ford did assign an engine code for use in the vehicle's VIN. In this way, you can at least tell by looking at a VIN what engine the car was built with. On 1954–1959 models, the engine code was the first digit of the vehicle's VIN. Beginning in 1960, the code was in the fifth position, and it remained in that position until 1981. Ford used the codes over and over, the same code standing for several different engines and years. These codes are listed in the tables.

There was an engine identification code stamped on engines from 1960 to 1964, but this code consisted of just the date the engine was built, the engine plant, and an inspector's identification code. It was located on the left front side of the engine. It didn't tie the engine in with the car.

From 1964, Ford placed a small metal tag (which was usually attached to the coil hold-down bolt) that included information about the engine. Most of these codes are included in the tables. These tags were easily lost, so they are often missing from engines today.

Engine Specifications

	Displacement	Carburetor	Horsepower	Torque	Compression Ratio	Notes
1962						
	221	2V	143@4,400	217@2,200	8.7	Fairlane, Meteor
	260	2V	164@4,400	258@2,200	8.7	Fairlane, Meteor
1963						
	221	2V	143@4,400	217@2,200	8.7	Fairlane, Meteor
	260	2V	164@4,400	258@2,200	8.7	Fairlane, Falcon, Meteor, Comet
	289	2V	195@4,400	282@2,400	9.0	Galaxie
	289	4V	271@6,000	312@3,400	10.5	Fairlane
1964						
	260	2V	164@4,400	258@2,200	8.7	Fairlane, Falcon, Mustang, Meteor, Comet
	289	2V	195@4,400	282@2,400	9.0	Fairlane, Galaxie, Mustang
	289	4V	210@4,400	300@2,400	9.0	Fairlane, Mustang, Galaxie, Comet
	289	4V	271@6,000	312@3,400	10.5	Fairlane, Mustang, Falcon, Comet
1965						
	289	2V	200@4,400	282@2,400	9.3	Fairlane, Mustang, Falcon, Galaxie, Comet
	289	4V	225@4,800	305@3,200	10.0	Fairlane, Mustang, Falcon, Galaxie, Comet
	289	4V	271@6,000	312@3,400	10.5	Fairlane, Mustang, Galaxie, Falcon, Comet
	289	4V	306@6,000	329@4,200	10.5	Shelby GT350
1966						
	289	2V	200@4,400	282@2,400	9.3	Fairlane, Mustang, Falcon, Galaxie, Comet
	289	4V	225@4,800	305@3,200	10.0	Fairlane, Mustang, Falcon, Galaxie, Comet
	289	4V	271@6,000	312@3,400	10.5	Fairlane, Mustang, Falcon, Galaxie, Comet
	289	4V	306@6,000	329@4,200	10.5	Shelby GT350
1967						
	289	2V	200@4,400	282@2,400	9.3	Fairlane, Mustang, Falcon, Ford, Cougar
	289	4V	225@4,800	305@3,200	10.0	Fairlane, Mustang, Falcon, Ford, Cougar
	289	4V	271@6,000	312@3,400	10.5	Fairlane, Mustang, Falcon, Ford, Cougar
	289	4V	306@6,000	329@4,200	10.5	Shelby GT350
1968						
	289	2V	195@4,400	288@2,400	8.7	Fairlane, Mustang, Falcon, Ford, Montego, Cougar

Engine Specifications

	Displacement	Carburetor	Horsepower	Torque	Compression Ratio	Notes
	289	2V	200@4,400	282@2,400	9.3	Bronco and F-series
	302	2V	210@4,400	300@2,600	9.0 (early), 9.5	Fairlane, Mustang, Falcon, Ford, Montego, Cougar
	302	2V	205@4,400	300@2,600	9.0	Bronco and F-series
	302	4V	230@4,800	310@2,800	10.0	Fairlane, Mustang, Falcon, Ford, Montego, Cougar
	302	4V	250@4,400	310@2,800	10.0	Shelby GT350
1969						
	302	2V	210@4,400	300@2,600	9.0	Ford, Falcon, Fairlane/Torino, Mustang, Comet, Montego, Cyclone, Cougar
	302	2V	205@4,400	300@2,600	9.0	Bronco and F-series
	302	4V	290@5,800	290@4,300	10.5	Boss 302
	351W	2V	250@4,600	355@2,600	9.5	Ford, Fairlane, Torino, Mustang, Comet, Montego, Cyclone, Cougar
	351W	4V	290@5,800	385@3,200	10.7	Fairlane, Mustang, Falcon, Ford, Montego, Cougar
1970						
	302	2V	205@4,400	300@2,600	9.0	Bronco and F-series
	302	2V	220@4,600	300@2,600	9.0	Fairlane, Mustang, Falcon, Ford, Torino, Montego, Cyclone, Cougar
	302	4V	290@5,800	290@4,300	10.5	Boss 302
	351W	2V	250@4,600	355@2,600	9.5	Fairlane, Mustang, Falcon, Ford, Torino, Montego, Cyclone, Cougar
1971						
	302	2V	205@4,400	300@2,600	9.0	Bronco and F-series
	302	2V	210@4,600	296@2,600	9.0	Fairlane, Mustang, Falcon, Ford, Maverick, Torino, Montego, Cyclone, Cougar, Comet
	351W	2V	240@4,600	350@2,600	9.0	Fairlane, Mustang, Falcon, Ford, Torino, Montego, Cyclone Cougar
1972						
	302	2V	140@4,000	239@2,000	8.5	Ford, Maverick, Mustang, Torino, Montego, Cougar, Comet
	302	2V	141@4,000	240@2,000	8.5	Bronco and F-series
	351W	2V	153@3,800	266@2,000	8.3	Ford, Mustang, Torino, Montego, Cougar
1973						
	302	2V	135@4,200	228@2,200	8.0	Ford, Maverick, Mustang, Torino, Montego, Cougar, Comet
	302	2V	136@4,200	232@2,200	8.0	Ford, Maverick, Mustang, Torino, Montego, Cougar, Comet
	302	2V	137@4,200	230@2,200	8.0	Ford, Maverick, Mustang, Torino, Montego, Cougar, Comet
	302	2V	138@4,200	234@2,200	8.0	Ford, Maverick, Mustang, Torino, Montego, Cougar, Comet
	302	2V	154@4,200	245@2,200	8.0	Bronco and F-series
	351W	2V	153@3,800	266@2,000	8.0	Ford, Mustang, Torino, Montego, Cougar
	351W	2V	154@3,800	256@2,400	8.0	Ford, Mustang, Torino, Montego, Cougar
	351W	2V	156@3,800	260@2,400	8.0	Ford, Mustang, Torino, Montego, Cougar
	351W	2V	157@3,800	246@2,400	8.0	Ford, Mustang, Torino, Montego, Cougar
	351W	2V	158@3,800	264@2,400	8.0	Ford, Mustang, Torino, Montego, Cougar
	351W	2V	159@4,000	250@2,400	8.0	Ford, Mustang, Torino, Montego, Cougar

This is the stock cast-iron four-barrel intake manifold for the small-block Ford. This particular one is for 1966 engines.

Displacement		Carburetor	Horsepower	Torque	Compression Ratio	Notes
	351W	2V	161@3,800	254@2,400	8.0	Ford, Mustang, Torino, Montego, Cougar
1974						
	302	2V	140@3,800	230@2,600	8.0	Ford, Torino, Granada, Maverick, Mercury, Montego, Cougar, Comet
	302	2V	154@4,200	245@2,200	8.0	Bronco and F-series
	351W	2V	162@4,000	275@2,200	8.0	Ford, Torino, Granada, Maverick, Mercury, Montego, Cougar
	351W	2V	163@4,200	278@2,000	8.0	Ford, Torino, Granada, Mercury, Montego, Cougar
1975						
	302	2V	115@3,600	203@1400	8.0	California, Comet, Maverick
	302	2V	115@3,600	203@1,800	8.0	California, Granada, Monarch
	302	2V	122@3,800	208@1,800	8.0	Ford, Elite, Granada, Maverick, Mercury, Montego, Cougar, Comet
	302	2V	129@3,800	220@1,800	8.0	Ford, Elite, Granada, Maverick, Mercury, Montego, Cougar, Comet
	302	2V	154@4,200	245@2,200	8.0	Bronco and F-series
	351W	2V	143@3,600	255@2,200	8.0	Granada, Monarch
	351W	2V	148@3,800	243@2,400	8.0	Ford, Elite, Mercury, Montego, Cougar
	351W	2V	150@3,800	244@2,800	8.0	Ford, Elite, Mercury, Montego, Cougar
	351W	2V	153@3,400	270@2,400	8.2	California
	351W	2V	154@3,800	268@2,200	8.0	Elite, Cougar

Engine Internal Dimensions

Displacement	Bore and Stroke	Rod Bearings	Main Bearings	Intake/Exhaust Valves
221	3.500x2.870	2.1228–2.1236	2.2482–2.2490	1.59/1.38
260	3.800x2.870	2.1228–2.1236	2.2482–2.2490	1.67/1.45
289	4.000x2.870	2.1228–2.1236	2.2482–2.2490	1.67/1.45 (1965–1968 1.78/1.45)
302	4.000x3.000	2.1228–2.1236	2.2482–2.2490	1.78/1.45 (TP 2.12/1.54)
302 Boss	4.000x3.000	2.1222–2.1223	2.2482–2.2490	2.23/1.72 (1970 2.19/1.72)
351W	4.000x3.500	2.599–2.600	2.8994–2.9003	1.84/1.54

Block, Head, and Manifold Part and Casting Numbers

Year	Engine	Part or Casting Number
Engine Blocks		
1962	221	C30Z-6010-B, casting C20E-G, C30E-
1963	221	C30Z-6010-B, casting C30E-A
1962	260	C30Z-6010-C, casting C30E-B
1963–1964	260	C30Z-6010-C, casting C30E-C, C40E-B,C40E-D, C40E-E
1963	289	C3AZ-6010-L, casting C3AE-N
	289	C3AZ-6010-D, casting C30E-B (High Performance-5 bolt bellhousing)
1964	289	C4AZ-6010-B to 08/20/64, casting C40E-C, C40E-F, C4AE, C4DE (5 bolt bellhousing)
	289	C40Z-6010-C, C40Z-6010-D, casting C40E-B (High Performance-5 bolt bellhousing)
1965–1968	289	C5AZ-6010-E to 12/01/67, C5AZ-6010-F after 12/01/67, casting C5AE-A, C50E-A,C6AE-C (6 bolt bellhousing)
1966–1967	289	C50Z-6010-C, casting C5AE-A (High Performance-6 bolt bellhousing)
1968–1969	302	casting C80E-A, C80E-B, C8TE-B
1970–1974	302	casting C8TE-B, D1TZ-E, D1QE-AA, D4DE-AA, D4DE-AA, D5ZY-AA
1969	Boss 302	C9ZZ-6010-B, casting C9ZE, C8FE
1970	Boss 302	D1ZZ-6010-A, casting D0ZE-B,
1970	Boss 302	casting D1ZE (service block)
1969–1970	351W	casting C90E-B
1971–1974	351W	casting D2AE-BA, D4AE-DA
1975	351W	casting D4AE-AA
Cylinder Heads		
1962–1963	221	C30Z-6049-C, casting C20E-A, C20E-B, C20E-C, C20E-D, C20E-E, C30E-A
	260	C30Z-6049-F, casting C20E-F
1963	260	C30Z-6049-F, casting C30E-E
1964	260	casting C40E-E
1963	289	casting C30E (High Performance)
1963–1964	289	C30Z-6049-H, casting C3AE-F, C30E-E, C30E-F
1964	289	casting C4AE-C
1964–1967	289	casting C40E-B, C50E-A, C5AE-E (High Performance)
1965–1966	289	casting C5DE-B, C6DE-G, C60E-M, C70E-C
1966–1967	289	C60Z-6049-C, C60Z-60490-E, C6AZ-6049-H, C70Z-6049-A, C70Z-6049-B, all with Thermactor, casting C60E-C, C60E-E, C70E-A, C70E-B, C70Z-B, C7ZE-A
1968	289	C80Z-6049-E
1968	289	C8DZ-6049-D, with Thermactor, casting C80E-D, C80E-L, C80E-M
1968	302	C8ZZ-6049-A, C80Z-6049-L, casting C80E-F, all with 4V carb
1968	302	C8AZ-6049-F, 2V carb with Thermactor, casting C80E-K, C80E-L
1968–1970	302	casting C70E0C, C70E-G, C8AE-J, C8DE-F, C80E-J, C80E-M, C9TE-C, D00E-B
1971–1974	302	casting D1TZ-A, D20E-BA
1975	302	casting D50E-GA, D50E-A3A, D50E-A3B
1969	Boss 302	C9ZE-6090-A, C9ZE-6090-C, casting C9ZE-A
1970	Boss 302	D0ZZ-6090-A, casting D0ZE-A
1970	Boss 302	D1ZE-6090-A, casting D1ZE-A (Service Head)
1969–1974	351W	casting C90E-B, C90E-D, D00E-C, D00E-G, D00Z-C
1975	351W	casting D5TE-EB
Intake Manifolds		
1962	221/260	C20Z-9424-F
1963	221/260	C30Z-9424-B
1963	260	C3AZ-9424-G, from 11/15/62
1963–1965	289 2V	C30Z-9424-C
1965	289 4V	S1MS-9424-A, Shelby, SFJD-9425, Shelby
1964–1967	289 4V	C40Z-9424-C, casting C50E-9425-A, C60E-9425-B
1965–1967	289 2V	C4AZ-9424-H
1967–1968	289 4V	casting S7MS-9424-A, Shelby
1965–1967	289 2x4V	casting C60A-9425, casting C622-63068-A

Year	Engine	Part or Casting Number
Intake Manifolds		
1968	289/302 2V	C4AZ-9424-J
1968	302 4V	C4OZ-9424-H, casting C8AE-9425-B
1969–1970	302	C4AZ-9424-J
1969	Boss 302	casting C9ZE-9424-E
1969–1970	Boss 302	C9ZZ-9424-C, D1ZZ-9424-E, casting C9FE-9424-F, casting
1971	Boss 302	casting D1ZE-9424-EA
1969	351 4V	C9OZ-9424, casting C8OE-9425-E, C9OE-9425-B
1969	351 4V	casting C8OX-9424-A, aluminum and C9OX-9424-A
1969–1971	351W	D1AZ-9424-C
1971–1972	302	D1OZ-9424-A
1973–1974	351W	D3OZ-9424-B
1973	302	D3OZ-9424-A
1974	302	D4DZ-9424
1975–1976	302	D5OZ-9424-G
1975–1976	351W	D5TZ-9424-T
1969	351 2V	casting C9OF-9425-F
Exhaust Manifolds		
1962	221/260	C2OZ-9430-C right, C2OZ-9431-B left
1963–1968	260/289/302	C3AZ-9430-H right, C3AZ-9431-H left
1963–1964	289 HP	C3OZ-9430-C right, C3OZ-9431-C left
1965–1967	289 HP	C5ZZ-9430-A right, C5ZZ-9431-A left
1965–1968	289/302	C5AZ-9431-E left
1967–1969	289/302	C7AZ-9430-A right, C7AZ-9431-A left
1970–1974	302	D4DZ-9430-E right, D4OZ-9430-B right, D4OZ-9431-B left, D0OZ-9431-D left
1969–1970	Boss 302	casting C9ZE-9430-A right, casting C9ZE-9431-A left
1969–1974	351W	C9AZ-9430-A right, C9OZ-9431-A left
1971–1974	351W	D0OZ-9430-B right, D0OZ-9431-B left
1975–1976	302	D5DZ-9430-A right, D5DZ-9431-C right, D4UZ-9431-A, B left

VIN Identification Codes

Code	Year	Engine
A	1965–1967	289 225 hp
C	1962	221, export
C	1963–1964	289 195 hp
C	1965–1967	289 200 hp
C	1968	289 195 hp
D	1964	289 210 hp
D	1969–1972	302 taxi/police
F	1962–1965	260 164 hp
F	1968–1971	302 210 hp
G	1969–1970	302 290 hp (Boss 302)
G	1970–1975	302 115–205 hp
H	1969–1970	351W 250 hp
H	1971	351W 240 hp
H	1972–1975	351W 151–163 hp
J	1968	302 230 hp (250 hp Shelby)
K	1963–1968	289 271 hp (306 hp Shelby)
L	1962–1963	221 145 hp
M	1969	351W 290 hp
3	1963	221, export
3	1965–1967	289, export
6	1968–1975	302, export

Engine-Tag Identification Codes

Code	Engine	VIN Code
200–207	351W 2V	H
208–213	351W 4V	M
231–233	289 2V	C
235	289 4V	A
236–241	289 2V	C
245, 246	289 4V	K
250	289 4V	A
252, 253, 257	289 2V	C
271–274	302 2V	F, G
275	302 2V	F
276	302 2V	D, F
277	302 2V	F
278	302 2V	D
279, 280	302 2V	F, G
281, 282	302 2V	F
283, 284	302 4V	J
285	302 2V	F
286	302 2V	D
287, 288	302 2V	F
289	352 4V	X
296	302 2V	G
299, 300	302 Boss 4V	G
491, 492	260 2V	F
500, 502, 504	260 2V	F
506, 534, 536	260 2V	F
538, 540	260 2V	F
548, 549	289 2V	C
550B	289 4V	D
550J	289 2V	C
551B	289 4V	D
551J	289 2V	C
552, 553	289 4V	A
554	289 4V	K
557, 558	289 2V	C
561, 562	289 2V	C
563, 564	289 4V	K
566, 567	289 4V	A

CHAPTER 15

FORD 335-SERIES

1970-1975

351 and 400

This was Ford's most modern V-8 engine family before Ford's modular V-8s of the 1990s. In the American idiom, the Cleveland engines, as they came to be known (the 335 series engines were built at Ford's Cleveland engine facility), were thoroughly modern—canted-valve cylinder heads and lightweight engine blocks made them compact, efficient mid-size powerplants. With two types of cylinder heads, the Cleveland engines were designed to breathe—on the street and on the track. Only a 351 cid version was offered for 1970, the 351C. Its bore and stroke was 4.00x3.50 in.

In typical Ford fashion, there is still come confusion as to the various 351 engines that were available in the late 1960s and 1970s. The 351W was the largest variant of the 90-degree V-8 engine family. The 351W has no connection or any resemblance to the 351C, which is of the 335 engine series.

The Cleveland series used an entirely different engine block and cylinder heads than those used on the 90-degree V-8s, although slightly modified Cleveland heads were used on one 90-degree V-8 engine—the Boss 302. The 351C was built in two- and four-barrel versions. The hot-dog 351C was the 1971 Boss 351 engine, which followed the same parameters as the Boss 302 engine it replaced. In 1972, for emission reasons, it was replaced by the 351 HO (for High Output). The performance 351Cs during 1972–1973 were the 351 CJs (Cobra Jets).

In 1971, the 400 cid version of the Cleveland family was introduced, with a square, 4.00x4.00 in. bore and stroke. Just as the 351W was an outgrowth of the 302, so was the 400 cid an outgrowth of the 351C engine. The 400 cid engine had a crank with a 1/2 in. longer stroke. To accommodate the 400's 4.00 in. stroke, the block's deck height was raised by an inch. Just as the 351 Windsor got larger main bearings than the 302, so did the 400. The 400's main bearings measured 3.00 in., the same size as those used on the 351W. However, the 400 cid engine and 351C still used the same size rod bearings, which also happened to be the same size as those used on the 351 Windsor. Thus the 351W and 400 cid crankshafts have the same size rod and main bearings.

What happens if you put the 351 Windsor crankshaft in the taller 400 cid block? They both have the same size main bearings so it will fit with no problems. This is what Ford did in 1975 and the result was the 351M, for 351 Modified.

351C Two-Barrel

The two-barrel carburetor 351C was rated at 250 hp in 1970 and 240 hp in 1971. The 1972 351C two-barrel was rated between 163 and 177 hp. In 1974, the engine's last year, it was rated at 163 hp.

All were equipped with the so-called two-barrel cylinder heads. These had smaller intake and exhaust ports when compared to the four-barrel cylinder heads, and also smaller intake and exhaust valves. All two-barrel carburetor engines came with a cast-iron crankshaft, two-bolt main-bearing caps, forged-steel connecting rods, cast-aluminum pistons, and a hydraulic camshaft with a nonadjustable valve train. Intake and exhaust manifolds were cast in iron.

351C Four-Barrel

The four-barrel version of the 351C came with a four-barrel intake manifold and carburetor and dual exhausts. More important, the engine's compression ratio was higher than that of the two-barrel engine, 11.0:1 for the 1970 engine, 10.7:1 for 1971, and 9.0:1 on 1972–1973 engines. Power ratings were 300 hp in 1970, 285 hp in 1971, between 248 and 266 hp in 1972 and 1973.

The engine also used the so-called four-barrel cylinder heads. These had larger intake and exhaust ports and larger valves as well, 2.19 in./1.71 in. intake/exhaust. The 1970 engines were also equipped with the four-bolt-main cap engine blocks, while 1971 and later blocks had the two-bolt variety.

The combustion chamber design used on these heads was of the smaller quench design for 1970–1971; the open chamber design was used on 1972–1973 engines. All four-barrel engines used a hydraulic-lifter camshaft and nonadjustable sled-fulcrum rockers. The fulcrums on these engines were made of sintered iron, which is stronger than the aluminum types used on the two-barrel engines.

351C Cobra Jet

The 351 CJ was introduced late in the 1971 model year. Instead of the quench chamber heads, the CJ used open chamber heads but with the larger ports and valves. In addition, the exhaust seats were induction-hardened for use with unleaded gasoline. Another difference was the use of a cast-iron intake manifold with a spread-bore bolt pattern to accommodate the Autolite 4300-D carburetor. Compression ratio on all the 1971–1973 engines was 9.0:1. Power output on the 1971 version was 280 hp. Power for the 1972–1973 CJs was rated using the SAE net method. Output thus went down to 266 hp.

Most CJs were generally equipped with a four-bolt-main engine block, but not all were. Like the four-barrel engines, the CJ came with a nonadjustable hydraulic-lifter camshaft and valvetrain.

Boss 351

This was the highest output 351C engine, and it was available only on the 1971 Boss 351 Mustang. Except for water passages, these heads are the same ones used on the 1970 Boss 302 engine, which meant the large-port, large-valve heads with the smaller quench combustion chambers. The Boss 351 engine used a solid-lifter camshaft with screw-in studs and adjustable rockers and an aluminum four-barrel intake manifold.

Also, the Boss was fitted with specially treated and prepared bottom-end components. The Boss 351 crankshaft, although cast

1971 Boss 351 was the high point in 351 Cleveland engine development. The cylinder heads, save for minor water passages, were identical to the Boss 302 heads.

of nodular iron like all 351C crankshafts, was chosen for hardness (90 percent nodularity). The four-bolt-main caps were also selected for hardness. The stock 351C connecting rods were used but were shot-peened, Magnafluxed, and fitted with special 180,000psi, 3/8 in. rod bolts. Forged aluminum pistons netted an 11.7:1 compression ratio.

Power output was 330 hp at 5,400 rpm with 370ft-lb torque at 4,000 rpm.

351 High Output

The 351 HO was the Boss 351 engine carried over and renamed for 1972. The major difference was the use of open chamber heads in order to reduce compression ratio to 9.2:1. The 351 HO also used a solid-lifter camshaft with milder cam timing, and although its intake manifold was similar to the Boss 351's, it used a spread-bore Autolite 4300-D carburetor. Even so, it was rated at 275 hp at 6,000 rpm with 286ft-lb torque at 3,800 rpm.

400 cid

The 400 was introduced in 1971 to replace the older FE-series 390 cid engine that Ford had used in larger passenger cars and trucks. This enlarged Cleveland V-8 used a taller engine block to accommodate its 4.00 in. stroke. As mentioned earlier, it had larger main-bearing journals, which meant that it used longer connecting rods than the 351C and different pistons. The cylinder heads were all of the open chamber design with the smaller 2.05 in./1.65 in. intake/exhaust valves. The 400 cid engine was rated at 260 hp in 1971; from 1972 on, the engine was rated between 143 and 180 hp. All 400s were equipped with a two-barrel carburetor and cast-iron intake manifold. The engine was used in Ford light trucks from 1977 to 1982.

351M

When the 351M was released in 1975, the 351C had already been retired from production. When the 351 Windsor crankshaft was used in the 400 cid engine block, the result was 351 cid. This makes the 351M a destroked 400. As such, it was visually identical to the 400. It used the two-barrel carburetor, Cleveland heads, two-barrel cast-iron intake manifold, and a hydraulic-lifter camshaft.

Engine Blocks

The 335 engine family has three basic engine blocks. The two-barrel engines were all equipped with two-bolt-main engine blocks.

The 1970 four-barrel carburetor engines and the Boss 351, HO, and CJ engines were all equipped with four-bolt blocks, although some engines came with the two-bolt blocks. According to top Ford engine builders, the four-bolt main-bearing caps don't add anything in the way of additional bottom-end strength on the 335-series block. There is also a small difference between the Boss 351 and HO blocks and other four-bolt blocks. The Boss 351 and HO used a split-rubber rear main seal, while the other blocks used a rope-type seal.

The 400 and 351M came with a block that had a 1.09-in. taller deck height and larger main bearings. It used the two-bolt-main caps.

Cylinder Heads

All 335-series engines came with canted-valve cylinder heads. Although Chevrolet used canted-valve cylinder heads on the big-block V-8, Ford initially used the design on the new-for-1968 460 cid engine and made several refinements, which were also carried over to the 351 Cleveland engines. The main refinement is that the Ford canted-valve engines have equal-length intake runners. The

1970 351 Cleveland with the four-barrel carburetor was rated at 300hp. The engine was equipped with the large port, large valve cylinder heads and small quench-type combustion chambers for 1970.

canted valve design allows for better engine breathing through superior valve placement and port configuration.

The most common Cleveland cylinder head is the so-called two-barrel head. These heads were used on all 351C two-barrel engines, the 351M, and the 400. The heads have smaller ports and valves than the four-barrel heads, and large, open-type combustion chambers. The valves measured 2.05 in./1.65 in. intake/exhaust. By way of comparison, they are considerably larger than the 351W's valves, which measured 1.84 in./1.54 in. intake/exhaust. These heads are probably better for street use than the larger four-barrel heads are. All two-barrel heads used nonadjustable stamped-steel rocker arms, which used sled fulcrums that bolted into slots in the cylinder head.

The 1970–1971 four-barrel Cleveland heads came with larger ports and valves. The valves measured 2.19 in./1.71 in. intake/exhaust, and these heads also had the smaller quench-type combustion chambers. The quench design makes more low- to mid-range torque, at the expense of greater emissions. The valvetrain on the four-barrel heads is identical to that of the two-barrel heads. The 1971–1973 four-barrel and CJ heads were identical with the 1970 quench chamber four-barrel heads except for the larger, open combustion chambers.

The "best" Cleveland heads were the ones used on the Boss 351 engine. They had the large ports and valves and quench-type combustion chambers and an adjustable valvetrain. Screw-in rocker studs, pushrod guide plates, and specially hardened rockers were used on the Boss 351, so the heads were modified for use of these components. The heads had machined spring seats, and the rocker arm pedestals were machined flat for use with the screw-in rocker studs. In addition, the Boss 351's valves used single-grooved valve keepers; these are better in a high-performance application because they hold the valve tighter. All other engines got multi-groove keepers.

The next best heads were used on the 351 HO. These heads were identical to the Boss 351's but used instead the larger, open-chamber design.

Intake Manifolds

All two-barrel engines came with a cast-iron intake manifold and a Ford two-barrel carburetor. All the four-barrel factory intake manifolds were of the same design and differed only in material they were cast in and the type of carburetor they were drilled to accept.

The 1970–1971 four-barrel engines got a cast-iron intake that used a conventional Autolite 4300-A carburetor. The 1972–1973 four-barrel engines and the CJ came with the same cast-iron intake manifold, but drilled to use the Ford Autolite 4300-D spread-bore carburetor.

The Boss 351 came with an aluminum version of the intake (which saved 31lb) and an Autolite 4300-A carburetor. The 351 HO got the same aluminum intake drilled to accept the Ford 4300-D spread-bore carburetor.

Exhaust Manifolds

All 351 Cleveland engines used cast-iron exhaust manifolds that exited downwards at the rear of the engine. There were no special exhaust manifolds for the Boss 351 or other performance variants.

Engine Identification

Ford's method of identifying engine parts follows typical industry procedures in that each part has a casting number cast onto it, and for Fords, that number consists of letters and numbers in a particular order. Let's look at a typical part number, in this case, D1ZZ-6069-B, which is the cylinder head for a 1971 351 Boss engine. It breaks down as follows: the D indicates the decade (D is 1970–1979); the 1 indicates the year of the decade (1971); the ZZ indicates the car line; the 6069 is a subgroup number (some Ford cylinder heads are numbered 6049); the E is an application suffix code (for example, on a camshaft, the letter A might stand for a high-performance solid-lifter cam, while the letter B might be for a two-barrel engine with hydraulic cam). The various codes and suffixes are listed in the tables.

Casting numbers are similar to part numbers, but there are major differences. Usually, the subgroup numbers were not used in the number cast on the part itself, but they will be indicated in the parts book, if the casting number is listed at all. However, sometimes the subgroup number is on the part itself, and sometimes the casting number is the same as the part number.

Date codes were also used. A typical date code might be as follows: 1 B 16, where the 1 indicates the last digit of the year (in this case it would be 1971); the B indicates the month, in this case February (the months were coded A for January through M for December, but I was not used); the 16 indicates the day of the month.

Depending on the part you're looking at, the date code is probably as important as the casting number itself, especially if you're trying to determine originality. To be considered original, parts installed in a Ford vehicle have to have been cast or manufactured before the car itself was built. This can be up to 30 days or more and still be considered original. On parts that were manufactured, the date codes were stamped on the part, rather than cast.

Beginning in 1970, Ford began stamping the car's VIN on the left rear side of the block just below the cylinder head, thereby making it fairly easy to determine an engine's origin. Ford also assigned a letter code for each engine installed in passenger cars and trucks, and this code appears in the VIN. This code is in the fifth position of the VIN. Ford used the codes over and over, the same code standing for different engines, which can cause some confusion. For example, the 351C two-barrel carburetor engine was first available on 1970 Ford and Mercury cars. The 351W was also available that year, and they both shared the same VIN letter code, "H." You have to actually look at the engine in order to determine if it is a Windsor or Cleveland.

The Windsor engines use a timing chain cover while the Cleveland engines have their blocks extended about 2 in. Inside this extension is the timing chain. Another way to differentiate a Cleveland from a Windsor is to look at the intake manifolds. All

Windsor intake manifolds incorporate water passages, and the thermostat housing is bolted on the front of the manifold. On the Cleveland engines, the thermostat housing is located on the block itself, on the block extension that houses the timing chain. There are no water passages in the intake manifold.

Engines produced between 1964 and 1972 had an aluminum ID tag, usually mounted under the coil mounting bolt. Stamped on the tag was information that included a numerical engine ID code, model year, engine plant code (usually), year and month of production, and engineering change level. It would have been nice if Ford had stamped this information on the engine block itself, as too often, tags got lost over the years. The engine ID codes are listed in the tables.

Engine Specifications

	Displacement	Carburetor	Horsepower	Torque	Compression Ratio	Notes
1970						
	351	2V	250@4,600	355@2,800	9.5	Ford, Mercury, Mustang, Torino, Cougar
	351	4V	300@5,400	380@3,400	11.0	Mustang, Mercury, Cougar, Cyclone
1971						
	351	2V	240@4,600	350@2,600	9.5	Mustang, Cougar
	351 CJ	4V	280@5,800	345@3,800	9.0	Mustang, Cougar
	351	4V	285@5,400	370@3,400	10.7	Ford, Mercury, Torino, Montego, Mustang, Cougar
	351 Boss	4V	330@5,400	370@4,000	11.7	Mustang
	400	2V	260@4,400	400@2,200	9.0	Ford, Mercury
1972						
	351	2V	154@3,800	266@2,000	8.3	Ford, Mercury
	351	2V	161@4,000	254@2,400	8.0	Torino, Montego
	351	2V	163@3,800	277@2,000	8.6	Ford, Mercury, Mustang, Cougar
	351	2V	177@3,800	284@2,000	8.6	Mustang, Cougar
	351	4V	248@5,400	301@3,600	8.6	Torino, Montego
	351 CJ	4V	266@5,400	301@3,600	9.0	Mustang, Cougar
	351 HO	4V	275@6,000	286@3,800	9.2	Mustang
	400	2V	172@4,000	298@2,200	8.5	Ford, Mercury
1973						
	351	2V	156@3,800	260@2,400	8.0	Torino, Montego
	351	2V	158@3,800	264@2,400	8.0	Ford, Mercury
	351	2V	159@3,800	250@2,400	8.0	Torino, Montego
	351	2V	161@4,000	254@2,400	8.0	Ford, Mercury
	351	2V	164@4,000	276@2,000	8.0	Mustang, Cougar
	351	2V	177@3,800	284@2,000	8.6	Mustang, Cougar
	351	4V	246@5,400	301@3,600	8.6	Torino, Montego
	351 CJ	4V	266@5,400	301@3,600	9.0	Mustang, Cougar
	400	2V	168@3,600	314@2,000	8.0	Torino, Montego
	400	2V	171@3,600	314@2,000	8.0	Ford, Mercury

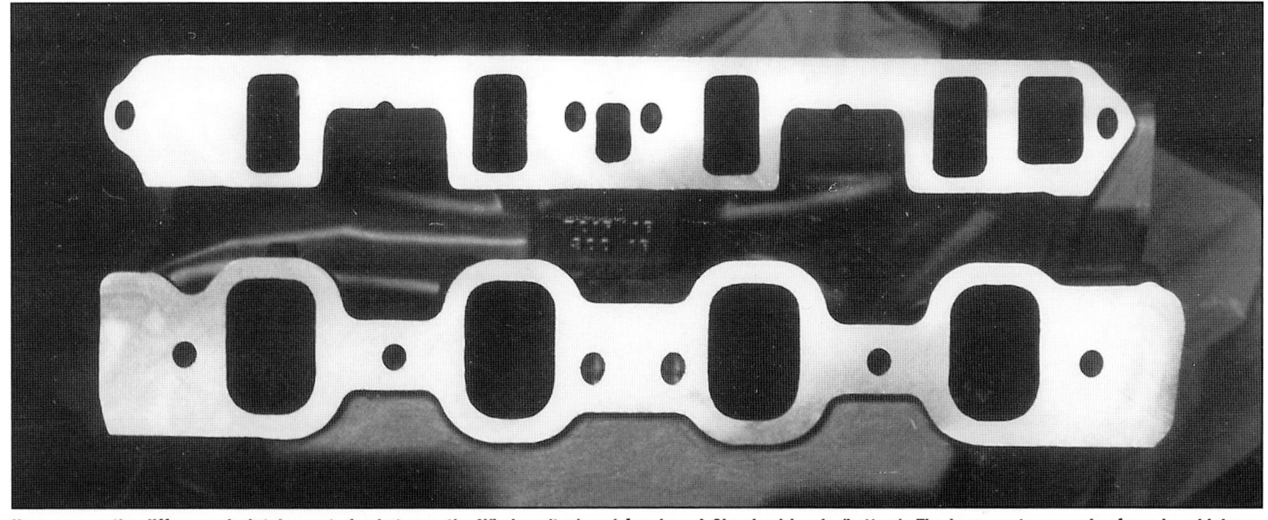

Here we see the difference in intake port size between the Windsor (top) and four-barrel Cleveland heads (bottom). The large ports are only of use in a high-performance situation. For regular everyday use, the Windsor heads are more economical.

Engine Specifications

	Displacement	Carburetor	Horsepower	Torque	Compression Ratio	Notes
1974						
	351	2V	163@4,200	278@2,000	8.0	Torino, Montego, Cougar
	351	4V	255@5,600	290@3,400	7.9	Torino, Cougar, Montego
	400	2V	170@3,400	330@2,000	8.0	Ford, Torino, Mercury, Montego
1975						
	351M	2V	148@3,800	243@2,400	8.0	Ford, Torino, Montego
	351M	2V	150@3,800	244@2,800	8.0	California, Ford, Torino, Montego, Elite
	400	2V	144@3,600	255@2,200	8.0	California, Ford, Torino, Montego, Elite
	400	2V	158@3,400	276@2,000	8.0	Ford, Mercury Torino, Montego, Elite

Engine Internal Dimensions

Displacement	Bore and Stroke	Rod Bearings	Main Bearings	Intake/Exhaust Valves
351C	4.000x3.500	2.3103–2.3111	2.7484-2.7492	2.05/1.65 (2.19/1.71 on 4V, CJ, HO, Boss)
351M	4.000x3.500	2.3103–2.3111	2.9994-2.3002	2.05/1.65
400	4.000x4.000	2.3103–2.3111	2.9994-2.3002	2.05/1.65

Block, Head, and Manifold Part and Casting Numbers

Year	Engine	Part or Casting Number
Engine Blocks		
1970–1974	351-2V	casting D0AZ-D
1971	351-4V	casting D0AE-J,D0AE-G, D2AE-CA
1971	351	Boss 351, HO, CJ, D1ZZ-6010-D, casting D2AE-CA
1972–1974	351-4V	D1ZZ-6010-A, casting D2AE-CA
1971–1974	400	D1AZ-6010-A, casting D1AE-A, D1AE-AC, D1AE-A2C, D4AE-B2A, D5AZ
1973	400	casting D3AE-B (has 351C bellhousing pattern)
1975	351M	D5AZ-6010-A, casting D5AZ, D7TE-A2B, D8
Cylinder Heads		
1970–1974	351-2V	D1AZ-6049-A D3AZ-6049-H, casting D0AE-E,D0AE-J,

Exhaust manifolds were usually cast with a date code (left) and casting code (right), as on this 1970 351 Cleveland exhaust manifold.

Intake ports on the 351C four-barrel heads were large; except for water passage configuration, they were identical to the 1970 Boss 302 head (shown).

Year	Engine	Part or Casting Number
Cylinder Heads		
		DOAZ-A, DOAZ-B, DOAZ-D
1975	351-2V	D5AZ-6049-B, casting D5AE-AA, D5AZ
1970–1971	351-4V	D1AZ-6049-B, casting DOAE-H, DOAE-R
1971	351-4V	BOSS 351, D1ZZ-6069-B, casting D1ZE-B
1971	351-4V	CJ, D1ZZ-6069-C, casting D1ZE-DA
1972–1974	351-4V	CJ, D1ZZ-6069-C, casting D1ZE-GA
1972	351-4V	HO, D2ZZ-6069-A, casting D2ZE-A
1971–1974	400	D1AZ-6049-A, casting D1AE-A, D3AE-G2B
1975	400	D5AZ-6049-B, casting D5AZ
Intake Manifolds		
1970–1972	351C 2V	D1AZ-9424-D
1970–1971	351C 4V	DOAZ-9424-C
1971	351C 4V CJ/Boss	D1ZZ-9424-B, D1ZX-9425-CA, casting
1972	351C 4V	D2ZZ-9424-A
1973	351C 2V	D30Z-9424-A
1973	351C 4V	D3AZ-9424-C
1974	351C 2V	D3AZ-9424-C w/o A.I.R.
1974	351C 2V	D4AZ-9424-C, w/ A.I.R.
1975	351M	D5AZ-9424-C, w/o EGR
1975	351M	D5AZ-9424-D, w/ EGR
1971	400	D1AZ-9424-A
1972	400	D2SZ-9424-A

Year	Engine	Part or Casting Number
Intake Manifolds		
1973	400	D3AZ-9424-B
1974	400	D3AZ-9424-B, w/o A.I.R.
1974	400	D4AZ-9424-B, w/ A.I.R.
1975	400	D5AZ-9424-C, w/o EGR
1975	400	D5AZ-9424-D, w/ EGR
Exhaust Manifolds		
1970	351C 2V	DOAZ-9430-B right, DOAZ-9431-A left, DOAE-9431-C, casting
1970	351C 4V	DOAZ-9430-B right, DOAZ-9431-B left, DOOE-9431-A, casting
1971–1972	351C 4V Boss/HO	D1ZZ-9430-B right, D1ZZ-9431-D
1971–1972	351C 2V	D20Z-9430-B right, D1ZZ-9431-A left
1971–1972	351C 4V	D20Z-9430-B right, D1ZZ-9431-B left, D1ZE-9431-BA, casting
1973–1974	351C 2V	D20Z-9430-B right, D1ZZ-9431-A left
1973–1974	351C 4V	D20Z-9430-B right, D1ZZ-9431-B left
1975	351M	D5AZ-9430-A right, D5AZ-9431-AZ left
1971–1974	400	D2AZ-9430-A right, D1AZ-9431-A left
1975	400	D5AZ-9430-A right, D5AZ-9431-AZ left

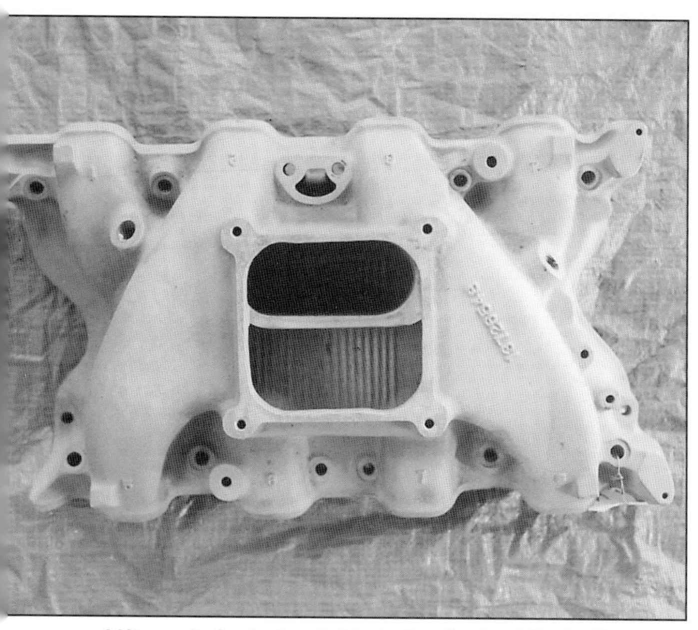

A bit excessive for street use is this aluminum four-barrel Cleveland intake manifold made to accept the Holley Dominator carburetor. This is an exact copy of the factory unit.

VIN Identification Codes

Code	Year	Engine
H	1970	351 250 hp
H	1971	351 240 hp
H	1972	351 154-77 hp
H	1975	351M 145–161 hp
M	1970	351 300 hp
M	1971	351 295 hp
Q	1972–1973	351 CJ 266 hp
Q	1974	351 CJ 255 hp
R	1971	351 Boss 330 hp
R	1972	351 HO 275 hp
S	1971–1975	400 144–260 hp

Engine-Tag Identification Codes

Code	Engine	VIN Code
219	400 2V	S
220	400 2V	S
221	400 2V	S
600	351C 2V	H
601	351C 2V	H
602	351C 2V	H
604	351C 2V	H
606	351C 2V	H
608	351C 4V	M
609	351C 4V	M
610	351C 2V	H
611	351C 2V	M
613	351C 4V	M
614	351C 2V	H
615	351C 2V	H
616	351C 4V	M
617	351C 4V	M
620	351C CJ 4V	Q
621	351C CJ 4V	Q
625	351C 4V	R
630	351C 4V	M
632	351C 2V	H

This is a view of the 400 cid block's bottom end. The 351C version was similar. The big difference between the 335 series engines and other Ford small-blocks was the extension that housed the timing chain.

CHAPTER 16

FORD 385-SERIES

1968-1975

429 and 460

Introduced in 1968, Ford's 385-series V-8s gradually replaced the tried and true FE-series big-block engines. It was Ford's first V-8 that used canted-valve "poly-angle" cylinder heads, very similar to those used on Chevrolet's big-block engine. The big Ford's heads are more refined than the Chevy's because they have equally spaced runners for better fuel mixture distribution. The 385-series engines are larger and heavier than the FE-series engines. They were also designed with plenty of room for future growth. Complementing the canted valve cylinder heads was a thin-wall, skirtless engine block that had the exact same oiling system that was later used on the 351C engines.

Ford 385-series big-blocks were made in two displacements, 429 and 460. The Thunder Jet 429 was first used on Ford's Thunderbird in 1968, and the 460 first saw service on the 1968 Lincoln. Both engines had the same 4.36 in. bore; the 429 cid engine had a relatively short stroke, at 3.59 in. (for comparison, the 351 Cleveland had a 3.50 in. stroke), while the 460 got a longer stroke, 3.85 in. As a result of their relatively short stroke, high-rpm capability was built into the 385 series.

429 cid

This was the basic 429 cid engine used as the optional engine on Ford and Mercury full-size and intermediate cars from 1968 to 1973. All base 429 cid engine used the regular two-bolt main-bearing cap engine block, cast-iron crankshaft, forged-steel connecting rods with 3/8 in. rod bolts and cast-aluminum pistons. All of these engines came with a hydraulic-lifter camshaft, the base small-port, small-valve 2.08 in./1.66 in. intake/exhaust valves, cylinder heads with nonadjustable rail-type rocker arms, cast-iron manifold, and Ford carb. Compression ratio on the two-barrel carburetor engine was 10.5:1: the four-barrel engine had a higher 11.0:1 ratio from 1968 to 1970; it was reduced to 10.5:1 in 1971 and again to 8.5:1 and 8.0:1 in 1972 and 1973, respectively.

In its first year of service, the 429 cid V-8 was available only with a four-barrel manifold and carburetor. It was rated at 360 hp. The engine was offered virtually unchanged in this guise through the 1971 model year in various Ford and Mercury full-size and intermediate cars. The 429 cid V-8 was available for another two model years, 1972 and 1973, and because Ford used the SAE net method to determine horsepower, output was in the low-200 hp range.

A two-barrel version, rated at 320 hp, was available from 1969 to 1971. The two-barrel carburetor engine didn't make it past 1971.

Depending on the application, these engines were equipped with either a two- or four-barrel cast-iron intake manifold and matching Ford carburetor.

429 Cobra Jet and Super Cobra Jet

Every Ford engine, at one time or another, seems to become a CJ engine, and the 429 was no exception. Two versions were made, the 429 CJ and the SCJ. Both were available on Ford and Mercury performance intermediates, the Ford Mustang and Mercury Cougar, during 1970–1971.

With the exception of the 1970 429 cid CJ engine, both the 1970–1971 CJ and SCJ used a four-bolt-main engine block. Four-bolt main-bearing caps were used in the numbers 2, 3, and 4 positions. The 1970 CJ appeared, with the base two-bolt-main engine block. As with the base 429s, the CJ and SCJ came with a cast-iron crankshaft and the regular 429 cid connecting rods. The CJ engines came with cast-aluminum pistons; the SCJ got stronger, forged-aluminum pistons. Compression ratio on both engines was listed at 11.3:1.

The big difference on the 429 CJ and SCJ was the cylinder heads. These were from the Ford school of thought that believed that if big was good, then really big must be a lot better. The ports on the CJ and SCJ engines were considerably larger, and so were the valves, 2.25 in./1.72 in. intake/exhaust. The CJ engine used a hydraulic-lifter camshaft, while the SCJ used a mechanical-lifter camshaft. Both engines used stamped-steel 1.73:1 ratio rocker arms on sled-type fulcrums, threaded screw-in rocker studs, and pushrod guide plates. The rockers on the SCJ engines were adjustable, and so were those of CJ engines built before November 1, 1969; later CJ engines used screw-in, positive-stop rocker studs, which were nonadjustable.

There was also a difference regarding intake manifolds and carburetors. The CJ engines used a Rochester Quadrajet carburetor

The Boss 429 hemi engine was Ford's best street engine to come out of the 1960s. In street trim, it was a little tame but that's to be expected. The engine wasn't a modified street engine but a race engine modified for the street.

This is the Boss 429 street cylinder head. Note O-rings around each cylinder. All oil and water passages were also perfectly round and designed to accept small Viton rubber O-rings. Each rubber O-ring was glued to each hole and then the head was installed on the block. Silicone sealer was used around the perimeter of the head to keep oil from the interior of the engine from leaking out. Most of these engines leak anyway.

mounted on a spread-bore cast-iron intake manifold; the SCJ engine used a similar intake manifold but with a Holley 780cfm four-barrel carburetor that used the Holley bolt pattern.

Interestingly, Ford said in its Off Highway Parts Manual that the small-port 429 and 460 cid cylinder heads, when equipped with the larger valves used on the CJ and SCJ engines, would outflow the CJ and SCJ heads and produce more power. Obviously, bigger is not always better.

Boss 429

The Boss 429 was the ultimate 429 cid engine. It was built so Ford could use the engine in NASCAR stock cars. The rules at the time stated that the engine had to be installed on at least 500 street cars, and Ford chose to install the engine in the 1969–1970 Boss 429 Mustang.

Just one look at the Boss engine will tell you that it is radically different from other 429s; the cylinder heads are massive and are cast in aluminum. The engine was designed to run at high rpm for extended periods of time, so Ford made sure that every component of the engine could withstand the punishment. In NASCAR racing, it was Ford's most reliable engine ever up to that time. Although the engine used in the Boss 429 Mustang resembled the race version, known as the NASCAR 429, there were quite a few differences between the street and race Boss 429 engines.

The aluminum Boss 429 cylinder heads had a modified hemi-type combustion chamber. Ford called these "crescent" chambers. They were a shallow type of hemi design with the sides filled in. The valves were big and located transversely for a cross-flow configuration. The street engine had intake/exhaust valves of 2.28 in./1.90 in. The intake ports were round, but the large exhaust ports were "D" shaped.

The cylinder heads did not use conventional head gaskets for sealing to the block. Each water and oil passage on the heads was completely round and made to accept rubber Viton O-rings. There was also a machined O-ring groove around each cylinder for use with metal copper rings. This level of attention to sealing was necessary because the engine used only 10 bolts to secure the cylinder head on the block.

The engine used individual shaft-mounted rockers with a 1.76:1 ratio for the exhaust rockers and 1.65:1 for the intakes.

Here is a group shot of some of the exotic Boss 429 and regular 429 intake setups. Tunnel ram on the lower right is the only non-factory manifold. It was made by Weiand.

The engine block used on the Boss 429 engines was also different from other 429 cid blocks. For one thing, there was a cast-in 429 HP identification on the left front of the block. Internally, four-bolt main-bearing caps were used on the numbers 1, 2, 3, and 4 positions, and the Boss blocks had a revised oiling system that had four oil galleries, whereas the regular 429 block had only two. There were two pedestals in the Boss 429 block's lifter gallery area (as opposed to one), and the cylinder walls on these blocks were much thicker than those of regular production blocks. Boss blocks could be overbored 0.160 in., according to Holman and Moody. They were also cast with higher nodularity iron.

There were two versions of the street Boss 429 engine, the 820-S and 820-T, as identified by the engine identification tag mounted underneath the coil. The S version, used only on early 1969 production Boss 429 Mustangs, had much stronger connecting rods with 1/2 in., 12-point rod bolts. These rods were 6.549 in. long. The T version used rods that were the same length as the regular 429 rods, but stronger. Both 1969 engines used a hydraulic-lifter camshaft and both had forged-aluminum pistons, forged-steel cross-drilled crankshafts, and a 10.5:1 compression ratio. The 1970 version T engine came with the 429 SCJ mechanical-lifter camshaft. Both engines used distinctive aluminum valve covers.

All street Boss 429s came with an aluminum dual-plane, high-rise type of intake manifold and a 735cfm Holley four-barrel carburetor. The cast-iron exhaust manifolds of the Boss 429 were also unique, made to fit within the tight confines of the Mustang engine compartment.

NASCAR 429

There was no "set" NASCAR 429 engine configuration, but these engines generally shared certain characteristics that made them different from the street engines, and these changed based on the requirements of each track and as the engine developed.

The NASCAR engine blocks were different from the street Boss; they had larger outboard bolts in the number one main-bearing cap, and it was the block's deck that was grooved for the O-rings. The blocks also had larger machined reliefs for the exhaust pushrods. The crankshaft of the NASCAR engines was forged steel. The rods were similar to the street S rods, but longer. Several types were made, and one even had an oil passage running through its center to bring oil up to the piston pin.

The cylinder heads were either of the crescent type or the full hemi design. The intake valves, usually stainless steel, were larger on the race engines, measuring 2.37 in. The rocker arms rotated on thinner shafts, and the intake valve rockers had a 1.75:1 ratio. The race engines also used lighter, magnesium valve covers.

There was a great variety of intake manifolds for the race engine—some cast in aluminum and some in magnesium. Unlike the street intake manifold, these did not have provision for a thermostat and water outlet; the race engines used a special water manifold that connected the cylinder heads.

The ultimate configuration of the race Boss engine was the all-aluminum block (reportedly some magnesium blocks were also cast) used in Ford's abbreviated Can Am race effort. The block used cast-iron liners bored out to 4.54 in. With the 460's 3.85 in. stroke, the result was 494 cid.

460 cid

The largest engine in this series, the 460 cid V-8 was available from 1968 through 1996; it was used to power Lincoln, Ford, and Mercury full-size cars, trucks, and vans.

This was the same engine as the base 429 four-barrel engine, but with a longer, 3.85 in. stroke. From 1968 to 1971, the engine was rated at 365 hp. From 1972 to 1975, the engine was rated between 208 and 275 hp.

Engine Blocks

The majority of 429 and 460 engines built have two-bolt main-bearing caps. The 1971 CJ and all SCJ engines got a block with four-bolt main-bearing caps in the numbers 2, 3, and 4 positions. Block deck height was increased 0.010 in 1970 1/2, and again in 1972 by 0.012.

The street Boss 429 block came with four-bolt main-bearing caps in the first position as well. It was a stronger, heavier casting (see the Boss 429 section).

Cylinder Heads

The base 429 and 460 cylinder heads featured oval intake and exhaust ports. Valves were 2.08 in./1.65 in. intake/exhaust. All these engines came with screw-in rocker studs with rail-type rocker arms. Later 460 cid engines came with slotted pedestals and nonadjustable rocker arms, similar to the ones used on the 351C engines.

The CJ and SCJ engines came with cylinder heads that had much larger intake and exhaust ports. Valves were also larger, 2.25 in./1.72 in. intake/exhaust. In addition, these heads came with screw-in rocker studs, adjustable rockers, and pushrod guide plates. The only exception are the CJ engines built after November 1, 1969, which came with screw-in positive-stop rocker studs.

Not commonly known is the fact that Ford used the big-valve, big-port CJ heads on the 1972–1974 429 and 460 PI (Police Interceptor) engines. Besides not having adjustable rocker arms, the heads also had larger combustion chambers.

The CJ and SCJ engines came with aluminum valve covers. All other 429 and 460 engines came with stamped-steel valve covers.

Intake Manifolds

Two- or four-barrel cast-iron intake manifolds were standard equipment on the 429 and 460 engines. The manifolds used on the CJ and SCJ engines have much larger passageways and ports and are designed to fit the larger CJ and SCJ heads. The 429 CJ engines were fitted with a cast-iron intake manifold that came with a Rochester Quadrajet four-barrel carburetor. The 429 SCJ used the same basic manifold, but it had its carburetor mounting pad drilled for the Holley bolt pattern. The SCJ came with a 780cfm Holley.

Exhaust Manifolds

Exhaust manifolds for the base 429 and 460 engines are made of cast iron and exit at the rear of the engine. The CJ and SCJ exhaust manifolds are also cast in iron but are considerably free-flowing and have larger outlets.

Engine Identification

Ford's method of identifying engine parts follows typical industry procedures in that each part has a casting number cast onto it, and for Fords, that number consists of letters and numbers in a particular order. Let's look at a typical part number, in this case, D0OZ-6049-H, which is the cylinder head for a 1970–1971 429 CJ engine. It breaks down as follows: the D indicates the decade (C is 1960–1969, D is 1970–1979); the 0 indicates the year of the decade (0 would be 1970 in our example); the OZ indicates the car line; the 6049 is a subgroup number (most Ford cylinder heads are numbered 6049, intake manifolds are 9424, camshafts 6250, and so on); the H is an application suffix code (for example, on a camshaft, the letter A might stand for a high-performance solid-lifter cam, while the letter B might be for a two-barrel engine with hydraulic cam). The various codes and suffixes are listed in the tables.

Casting numbers are similar to part numbers, but there are major differences. Usually, the subgroup numbers were not used in the number cast on the part itself, but they will be indicated in the parts book, if the casting number is listed at all. However, sometimes the subgroup number is on the part itself and sometimes the casting number is the same as the part number.

Date codes were also used. A typical date code might be as follows: 9 B 16, where the 9 indicates the last digit of the year (in

The bottom end of the 429/460 block is hefty, to say the least. Boss 429 and 429 CJ/SCJ blocks had four-bolt-main caps in the center three positions while the Boss 429 had an additional four-bolt-main cap in the front position as well.

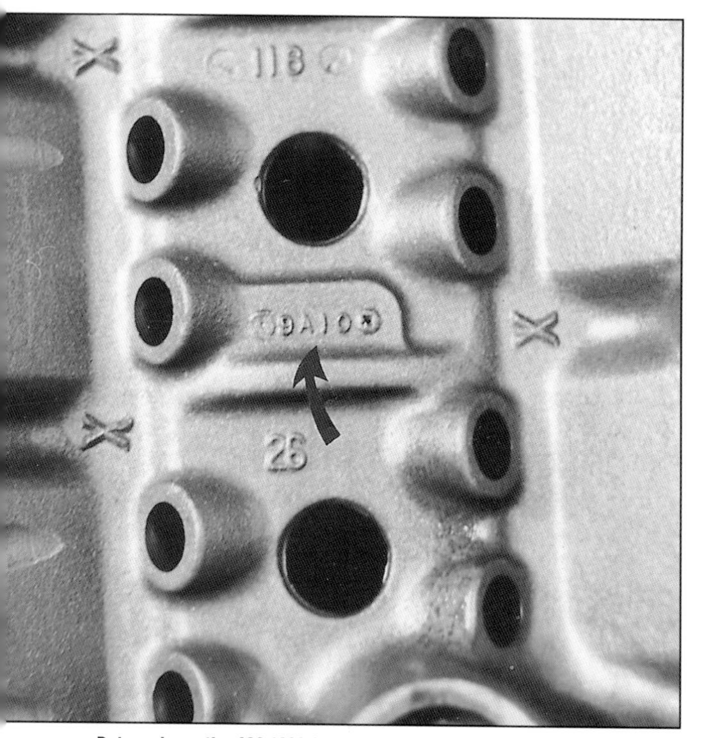

Date code on the 429/460 blocks can be found in the lifter valley area.

this case it could be 1969); the B indicates the month, in this case February (the months were coded A for January through M for December, but I was not used); the 16 indicates the day of the month.

Depending on the part you're looking at, the date code is probably as important as the casting number itself, especially if you're trying to determine originality. To be considered original, parts installed in a Ford vehicle have to have been cast or manufactured before the car itself was built. This can be up to 30 days or more and still be considered original. On parts that were manufactured, the date codes were stamped on the part, rather than cast.

There wasn't any engine identification in relation to the vehicle it was installed in until 1970, when Ford began stamping the car's VIN on the block, on the left rear side of the block just below the cylinder head. On pre-1970 Fords, you can't determine if a particular engine is original equipment in a particular car. The only exceptions to this were the Boss 429 engines. The car's VIN was stamped on the engine block itself, thereby tying the engine to the chassis it was installed in.

Ford did assign an engine code for use in the vehicle's VIN. In this way, you can at least tell by looking at a VIN what engine the car was built with. Beginning in 1960, the code was in the fifth position, and it remained in that position until 1981. Ford used the same codes over and over, and the same code can stand for different engines. These codes are listed in the tables.

Ford also placed a small metal tag on the engine through the 1972 model year, usually attached to the coil hold-down bolt, which included information about the engine. Most of these codes are included here, but it was very easy for this tag to get lost over the years.

Engine Specifications

	Displacement	Carburetor	Horsepower	Torque	Compression Ratio	Notes
1968						
	429	4V	360@4,600	480@2,800	10.5	Ford, Mercury
	460	4V	365@4,600	500@2,800	10.5	Lincoln
1969						
	429	2V	320@4,400	460@2,200	10.5	Ford, Mercury
	429	4V	360@4,600	476@2,800	11.0	Ford, Mercury
	429	4V	375@5,200	450@3,400	10.5	Mustang, Boss 429
	460	4V	365@4,600	500@2,800	10.5	Lincoln
1970						
	429	2V	320@4,400	460@2,200	10.5	Ford, Mercury
	429	4V	360@4,600	486@2,800	11.0	Ford, Mercury
	429	4V	370@5,400	450@3,400	11.3	CJ, Torino, Cyclone
	429	4V	375@5,600	450@3,400	11.3	SCJ, Torino, Cyclone
	429	4V	375@5,200	450@3,400	10.5	Boss 429, Mustang
	460	4V	365@4,600	500@2,800	10.5	Lincoln
1971						
	429	2V	320@4,400	460@2,200	10.5	Ford, Mercury
	429	4V	360@4,600	480@2,800	11.0	Ford, Mercury
	429	4V	370@5,400	450@3,400	11.3	CJ, Torino, Cyclone
	429	4V	375@5,600	450@3,400	11.3	SCJ, Torino, Cyclone
	429	4V	375@5,200	450@3,400	10.5	Boss 429, Mustang
	460	4V	365@4,600	500@2,800	10.2	Lincoln
1972						
	429	4V	205@4,400	322@2,600	8.5	Torino
	429	4V	208@4,400	322@2,800	8.5	Ford, T-Bird, Mercury
	429	4V	212@4,400	342@2,800	8.5	T-Bird
	460	4V	212@4,400	342@2,800	8.5	Lincoln
	460	4V	224@4,400	357@2,800	8.5	Lincoln, T-Bird
1973						
	429	4V	197@4,400	320@2,800	8.0	Ford, Mercury
	429	4V	201@4,400	322@2,800	8.0	Ford, Mercury

	Displacement	Carburetor	Horsepower	Torque	Compression Ratio	Notes
	429	4V	208@4,400	337@2,600	8.0	T-Bird
	460	4V	208@4,400	338@2,800	8.0	Lincoln
	460	4V	219@4,400	360@2,800	8.0	Lincoln
	460	4V	267@4,600	386@2,800	8.0	Mercury
	460	4V	274@4,600	392@2,800	8.8	Ford, PI
1974						
	460	4V	195@3,800	335@2,600	8.0	Ford, Mercury
	460	4V	215@4,400	342@2,600	8.0	Lincoln
	460	4V	220@4,400	357@2,600	8.0	Montego, Cougar, Lincoln, T-Bird
	460	4V	260@4,400	380@2,600	8.8	Ford, Mercury, PI
	460	4V	260@4,400	380@2,600	8.8	Ford, Mercury, Police Interceptor
1975						
	460	4V	194@3,800	347@2,600	8.0	Lincoln, T-Bird
	460	4V	206@4,400	338@2,800	8.0	Lincoln
	460	4V	218@4,000	369@2,600	8.0	Mercury
	460	4V	216@4,000	366@2,600	8.0	Montego, T-Bird, Cougar
	460	4V	218@4,000	369@2,600	8.0	Ford, Mercury, California
	460	4V	224@4,000	370@2,600	8.0	T-Bird
	460	4V	226@4,000	374@2,600	8.0	Ford, Mercury, PI

Engine Internal Dimensions

Displacement	Bore and Stroke	Rod Bearings	Main Bearings	Intake/Exhaust Valves
429	4.36x3.59	2.4992–2.5,000	2.9944–3.0002	2.08/1.66 (2.25–1.72 CJ/SCJ/PI 2.28/1.90 Boss)
460	4.36x3.85	2.4992–2.5,000	2.9944–3.0002	2.08/1.66 (2.19/1.66 PI, 1973–1974)

Block, Head, and Manifold Part and Casting Numbers

Year	Engine	Part or Casting Number
Engine Blocks		
1969–1970	429	NASCAR BOSS 429, casting C9AE-H
1969–1970	429	BOSS 429, casting C9AE-A, C9AE-B
1968–1970	429	casting C8VE-F, C8VY-A, C9VY-A, DOSZ-A, DOSZ-D
1971–1972	429	D1VZ-6010-A, casting D1VZ, D1VE, D1ZE-AZ
1970	429	CJ/SCJ, C9AZ-6010-B, casting DOOE-B
1970–1971	429	CJ/SCJ, D10Z-6010-A, casting DOOE-B
1971–1972	429	Police, D10Z-6010-A, casting DOOE-B
1968–1970	460	casting C8VE-F,C8VY-A, C9VY-A, DOSZ-A, DOSZ-D
1973	460 Police	D10Z-6010-A, casting DOOE-B
Cylinder Heads		
1968–1971	429/460	DOVZ-6049-D, casting C8SZ-B, C8VE-E, DOVE-C
1969–1970	429	BOSS 429 DOAZ-6049-C, casting C9AE-A
1970–1971	429	CJ/SCJ, DOOZ-6049-H, casting C9VE-A, DOAE-H
1970–1971	429	Police, DOOZ-6049-H, casting C9VE-A, DOAE-H

Casting number, D3VE-A2A, and date code, 3F16, are located on the top part of this 460 cylinder head.

Year	Engine	Part or Casting Number
1972–1974	429/460	D2VZ-6049-B, casting D2VE-AA, D3VE-AA, D3VE-A2A
1973–1974	460	D3VZ-6049-A, casting D3VE-AA, D3VE-A2A
1972–1974	429/460	Police D20Z-6049-A, casting D34E
1974	460	Police D3AZ-6049-F, casting D34E
1975	460	Police D4VZ-6049-C, casting D4VE
Intake Manifolds		
1969–1970	429 4V Boss	C9AZ-9424-D, aluminum
1969–1970	429 4V	D0VY-9424-A
1969–1970	429 2V	D0AZ-9424-A
1970–1971	429 4V CJ	D1AZ-9424-B, Quadrajet
1970–1971	429 4V SCJ	D00Z-9424-B, Holley
1971–1972	429 4V PI	D1AZ-9424-B
1971	429 2V	D1AZ-9424-E
1972	429 4V	D2VY-9424-A
1973	429 4V	D3VY-9424-A
1968–1971	460 4V	D1VY-9424-A
1972	460 4V	D2VY-9424-A
1973	460 4V	D3VY-9424-A
1974	460 4V	D4VY-9424-B, w/ A.I.R.
1974	460 4V	D4VY-9424-C, w/o A.I.R
1975	460 4V	D5VY-9424-A
1975	460 4V	D4VY-9424-C, w/o A.I.R
Exhaust Manifolds		
1969–1970	Boss 429	C9AE-9430-A right casting, C9AE-9431-A left casting
1969–1972	429	D3VY-9430-B right, D4VY-9431-A left
1971	429 CJ/SCJ/PI	D1ZZ-9430-C right, D1ZZ-9431-C, left
1972	429	D3VY-9430-B right, D4VY-9431-A left

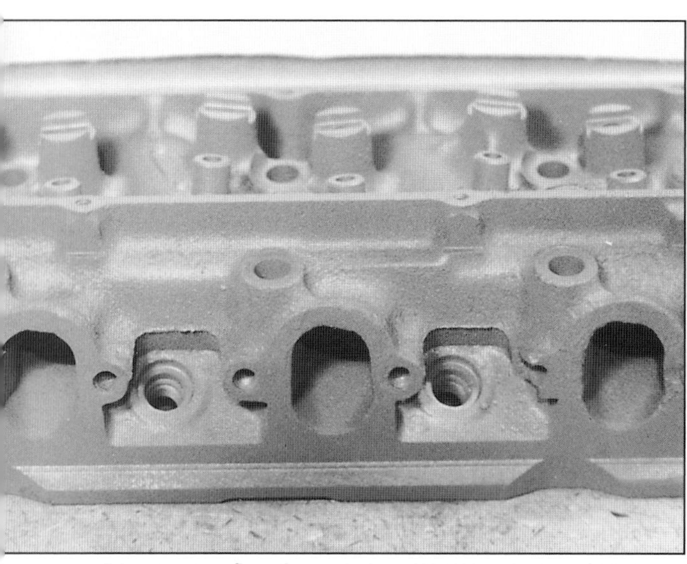

Exhaust port configuration on the base 429/460 engine looks fairly decent. The port floor gets higher as it gets closer to the valve, however, with the overall effect being to reduce the port's effectiveness.

Year	Engine	Part or Casting Number
1972	429 PI	D20Z-9430-C right, D20Z-9431-A left
1973	429	D3VY-9430-A right, D4VY-9431-A left
1969–1972	460	D3VY-9430-B right, D4VY-9431-A left
1973	460	D3VY-9430-A right, D4VY-9431-A left, before 03/15/73
1973	460	D3VY-9430-B right, D4VY-9431-A left, after 03/15/73
1973	460 PI	D30Z-9430-B right, D20Z-9431-A left
1973	460	D3TZ-9430-B right, D4VY-9431-A left, trucks
1974	460	D3VY-9430-B right, D4VY-9431-A left
1974	460	D3TZ-9430-B right, D4VY-9431-A left, trucks
1975	460	D5VY-9430-A right, D5VY-9431-A left
1975	460	D3TZ-9430-B right, D4VY-9431-A left, trucks, early
1975	460	D5TZ-9430-C right, D5TZ-9431-A, left, trucks, from s/n W00001

VIN Identification Codes

Code	Year	Engine
A	1968–1971	460 365 hp
A	1972–1975	460 200–212 hp
C	1971–1971	429 370 hp
C	1973–1975	460 275 hp
J	1970–1971	429 SCJ 375 hp
K	1971–1971	429 320 hp
K	1972	429 212 hp
N	1968–1971	429 360 hp
N	1972–1973	429 197-208 hp
P	1971	429 PI 360 hp
P	1972	429 PI 212 hp
Z	1969–1970	429 Boss 375 hp

Engine-Tag Identification Codes

Code	Engine	VIN Code
809	429 2V	K
810	429 2V	K
811–814	429 4V	N
815	429 2V	N
816	429 2V	K, N
817–819	429 4V	N
820-S	429 Boss 4V	Z
820-T	429 Boss 4V	Z
821, 822	429 4V	N
824, 826	429CJ 4V	C
828	429 4V	Z
829–831	429 SCJ 4V	C
832	429 CJ/SCJ 4V	C
832	429 PI 4V	P
833, 834	429 CJ 4V	C
835–838	429CJ/SCJ 4V	J
877	460 4V	A

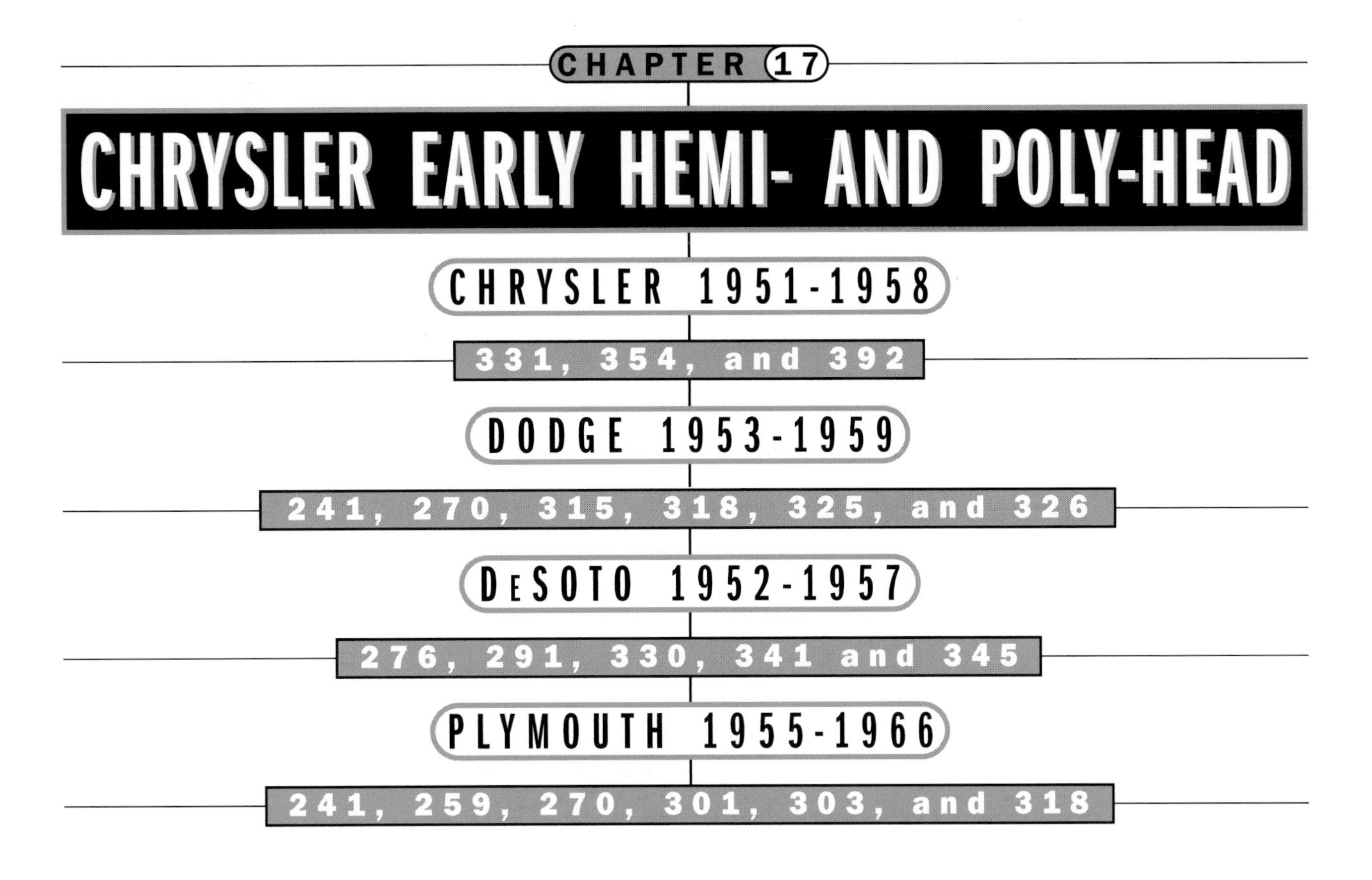

Chrysler's first V-8 engine was the Fire Power V-8, introduced in 1951. The first Fire Power V-8 had a bore and stroke of 3.8125x3.625 in. for a displacement of 331.1 cid. The engine's claim to fame was its hemispherical (hemi) combustion chambers. Chrysler had done quite a bit of research into cylinder head design and the conclusion was that the hemi-head design consistently got the most heat energy from the fuel used than from any other type of cylinder head design. In other words, it was much more efficient. Complementing the hemi combustion chamber design were large, free-flowing intake and exhaust ports and larger intake and exhaust valves with plenty of room around them for cooling. In addition, the valves were arranged opposite each other in a cross-flow arrangement—again increasing the engine's efficiency.

At the time, when fuel octane was considerably lower than it is today, and lower than it was in the 1960s, an engine's compression ratio was an important consideration. The higher the compression ratio, the higher the efficiency and power output of a given engine. Chrysler found out that the hemi-head design would accept a fuel octane rating that was lower than originally thought. This meant that as fuel octane got better during the 1950s, the Fire Power's output could increase at a greater rate than for engines using other cylinder head designs. The original Fire Power had only a 7.5:1 compression ratio for an output of 180 hp at 4,000 rpm with 312ft-lb torque at 2,000 rpm. As gasoline quality improved, the Fire Power V-8—through relatively small cubic displacement increases; normal carburetor, camshaft, and exhaust system modifications; and higher compression ratios—was able to reach close to a 400 hp power output by 1958.

Practically every four-cylinder engine, and most of the sixes, today are all a hemi-head design—or a variation thereof. The Chrysler hemi V-8 was indeed ahead of its time.

Chrysler followed up with the same hemi V-8 engines on its DeSoto division in 1952 and at Dodge in 1953. Chrysler used a lot of different names to describe these engines, but they all used the same basic block and cylinder head design. The major differences were in the bore and stroke dimensions.

The next development of the hemi-based engines occurred in 1955. A smaller, 301 cid version of the Chrysler hemi engine was released. It had a bore and stroke of 3.625x3.625 in. It also didn't have the hemi heads. It had what Chrysler called the Spitfire polyspherical cylinder heads. The combustion chamber wasn't a true hemi, but the valves were canted, and they were still located in a cross-flow arrangement. Rather than being directly opposite as in the hemi, the valves were diagonally opposed in the poly head. In many ways this cylinder head design resembled the well-known big-block Chevrolet engine introduced in 1965. These heads were also less expensive to manufacture than the full hemi heads and they also used one rocker shaft per head. Interestingly, Chrysler's 1999 Jeep V-8 engine has a similar combustion chamber design.

But by 1958, Chrysler stopped production of the Fire Power and all the other hemi-head engines it produced. The hemi was a complex design, so it was expensive to produce. Everyone else was building cheaper wedge-head engines and increasing displacement if more power was needed. The hemi was a very heavy engine as well. The 331 cid V-8, for example, weighed almost 800 pounds as installed in the typical Chrysler vehicle. That's a lot of weight. Still, even though Chrysler retired the hemi in 1958, it brought it back again in 1966, albeit in a very limited fashion.

Chrysler, 1951–1958: 331, 354, and 392

As mentioned previously, the original Chrysler hemi V-8 was the 331.1 cid Fire Power, introduced in 1951. It had a 3.81 in. bore and 3.63 in. stroke. Like all early hemi engines, the 331 came with a forged-steel crankshaft, forged connecting rods, and cast-aluminum pistons (except for the Chrysler 300 Letter car series engines). The 331.1 was also equipped with a hydraulic-lifter camshaft, a cast-iron two-barrel intake manifold and carburetor, and a 7.5:1 compression ratio, for an output of 180 hp at 4,000 rpm with 312ft-lb torque at 2,000 rpm.

The engine was carried over for 1952 and 1953, but in 1954 the two-barrel version was uprated to 195 hp, while a new four-barrel version was released for 235 hp. This, by the way, was the most powerful engine in an American production car for 1954.

There was a major change in the hemi's engine block in 1954. Earlier blocks had an extended bellhousing mounting area, but 1954 and later blocks had a conventional bellhousing mounting area.

In 1955, the 331's compression ratio was upped to 8.5:1, and with a four-barrel carburetor, power was up to 250 hp. More significant was the 331 cid engine powering the new Chrysler C300. Again, grabbing honors for the most powerful engine, the C300's 331 cid hemi, with its distinctive gold-painted valve covers and triangular air cleaner, put out 300 hp at 5,200 rpm and 345ft-lb torque at 3,200 rpm. The engine had a solid-lifter camshaft, two four-barrel carburetors, and forged aluminum pistons replacing the stock cast-aluminum ones.

Overshadowed by the C300's high output 331 V-8 was the release of the 301 cid head Spitfire 188 hp V-8 in 1953. This was the first Chrysler engine to have the polyspherical cylinder heads.

The Fire Power hemi was bored to 3.9375 in., and it displaced 354 cid in 1956. Compression ratio on the regular four-barrel version was 9.0:1 for 280 hp, while the high-performance 354 cid hemi with the dual four-barrel carburetors that powered the Chrysler 300B was up to 340 hp. The 301 cid Spitfire was replaced in 1956 with two 331 cid versions. The two-barrel version was rated at 225 hp, and the four-barrel version was 250 hp.

In 1957, the 354 cid engine became a Spitfire, while the regular hemi was bored and stroked to 4.00x3.906 in. for a 392 cid displacement. With a 9.25:1 compression ratio, the regular 392 cid Fire Power hemi was rated at 325 hp, while the 300C's version was up to 375 hp.

In its last year of production, 1958, the 392 cid hemi was pumping out 380 hp on the Chrysler 300D with the dual four-barrel carburetors and 390 hp with a dual throttle body EFI. Few of the 16 Chrysler 300Ds with the FI engine survived because the Bendix system proved to be unreliable. Most of these engines were later converted to the more reliable dual four-barrel setup.

The 354 cid poly head engines were also up in horsepower, to 290 and 310 hp, but it was their last year, too.

Dodge, 1953–1959: 241, 270, 315, 318, 325, and 326

Dodge's first V-8 engine, based on the 1951 Chrysler engine block, had the hemi cylinder heads. It was released in 1953. With a bore and stroke of 3.4375x3.25 in., it was the smallest hemi, with only a 241.3 cid. With a 7.1:1 compression ratio, the 1951 Red Ram engine was rated at 140 hp as installed in the Dodge Coronet. As with other hemi engines, the Red Ram had a forged-steel crankshaft, forged rods, cast-aluminum pistons, a hydraulic-lifter camshaft, and a two-barrel carburetor mounted on a cast-iron intake manifold.

Two versions of the 241 cid Red Ram engine were available in 1954. The engine installed in the Dodge Meadowbrook was rated 140 hp, as before. Engines installed in the Dodge Coronet and Royal had a 7.5:1 compression ratio, for 150 hp.

In 1955, the Super Red Ram, as it was now called, had its bore increased to 3.6250 in., for 270 cid. It was available in 183 and 193 hp versions. Also added was a 270 cid polyspherical head version, now called the Red Ram, rated at 175 hp.

Once again, the Dodge hemi engine got a displacement increase in 1956. This time, the 3.6250 in. bore remained the same, but the stroke was increased to 3.812 in., for 315 cid. With a 9.25:1 compression ratio, a solid-lifter camshaft, and a four-barrel carbure-

The 1955 331 cid Chrysler Fire Power in the new C-300 Chrysler was rated at 300hp, with two four-barrel carburetors. This was the most powerful engine in 1955 in the United States.

The 1956 DeSoto Adventurer was equipped with a 341 cid hemi. With its single four-barrel carburetor it was rated at 320hp.

tor, the D500 engine put out 260 hp, and 295 hp with two four barrels. Poly head versions, called Red Ram and Super Red Ram, were also available.

The bore and stroke were juggled again in 1957. With a bore of 3.6875 in. and a stroke of 3.797 in., the engine now displaced 325 cid. The Red Ram and Super Red Ram engines were poly-head versions; the D500 hemi was rated at 285 hp and 310 hp with the Power Pak, which included dual four-barrel carburetors.

The 325 cid (326 cid in 1959) Red Ram was available until 1959. It was a poly-head version rated at 252- and 255 hp.

The 241 cid poly-head V-8 engine was also used on Dodge light trucks, beginning in August of 1954. With a 7.5:1 compression ratio, it was rated at 145 hp. The 259 cid poly-head engine replaced it in 1955. It was rated at 169 hp and was also optional on 1956 Dodge light trucks.

The 315 cid poly-head engine was used in Dodge light trucks in 1957–1958. With an 8.5:1 compression ratio, it was rated at 204 hp.

Hemi-head V-8s were used only on medium and heavy-duty trucks.

DeSoto, 1952–1957: 276, 291, 330, 341, and 345

DeSoto got its hemi-head engine in 1952. The Fire Dome hemi had a 3.625x3.344 in. bore and stroke, for a 276.1 cid. As with other Chrysler hemi engines, the Fire Dome had a forged-steel crankshaft, forged rods, cast-aluminum pistons, a hydraulic-lifter camshaft, and a two-barrel carburetor mounted on a cast-iron intake manifold. It was rated at 160 hp with a 7.1:1 compression ratio.

The engine was carried over into 1953, and the 1954 version, with its slightly higher compression ratio of 7.5:1, was rated at 170 hp.

The 1955 version, now called the Firedome (one word) had a larger bore of 3.72 in., with the same stroke as before, for 291 cid. A four-barrel version was added, rated at 200 hp, while the two-barrel was 185 hp. The engine was called the Fireflite V-8 on DeSoto Fireflite models.

In 1956, the Firedome and Fireflite hemi engines got more stroke, 3.80 in., for 330 cid. Compression ratio was up to 8.5:1 and so was power, to 230 hp for the two-barrel engine and to 255 hp for the four-barrel. The DeSoto Adventurer got the same engine, but with a larger bore, 3.7812 in., for 341 cid. The compression ratio was raised to 9.25:1, and the engine was rated at 320 hp.

In 1957, the 330 cid hemi was dropped and replaced with the 341 cid version. The Firedome was rated at 270 hp with the two-barrel carburetor, while the four-barrel version, the Fireflite, was rated at 295 hp. Both engines had 9.25:1 compression ratio.

New for 1957 was the addition of the Firesweep poly-head V-8s. The Firesweep had a bore and stroke of 3.6875x 3.800 in. for 325 cid. The two-barrel version was rated at 245 hp, while the four-barrel was rated at 260 hp.

Plymouth, 1955–1966: 241, 259, 270, 301, 303, and 318

Lowly Plymouth never did get a hemi of its own in the 1950s. The division would have to wait until the 1960s, for the mighty 426 cid hemi V-8.

The closest the division got were poly-head V-8 engines introduced in 1955. The base engine was the 241.1 cid Hy-Fire V-8. This engine had the same dimensions as Dodge's 241 cid hemi but used the polyspherical heads instead. It was rated at 157 hp. With a bore and stroke of 3.5625x3.250 in., the next Hy-Fire engine displaced 259 cid. The two-barrel version was rated at 167 hp, while the four-barrel and dual-exhaust version (Power Pak) was good for another 10 hp. Both had a 7.6:1 compression ratio.

Nineteen fifty-six saw the introduction of another poly-head engine to replace the 259 cid version. The 270 cid V-8 had a bore

The last year for the Chrysler Fire Power hemi was 1958. This is the 380hp 392 cid engine was fitted in the 1958 Chrysler 300D. Two four-barrel carburetors, solid lifter camshaft, and 2-1/2 exhaust system were responsible.

and stroke of 3.6250x3.25 in., a two-barrel carburetor, and an 8.0:1 compression ratio, for 180 hp. The 270 cid engine was first used in 1955 in a Dodge.

Plymouth got a polyspherical cylinder head engine series of its own in 1956. The engine series was known as the "A" engine series, and it consisted of engines in four cubic displacements: 277-, 301-, 303-, and 318 cid. The engine was strictly conventional—two-bolt main-bearing caps and cast-iron block, heads, and manifolds. All engines, though, used a solid-lifter camshaft and had an adjustable valve train.

The first version of the engine was the 277 cid Hy-Fire, with a bore and stroke of 3.75x3.12 in. It was available only for two years, 1956–1957, in two-barrel form, for 187 hp. With the Power Pak, which meant dual exhausts and a four-barrel carburetor, output was up to 197 hp.

Plymouth's hot car in 1956 was the Fury. It was equipped with a 303 cid version of the engine, for 240 hp. During the model year, the company offered a dealer-installed dual four-barrel intake setup, which brought power up to 270 hp. The same setup was also made available on the 277 cid engine, for 230 hp.

In 1957, the block was bored to 3.91 in., for 301 cid, and it was called the "Fury 301." That displacement lasted only through 1957. The engine was rated at 215 hp with a two-barrel carburetor and 235 hp with the Power Pak. In this form, the engine was known as the Fury 301 Quad.

Also joining the lineup in 1957 was the Fury V-800 engine, a stroked version of the 301, displacing 318 cid. This was the most powerful A engine. With a dual four-barrel intake setup, the engine put out a healthy 290 hp on the special Fury model. The engine, without the dual four-barrel carburetors, was also available on the regular Plymouth models in 1958. With a two-barrel carb, it was rated at 225 hp.

The 290 hp 318 cid engine was available for only one more model year, 1958. The two-barrel 318 cid V-8 derivative continued on until 1966. A four-barrel version, rated at 260 hp, was available during 1960–1961.

Dodge also used the engine from 1960 to 1966. The engines paralleled those offered by Plymouth.

The 318 cid engine proved to be a capable truck engine as well. It was used on Dodge light trucks from 1959 through 1966. The engine was rated at 205 hp with an 8.25:1 compression ratio

This is a typical early hemi intake manifold, in this case a 1956 354 cid unit. Casting number, 155473-1, is located on the left front runner. Besides compensating for different deck heights, other hemi intake manifolds had different generator mounting bosses (arrow). 1954 and earlier manifolds had the thermostat mounted in the intake manifold; later intakes did not.

in 1959 and 200 hp from 1960 to 1966 with the same compression ratio. A heavy-duty version of the 318 cid V-8 was also used—this one was rated between 200 and 202 hp.

Engine Blocks

All Chrysler hemi and poly-head engines were cast in iron. This was before there were thin-wall casting techniques, so these blocks were heavy. They were all of a two-bolt-main design. There were two block designs: Chrysler blocks cast prior to 1954 had an extended integral rear flange at the top where the bellhousing would normally be attached to. The 1954 and later blocks are conventional and do not have the extended bellhousing section. Dodge and DeSoto blocks did not have the bellhousing extension.

Although all the early Chrysler hemi engines look generally the same, there are differences between each engine family group. The three groups were Chrysler, Dodge, and DeSoto.

Within the Chrysler family, the engines can be divided into low and high blocks. Most engines in this family were low-block engines, including the poly-head engines. The only high-block engines were the 1957–1958 392 cid engines. They have a 0.75 in.-taller deck height.

The high-block engines in the Dodge family were the 315- and 325 cid engines, whether they have hemi or poly heads. All the others were low-blocks.

With DeSoto, the low-blocks were the 276- and 291 cid displacement engines; the high-blocks were the 330-, 341-, and 345 cid engines.

Not all parts can interchange between each group and within each group. The major components that can interchange between the engine families are as follows:

- 1951–1953 Chrysler front covers will fit all DeSoto engines.
- 1956–1958 Chrysler front covers will fit all Dodge engines.
- Dodge high-block and DeSoto high-block connecting rods will interchange between them.

Major components that can interchange within each group are:

- Low- and high-block cylinder heads can interchange within an engine family. Hemi heads will fit poly-head engine blocks within the same family.
- Chrysler 392 hemi heads are wider than earlier Chrysler heads. A special spacer plate must be used if earlier intake manifolds and early heads are used on the 392 block.
- Camshafts will not interchange between low- and high-block engines in any engine family because of different valve-lifter bore angles.

Cylinder Heads

All hemi-head engines had the same type of combustion chamber, as did all polyspherical heads. The differences are in the valve sizes and the type of valvetrain components used.

Intake Manifolds

All hemi- and poly-head engines were equipped with cast-iron intake manifolds with either two-barrel, four-barrel, or dual four-barrel carburetor mounts. The manifolds were of a "low-rise" design. All were similar, except the manifolds for the 392 cid hemi. Because the 392 block was taller, other intake manifolds from other hemi engines will not fit the 392, unless a specially fabricated spacer block is used.

Exhaust Manifolds

All engines were equipped with cast-iron exhaust manifolds. There were various designs with differing outlet sizes and other differences, depending on engine size and application.

Engine Identification

All major Chrysler engine components were cast with a number to identify the part and a date code that indicated the date the part was cast. These numbers can be found in various locations. While the casting number is a series of numbers, the date code was expressed in various ways. A typical early hemi date code was 12-17-56, which decodes to December 17, 1956.

Completed engines were also stamped with additional numbers giving more information. Each engine was stamped with a series of numbers and letters that indicated what the engine was and an engine serial number indicating its place in the sequence. This sequence number usually began with 1001. Thus, for example, a 1956 Chrysler 300B 354 cid engine might have the following code: 3NE56-1015. This indicated that this was the fifteenth engine assembled for use in a 1956 Chrysler 300B. Most of these codes have the model year incorporated in them (the "56" in the example).

Unfortunately, Chrysler did not stamp the vehicle's VIN or any portion of it on the engine itself, so it is not possible to match an engine to a particular vehicle.

Chrysler Engine Specifications

	Displacement	Carburetor	Horsepower	Torque	Compression Ratio	Notes
1951–1953						
	331.1	2V	180@4,000	312@2,000	7.50	New York, Imperial, Saratoga
1954						
	331.1	2V	195@4,400	320@2,000	7.50	New Yorker
	331. 1	4V	235@4,400	330@2,600	7.50	Imperial
1955						
	301 (P)	2V	188@4,400	275@2,400	8.0	Windsor
	331.1	2V	250@4,600	340@2,800	8.50	New Yorker, Imperial
	331.1	2x4V	300@5,200	345@3,200	8.50	C300
1956						
	301 (P)	2V	225@4,400	310@2,400	8.0	Windsor
	331.1 (P)	4V	250@4,600	340@2,800	9.0	Windsor, Saratoga
	354	4V	280@4,600	380@2,800	9.0	New Yorker, Imperial
	354	2x4V	340@5,200	345@3,200	9.0	300B
	354	2x4V	355@5,400	405@3,400	10.0	300B
1957						
	354 (P)	2V	285@4,600	365@2,400	9.25	Windsor
	354 (P)	4V	295@4,600	390@2,800	9.25	Windsor, Saratoga
	392	4V	325@4,600	430@2,800	9.25	New Yorker, Imperial
	392	2x4V	375@5,200	420@4,000	9.25	300C
	392	2x4V	390@5,400	430@4,200	10.0	300C
1958						
	354 (P)	2V	290@4,600	385@2,000	10.0	Windsor
	354 (P)	4V	310@4,600	405@3,200	10.0	Saratoga
	392	4V	345@4,600	450@2,800	10.0	New Yorker, Imperial
	392	2x4V	380@5,200	435@3,600	10.0	300D
	392	2x4V	390@5,200	435@4,200	10.0	300D

(P) Polyspherical combustion chambers

Chrysler Engine Internal Dimensions

Displacement	Bore and Stroke	Rod Bearings	Main Bearings	Intake/Exhaust Valves
301	3.6250x3.625	2.249-2.250	2.499-2.500	1.81/1.50
331.1	3.8125x3.625	2.249-2.250	2.499-2.500	1.81/1.50
354	3.9375x3.625	2.249-2.250	2.499-2.500	1.94/1.75
392	4.000x3.906	2.374-2.375	2.687-2.688	2.00/1.75

Chrysler Block, Head, and Manifold Part and Casting Numbers

Year	Engine	Part or Casting Number
Engine Blocks		
1951–1954	301/331.1	1536302, 1330127, casting 1323329, 1330129
1955	301/331.1	1613127, casting 1618628, 1619629
1955	354	1556847, 1637798 (C300)
1956	331.1	1634849
1956	354	1619276
1956	354	1674732, 300B
1957	354	casting 1619829 (m/t), 1619829-2 (a/t)
1957	392	casting 1673729
1958	354	casting 1619829, 1819629
1958	392	casting 1673729-6
Cylinder Heads		
1951–1952	331.1	1323333, casting 1323337
1954–1955	331.1/354	1486832, casting 1486833
1955	301/331	1555767
1955	354	1556156
1956	331	1671143, poly
1956	354	casting 1619823, 1677441
1957–1958	354	1737805, casting 1733843, 1733463
1957–1958	392	1737809, casting 1731528, 1730438, 1731523, 1731528
1957–1958	392	casting 1735282, 300D

Year	Engine	Part or Casting Number
Intake Manifolds		
1951–1954	331.1 2V	1326812
1954	331.1 4V	1534501
1955	301 2V	1555473
1955–1956	354 2x4V	1634285, w/o a/c
1956	354 2x4V	1741686, w/ a/c
1956	301/331.1	1610472 w/o a/c, 1637709 w/ a/c
1957–1958	354 2V	1854818
1957–1958	354 4V	1945330
1957–1958	392 dual- 4V	1733477
1958	392 FI	1826105
Exhaust Manifolds		
1951–1953	331.1	1323315 right, 1323314 left
1951–1953	331.1	1535932 right, 1487817 left, with head casting 1486833
1954–1955	331.1	1535932 right, 1487817 left
1955	301	1558329 right, 1558397 left
1955–1956	331.1/354 2x4V	1536377 right and left
1956	302/331.1	1638343 right, 1638345 left
1956	354	1638346 right, 1638348 left
1957–1958	354	1730131 right, 1676372 left
1957–1958	392	1675932 right, 1674661 left
1957–1958	392 2x4V	1536377 right and left

Chrysler Engine Identification Codes

Code	Model	Engine
1951		
C51-8-1001	Chrysler	331 cid 180 hp
1952		
C52-8-1001	Chrysler	331 cid 180 hp
1953		
C53-8-1001	Chrysler	331 cid 180 hp
1954		
C541-8-1001	Chrysler	331 cid 195 hp
C542-8-1001	Chrysler	331 cid 235 hp
1955		
WE55-1001	Chrysler	301 cid 188 hp (poly)
NE55-1001	Chrysler	331 cid 250 hp
3NE55-1001	Chrysler 300	331 cid 300 hp
CE55-1001	Imperial	331 cid 250 hp
CE56-1001	Imperial	354 cid 280 hp
1956		
WE56-1001	Chrysler	331 cid 188/225/250 hp (poly)
NE56-1001	Chrysler	354 cid 280 hp
3NE56-1001	Chrysler 300	354 cid 340/355 hp
CE56-1001	Imperial	354 cid 280 hp
1957		
LE57-1001	Chrysler	354 cid 295 hp (poly)
WE57-1001	Chrysler	354 cid 280/285/295 hp (poly)
NE57-1001	Chrysler	392 cid 325/375 hp
3NE57-1001	Chrysler 300	392 cid 375 hp
CE57-1001	Imperial	392 cid 325 hp
1958		
58W-1001	Chrysler	354 cid 290 hp (poly)
58S-1001	Chrysler	354 cid 310 hp (poly)
58N-1001	Chrysler	392 cid 345 hp
58N3-1001	Chrysler 300	392 cid 380 hp w/ 2x4V, 390 hp w/FI
58C-1001	Imperial	392 cid 345 hp

DeSoto Engine Specifications

	Displacement	Carburetor	Horsepower	Torque	Compression Ratio	Notes
1952						
	276.1	2V	160@4,400	250@2,000	7.00	Firedome
1953						
	276.1	2V	160@4,400	250@2,000	7.00	Firedome
1954						
	276.1	2V	170@4,400	255@2,400	7.50	Firedome
1955						
	291	2V	185@4,400	245@2,800	7.50	Firedome
	291	4V	200@4,400	274@2,800	7.50	Fireflite
1956						
	330	2V	230@4,400	305@2,800	7.50	Firedome
	330	4V	255@4,400	350@3,200	7.50	Fireflite, Pacesetter
	341	2x4V	320@5,200	355@4,000	9.25	Fireflite, Adventurer
1957						
	325 (P)	2V	245@4,400	320@2,400	8.50	Firesweep
	325 (P)	4V	260@4,400	335@2,800	8.50	Firesweep
	341	2V	270@4,600	350@2,400	9.25	Firedome
	341	4V	295@4,600	375@2,800	9.25	Fireflite
	345	2x4V	345@5,200	355@3,600	9.25	Adventurer

(P) Polyspherical combustion chambers

DeSoto Engine Internal Dimensions

Displacement	Bore and Stroke	Rod Bearings	Main Bearings	Intake/Exhaust Valves
276.1	3.625x3.344	2.061–2.062	2.374–2.375	1.84/1.50
291	3.720x3.344	2.061–2.062	2.374–2.375	1.84/1.50
325	3.6875x3.80	2.249–2.250	2.499–2.500	1.87/1.53
330	3.720x3.800	2.249–2.250	2.499–2.500	1.94/1.75
341	3.7812x3.80	2.249–2.250	2.499–2.500	1.94/1.75
345	3.800x3.800	2.249–2.250	2.499–2.500	1.94/1.75

DeSoto Block, Head, and Manifold Part and Casting Numbers

Year	Engine	Part or Casting Number
Engine Blocks		
1952–1954	276.1	1409372, 1615512, casting 1327429
1955	291	1631227, casting 1558929
1956	330	1635786, casting 1636629
1957	315	1630029, 1731429
1957	341	casting 1636629, 1856629
1957	325	casting 1739429
Cylinder Heads		
1952–1953	276.1	1327372
1954	276.1	1327372, 1613606 (eng. no. 52860 and up)
1955	291	1613607, casting 1554132, 1635779
1956	330	1671100, casting 1635779
1957	325	1737816 (poly), casting 1628129, 1632099
Intake Manifolds		
1952	276.1 2V	1409376, 1327411 (to eng. no. 17102)
1953–1954	276.1 2V	1409376
1955	291 2V	1616833 w/o a/c, 1617178 w/ a/c
1955	291 4V	1618926
1956	330 2V	1671029
1956	330 4V	1671030
1956	341 2x4V	1731560
1957	325 2V	1738354
1957	325 4V	1735774
1957	341 2V	1730413
1957	341 4V	1730414
1957	345 2x4V	182139
Exhaust Manifolds		
1952–1955	276.1	1407719 right, 1328064 left
1956	330	1637389 right, 1637391 left
1957	325	1671128 right, 1634445 left, w/ a/c
1957	325	1737791 right, 1634445 left, w/o a/c

DeSoto Engine Identification Codes

Code	Model	Engine
1953		
S16-1001	Firedome	276 cid 160 hp
1952		
S17-1001	Firedome	276 cid 160 hp
1954		
S19-1001	Firedome	276 cid 170 hp
1955		
S21-1001	Fireflite	291 cid 200 hp
S22-1001	Fireflite	291 cid 185 hp
1956		
S23-1001	Firedome	330 cid 230 hp
S24-1001	Fireflite	330 cid 255 hp
S24A-1001	Adventurer	341 cid 320 hp
1957		
S27-1001	Firesweep	325 cid 245/260 hp
S25-1001	Firedome	341 cid 270 hp
S26-1001	Fireflite	341 cid 295 hp
S26A-1001	Adventurer	345 cid 345 hp

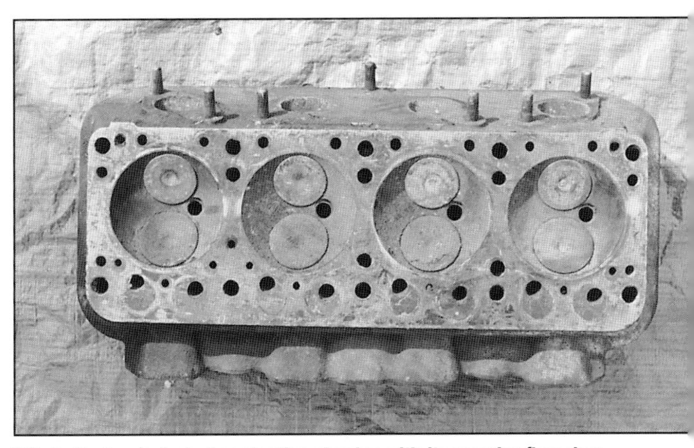

This is the hemispherical combustion chamber with its superior flow characteristics used on all early hemi engines. This is from a 330 cid engine, #1635779.

Dodge Engine Specifications

	Displacement	Carburetor	Horsepower	Torque	Compression Ratio	Notes
1953						
	241.3	2V	140@4,400	220@2,000	7.1	Coronet
1954						
	241.3	2V	140@4,400	222@2,000	7.5	Meadowbrook, m/t
	241.3	2V	150@4,400	222@2,000	7.5	Coronet, Royal, Sierra, a/t
1955						
	270 (P)	2V	175@4,400	240@2,400	7.6	Coronet, Royal
	270	2V	183@4,400	245@2,400	7.6	Custom Royal, Royal Lancer
	270	4V	193@4,400	245@2,400	7.6	Royal Lancer
1956						
	270 (P)	2V	189@4,400	266@2,400	8.0	Coronet
	315 (P)	2V	218@4,400	309@2,000	8.0	Royal, Custom Royal
	315 (P)	4V	230@4,400	316@2,400	8.0	Royal, Custom Royal
	315 (P)	4V	260@4,800	330@3,000	9.25	Dodge 500
	315	2x4V	295@4,800	335@3,000	9.25	Dodge 500
1957						
	325 (P)	2V	245@4,400	320@2,400	8.5	Coronet, Royal, Suburban, Sierra
	325 (P)	4V	260@4,800	335@3,800	8.5	Coronet, Royal, Suburban, Sierra
	325 (P)	4V	285@4,800	345@2,800	9.25	Coronet, Royal, Suburban, Sierra (D-500)
	325	2x4V	310@4,800	350@3,200	9.25	Coronet, Royal, Suburban, Sierra (D-500)
1958						
	325 (P)	2V	252@4,400	345@2,400	9.0	Coronet, Royal, Suburban, Sierra
	325 (P)	4V	265@4,400	355@3,800	10.0	Coronet, Royal
1959						
	326 (P)	2V	255@4,400	350@2,400	9.2	Coronet
1960						
	318 (P)	2V	230@4,400	340@2,800	9.0	Dart Seneca, Pioneer
	318 (P)	4V	255@4,400	345@2,800	9.0	Dart Phoenix
1961						
	318 (P)	2V	230@4,400	340@2,800	9.0	Dart
	318 (P)	4V	260@4,400	345@2,800	9.0	Dart
1962						
	318 (P)	2V	230@4,400	340@2,800	9.0	Dart
	318 (P)	4V	260@4,400	345@2,800	9.0	Dart
1963						
	318 (P)	2V	230@4,400	340@2,800	9.0	Polara
1964						
	318 (P)	2V	230@4,400	340@2,800	9.0	Dodge 330, 440, Polara
1965						
	318 (P)	2V	230@4,400	340@2,800	9.0	Coronet
1966						
	318 (P)	2V	230@4,400	340@2,800	9.0	Coronet, Charger, Polara

(P) Polyspherical combustion chambers

Dodge Engine Internal Dimensions

Displacement	Bore and Stroke	Rod Bearings	Main Bearings	Intake/Exhaust Valves
241.3	3.4375x3.250	2.061–2.062	2.374–2.375	1.75/1.41
270	3.6250x3.250	1.936–1.937	2.374–2.375	1.75/1.41
315	3.6250x3.812	2.249–2.250	2.499–2.500	1.87/153
318	3.9062x3.312	2.124–2.125	2.499–2.500	1.84/1.56
325	3.6875x3.797	2.249–2.250	2.499–2.500	1.87/1.53
326	3.9531x3.312	2.124–2.125	2.499–2.500	1.87/153

Dodge Block, Head, and Manifold Part and Casting Numbers

Year	Engine	Part or Casting Number
Engine Blocks		
1953–1954	241.3	1409528 (to eng. no. 173248), 1613745 (after eng. no. 173248), trucks to no. VT334 (1954)
1955	270	1672600 (poly), 1632231
1956	315	1619722 (poly), casting 1730429-5
1957	325	1630029, casting 1739429
1960–1966	318	1739429, 2264230, 2463930, 2532630
Cylinder Heads		
1953–1954	241.3	1617180, casting 1328362, 1327373
1955	270	1552947 (poly), 1632098 (poly), 1554131
1955	270	1554132 (hemi)
1956	315	1730540 casting 1635779, 1734049, 1828129-1
1956	315	1825923 (poly)
1960–1962	318	2402116, casting 2268341
1962–1966	318	2268593, casting 2268341
1957	325	1737816 (poly), casting 1628129, 1632099
1957	325	casting 1828129 (hemi)
Intake Manifolds		
1953–1954	241 2V	1409375
1955	270 2V	1615886
1955	270 4V	1639769
1956	315 2V	1639768
1956	315 4V	1639769
1956	315 2x4V	1731515
1957	325 2V	1738354
1957	325 4V	1735774
1959–1966	318 2V	2448757
1960–1962	318 4V	1859298, casting 1859229
Exhaust Manifolds		
1953–1954	241	1532891 right, 1532893 left
1955	270	1532891 right, 1558433 left
1955	270	1617786 right, 1553784 left, w/ p/s, poly
1955	270	1553782 right, 1553784 left, w/o p/s, poly
1956	270/315 2V	1638340 right, 1638342 left, w/o p/s
1956	315 4V	1638340 right, 1634445 left, w/o p/s
1956	270/315 2V	1671128 right, 1638342 left, w/ p/s
1956	315 4V	1671128 right, 1634445 left, w/ p/s
1957	325	1671128 right, 1634445 left, w/ a/c
1957	325	1737791 right, 1634445 left, w/o a/c
1957	325 2x4V	1532891 right, 1634446 left
1962	318	2129194 right
1962–1965	318	2268127 left
1960–1966	318	2536787 right, 2532414 left
1966	318	2536787 right, 2532525 left, intermediates

Dodge Engine Identification Codes

Code	Model	Engine
1953		
D44-1001	Dodge	241 cid 140 hp
D48-1001	Dodge	241 cid 140 hp
1954		
D50-1001	Dodge	241 cid 140 hp
D50A-1001	Dodge	241 cid 140 hp
D501-1001	Dodge	241 cid 140 hp
D502-1001	Dodge	241 cid 150 hp
D503-1001	Dodge	241 cid 150 hp
1955		
D551-1001	Dodge	270 cid 175 hp
D553-1001	Dodge	270 cid 183/193 hp
1956		
D63-1-1001	Dodge	270 cid 189 hp (poly)
D63-2-1001	Dodge	315 cid (poly)
D63-3-1001	Dodge	315 cid (poly)
D500-1001	Dodge D500	315 cid 260/295 hp
1957		
KDS-1001	Dodge	325 cid 245/260 (poly)
KD500-1001	Dodge D500	325 cid 285/310 hp
1958		
L325-1001	Dodge	325 cid 252/265 hp (poly)

Besides being big and heavy, the hemi heads required two rocker shafts to operate the valves, adding to manufacturing costs. This is one of the reasons why the engines were eventually dropped.

Plymouth Engine Specifications

	Displacement	Carburetor	Horsepower	Torque	Compression Ratio	Notes
1955						
	241.3 (P)	2V	157@4,400	217@2,400	7.6	
	259 (P)	2V	167@4,400	231@2,400	7.6	
	259 (P)	4V	177@4,400	231@2,800	7.6	
1956						
	270 (P)	2V	180@4,400	260@2,400	8.0	
	277 (P)	2V	187@4,400	265@2,400	8.0	
	277 (P)	4V	200@4,400	272@2,400	8.0	
	303 (P)	4V	240@4,800	310@2,800	9.25	Fury
1957						
	277 (P)	2V	197@4,400	270@2,400	8.0	
	301 (P)	2V	215@4,400	285@2,800	8.5	
	301 (P)	2V	235@4,400	305@2,800	8.5	
	318 (P)	2x4V	290@5,400	325@4,000	9.25	Fury
1958						
	318 (P)	2V	225@4,400	330@2,800	9.0	
	318 (P)	4V	250@4,400	340@2,800	9.0	
	318 (P)	4V	290@5,400	325@4,000	9.25	
1959						
	318 (P)	2V	230@4,400	340@2,800	9.0	
1960						
	318 (P)	2V	230@4,400	340@2,800	9.0	exc. Valiant
	318 (P)	4V	260@4,400	345@2,800	9.0	exc. Valiant
1961						
	318 (P)	2V	230@4,400	340@2,800	9.0	exc. Valiant
	318 (P)	4V	260@4,400	345@2,800	9.0	exc. Valiant
1962						
	318 (P)	2V	230@4,400	340@2,800	9.0	exc. Valiant
	318 (P)	4V	260@4,400	345@2,800	9.0	exc. Valiant
1963–1964						
	318 (P)	2V	230@4,400	340@2,800	9.0	exc. Valiant and Barracuda
1965						
	318 (P)	2V	230@4,400	340@2,800	9.0	Belvedere, Satellite, Fury
1966						
	318 (P)	2V	230@4,400	340@2,800	9.0	Belvedere, Satellite, Fury

(P) Polyspherical combustion chambers

Plymouth Engine Internal Dimensions

Displacement	Bore and Stroke	Rod Bearings	Main Bearings	Intake/Exhaust Valves
241.3	3.4375x3.250	2.061–2.062	2.374–2.375	1.75/1.41
259	3.5625x3.250	1.936–1.937	2.374–2.375	1.75/1.41
270	3.6250x3.250	1.936–1.937	2.374–2.375	1.75/1.41
277	3.750x3.125	1.936–1.937	2.374–2.375	1.75/1.41
301	3.9062x3.125	2.124–2.125	2.499–2.500	1.87/1.53
303	3.8125x3.312	2.124–2.125	2.499–2.500	1.87/1.53
318	3.9062x3.312	2.124–2.125	2.499–2.500	1.84/1.56

Plymouth Block, Head, and Manifold Part and Casting Numbers

Year	Engine	Part or Casting Number
Engine Blocks		
1955	259	1613970 to eng. no. 60201, 1630392 after no. 60201
1956	277	1618727, 1639609
1956	303	1630954
1957	277	1618729
1957	301	1737929
1957	318	1739429
1958	318	1739429
1960–1966	318	1739429, 2264230, 2463930, 2532630
Cylinder Heads		
1955	241.3/259	1552947
1956	270	1632098
1956	277	1618720
1956	303	1825964, casting 1618721
1957–1958	318	1825964, casting 1618721
1959–1962	318	2402116, casting 2268341
1962–1966	318	2268593, casting 2268341
Intake Manifolds		
1955	241/259 2V	1671780 w/ p/b
1956	270/277 2V	1671780, 1630944
1956	277 4V	1619826
1956	303 4V	1731609
1957	318 2x4V	1732479
1958	318 4V	1851762
1959–1966	318 2V	2448757
1960–1962	318 4V	1859298, casting 1859229
Exhaust Manifolds		
1955	241/259	1617786 right, 1553784 left w/ p/s
1955	241/259	1553782 right, 1553784 left, w/o p/s
1956	277 4V	1638340 right, 1634445 left
1957–1960	318	1634722 right, 1618650 left
1962	318	2129194 right
1962–1965	318	2268127 left
1960–1966	318	2536787 right, 2532414 left
1966	318	2536787 right, 2532525 left, intermediates

Plymouth Engine Identification Codes

Code	Model	Engine
1955		
P27-1001	Plymouth	241 cid 157 hp
P27-60201	Plymouth	259 cid 167/177 hp
1956		
P29-41001	Plymouth	270 cid 180 hp
P29-250001	Plymouth	270 cid 180 hp
P29-80001	Plymouth	277 cid 187 hp
P29-274101	Plymouth	277 cid 187 hp
P29-1618729	Plymouth	277 cid 200 hp
FP P29-1630429	Plymouth	303 cid 240 hp
1957		
LP31-1001	Plymouth	277 cid 197 hp
P31-1001	Plymouth	301 cid 215/235 hp
FP31-1001	Plymouth	303 cid 290 hp
1958		
LP8-1001	Plymouth	318 cid 225/250/290 hp
1959		
MP8-1001	Plymouth	318 cid 230/260 hp

The 1955–58 Spitfire engines used a single rocker shaft. The design was cheaper to manufacture and can easily be identified by the scalloped rocker covers. *Gary Stauffer*

CHAPTER 18

CHRYSLER B- AND RB-SERIES

1958-1977

350, 361, 383, 400, 413, 426, and 440

Chrysler replaced its line of hemi-head V-8 engines with the B engine series, first used by the Dodge, Plymouth, and DeSoto divisions in 1958. Curiously, Chrysler vehicles saw their first B engines in the 1959 model year.

The new engines were quite different from the hemi- and poly-head engines they replaced. There was no parts interchangeability between the two, and the most noticeable difference was the B-series' wedge-style combustion chambers. The new engine block was very similar to Ford's Y-block design, in that the sides of the block casting extended more than 2 in. below the crank centerline. This was supposed to increase the rigidity of the block's structure.

The block's big, 4.80 in. cylinder bore spacing meant that the engine had plenty of room for future growth. The first B engine displaced only 350 cid, yet the B engine's displacement was able to be increased to 440 cid in 1967—and that's with only a 3.75 in. stroke. By comparison, the well-known Chevrolet big-block engine used a 4.00 in. stroke in 1970 to attain 454 cid. Chrysler could have made the B even larger if it had resorted to increasing the stroke to the lengths that GM used.

It was obvious, based on the quality of the parts and components used, that the B and RB engines were meant to be durable and long lasting. The B and RB crankshafts were all forged steel (until 1971), and the forged-steel connecting rods were strong enough for high-performance use. In addition, the engine was designed with cylinder heads that breathed well, and over the years, the engine has had a great variety of high-performance intake manifolds—some of which were highly innovative and never duplicated by any other manufacturer. Even the exhaust manifolds were highly efficient. And of course, the famous 426 Hemi V-8 was based on the RB engine. The 426 Hemi is considered by many to be the strongest and most powerful V-8 engine to come out of the 1960s.

Dodge's first B engine was the 350 cid version, which had a 4.06x3.38 in. bore and stroke. The Super Red Ram V-8, as Dodge called it, was good for 295 hp. Also released at the same time in 1958 was the same engine, but with a 4.12 in. bore for 361 cid. On Dodge vehicles, this was the D-500 and was rated at 305 hp with its dual four-barrel carburetors. Some of the descriptive names Dodge used to describe its B-and RB-series engines over the years included the Super D-500 (1959), Ramcharger, and Magnum.

Plymouth's offerings in 1958 mirrored those of Dodge; Plymouth's engines were called Golden Commando.

DeSoto's B-series engines were named the Turboflash V-8. The series' most powerful engine in 1958 was the Turboflash 361 cid engine with dual four-barrel carburetors for 345 hp. A 355 hp version, with dual-throttle-body Bendix EFI, was offered, but the few that were sold were recalled, and the injection system was replaced with carburetors.

The 350 cid engine was dropped in 1959 by all Chrysler divisions. The 361 cid engine became the starting point for anyone opting for one of the big-block V-8s. Joining the 361 cid V-8 was a new 383 cid version that had a 4.03 in. bore and 3.75 in. stroke. The extra stroke was made possible by raising the deck height of the block, hence the "RB" (Raised Block) designation. The top version of the 383 cid engine had the dual four-barrel inline intake setup. From 1960 on, the 383 cid engine was destroked to an oversquare 4.25 in. bore and 3.38 in. stroke, thereby making it a B-series engine. The 383 cid engine was available through the 1972 model year in various configurations, most often serving as the base big-block passenger car V-8 engine.

The RB-series engines were part of the B-series engine family. By raising the 350- and 361 cid block's deck height by 0.745 in., an engine with a longer stroke and more cubic inches could be built. By using a 3.75 in. stroke on the 4.12 in. bore block, the 413 cid RB engine was created in 1959. Most parts interchange between the B and RB engines, parts that do not include intake manifolds and crankshafts. The RB-series engines had larger, 2.750 in. main-bearing journals, while the B used 2.625 in. mains. Rod journal sizes were identical at 2.380 in.

The 413 cid engine was initially used by the bigger, heavier Chrysler cars and the luxury Imperial. The most powerful 413 cid V-8 in 1959 was the one used on the Chrysler 300E, which had a 380 hp output with a dual four-barrel inline intake setup. Chrysler's name for the 413 cid V-8 was the Golden Lion.

One of the most interesting engines to come out of Detroit was the 413 cid V-8 that powered the 1960 Chrysler 300F. The Long Ram induction system used two sets of 30 in.-long intake tubes, each mounting a Carter AFB four-barrel carburetor. By shortening or lengthening the tubes, Chrysler engineers found that they could tailor the engine's performance characteristics, with the goal of providing more power in the midrange for better passing. A 30 in. tube was found to be optimum for these parameters. This was the standard 300F engine, and it produced 375 hp. It became known as the Long Ram 413. The Long Ram 413s would continue to be available through the 1964 model year.

The Long Ram tubes did have a drawback: They severely limited upper- rpm performance. By cutting the internal length of the tubes to 15 in., it was found that the torque peak was raised to 3,600 rpm, enabling the engine to keep on pulling to 5,200 rpm. Power output was also raised to 400 hp. The engines with the shorter tubes were called Short Ram 413s and were available from 1960 to 1964.

The Long Ram intake setup was also used on Plymouth cars during 1960–1961, but only with the 383 cid engine, called the SonoRamic Commando. Dodge used the engine as well, while in the few DeSoto cars that had it, it was called the Ram Charge.

Nineteen sixty-two saw the 413 cid RB engine get a major boost in the horsepower department with the introduction of the Max Wedge engine. This was a highly modified 413 cid V-8

This is the 375hp 440 cid big-block as installed in the 1969 GTS Dart. Engine barely fits.

designed to do battle with other similarly modified factory engines from Ford and Chevrolet, primarily on the drag strip. The engine was rated at 410–420 hp.

Regular Chrysler passenger cars received the 426 cid RB engine in 1962, with its 4.25 in. bore and 3.75 in. stroke. It was available in various states of tune through the 1965 model year, along with the 413 cid V-8.

The 426 Max Wedge Stage II engine replaced the 413 cid Max Wedge in 1963. Two versions were available, 415 hp and 425 hp. The Plymouth version was known as the Super Stock 426 while the Dodge was the 426 Ramcharger.

The 1964 426 Max Wedge Stage III was the final permutation of the Max Wedge concept. The engine featured many improvements over the previous versions, but it was rated at the same 425 hp.

Hemi cylinder heads returned to Chrysler, at least for track use, in 1964. Several versions of the 426 cid engine were made for different types of racing. However, in order to keep on using the engine on the track, Chrysler was forced to build a limited number of street versions. This was done in 1966, and the 425 hp 426 street Hemi became optionally available on certain Plymouth and Dodge cars. The engine remained in production through the 1971 model year.

Replacing the 426 and 413 cid engines in 1966 was 440 cid RB engine, which had a bore and stroke of 4.32x3.75 in. The 1966 version was not thought of as a high-performance motor, but in 1967 the engine received several modifications in the induction department, and the 440 cid V-8 became Chrysler's most powerful V-8, after the 426 Hemi. It was rated at 375 hp. During the 1969 model year, a specially modified version of the 440 cid engine was introduced, a triple two-barrel version rated at 390 hp. The Six Pack (Dodge) and Six Barrel (Plymouth) 440 were almost as fast on the street as the 426 Hemi, but the 440s cost quite a bit less. The engine lasted through the 1971 model year.

The last variation of the B block series was the 1972 400 cid V-8, which was the replacement for the 383 cid B engine. It had a 4.34 in. bore and a 3.38 in. stroke. The engine wasn't considered a performance engine because of its low compression ratio, emissions controls, and low power output.

350 cid

The first B series was the 350 cid version introduced in 1958, and available only for that year. It had a bore and stroke of 4.06x3.38 in. It set the pattern for the B and RB engines that followed it. The smallest B block, the 350 cid V-8 had two-bolt main-bearing caps, a forged-steel crankshaft, forged-steel connecting rods, a hydraulic-lifter camshaft, and either a two-barrel, four-barrel, or dual four-barrel intake manifold.

Plymouth's Golden Commando was rated at 305 hp at 5,000 rpm with 390ft-lb torque at 3,000 rpm. The engine had two four-barrel carburetors and a 10.0:1 compression ratio. The rare FI version added 10 hp.

The Turboflash 350 cid V-8, as installed in the DeSoto Firesweep, was rated at 280 hp with a two-barrel carburetor and 295 hp with a four-barrel. The compression ratio was 10.0:1.

Dodge's 350 cid V-8 was rated at 295 hp with the four-barrel carburetor and 320 hp with the dual four-barrel carbs. This was the D-500 engine.

361 cid

Also introduced in 1958, the 361 cid version of the B-series engine just had a wider bore of 4.125 in. and shared the 350's

The Short Ram 413 cid engine was a dealer-installed option on the 1962 Chrysler 300H. It was rated at 405hp.

stroke of 3.38 in. Like all Chrysler engines, the 361 cid V-8 had its day in the sun. There were four versions of the engine available in 1958. The base 10.0:1 compression two-barrel engine put out 295 hp. A four-barrel carburetor and intake brought power up to 305 hp. In the DeSoto Adventurer, a dual four-barrel intake manifold and 10.25:1 compression netted 345 hp. A FI version was rated at 355 hp. The D-500 Dodge version was rated at 320 hp.

During 1959–1960, there were only two versions of the engine optionally available, a two-barrel rated at 295 hp and a four-barrel rated at 305 hp. From then on, the engine became the base big-block option in Dodge, Plymouth, and Chrysler cars. With a two-barrel carburetor, 9.1:1 compression ratio, and a single exhaust system, the engine was rated at 295 hp. From 1962 on, it was rated at 265 hp, while the four-barrel remained at 305 hp. In its last year of production, the two remaining 1961 DeSoto models were both powered by the 265 hp two-barrel Turboflash 361 cid V-8.

383 cid

By far the most popular, at least in terms on how many were made, was the 383 cid version of the B-block engine. Early on, it was Chrysler's hot performance engine, and later on, as more emphasis was placed on larger engines, the 383 cid V-8 was downgraded, serving as a workhorse or as an entry-level performance engine. Like the other B-series engines, the 383 cid V-8 used a two-bolt-main engine block, forged-steel connecting rods, and a forged-steel crankshaft. The only deviation from this was in 1971 when Chrysler substituted a cast-iron crankshaft on the 1971 two-barrel 383 cid engines.

The first 383 cid V-8 was introduced in 1959. With a bore and stroke of 4.03 in.x3.75 in., it was an RB engine. The engine was made in several variations for Chrysler, DeSoto, and Dodge. For Chrysler, there were two versions of the 383 cid V-8, 305 hp with a two-barrel carburetor and 325 hp with a four-barrel. Both of these were also available in the DeSoto line. In addition, a 350 hp dual four-barrel version was available on the DeSoto Adventurer. Dodge got a 320 hp four-barrel version under the D-500 package and a dual four-barrel version under the Super D-500 package.

For 1960, the 383 cid V-8 became the hot Chrysler V-8—excluding the special 413 cid engines available on the Chrysler 300F. On Dodge vehicles the Super D-500 383 cid V-8 got the dual four-barrel Long Ram intake setup for 330 hp. The same engine in Plymouth guise was the Golden SonoRamic 383. A regular four-barrel 325 hp version was also available on both lines. DeSoto got along with three versions of the engine—the two-barrel motor was rated at 305 hp, the four-barrel (called the Adventurer Mark I) was rated at 325 hp, and the Long Ram 383 cid V-8 (the Ram Charger) was rated at 330 hp.

Although all of the above engines displaced 383 cid, the 1960 and later versions were based on the Low Block or regular B-series engine block. The 383 cid B-series V-8 had a bore and stroke of 4.25x3.38 in. The Chrysler division also used the Golden Lion, as it was called by Chrysler, 383 cid engine with the same two output ratings as in 1959. However, the 305 hp engine could have either been a B or an RB version of the engine; the 325 hp 383 cid V-8 was a B-series engine.

For 1961, the 330 hp 383 cid engine was carried over on Dodge and Plymouth, the four-barrel 325 hp on Dodge, and the 305 hp two-barrel on Chrysler vehicles. Nineteen sixty-one was the last year for the Long Ram 383. A special version of the Chrysler Golden Lion 383 cid engine, rated at 390 hp, was exported for use on the French Facel-Vega. It was also exported in 1962.

Nineteen sixty-two was a quiet year for the 383 cid V-8. It was used only on the Chrysler line. The engine was the 325 hp version.

For 1963 and 1964, the 383 cid V-8 was offered either as a 305 hp two-barrel engine or a 330 hp four-barrel. The 330 hp engine also included a hotter camshaft and a dual-point distributor. The 330 hp 383 cid V-8 was carried over to 1965, but it was reduced to 325 hp for 1966–1967; for 1968–1970 it was once again rated at 330 hp. The version used on the 1967 and 1968 Plymouth Barracuda was rated at 280- and 300 hp; the difference was due to the restrictive exhaust manifolds required in order for the engine to fit the Barracuda's engine compartment.

The two-barrel engine was reduced to 270 hp for 1965–1967; it was uprated to 290 hp for 1968–1970.

Nineteen sixty-eight saw the addition of a new 383 cid B engine. This version, which was rated at 335 hp, was for use on the Plymouth Road Runner and the Dodge Super Bee. The engine used cylinder heads that were similar to those used on the 1968 HP (High Performance) 440 cid engine, which had larger valves and better porting, the HP 440 cid camshaft, and Carter AVS carburetor on a high-rise-type cast-iron intake manifold. The Carter carburetor was replaced by a Holley unit in 1970. It was a very strong-running 383 and according to road tests at the time, 383 cid Road Runners and Super Bees were about as quick as other similar Dodge and Plymouth cars with the bigger, 440 cid engine.

The 383 cid B engine was also used on Dodge light trucks from 1967 to 1971. This was a 258 hp version. The engine had a hydraulic-lifter camshaft, a four-barrel carburetor, and a 9.2:1 compression ratio (8.7:1 in 1971).

400 cid

This B-block variation replaced the 383 cidV-8 in 1972. It had a 4.34 in. bore and a 3.38 in. stroke. With an 8.2:1 compression ratio, the 400 cid V-8 wasn't much of a performance engine. The 400 cid V-8s used with automatic transmissions were equipped with cast-iron crankshafts, but all engines used cast-iron two- or four-barrel intake manifolds, a hydraulic-lifter camshaft, and from 1973, an electronic ignition system that eliminated the previous points and condenser. Two versions were available in 1972, the two-barrel carburetor version was rated at 190 hp and the four-barrel at 255 hp. These were SAE net figures.

There were a few more 400s to choose from in 1973. Two-barrel engines were available in 175- and 185 hp versions. Four-barrel engines were rated 220-, 260- and 280 hp. The two-barrel engine in 1974 was rated 185 hp; four-barrel engines were rated at 200-, 205-, or 250 hp.

There was also a truck version of the 400 cid engine. It was used on Dodge trucks from 1974 to 1978. Power ranged from 185 hp in 1974, to 165 hp during 1976–1977, and to 170 hp in its last year of production in 1978.

413 cid

The 413 cid engine was first made available on the 1959 Chrysler full-size cars. The engine was an RB version of the B engine series. It had a 4.12 in. bore and a 3.70 in. stroke. Generally, these engines had cast-iron heads, an engine block that used two-bolt main-bearing caps, cast-iron exhaust manifolds, a cast-iron intake manifold with a four-barrel carburetor, and a hydraulic-lifter camshaft. High-performance renditions of the engine used a solid-lifter camshaft and multiple-carburetor intake setups.

The 413 cid V-8 was available in two forms in 1959. The 413 cid V-8 that powered Chrysler cars and the Imperial was rated at 350 hp with a single four-barrel carburetor. The 413 cid engine that was used on the high-performance Chrysler 300E was rated at 380 hp. The engine was equipped with an inline dual four-barrel intake manifold and a solid-lifter camshaft.

For 1960, the 350 hp 413 cid V-8 was carried over. A new 375 hp version of the 413 cid engine was now used to power the Chrysler 300F. The 375 hp engine used the Long Ram intake setup along with a hydraulic-lifter camshaft. There was also a Short Ram 400 hp optional engine for the 300F. The engine used a solid-lifter camshaft and the cylinder heads had larger, 1.74 in. exhaust valves. All three engines were carried over for the 1961 model year.

For 1962, the basic transportation 413 cid V-8 was downrated to 340 hp. In the Chrysler 300H, the Long Ram 413 was rated at 380 hp, while a dealer-installed version with the larger exhaust valve cylinder heads, a solid-lifter camshaft, and a Short Ram intake system was rated at 405 hp.

More significant, though, was the introduction of the 413 cid Max Wedge engine. Although the engine came to be known as the Max Wedge, it was officially known as the Ramcharger 413 (Dodge) or Super Stock 413 (Plymouth). This was really an all-out drag race engine that was available on special order. The cylinder heads featured ports that were 25 percent larger than those of the regular 413 cid engine and the exhaust valves were also larger, measuring 1.88 in. The engine was equipped with a solid-lifter camshaft and a special aluminum cross-ram intake manifold with two Carter AFB four-barrel carburetors. It even had unique cast-iron headers. The engine, with 11.0:1 compression, was rated at 410 hp; the 13.5:1 compression version was rated at 420 hp. Both engines were available only during 1962.

For 1963, the 340 hp engine was continued, as was the 390 hp Short Ram 413 cid V-8 on the Chrysler 300J.

Both engines were carried over into the 1964 model year, the 390 hp Short Ram available on the Chrysler 300K. The standard engine on the 300K was a single four-barrel 413 cid V-8 rated at 360 hp.

In the engine's last year of production, 1965, only the 340- and 360 hp versions were available.

426 cid

The next development of the RB series occurred in 1963 with the release of the 426 Max Wedge Stage II engine. A bore and stroke increase to 4.25x3.75 in. yielded 426 cid. The 1963 426 Max Wedge Stage II engine was essentially identical to the 413 Max Wedge, except for displacement and minor internal improvements such as camshaft timing. There were two power levels, 415 hp with an 11.0:1 compression ratio and 425 hp with 13.5:1 compression. Obviously, the 425 hp engine was a race-only engine, as even the premium gasoline available in 1963 wouldn't have been enough to stop the engine from detonating with such a high compression ratio.

The last Max Wedge engine was released in 1964. This was the 426 Max Wedge Stage III engine. The engine was equipped with larger bore Carter AFB carburetors and matching cross-ram intake manifold, a higher lift and longer duration solid-lifter camshaft, and reworked cylinder heads that produced more flow. The engine block was also notched for valve clearance. Even so, the engine was rated the same as before. Compression ratios for the two engines were 11.0:1 and 12.5:1.

Incidentally, all Max Wedge cylinder heads did not have provision for the exhaust crossover passage to heat the incoming fuel mixture.

Another 426 cid engine joined the lineup in 1964 and was available through the 1965 model year on Dodge and Plymouth cars. The single four-barrel 426 cid engine was rated at 365 hp. This was not a high-performance engine, as it used the standard cylinder heads, cast-iron intake manifold, and a hydraulic-lifter camshaft.

The 426 cid RB engine was also used on the 1964–1966 Dodge A100 Forward Control pickups. It was rated at 365 hp and used a four-barrel carburetor, a forged-steel crankshaft, forged connecting rods, and a hydraulic-lifter camshaft.

426 Hemi

Chrysler reintroduced hemispherical combustion chamber cylinder heads for use on the 426 cid RB engine block in 1964. Chrysler was heavily involved in racing at the time. The Max Wedge engines were doing well on the drag strip, but they weren't as competitive on the NASCAR circuits. The wedge just couldn't breathe as well as other engines. Chrysler, of course, knew that the hemi-head design was the best for producing the most power. Rather than build a completely new engine from the ground up, Chrysler chose to fabricate hemi cylinder heads and use them on the existing RB engine block. The result was the 426 Hemi, which was officially designated "Chrysler Corporation's Hemispherical Combustion Chamber Maximum Performance Engine." Chrysler built a great variety of race hemi-head engines during 1964–1965. The drag race hemi engines were different from the circle-track engines. Each used different intake setups, different internal components, and had different displacements. The drag engines were offered in 415- and 425 hp versions, while the circle-track engine was rated at 400 hp with a single four-barrel carburetor. These were just the starting point as competitors usually modified the engines to their needs. The factory also experimented with various hemi-head variations—even a double overhead camshaft version.

Chrysler first used the engine in the most prestigious NASCAR race of all—the Daytona 500. Hemi-powered Plymouths took the first three positions in the 1964 race. Although Ford won 30 races that year to Chrysler's 26, it was obvious the days of Ford's 427 Wedge were numbered—which resulted in Ford building its own hemi engine, the 427 SOHC.

At this point, it must be pointed out that the 426 Hemi and other engines used in sanctioned racing were special, low-production engines that were never really intended for use on any street vehicle. The problem, from the viewpoint of Bill France (who ran NASCAR), was that the factory racing engines and the manufacturers who built them took turns overwhelming each other, and that did not make for exciting racing to draw people to the track. France ruled that if Chrysler and Ford wanted to race their complex, expensive hemi-head engines, they would have to build a certain number of a street cars with these motors and sell them to the public. Ford declined, but Chrysler went ahead, and so the famous 426 street Hemi was born in 1966. Ford eventually did build its own street hemi—the Boss 429 in 1969.

The street Hemi used a specially modified RB engine block that had provision for cross-bolting the three center main-bearing caps. This added rigidity to the block and main cap structure. As one would expect, the Hemi used a forged-steel crankshaft, special forged-steel connecting rods and 10.25:1-compression forged-aluminum pistons, and a solid-lifter camshaft. The intake manifold was cast in aluminum and mounted two Carter AFB carburetors.

The cylinder heads on street Hemis were cast in iron and used 2.25 in. intake and 1.90 in. exhaust valves. Like other RB engines, the Hemi cylinder head was fastened down in 17 places; however, the Hemi used studs on the top four positions instead of bolts.

The 1968 version got a different camshaft; in 1970, the camshaft was changed to a hydraulic-lifter type. All 1966–1971 426 street Hemi engines were rated at 425 hp.

440 cid

Taking over the duties of the 365 hp 426 cid regular passenger car engine was the 440 cid version of the RB block in 1966. It had a bore and stroke of 4.32x3.75 in. and was equipped with all the non-performance factory parts for a 350 hp output and lots of low-end torque, 480ft-lb, to power the big, heavy Chrysler, Dodge, and Plymouth intermediates and full-size cars. In this form, the engine would be available through the 1970 model year. In 1971, it was rated at 335 hp, partly due to a lower, 9.0:1 compression ratio. During 1972–1978, the 440 cid engine was rated between 200 and 275 hp in various states of tune. Most of the passenger car 440 cid engines in this era also used a cast-iron crankshaft.

It really didn't take much to wake up the big 440 cid engine, which is what Chrysler did in 1967. The production heads were replaced with cylinder heads that had larger, 1.74 in. exhaust valves and larger ports. A higher performance hydraulic camshaft was substituted and a better flowing cast-iron intake manifold and Carter AVS carburetor were also added. The result was the 440 Magnum in Dodge cars and Super Commando 440 in Plymouths, both rated at 375 hp.

The 1968 engine was similar, but it used cylinder heads that had an open-chamber design.

The ultimate 440 cid V-8 was the 1969-1/2 440 Six Pack (Dodge) and the 440 Six Barrel (Plymouth). This engine was built to bridge the gap between the 375 hp 440 cid V-8 and the street Hemi. It was outfitted with an aluminum intake manifold that used three two-barrel Holley carburetors. The result was 390 hp. The 1970–1971 versions of the engine used a cast-iron version of the intake manifold as a cost savings measure, and the engine was also fitted with stronger connecting rods. Both of the HP 440 cid engines proved themselves to be capable performing street engines.

The 440 cid engine also found its way into Dodge light trucks, starting in 1974, when it was an optional V-8 engine on the new Ramcharger utility vehicle. The engine was rated at 230 hp. The 440 cid V-8 was rated at 235 hp in 1975, 220 hp in 1976–1977, and a paltry 200 hp in 1978, its last year of production. Unlike the passenger car 440s of that era, the truck version was equipped with a forged-steel crankshaft. By that time though, the need for a big-block V-8 had long passed.

Engine Blocks

There are two basic engine blocks to consider here, the B-series low-blocks and the raised-deck RB blocks. The RB blocks have a taller deck height, by 0.745 in. The B-series engines have main-bearing cap journals that measure 2.625 in., while the RB engines have larger journals, 2.750 in. This means that crankshafts are not interchangeable between the two. Forged-steel crankshafts were fitted to most B and RB engines. The only deviation from this are the 1971 383 cid engines with a two-barrel carburetor, 1972 and later 400 cid blocks, and most 440 cid engines. Truck engines were equipped with forged-steel crankshafts.

Both blocks have extended side walls, forming a Y-block design. The block used on the 426 Hemi engine is slightly different from other RB blocks. It was made in the same basic configuration, but there is provision for cross-bolting the numbers 2, 3, and 4 main-bearing caps for greater bottom-end rigidity.

While the Max Wedge blocks are basically the same as the regular RB blocks, they were equipped with main-bearing caps that were chosen for hardness, and the cylinder bores are notched so that the larger exhaust valves these engines are fitted with do not hit the cylinder bores.

Cylinder Heads

All B and RB engines except the 426 Hemi used cylinder heads with a wedge-style combustion chamber design. Engines built after the 1967 model year had a larger, open-type combustion chamber. The valves on all engines were operated by shaft-mounted rocker arms. On engines equipped with hydraulic-lifter camshafts, the rockers were made of stamped steel and had no provision for adjustment. The Max Wedge engines and the Chrysler 300 Letter cars that came with solid-lifter camshafts had adjustable cast-iron rockers. The ratio on all rockers was 1.50:1. Engines built until January 1963 used bolt-on rocker arm stands and four-bolt valve covers; later engines had integral rocker stands and six valve cover attaching bolts for better sealing.

In terms of porting, the Chrysler Letter car engines had ports that flowed better than regular production cylinder heads. The Max Wedge engines had much larger runners and port openings as well. In addition, the Max Wedge engines did not have provision for exhaust heat. The heads used on the 1967 and later HP 440 cid engines were also modified to flow better than the regular production cylinder heads.

Early production cylinder heads have 1.95 in./1.60 in. intake/exhaust valves; 1960 and later Letter series Chryslers have larger, 1.74 in. exhaust valves. This larger exhaust valve size was also used on the 1967 HP 440 cid engines and then on all engines beginning in 1968. All engines got larger, 2.08 in. intake valves in 1962, and this size remained unchanged from then on. All Max Wedge engines were equipped with larger, 1.88 in. exhaust valves.

The 1966–1971 426 Hemi engines came with the unique hemispherical combustion chamber cylinder heads. These used shaft-mounted adjustable rocker arms.

Intake Manifolds

The vast majority of B and RB engines were equipped with four-barrel cast-iron intake manifolds set up to accept Carter carburetors. The 1967 and later HP 440 cid intake manifolds flowed better than the previous designs. The 1968 and later 383 cid engines used on the Plymouth Road Runner and Dodge Super Bee also received a superior flowing cast-iron intake manifold.

In terms of multiple-carburetor setups, the 383- and 413 cid engines were available with cast-iron inline dual four-barrel intake manifolds. The 383 cid engine used such a manifold on Dodge D-500 engines and on the DeSoto Adventurer. The 413 cid engine used such a manifold in 1959.

The unique Long and Short Ram intake manifolds were also used on the 383 cid engine in 1960–1961; 413 cid engines used these manifolds from 1960 to 1964 as well.

The 413 and 426 cid Max Wedge engines used two four-barrel cross-ram-type manifolds cast in aluminum. Single four-barrel versions of the intake were available over the counter.

The only engine to get a triple two-barrel carburetor intake manifold was the 390 hp 440 cid engine used on Plymouth and Dodge high-performance cars. The 1969 versions were made by Edelbrock for Chrysler; 1970 and later versions were cast in iron by Chrysler.

The 1966–1971 426 street Hemi engine used a dual four-barrel Carter carburetor intake manifold cast in aluminum. There was also a great variety of race-only factory manifolds made for the 426 Hemi, in either aluminum or magnesium.

Exhaust Manifolds

All B and RB engines used cast-iron exhaust manifolds with various-length runners and outlet sizes to fit specific applications. The Max Wedge exhaust manifolds were unique, and probably the rarest of these were the Tri-Y manifolds used on the 1964 426 Max Wedge.

The 1967–1971 HP 440 cid engines have the best-flowing exhaust manifolds after the Max Wedge manifolds; the manifolds used on the 1967–1969 Barracuda are probably the most restrictive; otherwise the engine wouldn't have fit in the car's engine compartment.

The 426 street Hemi came with cast-iron exhaust manifolds that fit only that engine.

Engine Identification

All major Chrysler engine components were cast with a number to identify the part and a date code that indicated when the part was cast. These numbers can be found in various locations. The date codes used on blocks, intakes, and exhaust manifolds are fairly easy to decipher. As an example, 11-22–70 decodes to November 22, 1970.

Chrysler's engine-coding system, as used on the B/RB engines, evolved from the coding system used in the 1950s. The early coding system consisted of a series of numbers followed by a sequence number; for example, 3NE56-1001 was a 1956 Chrysler 300B 354 cid engine. The 3NE56 was the engine code, and 1001 was the sequence number showing what number the engine was out of the total produced during the year. This number usually began with 1001.

When the B and RB engines were introduced in 1958, the same system was used, but it was simplified somewhat. Just by looking at the code, you could quickly tell what engine it was, because engine size was obvious by just looking at the number. The 1958 Dodge, DeSoto, and Plymouth engines had the following ID codes: L350-1001 for the 350 cid engine and L361-1001 for the 361 cid engine.

In 1959, the codes were ML-361-1001 for the 361 cid and ML-383-1001 for the 383 on Dodge, DeSoto, and Plymouth; for Chrysler, the codes were MR-361-1001 (361 cid), MR-383-1001 (383 cid), and MR-413-1001 (413 cid).

These codes were stamped at the top of the block on a pad behind the water pump.

From 1960 on, a different engine code system was used. As an example, a typical code might be S42-222. The first letter in the code stood for the year. The year codes are as follows: P 1960, R 1961, S 1962, T 1963, V 1964, A 1965, B 1966, and C 1967.

The next two numbers are the first two numbers of the cubic-inch displacement of the engine, as follows: 36 was 361 cid, 38 was 383 cid, 40 was 400 cid, 41 was 413 cid, 42 was 426 cid, and 44 was 440 cid. Basically, all the companies did was drop the last number off the engine displacement size.

The final three numbers indicate the date and month. Thus in our example, S42-222 stands for a 426 cid engine assembled on February 22, 1962.

This code was stamped in one of several locations on the B and RB engine series, most often on the right side of the block below the distributor or on the left front of the block just behind the thermostat housing.

In 1965, all three numbers indicating engine size were stamped after the letter code for model year—for example, A383 322, which stands for a 383 cid engine assembled on March 22, 1965.

Besides the ID code, there were additional numbers and letters used to indicate a particular engine or an engine that required further clarification to whoever was reading the ID code. These were:

- A: 0.020 in. oversize cylinder bores
- B: 0.010 in. undersize main and rod bearings

The 426 Hemi. It's a great engine with the best that Chrysler had to offer in the 1960s. About the only thing it had going against it was cost.

- E: cast crankshaft
- H: standard 4V V-8
- HP: high performance
- LC: low compression
- O.S.: 0.005 in. oversize valve stems
- P: premium fuel recommended
- R: regular fuel may be used
- S: special engine (warranty replacement engines)
- SP: special engine
- WT: water test
- TW: water test
- X: oversize valve guides
- 2: 2nd shift
- Diamond symbol: 0.008 in. oversize tappets
- Maltese cross symbol: 0.001 in. undersize crankshaft
- Maltese cross and X: 0.010 in. undersize crankshaft

From 1968 to 1971, a different ID code system was used, and the ID code was relocated to the left side of the block, near the oil pan flange. A typical ID code might read as follows: PT38325920022. The first two letters indicate the engine plant where the engine was assembled. They are as follows:

- PT: Trenton Plant, which built 361-, 383-, 400-, 413-, 426-, and 440 cid engines
- PM, GM, HM: Mound Road plant, which built 318-, 340-, and 360 cid engines
- MV, MN: Marysville Plant, which built the 426 Hemi

The next three digits indicate engine displacement, which in this case is 383 cid. This is followed by a four-digit code that indicates the build date. This particular code, 2592, stands for September 1, 1969, and can be found in the 10,000-day calendar in the Chrysler service books. The date can usually be found next to or near the ID code, stamped in the conventional manner, 09-01-69 in this example. The last four numbers are the daily sequence number, which indicates the chronological number of each engine built that day. In this example, the 22nd built that day.

In 1972, with only the 400 and 440 cid engines in production, the engine code was relocated once again, but only for the 400 cid engine. It was moved to the right side of the block, next to the distributor. It remained by the oil pan flange for the 440 cid engine. For 1973–1975, the location for the 440 cid engine was on the left bank, adjacent to the front tappet rail.

The plant codes were also shortened in 1973. The letter P was dropped from the Trenton and Mound Road engine plant codes.

VIN Identification Codes

On this series of engines, there is no way to match a particular engine to a specific car. The car's VIN, or any portion of it, was not stamped on the engine itself. By 1967, though, Chrysler began including a letter code in the VIN for engines. Listed here are the VIN codes from 1967:

1967–1969
G: 383 cid
H: 383 cid HP
J: 426 cid Hemi
K: 440 cid
L: 440 cid HP
M: 440 cid 3x2V

1970–1975
L: 383 cid 2V
N: 383 cid 4V HP
M: 400 cid 2V
N: 400 cid 4V
P: 400 cid HP
R: 426 cid Hemi
T: 440 cid 4V
U: 440 cid 4V HP
V: 440 cid 3x2V HP

Engine Specifications

	Displacement	Carburetor	Horsepower	Torque	Compression Ratio	Notes
1958						
	350	2V	280@4,600	380@2,400	10.0	Firesweep
	350	4V	295@4,600	385@2,400	10.0	Royal, Sierra
	350	2x4V	305@5,000	370@3,600	10.0	Fury
	350	FI	315@5,200	375@3,600	10.0	Fury
	361	4V	295@4,600	390@2,400	10.0	Firesweep, Firedome
	361 D-500	4V	305@4,600	400@2,800	10.0	Fireflite, Sierra
	361 D-500	2x4V	320@4,600	420@2,800	10.0	Coronet, Royal, Sierra,
	361 D-500	FI	333@4,800	420@3,000	10.0	Coronet, Royal
	361	2x4V	345@5,000	400@3,600	10.25	Adventurer
	361	FI	355@5,200	400@3,600	10.25	Adventurer
1959						
	361	2V	290@4,600	390@2,400	10.0	Firesweep
	361	2V	295@4,600	390@2,400	10.1	Coronet, Royal
	361	4V	305@4,600	400@2,800	10.1	Coronet, Royal
	361	2x4V	305@4,600	395@2,800	10.0	Fury
	383	2V	305@4,600	410@2,400	10.0	Firedome, Windsor
	383 D-500	4V	320@4,600	420@2,800	10.0	Coronet, Royal
	383	4V	325@4,600	425@2,800	10.0	Saratoga, Fireflite
	383 Super D-500	2x4V	345@5,000	425@3,600	10.0	Coronet, Royal
	383	2x4V	350@5,000	425@3,600	10.0	Adventurer
	413	4V	350@4,600	470@2,800	10.0	New Yorker, Imperial
	413	2x4V	380@5,000	450@3,600	10.0	300E
1960						
	361	2V	295@4,600	390@2,400	10.0	Matador, Fireflite, Adventurer, Diplomat
	361	4V	305@4,600	395@2,800	10.0	Belvedere, Fury, Diplomat, Savoy, Fireflite, Adventurer, Diplomat
	361	2x4V	310@4,800	435@2,800	10.0	Dart, Belvedere, Fury
	383	2V	305@4,600	410@2,400	10.1	Windsor
	383	4V	325@4,600	425@2,800	10.1	Saratoga, Polara, Belvedere, Fury
	383	2x4V	330@4,800	460@2,800	10.0	Dart, Matador, Polara, Belvedere, Fury
	413	4V	350@4,600	470@2,800	10.1	Imperial, New Yorker, Saratoga
	413	2x4V	375@5,000	495@2,800	10.1	300F
	413	2x4V	400@5,200	465@3,600	10.1	300F
1961						
	361	4V	265@4,400	380@2,400	9.1	Newport, DeSoto, Diplomat, Dart, Polara
	361	4V	305@4,600	395@2,800	10.0	Belvedere, Fury, Savoy, Windsor, Dart, Polara
	383	4V	325@4,600	425@2,800	10.0	Belvedere, Savoy, Fury, Polara

Year	Displacement	Carburetor	Horsepower	Torque	Compression Ratio	Notes
	83	2x4V	330@4,800	460@2,800	10.0	Belvedere, Savoy, Fury, Dart, Polara
	413	4V	350@4,600	470@2,800	10.0	Imperial, Newport, New Yorker
	413	2x4V	375@5,000	495@2,800	10.1	300G
	413	2x4V	400@5,200	465@3,600	10.1	300G
1962						
	361	4V	265@4,400	380@2,400	9.0	Newport, Custom 880
	361	4V	305@4,600	395@2,800	10.0	Dart, Polara, Fury
	383	2V	305@4,600	410@2,400	10.0	300
	413	4V	350@4,600	470@2,800	10.0	Imperial, New Yorker
	413	4V	365@4,600	460@2,800	11.0	300
	413	2x4V	380@5,000	485@3,200	10.0	300H
	413 Max Wedge	2x4V	410@5,600	470@4,400	11.0	Dart, Polara
	413 Max Wedge	2x4V	420@6,000	480@4,400	13.5	Dart, Polara
1963						
	361	4V	265@4,400	380@2,400	9.0	Newport, Polara, 330, Custom 880, Fury
	383	2V	305@4,600	410@2,400	10.0	300, 330, 440, Polara, Custom 880
	383	4V	320@4,600	425@2,800	10.0	330, 440, Polara, 330, Custom 880, Fury, Belvedere
	413	4V	340@4,600	470@2,800	10.0	New Yorker, Imperial
	413	4V	365@4,600	460@2,800	11.0	300
	413	2x4V	390@4,800	485@3,600	9.6	Chrysler 300J
	426 Max Wedge	2x4V	415@5,600	470@4,400	11.0	330, 440, Polara, Belvedere, Fury
	426 Max Wedge	2x4V	425@6,000	480@4,400	13.5	330, 440, Polara, Belvedere, Fury
1964						
	361	4V	265@4,400	380@2,400	9.1	Newport, 880
	383	2V	305@4,600	410@2,400	10.0	300, 330, 440, 880, Polara
	383	4V	330@4,600	425@2,800	10.0	330, 440, Polara
	413	4V	340@4,600	470@2,800	10.0	New Yorker, Imperial
	413	4V	360@4,800	470@3,200	10.0	300, 300K
	413	2x4V	390@4,800	485@3,600	9.6	300K
	426	4V	365@4,600	465@2,800	10.5	330, 440, Polara, Coronet
	426 Max Wedge Stage III	2x4V	415@5,600	470@4,400	11.0	330, 440, Polara, Belvedere, Fury
	426 Max Wedge Stage III	2x4V	425@6,000	480@4,600	12.5	330, 440, Polara, Belvedere, Fury
1965						
	361	2V	265@4,400	380@2,400	9.1	Belvedere, Satellite, Coronet
	383	2V	270@4,400	390@2,800	9.2	Fury, Polara, Custom 880, Newport
	383	4V	315@4,400	420@4,800	10.0	Polara, Custom 880, Monaco, Newport, 300
	383	4V	330@4,600	425@2,800	10.0	Belvedere, Satellite, Coronet
	413	4V	340@4,600	470@2,800	10.1	Polara, Custom 880, Monaco, Imperial, New Yorker
	413	4V	360@4,800	470@3,200	10.1	300, 300L, New Yorker
	426	4V	365@4,600	465@2,800	10.5	Belvedere, Satellite, Fury, Coronet, Monaco
	426	2x4V	425@6,000	480@4,600	12.5	Coronet, Belvedere
1966						
	361	2V	265@4,400	380@2,400	9.1	Coronet, Charger, Belvedere, Satellite
	383	2V	270@4,400	390@2,800	9.2	Newport, Polara, Monaco, Fury
	383	4V	325@4,800	425@2,800	10.0	Newport, 300, Coronet, Charger, Belvedere, Satellite, Fury
	426	2x4V	425@5,000	490@4,000	10.25	Coronet, Charger, Belvedere, Satellite
	440	4V	350@4,400	480@2,800	10.0	Newport, 300, New Yorker, Imperial, Polara, Monaco

	Displacement	Carburetor	Horsepower	Torque	Compression Ratio	Notes
1967						
	383	2V	270@4,400	390@2,800	9.2	Belvedere, Satellite, Fury, Coronet, Deluxe, 440, 500, Polara, Monaco, Charger, Newport
	383	4V	280@4,200	400@2,400	10.0	Barracuda
	383	4V	325@4,800	425@2,800	10.0	Belvedere, Satellite, Fury, Coronet, Deluxe, 440, 500, Charger, Newport, T and C
	426	2x4V	425@5,000	490@4,000	10.25	Belvedere, Satellite, GTX, Coronet R/T, Charger
	440	4V	350@4,400	480@2,800	10.0	Polara, Monaco, 300, T and C, Imperial
	440	4V	375@4,600	480@3,200	10.0	GTX, Coronet R/T, Charger, Newport, New Yorker, 300, Polara, Monaco, Fury
1968						
	383	2V	290@4,400	380@2,400	9.2	Newport, T and C, Coronet, Coronet, Charger, Polara, Monaco, Belvedere, Satellite, Fury
	383	4V	300@4,200	400@2,400	10.0	Dart, Barracuda
	383	4V	330@5,000	425@3,200	10.0	Newport, T and C, Coronet, Charger, Polara Monaco, Fury
	383	4V	335@5,200	425@3,400	10.0	Road Runner, Super Bee
	426	2x4V	425@5,000	490@4,000	10.25	Dart, Road Runner, Super Bee, Charger, Coronet R/T, GTX, Barracuda
	440	4V	350@4,400	480@2,800	10.0	Imperial, 300, New Yorker, T and C
	440	4V	375@4,600	480@3,200	10.0	GTX, Coronet R/T, Charger, Newport, New Yorker, Polara, Monaco, 300, Fury
1969						
	383	2V	290@4,400	380@2,400	9.2	Newport, T and C, Coronet, 440, Charger, Polara, Monaco, Fury, Belvedere, Satellite
	383	4V	325@4,800	425@2,800	10.0	Newport, T and C, Dart, Coronet, 440, Charger, Polara, Monaco, Barracuda, Belvedere, Satellite, Fury
	383	4V	330@5,000	425@3,200	10.0	Newport, T and C, Dart, Coronet, 440, Charger, Polara, Monaco, Barracuda, Belvedere, Satellite, Fury
	383	4V	335@5,200	425@3,400	10.0	Road Runner, Super Bee
	426	2x4V	425@5,000	490@4,000	10.25	Coronet R/T, Charger R/T, Charger 500, GTX, Barracuda
	440	4V	350@4,400	480@2,800	10.0	Imperial, New Yorker, 300, T and C
	440	4V	375@4,600	480@3,200	10.0	Dart, Charger R/T, Coronet R/T, GTX, Newport, New Yorker, 300, Polara, Monaco, Fury
	440	3x2V	390@4,700	490@3,200	10.5	Road Runner, Super Bee
1970						
	383	2V	290@4,400	380@2,400	8.7	Barracuda, Belvedere, Challenger, Coronet, Charger, Fury, Satellite, Polara, Monaco, Newport, T and C
	383	4V	330@5,000	425@3,200	10.0	Barracuda, Challenger, Belvedere, Fury, Satellite, Charger, Coronet, Polara, Monaco, Newport, T and C
	383	4V	335@5,200	425@3,400	10.0	'Cuda, Challenger, GTX, Road Runner, Charger, Coronet

	Displacement	Carburetor	Horsepower	Torque	Compression Ratio	Notes
	426	2x4V	425@5,000	490@4,000	10.25	'Cuda, Challenger, GTX, Road Runner, Coronet, Charger
	440	4V	350@4,400	480@2,800	9.7	Imperial, Newport, New Yorker, T and C
	440	4V	375@4,600	480@3,200	9.7	'Cuda, Challenger, GTX, Road Runner, Coronet, Charger, Newport, 300, New Yorker, Polara
	440	3x2V	390@4,700	490@3,200	10.5	'Cuda, Challenger, Road Runner, Fury, Coronet, Charger
1971						
	383	2V	275@4,400	375@2,800	8.5	Newport, T and C, Challenger, Barracuda, Charger, Fury, Satellite
	383	4V	300@4,800	410@3,400	8.5	Newport, T and C, Challenger, Barracuda, Charger, Coronet, Fury, Satellite, Polara, Road Runner
	400	2V	190@4,400	310@2,400	8.2	
	426	2x4V	425@5,000	490@4,000	10.25	Challenger, 'Cuda, Charger, GTX, Road Runner
	440	4V	335@4,400	460@3,200	9.0	Imperial, New Yorker, T and C, Coronet, Polara
	440	4V	370@4,600	480@3,200	9.7	Newport, New Yorker, Charger, GTX, Newport, New Yorker, 300, Polara, Monaco, Fury
	440	3x2V	385@4,700	490@3,200	10.5	Challenger, 'Cuda, Charger, Road Runner, GTX
1972						
	400	2V	190@4,400	310@2,400	8.2	Fury, Satellite, Charger, Coronet, Polara, Monaco, T and C, Newport
	400	4V	255@4,800	340@3,200	8.2	Satellite, Road Runner, Charger
	440	4V	225@4,400	345@3,200	8.2	Fury, Imperial, T and C, Coronet, Polara, Monaco
	440	4V	245@4,400	360@3,200	8.2	Newport, New Yorker
	440	4V	280@4,800	380@3,200	8.2	Charger, Road Runner
1973						
	400	2V	175@3,600	305@2,400	8.2	Charger, Satellite
	400	2V	185@3,600	310@2,400	8.2	Newport, Coronet, Monaco, Fury, Satellite
	400	4V	260@4,800	335@3,600	8.2	Charger, Satellite
	440	4V	215@3,600	345@2,000	8.2	Newport, New Yorker, T and C, Imperial
	440	4V	220@3,600	350@2,400	8.2	Coronet, Monaco, Fury
	440	4V	280@4,800	380@3,200	8.2	Charger, Road Runner
1974						
	400	2V	185@4,000	315@2,400	8.2	Fury, Monaco, Newport
	400	2V	205@4,400	310@2,400	8.2	Fury, Satellite, Charger, Coronet, Monaco, Newport
	400	4V	250@4,800	330@3,400	8.2	Road Runner, Satellite, Charger
	440	4V	220@4,000	345@3,200	8.2	Chrysler
	440	4V	230@4,000	350@3,200	8.2	Fury, Monaco, Imperial, Newport, New Yorker
	440	4V	275@4,400	375@3,200	8.2	Road Runner, Charger
1975						
	400	2V	165@4,000	295@3,200	8.2	Road Runner, Fury, Cordoba, Coronet
	400	2V	175@4,000	300@2,400	8.2	Fury, Newport, New Yorker, Monaco
	400	4V	185@4,000	285@3,200	8.2	Coronet
	400	4V	190@4,000	290@3,200	8.2	Cordoba, Fury, Coronet
	400	4V	195@4,000	285@3,200	8.2	Newport, New Yorker

Displacement	Carburetor	Horsepower	Torque	Compression Ratio	Notes
400	4V	235@4,200	320@3,200	8.2	Road Runner, Fury, Cordoba, Coronet
440	4V	215@4,000	330@3,200	8.2	Fury, Newport, New Yorker, Monaco
440	4V	260@4,400	355@3,200	8.2	Chrysler

Chrysler models: Imperial, Windsor, Saratoga, Newport, 300, T and C, and Cordoba
DeSoto models: Firesweep, Firedome, Fireflite, Adventurer, and Diplomat
Dodge models: Coronet, Royal, Dart, Seneca, Pioneer, Phoenix, Matador, Polara, Custom 880, 330, 440, 880, Monaco, Charger R/T, Super Bee, Swinger, and Challenger
Plymouth models: Fury, Savoy, Plaza, Belvedere, Satellite, Barracuda, 'Cuda, GTX, and Road Runner

Engine Internal Dimensions

Displacement	Bore and Stroke	Rod Bearings	Main Bearings	Intake/Exhaust Valves
350	4.0625x3.375	2.379–2.380	2.629–2.630	1.95/1.60
361	4.1250x3.375	2.374–2.375	2.6245–2.6255	1.95/1.60 (1961–1967 2.08/1.60)
383	4.250x3.375	2.374–2.375	2.6245–2.6255	1.95/1.60 (1968-up 2.08/1.74)
383 (RB)	4.030x3.750	2.374–2.375	2.7495–2.7505	1.95/1.60
400	4.340x3.380	2.374–2.375	2.6245–2.6255	2.08/1.74
413	4.1875x3.750	2.374–2.375	2.7495–2.7505	1.95/1.60 (1961–1967 2.08/1.60)
426	4.250x3.750	2.374–2.375	2.7495–2.7505	2.08/1.60 (Max Wedge 1.88 ex.; Hemi 2.25/1.94)
440	4.320x3.750	2.374–2.375	2.7495–2.7505	2.08/1.74 (1966- 2.08/1.60)

Block, Head, and Manifold

Part and Casting Numbers

Year	Engine	Part or Casting Number
Engine Blocks		
1958	350	casting 1944929
1961–1964	361	casting 1737629
1958–1966	361	casting 2205712
1959–1964	383	casting 1851729, 2120329
1959–1971	383	casting 2468130
1971–1972	400	casting 3614230
1973–1978	400	casting 3698630
1962–1963	413	casting 1852029, 2120529
1959–1965	413	casting 2205697
1964	426	casting 2205697
1963–1965	426	casting 2406730, Max Wedge
1964–1966	426	casting 2532230, Max Wedge
1964–1971	426	casting 2468330, Hemi
Engine Blocks		
1966–1972	440	casting 2536430
1973–1975	440	casting 3698330
Cylinder Heads		
1958	350	2128553, casting 1737637, 1944705
1958	361	2128553, casting 1737637, 1944705
1959	361	2128553, casting 1737637, 1944705
1960	361	2448752, casting 1737637
1962	361	2128589, casting 2206324, 2206924
1963	361	2448752, casting 2463200
1964–1965	361	2406732, casting 2406516
1966–1968	361	2899940, casting 2899943, truck
1960	383	2448752, casting 1737637
1962	383	2128589, casting 2206324, 2206924
1964–1965	383	2406732, casting 2406516
1963	383	2448752, casting 2463200
1966–1967	383	2406732, casting 2406516
1968–1970	383	2843904, casting 2843906
1968	383	2843904, casting 2951250
1971–1972	383	3462344, casting 3462346
1972	400	3462344, casting 3462346
1973	400	3671640, casting 3462346
1974	400	3769910, casting 3769902
1974	400	3769954, casting 3769975
1975	400	3769954, casting 3769975
1962	413	2525053, casting 1944705
1962	413	2128589, casting 2206324, 2206924
1962	413	2402358, casting 2402286, Max Wedge

The date code and block casting number are located on the left rear of the block, as in this 1966 440 block.

Year	Engine	Part or Casting Number
Cylinder Heads		
1963	413	2448752, casting 2463200
1963	413	2202376, casting 2402527, 300J
1964	413	2406734, casting 2408520, 300K
1964–1965	413	2406732, casting 2406516
1963	426	2406754, casting 2463209, Max Wedge
1964	426	2406736, casting 2406518, Max Wedge
1964–1965	426	2406732, casting 2406516
1966–1971	426	2780557, casting 2780559, Hemi
1967	440	2806019, casting 2406158
1967	440	2806762, casting 2780915
1968–1970	440	2843904, casting 2843906
1968	440	2843904, casting 2951250
1971–1972	440	3462344, casting 3462346
1973	440	3671640, casting 3462346
1974	440	3769910, casting 3769902
1975	440	3769954, casting 3769975
Intake Manifolds		
1958	350 2x4V	1854852, casting 1827899
1962	361	1859300, casting 2205968
1959–1960	383 2V	casting 1851899, RB
1959–1960	383 4V	casting 1851898, RB
1962	383	1859300, casting 2205968
1959	383 2V	2120630
1959	383 4V	1858623
1960	383 2V	2120630
1961–1967	383 2V	1859299, casting 2205737/65
1960–1961	383/413 2x4V	2240394 left, 2240395 right, casting 1947162/1947163
1959–1961	383 2x4V	1854852, casting 1827899
1960–1967	383 4V	1859300, casting 2205968
1968–1969	383 4V	2843684, casting 2806301
1968	383 2V	2843683
1970	383 4V	2951665, casting 2951666
1970–1971	383 2V	3614020, casting 2951670
1970–1971	383 4V	2951665, casting 2951666
1972	400 4V	3614048, w/ A.I.R.
1972	400 4V	3614047, casting 3614046
1973	400 4V	3698583, casting 3698440
1973	400 4V	3671880, casting 3671879
1974	400 4V	3698584, casting 3698442
1974–1975	400 2V	3870024
1959	413 2x4V	1854817, casting 2264877, 300E
1960	413 2x4V	2240394, 300F
1959–1965	413 4V	1858623, casting 2206000
1962	413 2x4V	1854817, casting 2266487, 300H
1962	413 2x4V	casting 2402726, Max Wedge, aluminum
1963–1964	413 2x4V	2421368 right, 2421369 left, casting 2129985/2129987, 300J, 300K
1963	426 2x4V	2465214, casting 2402728, Max Wedge Stage II, aluminum
1964	426 2x4V	2465214, casting 2402720, Max Wedge Stage III

Chrysler big-block combustion chamber. This one has the more common open chamber. Casting number can be found on the underside of the head (arrow).

Year	Engine	Part or Casting Number
Intake Manifolds		
1964	426 4V	casting 2406185, Max Wedge, aluminum
1964	426 4V	casting 2465165, Max Wedge, aluminum
1964	426 2x4V	2468418, casting 2468045, Hemi S/S
1964	426 4V	casting 2468043, NASCAR, Hemi
1964–1965	426 4V	1858623, casting 2206000
1965	426 2x4V	2468418, casting 2536900, Hemi S/S, magnesium
1967	426 2x4V	2468418, casting 2536900, Hemi NASCAR
1966	426 2x4V	2780542, casting 2780543 (2780544, street Hemi)
1968	426 2x4V	2468418, casting 2536900, Hemi, Dart, Barracuda
1966	440 4V	1858623, casting 2206000
1967–1969	440 4V	2843031, casting 2806178
1971	440 4V	3512502, casting 3512501
1971	440 4V	3577164, Imperial
1970	440 4V	2951737, casting 2951736
1969–1970	440 3x2V	3412046, casting 3412046, aluminum
1970	440 3x2V	3418681, casting 3418681, aluminum
1970–1971	440 3x2V	2946275, casting 2946275, 2946276, iron
1971–1972	440 4V	3614015, casting 3614014
1972	440 4V	3614017
1972	440 4V	3614016, w/ A.I.R.
1973	440 4V	3698585, casting 3698444
1974	440 4V	3751729, casting 3751728
1974–1975	440 4V	3830731
Exhaust Manifolds		
1958	350	1851836 right, 1739600 left w/ FI, D500
1958	350	1844990 (2205535 casting) right, 1739600 (2205536 casting) left, w/ a/c
1958	350	1852599 right, 1739600 (2205536 casting) left
1958	361	1851836 right, 1739600 left w/FI, D500

This is a typical four-barrel cast-iron intake manifold for the "B" engine—in this case the 1966 383 cid engine.

Year	Engine	Part or Casting Number
Exhaust Manifolds		
1958	361	1844990 (2205535 casting) right, 1739600 (2205536 casting) left, w/ a/c
1958	361	1852599 right, 1739600 (2205536 casting) left
1959	361	1739597 (1739599 casting) right, 1739600 (2205536 casting) left
1960	361	1946969 right, 1739600 (2205536 casting) left
1961–1964	361	1844990 (2205535 casting) right, 1739600 (2205536 casting) left
1959	383	1739597 (1739599 casting) right, 1739600 (2205536 casting) left
1959	383	1844990 (2205535 casting) right, 1739600 (2205536 casting) left, w/ a/c
1960	383	1946969 right, 1739600 (2205536 casting) left
1961–1964	383	1844990 (2205535 casting) right, 1739600 (2205536 casting) left
1965	383	1844990 (2205535 casting) right, 2463106 (2461307 casting) left
1966–1969	383	2532459 (2532464 casting) right, 2463106 (2461307 casting) left
1968–1969	383	2863897 (2863900 casting) right, 2899001 (2899002 casting) left, Barracuda
1968–1969	383	2863897 (2863900 casting) right, 2946728 (2946720 casting) left, Barracuda, Dart
1968	383	2806898 (2806900 casting) right, 2843991 (2843992 casting) left, m/t
1969	383 2V	2532459 (2532464 casting) right, 2532627 left
1970–1971	383	2899968 (2899879 casting) right, 2951864 (2951865 casting) left, B/C body
1970–1971	383	2899968 (2899879 casting) right, 2951217 (2951216 casting) left, C body
1970–1971	383	2899954 (2899970 casting) right, 2951860 (2951861 casting) left, C body
1972	400	3614826 right, 2951860 (2951861 casting) left, C body
1973	400	3751794 right, 3744821 left
1973	400	3651072 (3751074 casting) right, 3744821 left B/C body
1974	400	3751791 right, 3698545 left
1975	400	3830041 right, 3830044 left w/ A.I.R.
1975	400	3830818 right, 3830799 left
1959	413	1739597 (1739599 casting) right, 1739600 (2205536 casting) left
1960	413	1947488 right, 1947432 left, 300F
1960	413	1946969 right, 1739600 (2205536 casting) left
1961	413	2205853 (2205830 casting) right, 1947432 (1947434 casting) left, 300G
1962	413	2268250 right, 1739600 (2205536 casting) left, 300H
1961–1964	413	1844990 (2205535 casting) right, 1739600 (2205536 casting) left
1962	413	2402335 (2402334 casting) right, 2402337 (2402336 casting) left, Max Wedge
1963–1964	413	2269093 (2402781 casting) right, 2269013 (2402782 casting) left, 300J, 300K
1965	413	1844990 (2205535 casting) right, 1739600 (2205536 casting) left
1963	426	2402335 (2402334 casting) right, 2402337 (2402336 casting) left, Max Wedge
1964–1965	426	2205905 (2205898 casting) right, 2203091 (2203262 casting) left
1965	426	1844990 (2205535 casting) right, 2463106 (2463107 casting) left
1964	426	2402335 (2402334 casting) right, 2402337 (2402336 casting) left, Max Wedge
1964	426	2468657 (2465657 casting) right, 2468658 (2468658 casting) left, Hemi
1965	426	2532236 (2465657 casting) right, 2532237 (2468658 casting) left, Hemi

Year	Engine	Part or Casting Number
Exhaust Manifolds		
1966–1969	426	2780506 (2780508 casting) right, 2780502 (2780501 casting) left, intermediates, Hemi
1970–1971	426	Challenger/Barracuda
1966–1968	440	2532459 (2532464 casting) right, 2463106 (2461307 casting) left
1967	440	2806898 (2806900 casting) right, 2843248, left, Fury, VIP
1967	440	2806898 (2806900 casting) right, 2806975 (2806974 casting) left, 375 hp, GTX, R/T
1968–1969	440	2806898 (2806900 casting) right, 2863408 (2843992 casting) left, 375 hp, GTX, R/T
1970–1971	440	2899968 (2899879 casting) right, 2951217 (2951216 casting) left, C body
1970–1971	440	2899968 (2899879 casting) right, 2951864 (2951865 casting) left, B/C body

Year	Engine	Part or Casting Number
Exhaust Manifolds		
1970–1971	440	2899954 (2899970 casting) right, 2951860 (2951861 casting) left, C body
1973	440	3751072 (3751074 casting) right, 3744821 left, B/C body
1973	440	3671934 right, 3698544 (3698546 casting) left, C body, w/ A.I.R.
1974	440	3751794 right, 3751193 left w/ A.I.R.
1974	440	3751791 right, 3698545 left, 230 hp
1974	440	3769208 right, 3744821 left, 250 hp
1974	440	3769208 right, 3751067 (3751068 casting) left, B body
1975	440	3830041 right, 3830044 left, w/ A.I.R.
1975	440	3830818 right, 3830799 left

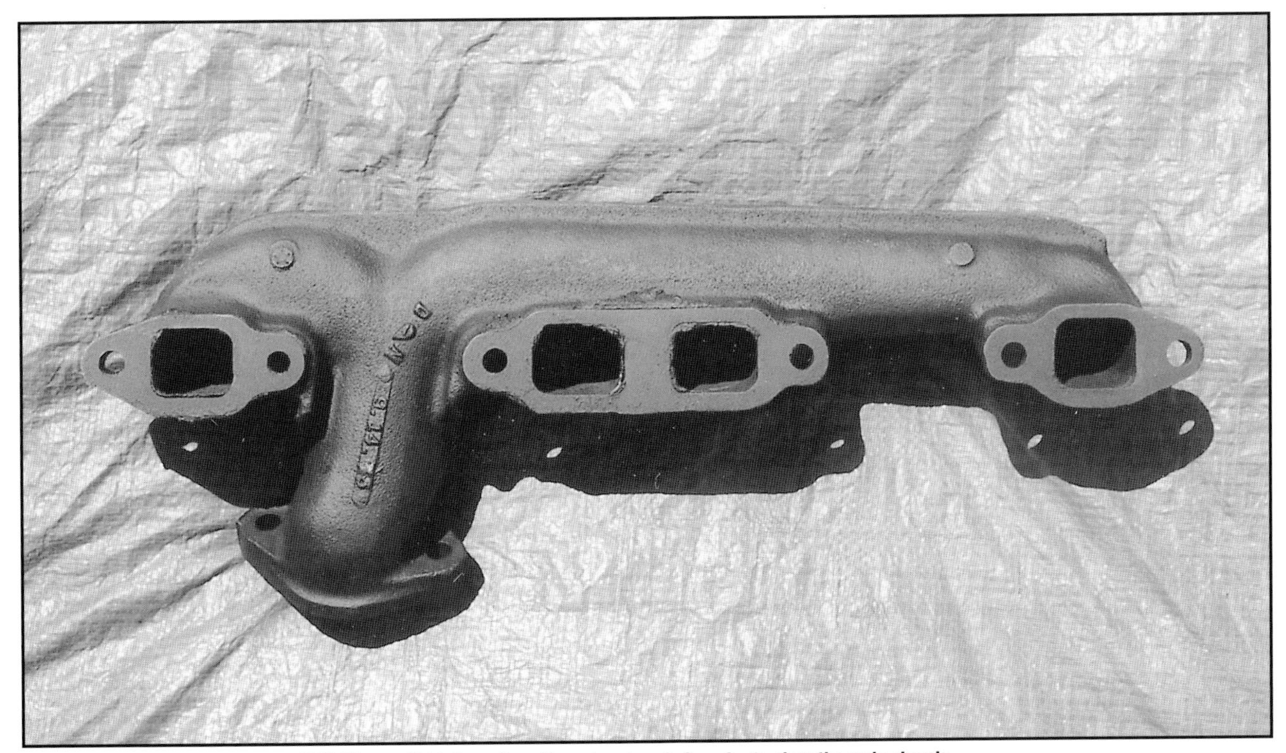

This is a typical B/RB exhaust manifold. The manifold rises above the exhaust ports in order to clear the car's chassis.

CHAPTER 19

CHRYSLER LA-SERIES

1964-1975

273, 318, 340, and 360

Chrysler's modern thin-wall-casting small-block V-8 engine made its debut in 1964. The engine series was known as the LA series, for "Lower A." The designation indicated that this was a lower-deck-height A-series engine. The A-series engines were available from 1958 to 1966, and the largest engine of that series, the 318 cid V-8, was still available and used on Dodge and Plymouth cars. In addition to the lowered deck height, there were a considerable number of other differences, so that components of the two engine families don't readily interchange with each other. The big difference, of course, was that the LA engines used cylinder heads with a new wedge combustion chamber design, whereas the older A-series used the polyspherical combustion chamber.

The LA engines were made from 100 percent pure Detroit cast iron—block, heads, and manifolds. Still, the thin-wall-casting techniques enabled Chrysler engineers to reduce the engine's weight by 55lb. The LA-series engines followed standard Chrysler practice of using rocker shafts, rather than the stamped-steel individual rockers used by Chevrolet and Ford. All engines, except for the 1964–1967 273 cid engines, used a hydraulic-lifter camshaft. All factory intake manifolds were made of cast iron, except the 1970 340 cid triple two-barrel intake setup, which was made of aluminum.

The high point in small-block development was the 340 cid engine used in the 1970 AAR 'Cuda and Challenger T/A. The actual race cars didn't used the street Tri-Power intake but rather a single four-barrel Holley carburetor. This is the original engine in the AAR 'Cuda as raced by the AAR team.

The 273 cid V-8 was the first engine of the reinvigorated LA series. It had a bore and stroke of 3.63x3.31 in. With a mechanical-lifter camshaft and two-barrel carburetor, it put out 180 hp.

The 318 cid version of the LA series was released in 1967. It had the same bore and stroke as the poly-head A series, 3.91x 3.31 in., but that's about all that was the same. The workhorse 318 remained basically unchanged through the 1971 model year, pumping out 230 hp. From 1972 on, the 318 cid engine's output was measured using the SAE net method for 150 hp.

As good as the 273- and 318 cid engines were, they didn't do much for the performance image of the Dodge and Plymouth cars that used them. The next development of the LA engine occurred in 1968 with the release of the 340 cid V-8. The 340 cid V-8 had a bore and stroke of 4.04x3.31 in. Rated at only 275 hp, this was an extremely strong-running engine. The 340 cid small-block lasted through the 1973 model year. Most notable of all was the special 340 cid triple two-barrel version that powered the 1970 Challenger T/A and the AAR 'Cuda.

The last variation of the LA series was the 360 cid version introduced in 1971. The 360 engine wasn't the performer the 340 cid engine was but it eventually replaced it.

LA engines have also powered Dodge light trucks. The 273 cid truck version, rated at 174 hp, was used during 1965–1966. The LA 318 cid engine replaced the A-series 318 cid V-8 in 1967, and it was rated at 210 hp until 1971. From 1971 to 1977, the 318 was rated at 150 hp. The engine is still in service today.

273 cid

First released in 1964, the 273 cid V-8 came with a forged-steel crankshaft, forged-steel rods, and cast-aluminum pistons. The 273 cid engine used a mechanical-lifter camshaft and with a two-barrel carburetor, it put out 180 hp. A hotter camshaft, a Carter AFB four-barrel carburetor, and a 10.5:1 compression ratio boosted power to 235 hp in 1965.

Both versions of the 273 cid engine were carried over into 1966–1967. A limited edition of the 273 cid V-8 put out 275 hp in 1966. The two-barrel 273 cid engine, rated at 190 hp with the two-barrel carburetor, was the only one available during 1968–1969. That engine also used a hydraulic-lifter camshaft and a cast-iron crankshaft.

318 cid

The 318 cid V-8 was your typical entry-level or base V-8 in Chrysler's cars from 1967 on. There was nothing that made it stand out. It came with a cast-iron intake manifold and two-barrel carburetor, a single exhaust system, and a hydraulic camshaft for 230 hp. The 1967 318 V-8 was the only one to come with a forged-steel crankshaft—all others were cast iron.

From 1971 on, power ratings on the 318 V-8 dropped to the 150–170 hp range. The engine continued on through the late 1990s.

340 cid

The 340 cid engine was introduced in 1968, with a bore and stroke of 4.04x3.31 in. The combination of larger cylinder head ports and valves, a 10.2:1 compression ratio, an improved intake manifold, and a Carter AVS combined to produce a strong 275 hp. The 340 cid also got a forged-steel crankshaft and a hydraulic camshaft. For 1968, the four-speed manual car's cam was a little more aggressive than that in an automatic-equipped engine. The engine would continue in this configuration through the 1971 model year. The Carter Thermoquad carburetor replaced the AVS from 1971 to 1973.

The most interesting 340 cid made was the one used on the 1970 Dodge Challenger T/A and Plymouth AAR 'Cuda. These were the cars that Chrysler was racing in SCCA's Trans Am series. In order to homologate the engine, at least 1,000 of each had to be built. Although the engine used in the actual races was a 305, it wasn't necessary for Chrysler to build a street 305 cid engine. The 340 used in the street cars had a special engine block with heavier bulkheads and webbing, and there was enough material so that four-bolt main-bearing caps could be installed. The engine also used a unique triple two-barrel carburetor aluminum intake manifold, and the cylinder heads had larger intake ports with 2.02 in. intake and 1.60 in. exhaust valves. It was rated at 290 hp.

All 1972 and later 340 cid engines were detuned. The 1972 automatic and all 1973 340 cid engines got a cast-iron crankshaft, cylinder heads that had smaller valves, and a lower compression ratio of 8.5:1, for a 240 hp output. The engine was dropped after the 1973 model year.

360 cid

The last engine of the LA family was the 360 cid version introduced in 1971. It had a smaller bore (4.00 in.) than the 340 cid engine but a longer stroke (3.58 in.). Because it used a cast-iron crank, Chrysler increased the engine's main-bearing cap journal size to 2.81 in. The 360 cid engine, in 1971, used the larger port and valve small-block cylinder heads. From 1972 on, the 360 cid V-8 came with the smaller-valve cylinder heads.

The 1971–1973 engines were low-performance engines; they all came with two-barrel carburetors. Some of the 360 cid engines from 1974 on were considered high performance, in the emission-era context, and they were equipped with four-barrel carburetors. The 360 cid engine was dropped from passenger car use in 1980, but continues on today in Dodge trucks.

Engine Blocks

All the LA engines use the same basic engine blocks, but there are detail differences, besides the various bore dimensions. All blocks except the 340 Challenger T/A, 'Cuda AAR, and Trans Am blocks have two-bolt main-bearing caps. The exceptions have four-bolt mains in the numbers 2, 3, and 4 positions and thicker bulkheads and filled-in pan rails. The main-bearing journals in all but 360 blocks were 2.50 in.; the 360 cid blocks have larger size journals, 2.81 in. Rod journals measure 2.125 in. on all engines. The 273 and 318 cid blocks also differ from 340 and 360 cid engines in that they have different left-side motor mount ears.

Cylinder Heads

All LA engines have wedge-type open-chamber combustion chambers with an inline-valve arrangement. The 273 and 318 cid cylinder heads have smaller ports and smaller valves, 1.75 in./1.50 in. intake/exhaust.

The 1968–1971 340- and 360 cid cylinder heads have larger ports and larger valves, 2.02 in./1.60 in. intake/exhaust. The 1972–1978 340- and 360 cid cylinder heads have smaller, 1.88 in./1.60 in. intake/exhaust valves, but still have the larger ports.

LA series blocks have the casting number on the left side of the block as shown. This one is a 360. Not all blocks have the engine displacement size casting.

The special 340 T/A and AAR cylinder heads have larger intake ports, which required special offset intake rocker arms and relocated pushrods. The T/A and AAR engines used the larger, 2.02 in./1.60 in. valves.

Intake Manifolds

The vast majority of LA engines were equipped with a cast-iron two-barrel intake manifold, simply because most of these engines were 318s. Four-barrel intake manifolds were used by all engines at one time or another, except for the 318 cid engine.

The triple two-barrel intake manifold used on the 1970 340 T/A and AAR engines was made from cast aluminum. It used three Holley two-barrel carburetors.

Exhaust Manifolds

All LA engines used cast-iron exhaust manifolds with various sizes of outlets, depending on application. The manifolds used on the 340 cid engines flowed better than other LA exhaust manifolds.

Engine Identification

All major Chrysler engine components were cast with a number to identify the part and a date code that indicated the date that part was cast. These numbers were cast in a variety of locations. The date codes used on blocks, intakes, and exhaust manifolds were fairly easy to decipher. As an example, 11-22-70 decodes to November 22, 1970.

The engine ID code on the LA series varied quite a bit from 1964 to 1975. Initially, the code consisted of a single letter code indicating model year, followed by an engine displacement code and a date code. From 1964 to 1967, the year letter codes were as follows: V is 1964, A is 1965, B is 1966, and C is 1967.

The engine displacement code for 1964 was 27 for 273 cid. The engine displacement codes for 1965–1967 were 273 for 273 cid and 318 for 318 cid.

The last three digits in the ID code were three numbers indicating month and date. An example for a 1964 engine would be V 27 -4- 26. It decodes to a 273 cid engine assembled on April 26, 1964.

The code could be found on the left front side of the engine block below the cylinder head.

Besides the ID code, there were additional numbers and letters used to indicate the characteristics of a particular engine:

- A: 0.020 in. oversize cylinder bores
- B: 0.010 in. undersize main and rod bearings
- E: cast crankshaft
- H: standard 4V V-8
- HP: high performance
- LC: low compression
- O.S.: 0.005 in. oversize valve stems
- P: premium fuel recommended
- R: regular fuel may be used
- S: special engine (warranty replacement engines)
- SP: special engine
- WT: water test
- TW: water test
- X: oversize valve guides
- 2: 2nd shift
- Diamond symbol: 0.008 in. oversize tappets (lifters)
- Maltese cross symbol: 0.001 in. undersize crankshaft
- Maltese cross and X: 0.010 in. undersize crankshaft

From 1968 to 1971, a different ID code system was used. A typical ID code might read as follows: PM31825920022.

The first two letters indicate the engine plant where the engine was assembled. They are as follows: PT for the Trenton plant, which built 361-, 383-, 400-, 413-, 426-, and 440 cid engines; PM, GM, and HM for the Mound Road plant, which built 318-, 340-, and 360 cid engines; and MV and MN for the Marysville plant, which built the 426 Hemi.

The next three digits indicate engine displacement, which in this case is 318 cid. This is followed by a four-digit code that indicates the build date. This particular code, 2592, stands for September 1, 1969, and can be found in the 10,000-day calendar in the Chrysler service books. The date can usually be found next to or near the ID code, stamped in the conventional manner, 09-01-69. The last four numbers indicate what number the engine was in the sequence of engines built that day—in this case the 22nd.

In 1973, the plant code was shortened to one letter, with the letter "P" being deleted.

VIN Identification Codes

In spite of having fairly thorough engine identification codes, there is no way to match a particular engine with a specific car. Neither the car's VIN, nor any portion of it, was stamped on the engine itself. By 1967, though, Chrysler began including a letter code in the VIN for engines. Listed below are the VIN codes from 1967 on.

1967–1969

D: 273 cid
E: 273 cid HP
F: 318 cid
P: 340 cid

1970–1975

G: 318 cid
H: 340 cid
J: 340 cid 3x2V
K: 360 cid 2V
J: 360 cid 4V
L: 360 cid HP

Engine Specifications

	Displacement	Carburetor	Horsepower	Torque	Compression Ratio	Notes
1964						
	273	2V	180@4,200	260@1,600	8.8	Barracuda, Valiant, Dart
1965						
	273	2V	180@4,200	260@1,600	8.8	Barracuda, Valiant, Belvedere, Satellite, Dart, Coronet
	273	4V	200@5,200	280@4,000	10.5	Barracuda, Valiant, Dart
1966						
	273	2V	180@4,200	260@1,600	8.8	Barracuda, Valiant, Belvedere, Satellite, Dart, Coronet
	273	4V	200@5,200	280@4,000	10.5	Barracuda, Valiant, Dart
1967						
	273	2V	180@4,200	260@1,600	8.8	Barracuda, Valiant, Belvedere, Satellite, Dart, Coronet
	273	4V	200@5,200	280@4,000	10.5	Barracuda, Valiant, Dart
	318	2V	230@4,400	340@2,400	9.2	Belvedere, Satellite, Fury, Coronet, Polara, Charger
1968						
	273	2V	190@4,400	260@2,000	9.0	Valiant, Belvedere, Satellite, Dart, Coronet
	318	2V	230@4,400	340@2,400	9.2	Barracuda, Valiant, Belvedere, Satellite, Fury, Dart, Coronet, Charger, Polara
	340	4V	275@5,000	340@3,200	10.5	Barracuda, Dart GTS
1969						
	273	2V	190@4,400	260@2,000	9.0	Valiant, Dart
	318	2V	230@4,400	340@2,400	9.2	Barracuda, Belvedere, Satellite, Fury, Dart, Coronet, Charger, Polara
	340	4V	275@5,000	340@3,200	10.5	Barracuda, Swinger, Dart GTS

	Displacement	Carburetor	Horsepower	Torque	Compression Ratio	Notes
1970						
	318	2V	230@4,400	320@2,400	8.8	Barracuda, Belvedere, Duster, Fury, Satellite, Valiant, Challenger, Charger, Coronet, Dart
	340	4V	275@5,000	340@3,200	10.5	'Cuda, Duster, Challenger
	340	3x2V	290@5,000	340@3,200	10.5	'Cuda, Challenger
1971						
	318	2V	230@4,400	320@2,400	8.6	Barracuda, Duster, Valiant, Fury, Satellite, Challenger, Charger, Dart, Coronet, Polara, Monaco
	340	4V	275@5,000	340@3,200	10.3	Barracuda, Duster, Valiant, Road Runner, Fury, Challenger, Dart
	360	2V	255@4,400	360@2,400	8.7	Fury, Satellite, Coronet, Monaco, Polara
1972						
	318	2V	150@4,000	260@1,600	8.6	Barracuda, Duster, Valiant, Fury, Satellite, Challenger, Charger, Dart, Coronet, Polara, Monaco
	340	4V	240@4,800	290@3,600	8.5	Barracuda, Duster, Valiant, Road Runner, Challenger, Charger, Dart
	360	2V	175@4,000	285@2,400	8.8	Fury, Coronet, Polara, Monaco
1973						
	318	2V	150@4,000	260@1,600	8.6	Barracuda, Duster, Valiant, Fury, Satellite, Road Runner, Charger, Coronet, Polara, Dart
	340	4V	240@4,800	295@3,600	8.5	Barracuda, Duster, Valiant, Road Runner, Challenger, Charger
	360	2V	170@4,000	285@2,000	8.8	Fury, Coronet, Polara, Monaco
1974						
	318	2V	150@4,000	255@2,000	8.6	'Cuda, Challenger, Duster, Valiant, Satellite, Charger, Dart
	318	2V	170@4,000	265@2,600	8.6	Road Runner
	360	2V	180@4,000	290@2,400	8.4	Fury
	360	4V	200@4,000	290@3,200	8.4	Fury, Charger, Newport
	360	4V	245@4,800	320@3,600	8.4	'Cuda, Challenger, Duster, Valiant, Road Runner, Charger, Dart
1975						
	318	2V	150@4,000	255@1,600	8.5	Fury, Road Runner, Cordoba, Coronet, Monaco
	318	2V	145@4,000	255@1,600	8.5	Valiant, Duster, Dart
	360	2V	180@4,000	290@2,400	8.4	Fury, Road Runner, Cordoba, Newport, Coronet, Monaco
	360	4V	230@4,400	300@3,600	8.4	Dart
	360	4V	190@4,000	270@3,200	8.4	Newport

Engine Internal Dimensions

Displacement	Bore and Stroke	Rod Bearings	Main Bearings	Intake/Exhaust Valves
273	3.63x3.31	2.124–2.125	2.499–2.500	1.78/1.50
318	3.91x3.31	2.124–2.125	2.499–2.500	1.78/1.50
340	4.04x3.31	2.124–2.125	2.499–2.500	2.02/1.60 (1972–1975 1.88/1.60)
360	4.00x3.58	2.124–2.125	2.8095–2.8105	2.02/1.60 (1972–1975 1.88/1.60)

Block, Head, and Manifold Part and Casting Numbers

Year	Engine	Part or Casting Number
Engine Blocks		
1964–1966	273	casting 2465330
1965	273	casting 2536130
1965–1969	273	casting 2806130
1967–1975	318	casting 2466090, casting 2536030, casting 2566080, casting 2806030
1968–1973	340	casting 2780930
1970	340 290 hp	casting 3577130TA
1971–1974	360	casting 3418496
1975	360	casting 3870230
Cylinder Heads		
1964–1965	273	casting 2465315, casting 2532080
1966	273	casting 2536178, casting 2658234, casting 2658920
1968–1969	273	casting 2843675
1967	318	casting 2658920
1968–1974	318	casting 2843675
1975	318	casting 3769973, w/ A.I.R.
1968–1970	340	casting 2531894
1970–1972	340	casting 3418915
1973	340	casting 3671587
1970–1972	360	casting 3418915
1973–1974	360	casting 3671587
1975	360	casting 3769974 , w/ A.I.R.
Intake Manifolds		
1965	273 2V	casting 2463253
1965	273 4V	casting 2465726
1966–1968	273 2V	casting 2536560
1966	273 4V	casting 2536636
1966–1967	273 4V	casting 2536563, casting 2536771, w/ C.A.P. emissions system
1967–1969	318 2V	casting 2468959

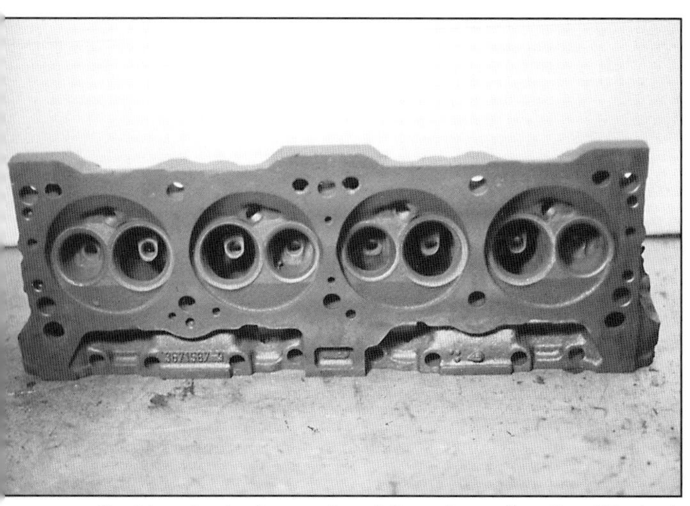

The LA series heads are of an inline valve configuration. This head, #3671587, is made for the 1973 340 and 1974 360 cid engines.

Year	Engine	Part or Casting Number
Intake Manifolds		
1970	318 2V	casting 2951185
1972	318 2V	casting 3671466
1973	318 2V	casting 3698431
1968	340 4V	casting 2531915
1970	340 4V	casting 3462848
1970	340 3x2V	casting 3418681, aluminum
1971	340 4V	casting 3512100
1972	340 4V	casting 3614025
1972	340 4V	casting 3671918, California
1973	340 4V	casting 3671918
1972	360 4V	part number 3671468 w/ NOX emission system
1972	360 4V	part number 3671467 w/o NOX emission system
1973	360 4V	casting 3698437
1974	360 4V	casting 3698434, casting 3668435
1974	360 2V	part number 3769993
Exhaust Manifolds		
1965–1968	273/318	2465766 (casting 2465769) right, 2465718 (casting 2475719) left, Dodge, Plymouth
1964–1966	273	2465766 (casting 2465769) right, 2465848 (casting 2465857) left, Dart, Barracuda
1967–1968	273/318	2465766 (casting 2465769) right, 2780946 (casting 2780945) left, Dart, Barracuda
1967–1968	318	2465766 (casting 2465769) right, 2465718 (casting 2475719) left, Charger
1968–1969	318	2843966 (casting 2843953) right, 2465718 (casting 2475719) left, Barracuda
1969	318	2843966 (casting 2843953) right, 2951124 (casting 2951123) left, Dart, Valiant
1970–1973	318	2843966 (casting 2843953) right, 3512076 (casting 3512077) left, Barracuda, Challenger, Charger, Dodge
1969	318	2843966 (casting 2843953) right, 2465718 (casting 2475719) left, Charger, Dodge
1969–1971	318	2843966 (casting 2843953) right, 2465718 (casting 2475719) left, Dart, Valiant
1972–1973	318	2843966 (casting 2843953) right, 3614396 (casting 3614395) left, Dart, Valiant
1973	318	3671396 right, 3671399 (casting 3671400) left, Road Runner
1974	318	3769406 right, 3671399 (casting 3671400) left, Road Runner

Year	Engine	Part or Casting Number
Exhaust Manifolds		
1974	318	2843966 (casting 2843953) right, 2843966 (casting 2843953) left, truck
1974	318	3751607 right, 3512076 (casting 3512077) left, Barracuda, Challenger, Charger
1974	318	3751607 right, 3512076 left, Dodge, Plymouth
1974	318	3751607 right, 3614396 left, Dart, Valiant
1975	318	3879721 right, 3671914 left, w/ A.I.R., Dart, Valiant
1975	318	3870059 right, 3830904 left, Dart, Valiant
1968	340	2863546 right, 2863552 (casting 2863553) left, Dart, Barracuda
1969–1970	340	2863545 (casting 2863549) right, 3418624 (casting 3418623) left, Barracuda, 1970 Challenger
1969–1970	340	2863545 (casting 2863549) right, 3614367 (casting 3614368) left, Dart, Valiant
1971–1973	340	3418624 (casting 3418623) right, 3614396 (casting 3614395) left, Dart, Valiant
1971–1972	340/360	3418624 (casting 3418623) right, 3418620 (casting 3418621) left, Barracuda, Challenger, Charger, Dodge, Plymouth
1973	340	3418624 (casting 3418623) right, 3751083 left, Barracuda, Challenger, Charger
1973	340/360	3671634 right, 3671583 left, w/ A.I.R., Dodge, Plymouth
1973	340/360	3418624 (casting 3418623) right, 3751083 left, Dodge, Plymouth
1974	360	3751393 right, 3751083 left, Barracuda, Challenger, Charger
1974	360	3751393 right, 3614367 left, Dart, Valiant
	360	3751393 right, 3751083 left, Dodge, Plymouth
1974	360	3671634 right, 3751393 left, truck
1975	318/360	3879721 right, 3830205 left w/ A.I.R., Charger, Cordoba, Chrysler, Dodge, Plymouth
1975	318/360	3870059 right, 3870366 left, Charger, Cordoba, Chrysler, Dodge, Plymouth
1975	318/360	3870059 right, 3870057 left, w/ A.I.R., light truck
1975	318/360	3870057 right, 3870057 left, truck

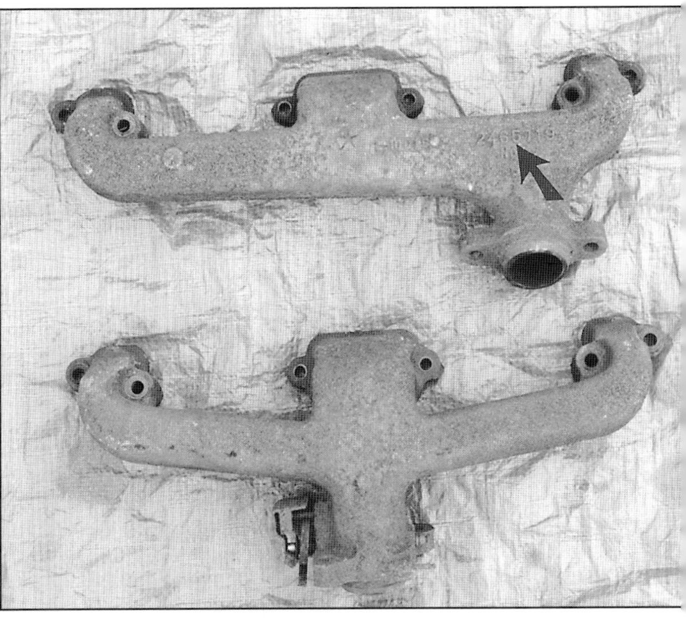

These exhaust manifolds are for the 1965–69 273-318 cid engine in a "B" or "C" body chassis. Casting number, 2465719, is still visible on this weathered manifold.

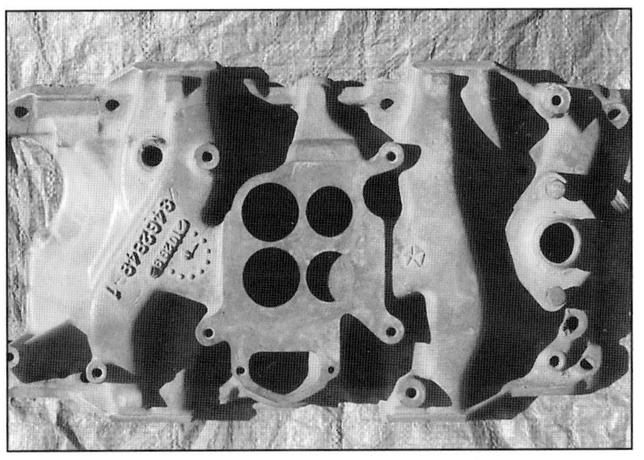

This is a typical 340/360 factory cast-iron intake manifold for four-barrel applications.

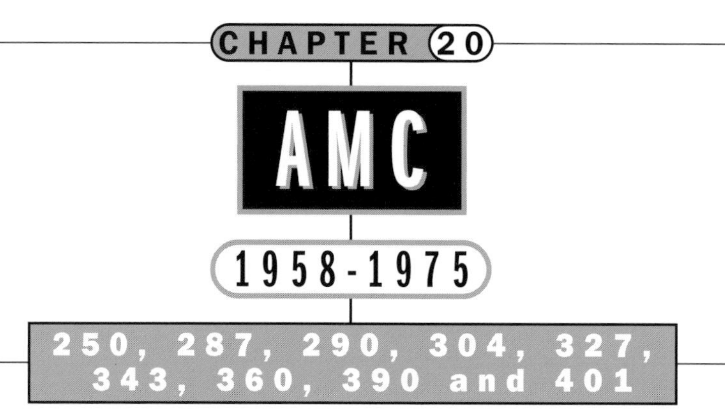

CHAPTER 20

AMC

1958-1975

250, 287, 290, 304, 327, 343, 360, 390 and 401

In 1954, Hudson Motor Company and Nash-Kelvinator Company merged to form American Motors. The cars that the new company chose to promote were the Rambler from Hudson and the Ambassador from Nash. The timing was good because the big three, with their styling excesses and larger and larger cars, managed to turn off a significant part of the public who preferred smaller, economical cars. AMC proved to be successful in that respect. By the mid-1960s, the company changed its focus and tried to compete head to head with the big three by offering larger cars as well. That eventually proved to be the undoing of the company, because it did not have the resources and plant capacity to do so. AMC should have continued producing and refining its small cars. Still, in the process, AMC did produce some interesting cars, and at the same time, a well-designed new V-8 engine in 1966.

The AMC V-8 engines eventually showed themselves to be able passenger car performers that also had considerable high-performance potential. The 390- and 401 cid engines were strong street performance engines. This was due to an excellent cylinder head design that featured large ports and valves. The engine, when modified, proved to be an able performer on the track as well. AMC won the 1971–1972 Trans Am Series, and the engine was also used in NASCAR racing, Formula 5000, and on the drag strip with good results. All these racing efforts were made to promote the company's passenger cars, but as said earlier, the problem was that AMC didn't have the means to compete successfully, no matter how many races they won.

The first official AMC cars were introduced in 1958—the Rambler, Rebel, and Ambassador. Two V-8 engines were used, a

All 1967 and later AMC V-8s looked the same externally. Good port design and valve sizing made it possible for the engine to produce more than respectable power in stock applications. This is a 1969 390 cid in an AMX. Note ID tag on right valve cover.

250 cid and a 327 cid. The 250 cid Rebel V-8 had a bore and stroke of 3.50x3.250 in., and it was used first in Hudson cars in 1956. In 1957, the engine was used on Nash and Rambler models as well. The engine had a cast-iron engine block, cylinder heads, and manifolds, and a forged-steel crankshaft and forged-steel connecting rods. This V-8 was in production until 1962. During this time period, the engine developed between 200 and 215 hp.

The Ambassador V-8 was introduced in 1957 and was carried over to the AMC line. The Ambassador had a bore and stroke of 4.00x3.25 in., for 327 cid. It was rated at 255 hp. The high point, in terms of power output for the engine, came in 1959, when it was rated at 270 hp.

As 1962 was the final year for the 250 cid engine, a 3.75x3.25 in. bore and stroke version of the engine was introduced in 1963, which had a displacement of 287 cid. The 287- and 327 cid engines were in production through the 1966 model year. These engines had a reputation for reliability, but didn't offer much in terms of high performance. They were also on the heavy side. In addition to passenger car duty, these engines were used in various Jeep vehicles and trucks.

AMC designed a new engine series in the mid-1960s. The engine was completely new from the ground up. It had a new, thin-wall-casting block, heads, and manifolds. There was no interchangeability between the new engine and the old heavyweights. The engine, with a bore spacing of 4.75 in. (which was bigger than that of the small-block Chevy, Ford's FE and 351C families, and the Pontiac and Oldsmobile V-8s), had plenty of room for future growth, eventually reaching 401 cid in 1971.

The first version of the new engine was a late-1966 release, with a bore and stroke of 3.75x3.28 in., displacing 290 cid. With a two-barrel carburetor, the Typhoon V-8 was rated at 200 hp; the four-barrel was rated at 225 hp. A 343 cid version was released in 1967 and a 390 cid engine in 1968. All three were in production through the 1969 model year.

In 1970, the 290 cid was used as a basis for two new engines by modifying it with new bore and stroke dimensions, resulting in 304- and 360 cid engines; the 390 cid engine was similarly modified for 401 cid in 1971. The 401 cid engine was in production through the 1974 model year in cars and throughout 1978 in Jeep trucks; the 304- and 360 cid engines were in production well into the 1980s, and the 360 cid engine until 1991, in the Jeep Grand Wagoneer. Both the 304- and 360 cid engines were also used in various Jeep vehicles through the 1970s and '80s.

250-, 287-, and 327 cid

The first generation AMC engines were heavy passenger car engines. As stated earlier, they all used cast-iron blocks and heads with forged-steel crankshafts and connecting rods. They were available with two- or four-barrel carburetors. The 327 cid engine was also used on the Kaiser Jeep Wagoneer and Gladiator 1/2- and 3/4-ton pickups. These vehicles all used the 250 hp version of the engine.

290 cid

The first engine in the new AMC engine series was the 290 cid version, introduced in 1966. It had a bore and stroke of 3.75x3.28 in. The 290 cid engine came with either a two-barrel (200 hp) or four-barrel (225 hp) carburetor; the four-barrel engine was equipped with dual exhausts. The engine would remain in production through the 1969 model year.

304 cid

The 304 cid AMC had a 3.75 in. bore and a 3.44 in. stroke. All 304 cid engines came with a two-barrel carburetor and a single exhaust system. The 1970–1971 versions were rated at 210 hp; 1972–1975 engines were rated at 150 hp.

1967 and later AMC cylinder blocks. All factory blocks came with hefty two-bolt main bearing caps. The one on the left is a 390 while the one on the right is a 401. All blocks were cast with displacement size on both sides of block. *A.J. Jacobs*

343 cid

Increasing the bore on the block to 4.08 in. and using the 290's 3.28 in. stroke resulted in a 343 cid version AMC V-8. The 1967 version of the engine came with a four-barrel carburetor and was rated at 280 hp. In 1968, a two-barrel version was added, rated at 235 hp. Both variations were available through the 1969 model year.

360 cid

The 360 cid variation was introduced in 1970. It was basically a stroked 343 cid engine (they both had the same 4.08 in. bore). The 360's stroke was 3.44 in. There were two- and four-barrel versions available. The two-barrel engine was rated at 245 hp, while the four-barrel put out an advertised 290 hp. Both engines were available in 1971, but the four-barrel was rated at 5 hp less. Through the 1973 model year, the two versions of the engine were rated at 150 and 175 hp. In 1974, a 220 hp version was added.

390 cid

This was AMC's biggest engine through the 1969 model year. Introduced in 1968, the engine had a 4.165 in. bore and a 3.574 in. stroke. The engine was equipped with a four-barrel carburetor. The 1969 version of the engine was rated at 315 hp, and the 1970 version was rated at 325 hp. The 390 cid engine used on the 1970 Rebel Machine model was rated at 340 hp.

Although the engine looked the same as other AMC engines, the 390 cid version had larger rod bearings, 2.250 in. vs. 2.090 in. The crankshaft and connecting rods were also made of forged steel instead of the cast nodular iron used on the 290- and 343 cid engines.

401 cid

The biggest AMC V-8 had a 4.165 in. bore and a 3.68 in. stroke. The 1971 version was rated at 330 hp. The 1972–1975 engines were rated (using the SAE net method) at 255 hp. The compression ratio was lowered, to 8.5:1.

As with the 390 cid engine, the 401 cid V-8 was also equipped forged-steel connecting rods and a forged-steel crankshaft. All 401 cid engines were equipped with a four-barrel carburetor.

Engine Blocks

All AMC V-8 engine blocks were made of cast iron. The only exception were the few blocks AMC cast in aluminum for Indy car use. All engines used two-bolt main-bearing caps. The 401 cid blocks and a special 1970 360 cid block that was used for Trans Am racing could be fitted with four-bolt-main caps. The 250-, 287-, and 327 cid blocks had 2.500 in. main-bearing journals; the later design AMC blocks had 2.747 in. mains. Rod bearings measured 2.245 in. on the early engines and 2.095 in. on the later engines, except the 390- and 401 cid engines, which had larger, 2.247 in. journals.

All early engines used a forged-steel crankshaft and forged-steel connecting rods. Later, the 290-, 304-, 343-, and 360 cid engines used cast nodular iron connecting rods and crankshafts. The 390-401 cid engines got forged-steel connecting rods and crankshafts. Forged-steel crankshafts and forged-steel connecting rods were available as an over-the-counter option for the later engines. These and other high-performance parts were part of AMC's Group 19 performance parts program.

All 1972 and later automatic engines have a different crankshaft than earlier engines, because AMC switched to the Chrysler Torqueflite transmission in 1972, which required a different crankshaft flange.

Cylinder Heads

Pre-1966 AMC engines had cast-iron cylinder heads with wedge-style combustion chambers. The valves were actuated by shaft-mounted rockers. The 250 cid engines used a mechanical-lifter camshaft, while the 287- and 327 cid engines used hydraulic-lifter camshafts. These engines were equipped with 1.787 in./1.406 in. intake/exhaust valves.

All later AMC V-8 engines came with hydraulic-lifter camshafts, and all engines used individual stud-mounted stamped-steel rocker arms. The 1973 304 cid engines and all 1974 and later V-8 engines used stamped rocker arms that were bridged together in pairs.

The 1966–1969 engines had rectangular intake and exhaust ports. Nineteen seventy and later cylinder heads had the so-called dog-leg style exhaust ports, which flowed considerably better than the previous design. Combustion chamber design was similar on all engines, but chamber volume differed, depending on compression ratio.

There was also the SS and AMX cylinder heads that were used for NHRA competition. These were specially prepared by Crane Engineering and featured 2.08 in./1.74 in. intake/exhaust valves, along with modified intake and exhaust ports.

Valve sizes differed as well. The 290- and 304 cid engines have valves of 1.787 in./1.406 in. intake/exhaust. The 343-, 360- (1970 only), and 390 cid engines used larger, 2.02 in./1.625 in. intake/exhaust valves. The 1970 and later 360- and 401 cid engines had 2.02 in./1.68 in. exhaust valves.

All 1969 and earlier engines had 7/16 in. head bolts; later engines used 1/2 in. bolts.

Intake Manifolds

All AMC intake manifolds, two- and four-barrel, were made from cast iron. The stock intake manifold used on the 1970 Rebel Machine, also made of cast iron, flowed better than all other stock intake manifolds because it had larger passages. The Edelbrock R4B aluminum intake manifold, along with a dual-quad cross-ram intake, was available as part of the Group 19 program.

There are differences between the 1966–1969 manifolds and those from 1970 and later. The earlier manifolds have the center mounting bolts lower than the outer ones; 1970 and later bolts all line up on a single plane.

Exhaust Manifolds

All AMC engines use log-type cast-iron exhaust manifolds with outlets toward the rear of the engine, pointing downward.

All 1966–1969 exhaust manifolds have rectangular exhaust ports; later engines have exhaust manifolds that match the dog-leg-style exhaust ports. The exhaust manifolds used on the 1970 Rebel Machine have 2.25 in. outlets; most other engines use a 2.00 in. outlet.

Engine Identification

Each AMC part was cast with a number and a date code, located in various locations. It's fairly easy to locate these numbers on intake and exhaust manifolds. On cylinder heads, the casting numbers were located under the valve cover area. On engine blocks, the date codes were located generally in the lifter valley area. All 1967–1975 AMC engines (and the 1966 290 cid engines) had the engine displacement size cast on both sides of the block, making it easy to tell what displacement a particular block was.

Additional engine information can be found on a metal tag attached to the front of the right valve cover on the 1966–1975 AMC V-8 engines. On earlier engines, this information was either on a tag or stamped on the generator or alternator support bracket. A typical code might read "11 3 W 21." The first two-digit number is the year code. Year codes 2–16 represent the years 1960–1975; thus the 11 code represents 1969. The one- or two-digit number following the year code, "3" in this example, is the month code. Month codes range from 1 to 12, with 3 representing March. The letter following the month code is the engine code. These codes are listed in the tables. The "W" in the example denotes the 390 cid engine. The two-digit number at the end of the tag code, "21" in this example, is the day-of-the-month code, ranging from 01 to 31. Thus, our example decodes to a 390 cid engine assembled on March 31, 1969.

1966–1967 VIN Engine Codes

Listed here are the 1966–1967 VIN engine codes, which are different from those found on the engine tag.

Code	Engine
1966 American	
C	290 cid 200 hp
D	290 cid 225 hp
1966 Classic	
H	287 cid 198 hp
J	327 cid 250 hp
K	327 cid 270 hp
1966 Ambassador	
N	287 cid 198 hp
P	327 cid 250 hp
Q	327 cid 270 hp
1966 Marlin	
T	287 cid 198 hp
U	327 cid 250 hp
W	327 cid 270 hp
1967 American	
C	290 cid 200 hp
D	290 cid 225 hp
X	343 cid 280 hp
1967 Ambassador	
N	290 cid 200 hp
R	343 cid 235 hp
Q	343 cid 280 hp
1967 Rebel	
H	290 cid 200 hp

Code	Engine
J	343 cid 235 hp
K	343 cid 280 hp
1967 Marlin	
U	290 cid 200 hp
V	343 cid 235 hp
W	343 cid 280 hp

Engine Identification Codes

Code	Engine
1958	
G-24001 and up	250 cid
N-17001 and up	327 cid
1959	
G-34501 and up	250 cid
N-32501 and up	327 cid
1960	
G	250 cid 215 hp
E	327 cid 250 hp
F	327 cid 270 hp
1961	
G	250 cid 200/215 hp
E	327 cid 250 hp
F	327 cid 270 hp
1962	
G	250 cid 200 hp
E	327 cid 250 hp
F	327 cid 270 hp
1963–1966	
G	287 cid 198 hp
E	327 cid 250 hp
F	327 cid 270 hp
H	290 cid 200 hp
N	290 cid 225 hp
1967	
H	290 cid 200 hp
N	290 cid 225 hp
Z	343 cid 280 hp
1968	
H	290 cid 200 hp
N	290 cid 225 hp
S	343 cid 235 hp
Z	343 cid 280 hp
W	390 cid 315 hp
1969	
H	290 cid 200 hp
N	290 cid 225 hp
S	343 cid 235 hp
Z	343 cid 280 hp
W	390 cid 325 hp
1970	
H	304 cid 210 hp

The weakness of the 1967–69 AMC heads were the rectangular exhaust ports. In 1970, AMC went to this "dog-leg" exhaust port design, which flowed considerable better than the previous rectangular ports, even with larger valves.

Code	Engine
N	360 cid 245 hp
P	360 cid 290 hp
X	390 cid 325 hp
Y	390 cid 340 hp
1971	
H	304 cid 210 hp
N	360 cid 245 hp
P	360 cid 285 hp
Z	401 cid 330 hp
1972	
H	304 cid 150 hp
N	360 cid 175 hp
P	360 cid 195/220 hp
Z	401 cid 255 hp
1973	
H	304 cid 150 hp
N	360 cid 175 hp
P	360 cid 195/220 hp
Z	401 cid 255 hp
1974	
H	304 cid 150 hp
N	360 cid 175 hp
P	360 cid 195/220 hp
Z	401 cid 255 hp
1975	
H	304 cid 150 hp
N	360 cid 175 hp
P	360 cid 195/220 hp

Engine Specifications

Year	Displacement	Carburetor	Horsepower	Torque	Compression Ratio	Notes
1958						
	250	4V	215@4,900	260@2,500	8.70	Rebel
	327	4V	255@4,700	345@2,600	9.70	Ambassador
1959						
	250	4V	215@4,900	260@2,500	8.70	Rebel
	327	4V	270@4,700	360@2,600	9.70	Ambassador
1960						
	250	4V	215@4,900	260@2,500	8.70	Rebel
	327	4V	270@4,700	360@2,600	9.70	Ambassador
1961						
	250	2V	200@4,900	245@2,500	8.70	Classic
	250	4V	215@4,900	260@2,500	8.70	Classic
	327	4V	250@4,700	340@2,600	8.70	Ambassador
	327	4V	270@4,700	360@2,600	9.70	Ambassador
1962						
	250	2V	200@4,900	245@2,500	8.70	Classic
	327	4V	250@4,700	340@2,600	8.70	Ambassador
	327	4V	270@4,700	360@2,600	9.70	Ambassador
1963						
	287	2V	198@4,700	280@2,600	8.70	Classic, American
	327	4V	250@4,700	340@2,600	8.70	Ambassador
	327	4V	270@4,700	360@2,600	9.70	Ambassador
1964						
	287	2V	198@4,700	280@2,600	8.70	Ambassador, Classic, American
	327	4V	250@4,700	340@2,600	8.70	Ambassador, Classic
	327	4V	270@4,700	360@2,600	9.70	Ambassador
1965						
	287	2V	198@4,700	280@2,600	8.70	Ambassador, Classic, American
	327	4V	250@4,700	340@2,600	8.70	Ambassador, Classic
	327	4V	270@4,700	360@2,600	9.70	Ambassador, Classic
1966						
	287	2V	198@4,700	280@2,600	8.70	Ambassador, Classic, Marlin
	290	2V	200@4,600	285@2,800	9.0	American
	290	4V	225@4,700	300@3,200	10.0	American
	327	4V	250@4,700	340@2,600	8.70	Ambassador, Classic, Marlin
	327	4V	270@4,700	360@2,600	9.70	Ambassador, Classic, Marlin
1967						
	290	2V	200@4,600	285@2,800	9.0	American, Ambassador, Rebel, Marlin
	290	4V	225@4,700	300@3,200	10.0	American
	343	2V	235@4,400	345@2,600	9.0	Marlin, Rebel, Ambassador
	343	4V	280@4,800	365@3,000	10.2	American, Ambassador, Rebel, Marlin
1968						
	290	2V	200@4,600	285@2,800	9.0	American, Ambassador, Rebel
	290	4V	225@4,700	300@3,200	10.0	American, Rebel, AMX, Javelin
	343	2V	235@4,400	345@2,600	9.0	Ambassador, Javelin
	343	4V	280@4,800	365@3,000	10.2	Ambassador, Rebel, Javelin, AMX
	390	4V	315@4,600	425@3,200	10.2	AMX, Javelin
1969						
	290	2V	200@4,600	285@2,800	9.0	Rambler, Ambassador, Rebel
	290	4V	225@4,700	300@3,200	10.0	Rebel, AMX, Javelin, Rogue
	343	2V	235@4,400	345@2,600	9.0	Ambassador, Javelin
	343	4V	280@4,800	365@3,000	10.2	Ambassador, Rebel, Javelin, AMX
	390	4V	315@4,600	425@3,200	10.2	AMX, Javelin, Ambassador, Hurst SC/Scrambler
1970						
	304	2V	210@4,400	305@2,800	9.0	Hornet, Rebel, Javelin, Ambassador
	360	2V	245@4,400	365@2,600	9.0	Rebel, Javelin, Ambassador
	360	4V	290@4,800	395@3,200	10.0	Rebel, Javelin, Ambassador, AMX
	390	4V	325@5,000	420@3,200	10.0	Rebel, Javelin, Ambassador, AMX
	390	4V	340@5,100	430@3,600	10.0	Rebel Machine

	Displacement	Carburetor	Horsepower	Torque	Compression Ratio	Notes
1971						
	304	2V	210@4,400	300@2,800	8.4	Hornet, Gremlin, Matador, Javelin, Ambassador
	360	2V	245@4,400	365@2,600	8.5	Hornet SC/360, Matador, Javelin, Ambassador
	360	4V	285@4,800	390@3,200	8.5	Matador, Javelin, Ambassador, Javelin
	401	4V	330@5,000	430@3,400	9.5	Javelin, Ambassador, Matador, Javelin
1972						
	304	2V	150@4,200	245@2,500	8.4	Hornet, Gremlin, Matador, Javelin, Ambassador
	360	2V	175@4,000	285@2,400	8.5	Hornet, Matador, Javelin, Ambassador
	360	4V	195@4,800	295@2,900	8.5	Matador, Javelin, Ambassador
	360	4V	220@4,400	315@3,100	8.5	Matador, Javelin, Ambassador
	401	4V	255@4,600	345@3,300	8.5	Matador, Javelin, Ambassador
1973						
	304	2V	150@4,200	245@2,500	8.4	Hornet, Gremlin, Matador, Javelin, Ambassador
	360	2V	175@4,000	285@2,400	8.5	Hornet, Matador, Javelin, Ambassador
	360	4V	195@4,800	295@2,900	8.5	Matador, Javelin, Ambassador
	360	4V	220@4,400	315@3,100	8.5	Matador, Javelin, Ambassador
	401	4V	255@4,600	345@3,300	8.5	Matador, Javelin, Ambassador
1974						
	304	2V	150@4,200	245@2,500	8.4	Hornet, Gremlin, Matador, Javelin, Ambassador
	360	2V	175@4,000	285@2,400	8.5	Hornet, Matador, Javelin
	360	4V	195@4,800	295@2,900	8.5	Matador, Javelin, Ambassador
	360	4V	220@4,400	315@3,100	8.5	Matador, Javelin, Ambassador
	401	4V	255@4,600	345@3,300	8.5	Matador, Javelin, Ambassador
1975						
	304	2V	150@4,200	245@2,500	8.4	Hornet, Gremlin, Matador
	360	2V	175@4,000	285@2,400	8.5	Hornet, Matador
	360	4V	195@4,800	295@2,900	8.5	Matador, Javelin
	360	4V	220@4,400	315@3,100	8.5	Matador, Javelin

Engine Internal Dimensions

Displacement	Bore and Stroke	Rod Bearings	Main Bearings	Intake/Exhaust Valves
250	3.500x3.250	2.2483–2.2490	2.4988–2.4995	1.787/1.406
287	3.750x3.250	2.2483–2.2490	2.4988–2.4995	1.787/1.406
290	3.750x3.280	2.0934–2.0955	2.7469–2.7489*	1.787/1.406
327	4.000x3.250	2.2483–2.2490	2.4988–2.4995	1.787/1.406
304	3.750x3.440	2.0934–2.0955	2.7469–2.7489*	1.787/1.406
343	4.080x3.280	2.0934–2.0955	2.7469–2.7489*	2.02/1.625
360	4.080x3.440	2.0934–2.0955	2.7469–2.7489*	2.02/1.625**
390	4.165x3.574	2.2402–2.2471	2.7469–2.7489*	2.02/1.625
401	4.170x3.680	2.2471–2.2485	2.7469–2.7489*	2.02/1.68

* Rear main 2.7464–2.7479
** 1971-up, 2.02/1.68

Block, Head, and Manifold Part and Casting Numbers

Year	Engine	Part or Casting Number
Engine Blocks		
1958–1962	250	3200557, 3153077
1963–1966	287	3204559, 3169824
1958–1961	327	3144932, 3153677
1958–1962	327	3147230, 3153044, 3153055
1963–1966	327	3166463
1958–1966	327	3203950, 440275
1966–1967	290	3207405 (to eng. code 908-H-18), 3208950, 3179062
1969	290	4486278
1970–1971	304	3195292
1970–1975	304	3195527
1970–1975	304	4487311
1967	343	3207978 to (eng. code 908-7-18), 3208951, 3179063
1968	343	3208951, 3179063
1969	343	4486279, 3179063
1970	360	4488937 Trans Am block
1970	360	3195528
1971–1975	360	3195528
1968	390	4486279, 4486280, 3190806, 3190808
1969	390	4486279, 4486280
1970	390	4487213, 3195528
1971	401	3190079
1971–1974	401	4488874, 3198951, 3195528
Cylinder Heads		
1958	250/327	3152938
1963–1966	287	3169513, 3152930, Jeep
1959–1966	250/287/327	3207349
1959–1966	327	3145596, Jeep
1966	327	3206988, w/ A.I.R.
1966	327	3207349 w/o A.I.R.
1966–1969	290	3206989 (casting 3178453, casting 3207989)
1970	304	4487242 (to eng. 303H20), 4488894
1971–1972	304	8120125 (casting 3212990 late 1971)
1973	304	8122376
1974–1975	304	8123302
1967–1969	343	3208081 (casting 3188558)
1970	360	4488895, to eng. no. 306N, P, X26 (casting 3196291)
1970	360	8120126, after eng. no. 306X26 (casting 3196291)
1971–1972	360	8120126 (casting 3196291, early 1971))
1973	360	8122377
1974–1975	360	8123303
1968–1969	390	3208081 (casting 3188558)
1970	390	4488895, to eng. no. 306N,P, X26 (casting 3196291)
1970	390	8120126, after eng. no. 306X26 (casting 3196291)
1971–1972	401	8120126 (casting 3196291, early 1971)
1973	401	8122377
1974	401	8123303
Intake Manifolds		
1958	327	3153706
1959–1966	250/287/327 2V	3201779
1959–1966	250/287/327 4V	3201173
1966–1967	290 2V	3181896
1968–1969	290 2V	3192462
1966–1969	290 4V	3187000
1967	343 2V	3181896
1968–1969	343 2V	3192462
1967–1969	343 4V	3187000
1970	304 2V	3197075 (casting 3195530)
1971–1972	304 2V	3198953 (casting 3195530)
1973–1974	304 2V	3218356 (casting 3217561)
1975	304 2V	3224360
1970	360 2V	3197075 (casting 3195530)
1970	360 4V	3197035 (casting 3195532)
1971–1972	360 2V	3198953 (casting 3195530)
1971–1972	360 4V	3213991 (casting 3213989)
1973–1974	360 2V	3218356 (casting 3217561)
1973–1974	360 4V	3218357 (casting 3217486)
1975	360 2V	3224360
1975	360 4V	3224361
1968–1969	390 4V	3191737
1970	390 4V	3197035 (casting 3195532)
1970	390 4V	3199763 (casting 3199762), Rebel Machine
1971–1974	401 4V	3218357 (casting 3217486)
1966–1969	290/343	3191737, Group 19, iron, 4V

AMC cylinder heads had their head casting number located underneath the valve cover area.

Year	Engine	Part or Casting Number
Intake Manifolds		
1970–up	304	3197035, Group 19, iron 4V
1966–1969	all	4485729, Group 19 Edelbrock, aluminum
1970–up	all	4488409, Group 19 Edelbrock, aluminum
1966–1969	all	4486268, Group 19 Cross Ram, Edelbrock, aluminum
1970–up	all	4488411, Group 19 Cross Ram, Edelbrock, aluminum
Exhaust Manifolds		
1958	250/327	3151241 right, 3153054 left (early), 3203407 left (late)
1959–1962	250/327	3151241 right, 3203407
1963–1966	287/327	3166824 right, 3166825 left
1967–1969	290/343/390	3207865 right, 3207864 left
1967–1969	290/343/390	3207863 right, 3207862 left, w/ A.I.R.
1970	304/306/390	4487379 right, 4487378 left
1970	304/306/390	4487375 right, 4487374 left, w/ A.I.R.

Year	Engine	Part or Casting Number
Exhaust Manifolds		
1970	390	4488356 right, 4488355 left, Rebel Machine
1970	390	4488354 right, 4488353 left, w/ A.I.R., Rebel Machine
1971	304/360/401	4488900 right, 4488899 left
1971	304/360/401	4488903 right, 4488802 left, w/ A.I.R.
1972	304/360/401	8121271 right, 4488899 left
1972	304/360/401	4488901 right, 4488902 left, w/ A.I.R.
1973	304	8121274 right, 8122442 left, w/ shroud
1973	304	4488901 right, 8122442 left, w/o shroud
1973	360/401	4488901 right, 8122442 left
1974	304/360/401	4488901 right, 8122442 left
1975	304/360	4488901 right, 8122442 left
1975	304/360	8125521 right, 8122442 left, California

CHAPTER 21

STUDEBAKER

1951-1964

224.3, 232.6, 259.2, 289 and 304.5

Studebaker came out with its ohv V-8 engine before most other American manufacturers, in 1951. The engine was entirely conventional with cast-iron two-bolt-main engine block, heads, and manifolds. The engine had a forged-steel crankshaft and forged-steel connecting rods, and the valves were operated by shaft-mounted rocker arms. Unlike most other manufacturers of the day, Studebaker used a solid-lifter camshaft.

The initial Studebaker engine was the Commander V-8. With a bore and stroke of 3.375x3.25 in., the Commander displaced 232.6 cid. The Commander had a 7.0:1 compression ratio, and it was rated at 120 hp. It was available from 1951 to 1954 at the same power rating.

The next variation of the engine occurred in 1955, when the Commander's displacement was increased. The new bore and stroke of 3.5625x3.25 in. yielded 259.2 cid. With a two-barrel carburetor, the engine was rated at 140 hp and later in the year at 162 hp. The engine from 1957 to 1964 was rated at 180 hp with a two-barrel and 195 hp with a four-barrel.

In 1956, the President 289 cid V-8 was released. The engine's bore remained at 3.5625 in., but the stroke was increased to 3.625 in. The two-barrel version was rated at 195 hp and the four-barrel at 210 hp. The engine was available in these two power ratings through the 1964 model year.

The 1957–1958 289 cid V-8 that powered the Golden Hawk was supercharged. It was rated at 275 hp. The 289 would again be supercharged in 1964–1965, for 289 hp as installed in the Avanti. A larger version of the engine, displacing 304.5 cid, also supercharged, was rated at 335 hp.

The 352 cid Golden Hawk V-8 that Studebaker used in 1956 was actually an engine built by Packard; see the Packard V-8 chapter for further details. In the same way, Studebaker supplied supercharged 289 cid engines to Packard in 1958.

Studebaker also produced trucks. In 1955, Studebaker installed a smaller displacement version of its V-8 in light trucks. With a bore and stroke of 3.5625x2.812 for 224.3 cid, the engine produced 140 hp. The engine was carried over into 1956 production as well.

Studebaker production ended in the United States during 1964. The 1965 and 1966 Studebaker models were built in Canada. V-8 equipped vehicles were powered by the 283 cid Chevrolet small-block V-8. Production of the Avanti continued under private ownership through the 1990s. These vehicles used various Chevrolet engines.

Engine Identification

Studebaker stamped each engine block with an engine number to the right of the distributor mounting pad. If a letter C follows the engine code, it indicates Canadian origin. The numbers are as follows:

Engine	Code
1951	
232.6 cid	V-101 and up
1952	
232.6 cid	V-123001 and up
1953	
232.6 cid	V-207001 and up
1954	
232.6 cid	V-285501 and up
1955	
224 cid Commander	V-312701 and up, VL-312701 and up (Los Angeles engine plant)
259 cid Commander	V-331101 and up, VL-101 and up (Los Angeles engine plant)
259 cid President	P-101 and up, PL-101 and up (Los Angeles engine plant)
1956	
259 cid Commander	V-363751 and up, VL-6301 and up (Los Angeles engine plant)
259 cid President	P-2201 and up, PL-2701 and up (Los Angeles engine plant)
1957	
259 cid	V-390001 and up
289 cid	P-39601 and up
289 cid	PS-1001 and up, Golden Hawk
1958	
259 cid	V-407501 and up
289 cid	P-60701 and up
289 cid	PS-5501 and up, Golden Hawk
1959	
259 cid	V-418701 and up
1960	
259 cid	V-454701 and up
289 cid	S-70501 and up
1961	
259 cid	V-510401 and up
289 cid	P-74701 and up
1962	
259 cid	V-534901 and up
289 cid	P-79801 and up
1963	
259 cid	V-1001 and up
289 cid	P-1001 and up
1964	
259 cid	V-1001 and up
289 cid	P-1001 and up
R1 289 cid	R-1001 and up
R2 289 cid	RS-1001 and up

Engine Specifications

	Displacement	Carburetor	Horsepower	Torque	Compression Ratio	Notes
1951–1954						
	232.6	2V	120@4,000	190@2,000	7.00	Commander
1955						
	224.3	2V	140@4,500	202@2,800	7.50	Commander
	259.2	2V	162@4,500	250@2,800	7.50	Commander
	259.2	4V	175@4,500	250@3,000	7.50	President
	259.2	4V	185@4,500	258@2,800	7.50	President
1956						
	259.2	2V	170@4,500	260@2,800	7.80	Champion, Commander, President
	259.2	4V	185@4,500	258@2,800	7.80	Champion, Commander, President
	289	2V	195@4,500	286@2,800	7.80	Champion, Commander, President
	289	4V	210@4,500	300@2,800	7.80	Champion, Commander, President
	352	4V	275@4,600	380@2,800	9.50	Golden Hawk (Packard V-8)
1957						
	259.2	2V	180@4,500	260@2,800	8.00	Champion, Commander, President
	259.2	4V	195@4,500	265@2,800	8.00	Champion, Commander, President
	289	2V	195@4,500	286@2,800	8.00	Champion, Commander, President
	289	4V	210@4,500	300@2,800	8.00	Champion, Commander, President
	289	4V	225@4,500	305@2,800	8.00	Champion, Commander, President
	289	2V	275@4,600	380@2,800	7.50	Golden Hawk (supercharged)
1958						
	259.2	2V	180@4,500	260@2,800	8.30	Champion, Commander, President
	289	4V	210@4,500	300@2,800	8.30	Champion, Commander, President
	289	4V	225@4,500	305@2,800	8.30	Champion, Commander, President
	289	2V	275@4,600	380@2,800	7.30	Golden Hawk (supercharged)
1959						
	259.2	2V	180@4,500	260@2,800	8.80	Lark, Hawk
	259.2	4V	195@4,500	265@2,800	8.80	Lark, Hawk
1960						
	259.2	2V	180@4,500	260@2,800	8.50	Lark, Hawk
	259.2	4V	195@4,500	265@2,800	8.50	Lark, Hawk
	289	4V	210@4,500	300@2,800	8.50	Lark, Hawk
	289	4V	225@4,500	305@2,800	8.50	Lark, Hawk
1961						
	259.2	2V	180@4,500	260@2,800	8.50	Lark, Hawk
	259.2	4V	195@4,500	265@2,800	8.50	Lark, Hawk
	289	4V	210@4,500	300@2,800	8.50	Lark, Hawk
	289	4V	225@4,500	305@2,800	8.50	Lark, Hawk
1962						
	259.2	2V	180@4,500	260@2,800	8.50	Lark, Hawk
	259.2	4V	195@4,500	265@2,800	8.50	Lark, Hawk
	289	4V	210@4,500	300@2,800	8.50	Lark, Hawk, Gran Turismo Hawk
	289	4V	225@4,500	305@2,800	8.50	Lark, Hawk, Gran Turismo Hawk
1963						
	259.2	2V	180@4,500	260@2,800	8.50	Lark, Hawk
	259.2	4V	195@4,500	265@2,800	8.25	Lark, Hawk
	289	4V	210@4,500	300@2,800	8.25	Lark, Hawk, Gran Turismo Hawk
	289	4V	225@4,500	305@2,800	8.25	Lark, Hawk, Gran Turismo Hawk
	289	4V	240@4,500	305@2,800	10.25	Avanti
	289	4V	289@4,500	305@2,800	9.00	Avanti (supercharged)
	304.5	4V	335 hp–estimated	NA	9.75	Avanti (supercharged)
1964						
	259.2	2V	180@4,500	260@2,800	8.50	Lark, Hawk
	259.2	4V	195@4,500	265@2,800	8.25	Lark, Hawk
	289	4V	210@4,500	300@2,800	8.25	Lark, Hawk, Gran Turismo Hawk
	289	4V	225@4,500	305@2,800	8.25	Lark, Hawk, Gran Turismo Hawk
	289	4V	240@4,500	305@2,800	10.25	Avanti
	289	4V	289@4,500	305@2,800	9.00	Avanti (supercharged)
	304.5	4V	335 hp–estimated	NA	9.75	Avanti (supercharged)

Engine Internal Dimensions

Displacement	Bore and Stroke	Rod Bearings	Main Bearings	Intake/Exhaust Valves
224.3	3.5625x2.812	2.000	2.5000	1.28/1.28
232.6	3.3750x3.250	2.000	2.5000	1.28/1.28*
259	3.5625x3.250	2.000	2.5000	1.65/1.53
289	3.5625x3.625	2.000	2.5000	1.65/1.53
304.5	3.6500x3.625	2.000	2.5000	1.65/1.53

*1953–1955 = 1.46/1.28

Studebaker offered two V-8 engines in the late 1950s and early 1960s: the 259 and the 289. This is the 1961 289 version.

Block, Head, and Manifold Part and Casting Numbers

Year	Engine	Part or Casting Number
Engine Blocks		
1951–1954	232.6	529464
1955–1964	259.2/289	535601
Cylinder Heads		
1951–1954	232.6	527772, 535298
1955–1964	259.2/289	536097, 537571
Intake Manifolds		
1951–1952	2V	534854, to eng. no. 95954
1951–1952	2V	532389, after eng. no. 95954
1952–1958	2V	534854
1955–1958	4V	536303
1956–1957	2V	440891, Golden Hawk
1959–1964	2V	1551330
1959–1964	4V	1547718
Exhaust Manifolds		
1951–1952	232.6	529489 right, 529490 left
1953	232.6	529489 right, 532424 left, w/o p/s
1953	232.6	59489 right, 534414 left, w/ p/s
1954	232.6	529489 right, 534414 left
1955–1964	259.2/289	536194 right, 5361995 left

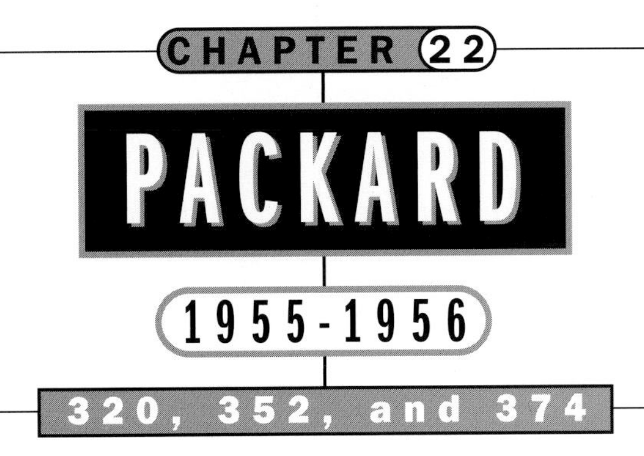

By the time Packard brought out its ohv engines in 1955, it was a situation of too little, too late—much too late. Not that the engines were bad, but the company had been in decline for some time, and the merger with Studebaker in 1954 didn't do much to turn things around.

For 1955, Packard released two V-8 engines. The first was a 320 cid V-8 with a bore and stroke of 3.8125x3.50 in. and a 225 hp rating. Also introduced was a larger 352 cid engine, with a bore and stroke of 4.00x3.50 in., rated at 245-, 260-, and 275 hp. The 275 hp engine used a dual four-barrel intake setup.

In 1956, the 320 cid engine was dropped, the 352 cid continued unchanged, and a 374 cid version was introduced, with a bore and stroke of 4.125x3.50 in. There were two versions to choose from, rated at 290 hp and 310 hp. The 310 hp engine featured a dual-quad system using Rochester carburetors.

The engines were strictly conventional, with cast-iron block, heads, and manifolds. Shaft-mounted rockers were used, and all engines were equipped with a hydraulic-lifter camshaft. The block had two-bolt main-bearing caps, and all engines used forged-steel crankshafts and connecting rods.

The 352 cid engine was also used in the 1955–1956 Nash Ambassador (which by then was part of AMC) and also on the 1956 Studebaker Golden Hawk.

Engine Identification

The engine identification codes used on Packard engines were the same as the vehicle's serial number. It was stamped at the front of the engine block, behind the water pump. An example of a serial number is 5540-1001. The number consisted of the engine model-number code (5540 in the example), followed by a four-digit consecutive number beginning with 1001. The codes are listed in the following table.

Code	Model	Engine
1955		
5522	Clipper Deluxe	320 cid 225 hp
5542	Clipper Super	320 cid 225 hp
5547	Panama	320 cid 225 hp
5562	Clipper Custom	352 cid 245 hp
5567	Constellation	352 cid 245 hp
5582	Patrician	352 cid 260 hp
5587	Four Hundred	352 cid 260 hp
5588	Caribbean	352 cid 275 hp
1956		
5622	Clipper Deluxe	352 cid 240 hp
5642	Clipper Super	352 cid 240 hp
5647	Clipper Super	352 cid 240 hp
5662	Clipper Custom	352 cid 275 hp
5667	Constellation	352 cid 275 hp
5672A	Executive	352 cid 275 hp
5687	Executive	352 cid 275 hp
5682	Patrician	374 cid 290 hp
5687	Four Hundred	374 cid 290 hp
5697	Caribbean	374 cid 310 hp
5699	Caribbean	374 cid 310 hp

Engine Specifications

	Displacement	Carburetor	Horsepower	Torque	Compression Ratio	Notes
1955						
	320	4V	225@4,600	325@2,600	8.5	Clipper
	352	4V	245@4,600	355@2,600	8.5	Clipper
	352	4V	260@4,600	355@2,600	8.5	Packard Patrician, 400, Caribbean
	352	2x4V	275@4,600	355@2,800	8.5	Caribbean
1956						
	352	4V	245@4,600	355@2,600	9.5	Clipper
	352	4V	275@4,600	355@2,800	9.5	Clipper, Executive
	374	4V	290@4,600	405@2,800	10.0	Packard Patrician, 400
	374	2x4V	310@4,600	405@2,800	10.0	Caribbean

Engine Internal Dimensions

Displacement	Bore and Stroke	Rod Bearings	Main Bearings
320	3.8125x3.500	2.250	2.4990
352	4.000x3.500	2.250	2.4990
374	4.125x3.500	2.250	2.4990

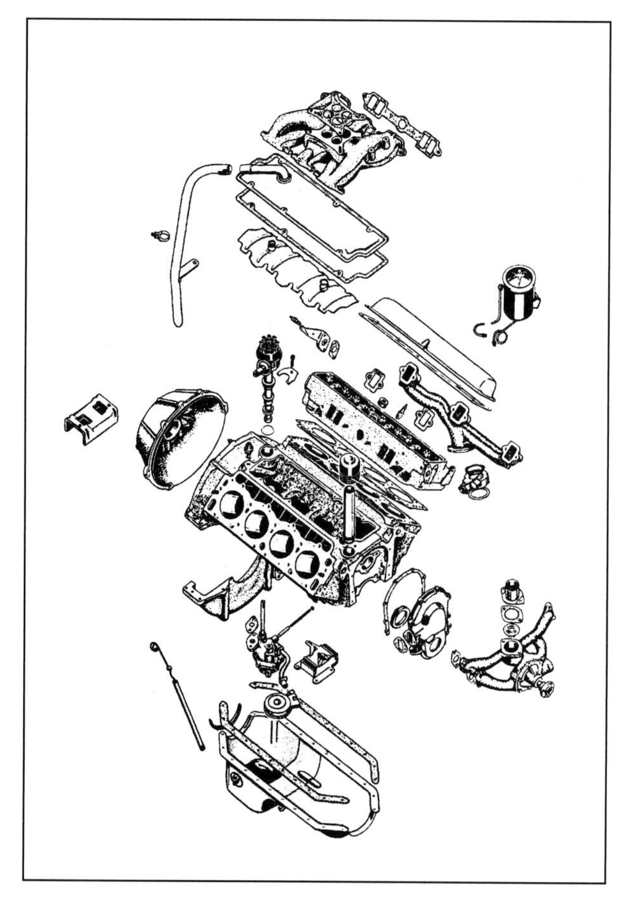

The Packard V-8 was a conventionally designed engine but because it was big, it had potential for 500 cubic inches and more.

Block, Head, and Manifold Part and Casting Numbers

Year	Engine	Part or Casting Number
Engine Blocks		
1955	320	6440570
Cylinder Heads		
1955	320	440689 early, 440854 late
Intake Manifolds		
1955–1956	320/352 4V	440893
1955–1956	352/374 2x4V	440856, 4400857
1956	352 4V	471081
Exhaust Manifolds		
1955–1956	all	446740 right, 446741 left

CHAPTER 23

INTERNATIONAL HARVESTER CORPORATION

1959-1975

266, 304, 345, and 392

International Harvester Corporation built many types of trucks. The Scout, introduced in 1961, was one of the first American sport utility vehicles. The company did very well during the 1960s and took pride in the fact that it didn't have yearly model changes like other manufacturers did. "We haven't had a model year since 1907," proclaimed the company in a 1971 ad. In the 1970s, the company found it harder and harder to compete with the big three, and by the mid-1980s, it was forced to abandon the light truck market.

In 1959, the company made its V-266 engine available on light trucks. The V-266 was an ohv V-8 engine with a bore and stroke of 3.625x 3.21875 in., for a 266 cid. The engine was rated at 154.8 hp. In keeping with the company's policy of no model-year changes, the engine was available in this configuration through the 1970 model year.

The 304 cid engine was introduced in 1964. It was basically a bored-out 266. It had a bore of 3.875 in. and the same 3.21875 in. stroke as the 266 cid engine. The engine was rated at 193.1 hp. The engine continued in this configuration through 1972. In 1973, two versions of the engine were available: The two-barrel was rated at 147 hp and the four-barrel at 153 hp. These were SAE net figures. The engine continued to be available beyond 1975.

In 1971, IHC introduced a larger V-8, a 345 cid engine with a bore and stroke of 3.875x3.65625 in. With a two-barrel carburetor, it was rated at 196.7 hp. The engine was available past 1975 in various configurations.

In 1972, IHC introduced its 392 cid engine in light trucks. This one had a bore and stroke of 4.125x3.65625 in. With a two-barrel carburetor it was rated at 253.4 hp.

There's not much you can do to IHC V-8 engines from an aftermarket standpoint, but you can dress them up like this Scout II owner did.

Engine Specifications

	Displacement	Carburetor	Horsepower	Torque	Compression Ratio	Notes
1959–1970						
	266	2V	155@4,400	227@2,800	8.4	
1964–1975						
	304	2V	193.1@4,400	272.5@2,800	8.19	
1971–1975						
	345	4V	196.7@4,000	309@2,200	8.28	
1972						
	392	2V	235.6@4,000	356.5@2,800	8.5	
1974						
	392	4V	196@3,600	316@2,400	8.0	

Engine Internal Dimensions

Displacement	Bore and Stroke	Rod Bearings	Main Bearings	Intake/Exhaust Valves
266	3.6250x3.21875	2.2483–2.2490	2.4988–2.4995	1.969/1.609
304	3.875x3.21875	2.373–2.379	2.7484–2.7494	1.969/1.609
345	3.6250x3.65625	2.373–2.379	2.7484–2.7494	1.969/1.609
392	4.1250x3.65625	2.373–2.379	2.7484–2.7494	2.078/1.734

Block, Head, and Manifold Part and Casting Numbers

Year	Engine	Part or Casting Number
Engine Blocks		
N/A	266	338629C91, Scout
N/A	266	217145R (casting 217145R)
N/A	304	217144R21 (casting 217144R)
N/A	345	151023R31 (casting 151023R)
N/A	392	151339R51 (to eng. no. 1013196), 436782C91 (after eng. no. 1013196)
Cylinder Heads		
N/A	266	326389C91 w/ A.I.R., early
N/A	266	337133C91 w/ A.I.R. after chassis H668260
N/A	266	216373R91 (casting 216364R), w/o A.I.R.
N/A	304	326389C91 w/ A.I.R.
N/A	304	215591R91 (casting 216368R), w/o A.I.R.
N/A	304	361665C92, w/ A.I.R., Scout 800A, 800B
N/A	304	337135C91, w/ A.I.R., Scout II
N/A	304	casting 216368R, w/o A.I.R.
N/A	304	361665C92, w/ A.I.R., after chassis H673942, Scout 800A, 800B
N/A	304	337135C91, w/ A.I.R., chassis H668260–H765353, Scout II, 1010–1510, 100–500
N/A	345	216369R91 (casting 216368R)
N/A	345	337133C91 w/ A.I.R., late
N/A	345	casting 216364R, w/o A.I.R., late
N/A	345	w/ exhaust emissions 1000B-C through 1500B-C, early 336846C91, late 432091C91, others 432091C91
N/A	345	w/o exhaust emissions, 216369R91 (casting 216368R)
N/A	392	w/ exhaust emissions, through 1971: 433012C91. 1972-up: 43676C91 w/o exhaust emissions, 352119C91

It's hard to tell the difference between the V-392 (shown) and other smaller IHC V-8 engines as they all used the same basic block and heads. *Navistar International*

The V-304 engine shows its typical American V-8 engine design. The exhaust manifold can be used on either side of the engine. *Navistar International*

Year	Engine	Part or Casting Number
Intake Manifolds		
N/A	266/304	2V 217947R92
N/A	345	2V 217948R92
N/A	392	2V 15153R31
N/A	266	2V 338688C11
N/A	304	2V 449536C91, w/ EGR
N/A	304	2V 338688C11, w/o EGR
N/A	345	2V 449535C91, w/ EGR
N/A	345	4V 451019C91, w/ EGR
N/A	392	4V 449534C91, w/ EGR
N/A	392	4V 151539R31, w/o EGR
Exhaust Manifolds		
through 1966	266/304	323518C11
through 1975	266/304/345	323518C12
	392	441116C91 right, 441119C1 left